Great Brand Name
BAKING

Great Brand Name
BAKING

Edited by Hedi Levine
Photographs by George G. Wieser

TRIPART

Copyright © 1997 Tripart, Ltd.
Photographs © 1997 George G. Wieser
All rights reserved.
No part of this book may be reproduced or transmitted in any form or by any means, electronic or mechanical, including photocopying, recording, or by any information storage and retrieval system, without permission in writing from the Publisher.

Produced by Tripart, Ltd.
118 East 25th Street
New York, NY 10010

Publisher: George Wieser
Creative Director: Tony Meisel
Editorial Director: Hedi Levine
Photographer: George G. Wieser
Production: Jake Elwell
Composition: Diane Specioso
Copy Editor: Sarah May Clarkson
Food Stylist: Hillary Snyder
Head Baker: Felice Ramella
Color separations and film production
Creative Edge Graphics Edmonton Alberta

Manufactured in Canada

ISBN 0-914373-42-0

Tripart would like to thank the following for their contributions of tableware, flowers and props:
Fishs Eddy, 889 Broadway, New York, NY 10003, 212-420-9020
Zona, 97 Greene Street, New York, NY 10012, 212-925-6750
Second Hand Rose, 270 Lafayette Street, New York, NY 10012, 212-431-7673
Elan Flowers, 108 Wooster Street, New York, NY 10012, 212-343-2426
University Flower Shoppe, 51 University Place, New York, NY 10003, 212-673-5004
Ad Hoc, 410 West Broadway, New York, NY 10012, 212-925-2652

Tripart would also like to thank the following manufacturers for their contributions of recipes and photographs:
American Egg Board
Blue Diamond Growers
Arm & Hammer
Mott's
Grandma's Molasses
Chiquita
Comstock
Thank You Brands
Domino Sugar
Canned Fruit Promotion Service
Northwest Cherry Growers
Oregon Washington California Pear Bureau
National Cherry Growers & Industries Foundation
California Grape Commission
Presto Cake Flour
General Mills
Ghirardelli
Hershey
Baker's Chocolate
Minute Brand Tapioca
Tabasco Sauce
California Prune Board
California Strawberry Commission
Sonoma Dried Tomatoes
Almond Board of California
Musselman's Applesauce
Lucky Leaf Applesauce
Apple Time
Heath Bits of Brickle
North American Blueberry Council
McCormick & Company
Nabisco
Nestles
Bailey's Irish Cream
Roman Sambucca
Di Saronno Amaretto
The Pillsbury Company
Red Star Yeast
Jack Frost Sugar
Swan's Down Cake Flour
Saco Chocolate Chunks
Sokol & Co. Pastry Fillings
Sunmaid Raisins
Diamond Walnuts
Hecker's Flour
Indian Head Stone Ground Cornmeal
Washington Flour & Cornmeal & Cornmeal

Contents

Introduction

Nothing can compare to the aroma and fragrance of freshly-baked bread, except perhaps for a plateful of delicate but rich little cookies or a moist and rich torte or cake. Home baking is one of those quiet yet deeply satisfying pleasures that not only supply satisfaction in the doing but also delirium in the tasting.

Considering the vast variety of baked goods available in supermarkets and stores, why bake? Just look at the labels: artificial ingredients, peculiar shortenings, preservatives. These may not be bad for you, but they produce a product designed for shelf life, not for your enjoyment. After you have tasted real chocolate, butter, less sugar and real vanilla or fresh citrus zest, will you be able to go back to tearing a package open with your teeth?

This is not to say that there are not good bakeries around. There are, but they are not numerous outside of big cities and they are certainly not cheap. Good ingredients cost.

What makes good baking? First-rate ingredients and careful measurement, followed by precise execution. And anything homemade will taste better than what can be store bought. This doesn't mean you can get away with baking from a mix and calling it homemade, despite the fact that many of today's baking mixes are quite good.

The effort expended in starting with flour, butter, sugar, eggs and natural flavorings is actually very little greater than opening a box, and the results will win many more compliments. With modern electric mixers, blenders and food processors, and an accurate oven, anyone who can follow a recipe can produce savory and satisfying baked goods. And follow you must! Unlike all other cooking, baking demands precise measurement. Chemical reactions between yeasts, sugars, fats and heat demand that you take care in sifting, leveling and apportioning your ingredients. If a recipe states to let the dough rise for two hours, don't think you can get by with one hour at a higher temperature. It won't work!

Of course, at the end of the day, you will have some splendid food. All of it filling, sometimes fattening, loaded with carbohydrates and sugar and deeply satisfying. Serve the cakes and cookies by themselves, with first-class tea or coffee. Serve the plain breads, muffins, scones and biscuits with the best butter money can buy, perhaps with jam or honey. The fancy breads and fruit loaves can make light desserts or breakfast treats with fresh fruit. And a slice of pie or cake or a plate of cookies or brownies is just the treat for a long afternoon.

And do remember, it's the taste of the cake that matters. Try to avoid the school of cake decorating that makes everything into an icing sculpture. You want to taste the cake. And, all that added sugar isn't very good for you.

Almost everything that can be baked can be frozen. But be warned, the flavor and texture will change once it's defrosted. The moister breads respond best to freezing and reheating. And most all breads and muffins can be toasted.

These recipes have been tested and carefully edited to make your baking a pleasure. You will find old favorites and lots of new ideas here. Just imagine the your family's reaction when you bring out that home-baked delight!

The recipes in this book have been chosen from those of the best-known manufacturers and brands available. However, please feel free to substitute a particular ingredient if the listed brand is not available in your area.

Muffins

Bran
Fruit
Vegetable
Nut
Whole Wheat
MUFFINS

Muffins Plain and Fancy

2 cups (480 ml) all-purpose flour
3 tbs (45 ml) sugar
3 tsp (15 ml) baking powder
½ tsp (3 ml) salt
1 egg
1 cup (240 ml) milk
3 tbs (45 ml) vegetable shortening, melted
1 tsp (5 ml) McCORMICK/SCHILLING Pure Vanilla Extract

Preheat oven to 425°F (220°C). Grease 12-cup muffin pan or line cups with paper baking cups and set aside.

Combine sifted flour, sugar, baking powder and salt. Sift into large bowl and set aside. Place egg in separate bowl and beat lightly. Add milk, shortening and vanilla and beat until well combined. Make a well in center of dry ingredients and stir in egg mixture with spoon just until dry ingredients are moistened.

Spoon into prepared muffin cups, filling cups no more than ⅔ full. Bake 20-25 minutes or until toothpick inserted in center of muffin comes out clean. Remove from pan immediately and serve hot. Yields 12 muffins.

Blueberry-Nutmeg Muffins: Add dash McCormick/Schilling Ground Nutmeg to dry ingredients. Reduce milk to ¾ cup (180 ml) and add 1 cup (240 ml) blueberries with milk. Bake as directed above.

Orange Muffins: Add 2 tsp (10 ml) McCormick/Schilling Orange Peel to dry ingredients. Bake as directed above. Combine ½ cup (120 ml) confectioners sugar, 2 tsp (10 ml) water, ½ tsp (3 ml) McCormick/Schilling Orange Peel and ½ tsp (3 ml) McCormick/Schilling Pure Orange Extract. Mix well and drizzle over tops of hot baked muffins.

Spice Muffins: Add 1 tsp (5 ml) McCormick/Schilling Pumpkin Pie Spice to dry ingredients. As an alternative, make your own spice mixture by combining ¼ tsp (1 ml) each McCormick/Schilling Ground Cinnamon, Ground Ginger, Ground Nutmeg and Ground Cardamom. Bake as directed above.

Cinnamon-Streusel Muffins: Combine 1 tbs butter or margarine with ¼ cup (60 ml) McCormick/Schilling Cinnamon Sugar. Sprinkle over top of muffin batter just before baking. Bake as directed above.

Opposite: **Muffins Plain and Fancy**

Marvelous Oatmeal Muffins

¼ cup (60 ml) IMPERIAL Granulated Sugar
1½ cups (355 ml) all-purpose flour
2 tsp (10 ml) baking powder
1 tsp (5 ml) salt
1 cup (240 ml) quick-cooking oatmeal, uncooked
1 egg, well beaten
¾ cup (180 ml) milk
¼ cup (60 ml) butter or margarine, melted
¼ cup (60 ml) molasses

Preheat oven to 400°F (205°C). Grease 12-cup muffin pan or line with paper baking cups.

Combine granulated sugar, flour, baking powder and salt in medium size bowl; stir in oatmeal. Combine egg, milk, melted butter or margarine and molasses in small bowl and add all at once to flour mixture, stirring only enough to combine liquid with dry ingredients. Do not overmix.

Spoon batter into muffin cups. Bake in preheated oven 20 minutes or until richly browned. Remove from pan at once. Yields 12 muffins.

Variation: After spooning batter into muffin cups, add 1 tsp (5 ml) of any of the following to top of batter, then press gently into batter: chopped nuts, chocolate morsels, raisins.

Basic Buttermilk Muffins

1 egg
1 cup (240 ml) water
¼ cup (60 ml) vegetable oil
2 cups (480 ml) all-purpose flour
¼ cup (60 ml) SACO Buttermilk Blend
¼ cup (60 ml) sugar
1 tsp (5 ml) baking powder
1 tsp (5 ml) salt
½ tsp (3 ml) baking soda

Preheat oven to 400°F (205°C). Grease bottoms of 12-cup muffin pan or line with paper baking cups.

In a mixing bowl, beat egg. Stir in water and oil. Mix in dry ingredients just until flour is moistened. Batter should be lumpy. Do not overbeat.

Fill muffin cups ⅔ full. Bake 20-25 minutes or until golden brown. Immediately remove from pan. Yields 12 muffins.

Whole Wheat Muffins

1 cup (240 ml) HECKERS/CERESOTA Unbleached Flour
½ tsp (3 ml) salt
2 tsp (10 ml) baking powder
1 cup (240 ml) HECKERS/CERESOTA Whole Wheat Flour
1 cup (240 ml) milk
1 egg
1 tsp (5 ml) vegetable oil
½ cup (120 ml) raisins
½ cup (120 ml) finely chopped nuts
¼ tsp (1 ml) cinnamon
2 tsp (10 ml) sugar

Preheat oven to 425°F (220°C). Grease 12-cup muffin pan or line with paper baking cups.

Sift unbleached flour, salt and baking powder together. Combine with whole wheat flour. Mix milk, egg and oil together; add to dry ingredients and mix only to incorporate (do not beat, batter will not be smooth). Fold in raisins and nuts.

Fill prepared muffin cups ⅔ full. Mix cinnamon and sugar together and sprinkle over top. Bake 20-25 minutes or until a muffin tests done. Serve warm.
Yields 12 muffins.

Whole Wheat Muffins

Apple Muffins

2 cups (480 ml) HECKERS/CERESOTA Unbleached Flour
4 tbs (60 ml) sugar
3 tsp (15 ml) baking powder
½ tsp (3 ml) salt
½ tsp (3 ml) cinnamon
1 egg, beaten
¼ cup (60 ml) shortening, melted
1 cup (240 ml) milk
1 cup (240 ml) grated raw apple

Preheat oven to 400°F (205°C). Grease 12-cup muffin pan or line with paper baking cups.

Sift flour, sugar, baking powder, salt and cinnamon together. Blend egg, shortening and milk together. Combine flour mixture and egg mixture. Mix only until blended. Blend in grated raw apple.

Fill muffin cups ⅔ full. Bake about 25 minutes or until muffins test done. Yields 12 muffins.

Applesauce Maple Muffins

Applesauce Maple Muffins

2 cups (480 ml) whole wheat flour
1 tbs (15 ml) baking powder
1¼ cups (295 ml) LUCKY LEAF Natural Apple Sauce, unsweetened
½ cup (120 ml) maple syrup
2 egg whites
½ cup (120 ml) raisins or chopped walnuts.

Preheat oven to 350°F (180°C). Grease 12-cup muffin pan with nonstick cooking spray or line with paper baking cups.

Combine the flour and baking powder; stir to mix well. Add the applesauce, maple syrup and egg whites, stir just until the dry ingredients are moistened. Fold in the raisins or walnuts.

Fill muffins cups ⅔ full. Bake for 16-18 minutes or until a wooden toothpick inserted in the center of a muffin comes out clean. Remove the muffin pan from the oven and allow to sit for 5 minutes before removing the muffins. Serve warm or at room temperature. Yields 12 muffins.

Apple Muffins

Apple Streusel Muffins

Apple Streusel Muffins

2½ cups (590 ml) all-purpose flour
2 cups (480 ml) granulated sugar
1 tbs (15 ml) pumpkin pie spice
1 tsp (5 ml) baking soda
½ tsp (3 ml) salt
2 eggs
1 cup (240 ml) LIBBY'S Solid Pack Pumpkin
½ cup (120 ml) vegetable oil
2 cups (480 ml) peeled, finely chopped apple

Streusel Topping:
2 tbs (30 ml) all-purpose flour
¼ cup (60 ml) granulated sugar
½ tsp (3 ml) ground cinnamon
4 tsp (20 ml) butter

Preheat oven to 350°F (180°C). Grease 12-cup muffin pan or line with paper baking cups.

Combine flour, sugar, pumpkin pie spice, baking soda and salt in large bowl. Beat eggs, pumpkin and oil in medium bowl. Add to flour mixture; stir just until moistened. Stir in apples.

Spoon into muffin cups. Sprinkle with Streusel Topping. Bake for 35-40 minutes or until wooden pick inserted in center comes out clean. Remove to wire rack; cool slightly. Serve warm.

Streusel Topping: Combine flour, granulated sugar and ground cinnamon in small bowl. Cut in butter with pastry blender or two knives until mixture is crumbly.

16

Orange Zucchini Muffins

2 tbs (30 ml) vegetable oil
½ cup (120 ml) MOTT'S Natural Apple Sauce
½ cup (120 ml) granulated sugar
¼ cup (60 ml) honey
1 whole egg
1 egg white
1¾ cups (415 ml) all-purpose flour
¼ cup (60 ml) whole wheat flour
2 tsp (10 ml) baking powder
½ tsp (3 ml) salt
1 tsp (5 ml) cinnamon
1 tsp (5 ml) grated orange peel
½ cup (120 ml) skim milk
¼ cup (60 ml) orange juice
1 cup (240 ml grated zucchini

Preheat oven to 350°F (180°C). Line a 12-cup muffin pan with paper baking cups or spray with nonstick cooking spray.

In a large bowl, mix oil, applesauce, sugar, honey, egg and egg white. In a separate medium bowl, mix flours, baking powder, salt, cinnamon and orange peel. In a small bowl, combine skim milk and orange juice. Add flour mixture to applesauce mixture alternately with milk mixture. Fold in zucchini. Do not overmix.

Fill muffin cups ¾ full. Bake 25-30 minutes. Remove from oven and cool 20 minutes before serving. Yields 12 muffins.

Orange Zucchini Muffins

Cran-Apple Muffins

8-oz can (240 g) DEL MONTE Crushed Pineapple In Its Own
Juice
1 egg, beaten
¼ cup (60 ml) milk
⅓ cup (80 ml) sugar
2 cups (480 ml) biscuit mix
2 tbs (30 ml) butter or margarine, melted
½ cup (120 ml) chopped fresh or frozen cranberries

Preheat oven to 400°F (205°C). Grease 12-cup muffin pan
or line with paper baking cups.

Drain pineapple reserving ¼ cup juice. Combine
reserved juice, egg, milk, sugar, biscuit mix and butter;
beat vigorously ½ minute. Fold in pineapple and cranberries.

Fill muffin cups ⅔ full. Bake 15-20 minutes or until a
muffin tests done. Serve warm. Yields 12 muffins.

Buttermilk Bran Muffins

1¼ cups (295 ml) all-purpose flour
1 tsp (5 ml) baking powder
½ tsp (3 ml) baking soda
½ tsp (3 ml) salt
½ cup (120 ml) sugar
¼ cup (60 ml) SACO Buttermilk Blend
1½ cups (355 ml) all-bran cereal
1¼ cups (295 ml) water
1 egg
⅓ cup (80 ml) vegetable oil or soft shortening

Preheat oven to 400°F (205°C). Grease 12-cup muffin pan
or line with paper baking cups.

Sift together flour, baking powder, baking soda, salt,
sugar and buttermilk blend and set aside. In a separate
mixing bowl, add all-bran cereal and water. Stir to combine. Let stand 1-2 minutes or until cereal is softened. Add
egg and oil or shortening and beat well. Add dry ingredients to cereal mixture, stirring only until moistened. Do
not overbeat.

Portion batter evenly into muffin cups. Bake 20-25
minutes, or until muffins are golden brown. Yields 1 dozen
muffins.

Double Apple Pumpkin Muffins

2 tbs (30 ml) vegetable oil
½ cup (120 ml) MOTT'S Apple Sauce
½ cup (120 ml) canned pumpkin
½ cup (120 m) granulated sugar
1 whole egg
1 egg white
¼ cup (60 ml) MOTT'S Apple Juice
2 cups (480 ml) all-purpose flour
2 tsp (10 ml) baking powder
½ tsp (3 ml) pumpkin pie spice
1 tsp (5 ml) salt
1 cup (240 ml) cored and chopped apple, with peel on
     (about 2 medium apples)

Preheat oven to 375° (190°C). Line a 12-cup muffin pan
with paper baking cups or spray with nonstick cooking
spray.

In a large bowl mix oil, applesauce, pumpkin, sugar,
egg, egg white and apple juice. In a separate medium
bowl, mix flour, baking powder, pumpkin pie spice, and
salt. Add flour mixture to applesauce mixture. Fold in
chopped apple.

Fill muffins cups ¾ full. Bake 20-25 minutes. Cool
15 minutes before serving. Yields 12 muffins.

Opposite: Double Apple Pumpkin Muffins

Garden Bounty Muffins

2 tbs (30 ml) vegetable oil
½ cup (120 ml) MOTT'S Natural Apple Sauce
1 cup (240 ml) granulated sugar
1 whole egg
2 egg whites
1 tsp (5 ml) vanilla extract
1 cup (240 ml) shredded carrots
1 cup (240 ml) shredded zucchini
½ cup (120 ml) raisins
2 cups (480 ml) all-purpose flour
2 tsp (10 ml) baking powder
½ tsp (3 ml) baking soda
1 tsp (5 ml) ground nutmeg
1 tsp (5 ml) salt
1 tsp (5 ml) grated orange peel

Preheat oven to 400°F (205°C). Spray a 12-cup muffin pan with nonstick cooking spray or line with paper baking cups.

In a large bowl, combine vegetable oil, applesauce, sugar, egg, egg whites, vanilla extract, shredded carrots, shredded zucchini, and raisins. In a separate medium bowl, combine flour, baking powder, baking soda, ground nutmeg, salt and orange peel. Add flour mixture to applesauce mixture. Mix until moistened.

Fill muffin cups ¾ full and place in oven. Decrease oven temperature to 375°F (190°C) and bake 25-30 minutes. Remove from oven and let cool 10 minutes before serving. Yields 12 muffins.

Above: Garden Bounty Muffins

Raisin Bran Muffins

3 cups (720 ml) whole wheat flour
2 cups (480 ml) toasted bran flake cereal
1 cup (240 ml) toasted wheat germ
1 cup (240 ml) brown sugar, firmly packed
2½ tsp (13 ml) baking soda
½ tsp (3 ml) salt
2 cups (480 ml) buttermilk
1 cup (240 ml) water
2 eggs, beaten
½ cup (120 ml) vegetable oil
½ cup (120 ml) honey
¼ cup (60 ml) molasses
2 cups (480 ml) SUN•MAID Raisins

In large bowl, combine whole wheat flour, bran flakes, wheat germ, brown sugar, baking soda and salt; mix well. Combine buttermilk, water, eggs, oil, honey and molasses; blend well. Add to flour mixture; stir just until dry ingredients are moistened. Fold in raisins.

Pour into glass or plastic container. Cover and store in refrigerator for a minimum of 4 hours and a maximum of 4 weeks.

To bake, heat oven to 400°F (205°C). Grease or line muffin pan with paper baking cups. Spoon ¼ cup batter into prepared muffin cups. Bake in upper third of oven for 20-25 minutes. Yields 3 dozen muffins.

Microwave Directions: Prepare as above. Line microwave muffin pan with paper baking cups. Fill cups with ¼ cup batter. Microwave on high for 3-3½ minutes for 6 muffins; rotate pan halfway through. For 1 muffin, microwave at high for 30-45 seconds.

Raisin Oatmeal Muffins

1 cup (240 ml) rolled oats
1 cup (240 ml) buttermilk
1 cup (240 ml) all-purpose flour
1½ tsp (8 ml) baking powder
1 tsp (5 ml) cinnamon
½ tsp (3 ml) baking soda
¼ tsp (1 ml) salt
½ cup (120 ml) butter or margarine, melted
½ cup (120 ml) brown sugar, firmly packed
1 egg, beaten
½ tsp (3 ml) grated orange peel
1 cup (240 ml) SUN•MAID Raisins

Preheat oven to 350°F (180°C). Grease or line 12-cup muffin pan with paper baking cups. Combine oats and buttermilk; let stand. Combine flour, baking powder, cinnamon, baking soda and salt in large bowl; mix well. Combine butter, brown sugar, egg and orange peel. Stir into oat mixture; mix well. Add to flour mixture; stir just until dry ingredients are moistened. Fold in raisins.

Spoon batter into prepared muffin cups. Bake for 25-30 minutes or until toothpick inserted in center comes out clean. Yields 12 muffins.

Microwave Directions: Prepare as above. Line microwave muffin pan with paper baking cups. Fill cups with ¼ cup batter. Sprinkle with cinnamon sugar, if desired. Microwave on high for 3-3½ minutes for 6 muffins; rotate pan halfway through. Repeat with remaining batter.

Refrigerator Bran Muffins

2½ cups (590 ml) all-purpose flour
½ cup (120 ml) SACO Buttermilk Blend
2½ tsp (13 ml) baking soda
½ tsp (3 ml) salt
1 cup (240 ml) boiling water
3 cups (720 ml) all-bran cereal
1 cup (240 ml) boiling water
2 cups (480 ml) water
½ cup (120 ml) vegetable oil
1½ cups (355 ml) sugar
2 eggs

Preheat oven to 400°F (205°C).

Sift together flour, buttermilk blend, baking soda and salt and set aside. Pour boiling water over bran cereal; let stand until cereal has absorbed all the water. Stir in 2 additional cups water. In a separate mixing bowl thoroughly mix oil and sugar; add eggs, one at a time, mixing well after each addition. Stir cooled bran into oil and sugar mixture. Add dry ingredients and stir only until mixed. Do not overbeat.

Either use immediately or refrigerate batter, covered, up to five weeks. When ready to use, drop batter from container (without stirring) into greased muffins tins or cupcake liners. Bake at 400°F (205°C) for 20-25 minutes. Recipe can easily be doubled. Yields about 3 dozen muffins.

Whole Wheat Buttermilk Muffins

1 cup (240 ml) all-purpose flour
¼ cup (60 ml) sugar
1 tsp (5 ml) baking powder
½ tsp (3 ml) baking soda
¼ cup (60 ml) SACO Buttermilk Blend
1 tsp (5 ml) salt
1 cup (240 ml) whole wheat flour
1 egg
1 cup (240 ml) water
¼ cup (60 ml) vegetable oil

Preheat oven to 400°F (205°C). Grease bottom of 12-cup muffin pan or line with paper baking cups.

Into medium bowl sift together all-purpose flour, sugar, baking powder, baking soda, buttermilk blend, and salt. Stir in whole wheat flour. Set aside. In another mixing bowl, beat egg; stir in water and oil. Add dry ingredients to liquid mixture, stirring just until flour is moistened. Do not overbeat.

Fill muffin cups ⅔ full. Bake 20-25 minutes. Immediately remove from pan. Yields 10-12 muffins.

Oatmeal Muffins

1 egg
1 cup (240 ml) water
1 cup (240 ml) quick-cooking oats
1 cup (240 ml) flour
1 tsp (5 ml) baking powder
1 tsp (5 ml) salt
½ tsp (3 ml) baking soda
¼ cup (60 ml) SACO Buttermilk Blend
½ cup (120 ml) brown sugar
⅓ cup (80 ml) salad oil

Preheat oven to 400°F (205°C). Grease bottoms of 12-cup muffin pan or line with paper baking cups.

Beat egg in medium bowl. Add water and oats and let stand 3-5 minutes. Sift together flour, baking powder, salt, baking soda and buttermilk blend and set aside. Stir brown sugar and oil into oatmeal mixture. Mix in dry ingredients just until flour is moistened. Do not overbeat.

Fill muffin cups ⅔ full and bake for 20-25 minutes or until light brown. Immediately remove from pan. Yields 10-12 muffins.

Oatmeal Muffins

Bran Muffins

2½ cups (590 ml) whole bran
1 cup (240 ml) milk
1 egg, beaten
¼ cup (60 ml) vegetable oil
⅔ cup (160 ml) GRANDMA'S Molasses
1 cup (240 ml) sifted all-purpose flour
1 tsp (5 ml) baking soda
1 tsp (5 ml) salt
⅔ cup (160 ml) raisins or chopped dates

Preheat oven to 400°F (205°C). Grease 12-cup muffin pan or line with paper baking cups.

Soak bran in milk. Add beaten egg, oil and molasses. Mix dry ingredients with raisins or dates. Mix everything together.

Spoon batter into muffin cups, and bake 20 minutes. Yields 12 muffins.

Microwave Method: Spoon batter into microwave muffin pan. Cook 6 muffins for 2½ minutes on high.

Grandma's Buttermilk Bran Muffins

2½ cups (590 ml) bran cereal
1 cup (240 ml) raisins
1 cup (240 ml) boiling water
1 cup (240 ml) GRANDMA'S Mild Flavor Molasses
½ cup (120 ml) canola oil
2 eggs, beaten
2 cups (480 ml) buttermilk
2¾ cups (660 ml) all-purpose flour
2½ tsp (13 ml) baking soda
½ tsp (3 ml) salt

Preheat oven to 400°F (205°C). Grease 12-cup muffin pan or line with paper baking cups.

In medium bowl, mix 1 cup bran cereal, raisins and water. Set aside. In large bowl, combine remaining ingredients. Mix in bran-raisin mixture.

Fill each muffin cup ⅔ full. Bake for 20 minutes. Remove muffins onto rack to cool. Yields 3-4 dozen muffins.

Blueberry Bran Muffins

½ cup (120 ml) skim milk
1 cup (240 ml) all-bran cereal
1¼ cups (295 ml) all-purpose flour
2½ tsp (13 ml) baking powder
½ tsp (3 ml) salt
½ tsp (3 ml) cinnamon
2 tbs (30 ml) vegetable oil
½ cup (120 ml) MOTT'S Apple Juice
½ cup (120 ml) MOTT'S Natural Apple Sauce
⅓ cup (80 ml) GRANDMA'S Molasses
⅓ cup (80 ml) granulated sugar
1 whole egg or ¼ cup (60 ml) egg substitute
1 egg white
½ cup (120 ml) blueberries, dusted with
¼ cup (60 ml) all-purpose flour

Preheat oven to 400°F (1205°C). Line a 12-cup muffin pan with paper baking cups or spray with cooking spray.

In a small bowl, add skim milk to bran cereal. Let soak for 5 minutes.

In a large bowl, mix flour, baking powder, salt and cinnamon. In a separate bowl, blend oil, apple juice, applesauce, molasses, sugar and bran mixture. Mix well. Add egg and egg white. Mix well. Fold in dusted blueberries. Add applesauce mixture to flour mixture. Mix until moistened.

Fill muffin cups ¾ full. Bake 20-25 minutes. Remove from oven and cool 20 minutes. Yields 12 muffins.

Blueberry Bran Muffins

Blueberry Muffins

2 cups (480 ml) flour
2 tsp (10 ml) baking powder
1 tsp (5 ml) ground cinnamon
¼ tsp (1 ml) salt
2 eggs
1 cup (240 ml) milk
¾ cup (180 ml) sugar
½ cup (120 ml) vegetable oil
1 cup (240 ml) fresh or frozen North American blueberries,
    thawed, if necessary

Preheat oven to 400°F (205°C). Grease 12-cup muffin pan or line with paper baking cups.

Combine flour, baking powder, cinnamon and salt in a large bowl; mix well. Beat eggs lightly; stir in milk, sugar and oil. Quickly stir egg mixture into dry ingredients; carefully stir in blueberries.

Spoon into muffin cups; bake 15-17 minutes. Yields 18 muffins.

Courtesy of the North American Blueberry Council.

Quick Raisin Bran Muffins

1¼ cups (295 ml) milk
2½ cups (590 ml) bran flakes cereal
1½ cups (355 ml) BISQUICK Original Baking Mix
½ cup (120 ml) sugar
2 tbs (30 ml) vegetable oil, margarine or butter, melted
1 egg
½ cup (120 ml) raisins

Preheat oven to 400°F (205°C). Grease bottoms of 12-cup muffin pan or line with paper baking cups.

Pour milk over cereal in large bowl; let stand 2 minutes. Stir in remaining ingredients until moistened.

Fill muffin cups about ⅔ full. Bake 20-25 minutes or until golden brown. Yields 12 muffins.

Golden Banana Oat Bran Muffins

1¼ cups (295 ml) whole wheat flour
¾ cup (180 ml) oat bran
½ cup (120 ml) brown sugar, firmly packed
2 tsp (10 ml) baking powder
½ tsp (3 ml) salt
½ tsp (3 ml) cinnamon
¼ tsp (1 ml) nutmeg
½ cup (120 ml) raisins
¾ cup (180 ml) skim milk
2 egg whites, slightly beaten
2 tbs (30 ml) vegetable oil
1 tsp (5 ml) vanilla
½ cup (120 ml) CHIQUITA Banana, mashed

Preheat oven to 425°F (220°C). Prepare 12 muffin cups with nonstick baking spray or paper baking cups.

Combine all dry ingredients. Add all remaining ingredients and mix just until dry ingredients are moistened.

Fill muffin cups ¾ full. Bake 20-25 minutes or until golden brown. Yields 12 muffins.

Golden Banana Oat Bran Muffins

Opposite: Blueberry Muffins

Coconut Crusted Date Muffins

1 pkg PILLSBURY Date Quick Bread Mix
⅔ cup (160 ml) dairy sour cream
½ cup (120 ml) orange juice
½ tsp (3 ml) grated orange peel
1 egg

Topping:
⅓ cup (80 ml) powdered sugar
¼ cup (60 ml) coconut
2-3 tsp (10-15 ml) orange juice

Preheat oven to 400°F (205°C). Grease bottoms only of 12-cup muffin pan or line with paper baking cups.

In large bowl, combine all muffin ingredients; stir 50-75 strokes until dry particles are moistened.

Fill greased muffin cups ¾ full. Bake for 15-18 minutes or until golden brown.

Topping: In small bowl, blend powdered sugar, coconut and enough orange juice for desired spreading consistency. Spoon and gently spread topping mixture over warm muffins. Bake an additional 2-4 minutes or until topping is bubbly. Cool 5 minutes; remove from pan. Serve warm or cool. Store tightly covered in refrigerator. Yields 12 muffins.

Gingerbread Streusel Raisin Muffins

1 cup (240 ml) raisins
½ cup (120 ml) boiling water
⅓ cup (80 ml) margarine or butter, softened
¾ cup (180 ml) GRANDMA'S Molasses, Unsulphured
1 egg
2 cups (480 ml) all-purpose flour
1½ tsp (8 ml) baking soda
½ tsp (3 ml) salt
1 tsp (5 ml) cinnamon
1 tsp (5 ml) ginger

Topping:
⅓ cup (80 ml) all-purpose flour
¼ cup (60 ml) brown sugar, firmly packed
3 tbs (45 ml) margarine or butter
1 tsp (5 ml) cinnamon
¼ cup (60 ml) chopped nuts

Preheat oven to 375°F (190°C). Grease bottoms only of 12-cup muffin pan or line with paper baking cups.

In small bowl, cover raisins with boiling water; let stand 5 minutes. In large bowl, beat margarine or butter and molasses until light. Add egg; beat well. Stir in flour, baking soda, salt, cinnamon and ginger. Blend just until dry ingredients are moistened. Gently stir in raisins and water.

Fill prepared muffin cups ¾ full. In small bowl, combine all Topping ingredients. Sprinkle over batter. Bake for 20-25 minutes or until toothpick inserted in center comes out clean. Cool 5 minutes; remove from pan. Serve warm. Yields 12 muffins.

Coconut Crusted Date Muffins

Opposite: Gingerbread Streusel Raisin Muffins

Carrot and Cream Cheese Muffins

1 cup (240 ml) bran cereal
½ cup (120 ml) boiling water
2 eggs
1 cup (240 ml) JACK FROST Granulated Sugar
1 cup (240 ml) JACK FROST Brown Sugar, packed
½ cup (120 ml) cooking oil
2 cups (480 ml) buttermilk
2 cups (480 ml) quick-cooking oats
2½ tsp (13 ml) baking soda
½ tsp (3 ml) salt
2½ cups (590 ml) flour
1 cup (240 ml) shredded carrots
½ cup (120 ml) chopped walnuts

Cream Cheese Filling:
⅔ cup (160 ml) JACK FROST Confectioners Sugar
8-oz pkg (240 g) cream cheese

Preheat oven to 350°F (180°C). Grease 12-cup muffin pan or line with paper baking cups.

In small bowl, stir together bran cereal and boiling water, set aside to cool. In large bowl, beat eggs. Stir in granulated sugar, brown sugar, oil, buttermilk and oats. Mix well. Add baking soda, salt and flour, stirring just until moistened. Stir in cooled bran mixture, carrots and walnuts.

Fill muffin cups ⅔ full, add 1 tbs Cream Cheese Filling. Add 2-3 tbs more muffin batter. Bake 18-20 minutes. This batter can be refrigerated up to 1 week, so you can bake only what you need at a time. Yields 2 dozen muffins.

Cream Cheese Filling: In small mixing bowl, beat sugar and cream cheese until smooth.

Hazelnut Muffins

2 tbs (30 ml) McCORMICK/SCHILLING Sesame Seed
1 cup (240 ml) apple juice
½ cup (120 ml) molasses
¼ cup (60 ml) butter or margarine, melted
¼ cup (60 ml) milk
2 eggs, beaten
2 cups (480 ml) whole wheat flour
1 cup (240 ml) all-purpose flour
¾ cup (180 ml) sugar
4 tsp (20 ml) baking powder
1 tsp (5 ml) baking soda
1 tsp (5 ml) salt
¼ tsp (1 ml) McCORMICK/SCHILLING Ground Ginger
dash McCORMICK/SCHILLING Ground Allspice
dash McCORMICK/SCHILLING Ground Cardamom
½ cup (120 ml) chopped hazelnuts (filberts)

Preheat oven to 400°F (205°C). Lightly grease 12-cup muffin pan.

Spread sesame seeds on cookie sheet and toast in preheated oven 10 minutes or until lightly browned. Remove from cookie sheet and set aside. Do not turn off oven.

Place apple juice, molasses, melted butter or margarine, milk and beaten eggs in bowl and mix well. Place whole wheat flour, all-purpose flour, sugar, baking powder, baking soda, salt and spices in large bowl and stir until well combined. Add liquid ingredients and hazelnuts to dry ingredients and stir just until dry ingredients are moistened. Do not overmix.

Spoon into prepared muffin pans, filling cups no more than ⅔ full. Sprinkle ¼ tsp reserved, toasted sesame seeds over each muffin.

Bake 15 minutes or until toothpick inserted in center of muffin comes out clean. Remove from pan immediately and serve hot. Yields 2 dozen muffins.

Opposite: **Carrot and Cream Cheese Muffins**

Best-Ever Blueberry Streusel Muffins

2 cups (480 ml) all-purpose flour
1 cup (240 ml) JACK FROST Granulated Sugar
1 tbs (15 ml) baking powder
½ tsp (3 ml) baking soda
¼ tsp (1 ml) salt
1 cup (20 ml) buttermilk
1 egg, beaten
¼ cup (60 ml) butter, melted
1 tsp (5 ml) vanilla
1 cup (240 ml) fresh or frozen blueberries, slightly thawed
1 tbs (15 ml) flour

Streusel Topping:
¼ cup (60 ml) all-purpose flour
2 tbs (30 ml) JACK FROST Granulated Sugar
¼ tsp (1 ml) cinnamon
2 tbs (30 ml) butter
¼ cup (60 ml) sliced almonds

Preheat oven to 400°F (205°C). Lightly grease 12-cup muffin pan or line with paper baking cups.

In a large bowl, combine flour, sugar, baking powder, baking soda and salt. Set aside. In a small bowl, combine buttermilk, beaten egg, butter and vanilla. Add liquid ingredients to dry ingredients all at once, stirring until flour is moistened (batter will be lumpy). In a small bowl, stir together blueberries and flour until blueberries are coated; fold into batter.

Fill muffin cups ¾ full. Sprinkle with Streusel Topping. Bake 20 minutes. Yields 18 medium muffins.

Streusel Topping: Combine flour, sugar and cinnamon; cut in butter until crumbly. Stir in sliced almonds. Sprinkle approximately 1 tbs streusel on each muffin.

Brown Bag Peach Muffins

1½ cups (355 ml) all-purpose flour
¾ tsp (4 ml) salt
½ tsp (3 ml) baking soda
1 cup (240 ml) IMPERIAL Granulated Sugar
2 eggs, well beaten
½ cup (120 ml) salad oil
½ tsp (3 ml) vanilla
dash almond extract
1¼ cups (295 ml) fresh or canned peaches, coarsely chopped
½ cup (120 ml) almonds, chopped

Preheat oven to 350°F (180°C). Grease 12-cup muffin pan or line with paper baking cups.

Combine flour, salt, baking soda and granulated sugar. Make a well in center of dry ingredients. Add beaten eggs, salad oil, vanilla and almond extract. Stir only until dry ingredients are moistened. Stir in peaches and nuts.

Fill each muffin cup with ⅓ cup batter. Bake for 20-25 minutes or until muffins test done. Yields 12 muffins.

Best-Ever Blueberry Streusel Muffins

Almond Sticky Muffins

1 cup (240 ml) toasted chopped almonds
½ cup (120 ml) butter, melted
¾ cup (180 ml) brown sugar
1 tsp (5 ml) light corn syrup
1½ cups (355 ml) flour
½ cup (120 ml) natural, unprocessed bran
1 tbs (15 ml) baking powder
1 tsp (5 ml) cinnamon
¼ tsp (1 ml) salt
2 eggs
1 cup (240 ml) milk
1 tsp (5 ml) vanilla extract
¼ tsp (1 ml) almond extract
¼ tsp (1 ml) grated orange peel
¼ cup (60 ml) currants

Preheat oven to 350°F (180°C).

Sprinkle ½ cup toasted almonds equally among 4 dozen minimuffin cups or 12 regular muffin cups. Stir together ¼ cup butter, ¼ cup brown sugar and the corn syrup; divide between muffin cups. Set aside.

Combine flour with remaining ½ cup brown sugar, bran, baking powder, cinnamon and salt; mix well. Whisk together eggs, remaining ¼ cup butter, milk, vanilla, almond extract and orange peel. Pour wet ingredients into dry ingredients and mix until just moistened. Fold in remaining ½ cup almonds and currants.

Spoon batter into prepared muffin cups. Bake 20 minutes for minimuffins or 25-30 minutes for regular muffins, until tops are golden brown. Remove from oven and turn pans upside down on baking sheet. Let pans stand upside-down several minutes to allow sticky mixture to coat muffins. Remove from pan and scrape any remaining mixture onto muffins. Yields 4 dozen minimuffins or 12 regular muffins.

Courtesy of the Almond Board of California.

Merry Muffins

2 cups (480 ml) all-purpose flour
½ cup (120 ml) sugar
1 tbs (15 ml) baking powder
½ tsp (3 ml) salt
1 large egg, beaten
¾ cup (180 ml) milk
⅓ cup (80 ml) oil
1 tsp (5 ml) vanilla
⅔ cup (160 ml) chopped DIAMOND Walnuts
¼ cup (60 ml) chopped maraschino cherries
¼ cup (60 ml) unsweetened cocoa
powdered sugar

Preheat oven to 400°F (205°C). Grease 12-cup muffin pan or line with paper baking cups.

Combine flour, sugar, baking powder and salt; mix well. Combine beaten egg, milk, oil and vanilla; blend well. Add to flour mixture; stir just until dry ingredients are moistened. Fold in walnuts. Divide batter in half; stir cherries into one half and cocoa into the other half.

Spoon some of each batter into each muffin cup, using 2 spoons and placing batters "side-by-side." Bake for 20 minutes or until toothpick inserted in center comes out clean. Sprinkle with powdered sugar. Serve warm. Yields 12 muffins.

Upside-Down Sticky Muffins

½ cup (120 ml) butter or margarine, melted
¾ cup (180 ml) brown sugar, firmly packed
1 tsp (5 ml) light corn syrup
¾ cup (180 ml) finely chopped DIAMOND Walnuts
1½ cups (355 ml) all-purpose flour
1 tbs (15 ml) baking powder
2 tsp (10 ml) cinnamon
¼ tsp (1 ml) salt
1 egg
½ cup (120 ml) milk
1 tsp (5 ml) vanilla

Preheat oven to 350°F (180°C). Lightly grease 12-cup muffin pan or line with paper baking cups.

Combine ¼ cup butter, ¼ cup brown sugar and the corn syrup; mix well. Spoon into muffin cups; sprinkle each with walnuts.

Combine remaining ½ cup brown sugar, flour, baking powder, cinnamon and salt; mix well. Combine remaining ¼ cup butter, egg, milk and vanilla; blend well. Add to flour mixture; stir just until dry ingredients are moistened.

Spoon over walnuts in muffin cups. Bake in upper third of oven for 20 minutes or until lightly browned. Remove from oven; loosen edges. Invert onto cooling surface. Place any walnut mixture left in cups on top of muffins. Yields 12 muffins.

Upside Down Sticky Muffins

Opposite: **Merry Muffins**

Almond-Pineapple Muffins

3 cups (720 ml) all-purpose flour
1 cup (240 ml) granulated sugar
1¼ tsp (6 ml) baking soda
1½ tsp (8 ml) ground cinnamon
2 eggs, lightly beaten
1⅔ cups (400 ml) buttermilk
⅔ cup (160 ml) butter, melted and cooled
1½ cup (240 ml) BLUE DIAMOND Slivered Almonds
1⅓ cups (320 ml) crushed pineapple, drained

Preheat oven to 400°F (205°C). Grease 12-cup muffin pan or line with paper baking cups.

In a large mixing bowl stir together flour, sugar, baking soda and cinnamon until well combined. In a separate container, whisk together beaten eggs, buttermilk and cooled melted butter until well blended. Stir buttermilk mixture into dry mixture with crushed pineapple and 1 cup almonds, just until dry ingredients are blended. Do not overmix.

Fill muffin cups ¾ full with batter. Sprinkle remaining almonds over batter in each muffin cup. Bake for 18-22 minutes, or until wooden pick inserted in center comes out clean. Cool on racks. Serve warm. Yields 2 dozen muffins.

Sherry Tea Muffins

2 cups (480 ml) unsifted flour
⅓ cup (60 ml) GHIRARDELLI Ground Chocolate
⅓ cup (80 ml) sugar
1 tbs (15 ml) baking powder
½ tsp (3 ml) salt
½ tsp (3 ml) cinnamon
¼ tsp (1 ml) nutmeg
½ cup (120 ml) currants
2 eggs
½ cup (120 ml) sweet sherry wine
¼ cup (60 ml) milk
½ cup (120 ml) oil
2 tbs (30 ml) sugar
1 tbs (15 ml) GHIRARDELLI Ground Chocolate

Preheat oven to 375°F (190°C). Grease 12-cup muffin pan or line with paper baking cups.

In a bowl, sift flour with ground chocolate, sugar, baking powder, salt, cinnamon and nutmeg; stir in currants. Make a well in center of dry ingredients. Beat eggs with sherry wine, milk and oil. Add liquids all at once to dry ingredients, stirring only until moistened. Do not overmix.

Spoon batter into muffin cups, ⅔ full. Sprinkle tops with mixture of 2 tbs sugar and 1 tbs ground chocolate. Bake for 20 minutes. Serve warm. Yields 12 muffins.

Note: Wrap leftover muffins in foil; reheat in oven. Muffins may also be frozen. To reheat in microwave oven, wrap muffins in paper towel, heat on high for 30-60 seconds.

Sherry Tea Muffins

Opposite: Almond-Pineapple Muffins

Bayou Yam Muffins

1 cup (240 ml) flour
1 cup (240 ml) yellow cornmeal
¼ cup (60 ml) sugar
1 tbs (15 ml) baking powder
1¼ tsp (6 ml) ground cinnamon
½ tsp (3 ml) salt
2 eggs
½ cup (120 ml) cold strong coffee
¼ cup (60 ml) butter or margarine, melted
1 cup (240 ml) mashed yams or sweet potatoes
½ tsp (3 ml) TABASCO Pepper Sauce

Preheat oven to 425°F (220°C). Grease 12-cup muffin pan or line with paper baking cups.

In large bowl, combine flour, cornmeal, sugar, baking powder, cinnamon and salt. In medium bowl, beat eggs; stir in coffee, butter or margarine, yams and pepper sauce. Make a well in center of dry ingredients; add yam mixture and stir just to combine.

Spoon batter into muffin cups. Bake 20-25 minutes or until a cake tester inserted in center comes out clean. Cool 5 minutes on wire rack. Remove from pans. Serve warm or at room temperature. Yields 12 muffins.

Microwave Directions: Prepare muffin batter as directed above. Spoon approximately ⅓ cup batter into each of 6 paper baking cup-lined 6-oz custard cups or microwave-safe muffin pan cups. Cook uncovered on high 4-5½ minutes or until cake tester inserted in center comes out clean; turn and rearrange cups or turn muffin pan ½ turn once during cooking. Cool 5 minutes on wire rack. With small spatula, remove muffins from pans. Repeat procedure with remaining batter. Serve warm or at room temperature.

Tex-Mex Cornmeal Muffins

1¼ cups (295 ml) SONOMA Dried Tomato Bits
1½ cups (355 ml) milk
1½ cups (355 ml) yellow cornmeal
1½ cups (355 ml) buttermilk baking mix
2¼ tsp (11 ml) baking powder
1¼ tsp (6 ml) garlic powder
¾ tsp (4 ml) salt
½ cup (120 ml) vegetable oil
3 eggs
4-oz can (120 g) diced mild green chiles
1-2 fresh or canned jalapeño chiles, minced
¾ cup (180 ml) sliced green onions
¾ cup (180 ml) shredded sharp cheddar cheese
⅔ cup (160 ml) grated Parmesan cheese

Preheat oven to 375°F (190°C). Grease 12-cup muffin pan or line with paper baking cups.

In small bowl, mix tomato bits and milk; set aside. In large bowl, mix cornmeal, buttermilk baking mix, baking powder, garlic powder and salt. Add oil, eggs, chiles and onions; whisk to blend thoroughly. Add tomato mixture; mix just to blend thoroughly. Mix in cheeses.

Spoon into muffin cups until ½ full. Bake 25-35 minutes or until springy to the touch and pick inserted into centers comes out clean. Yields 12 muffins.

Opposite: Bayou Yam Muffins

Sweet Corn Muffins

1½ cups (355 ml) INDIAN HEAD Corn Meal
½ cup (120 ml) WASHINGTON All-Purpose Flour
4 tsp (20 ml) baking powder
1¼ tsp (6 ml) salt
1 tbs (15 ml) sugar
1 egg, beaten
1⅓ cups (320 ml) milk
2 tbs (30 ml) vegetable oil

Preheat oven to 425°F (220°C). Grease 12-cup muffin pan or line with paper baking cups.

Stir together all dry ingredients. In a separate bowl, combine wet ingredients. Add to dry ingredients. Stir just until blended.

Fill muffin cups ⅔ full. Bake about 20 minutes. Yields 12 muffins.

Crumble-Top Pumpkin Muffins

4 cups (960 ml) buttermilk baking mix
⅔ cup (160 ml) wheat germ
⅔ cup (160 ml) granulated sugar
1 tsp (5 ml) ground cinnamon
1 cup (240 ml) raisins, optional
3¼ cups (780 ml) LIBBY'S Pumpkin Pie Mix
2 eggs

Streusel Topping:
3 tbs (45 ml) all-purpose flour
3 tbs (45 ml) granulated sugar
¾ tsp (4 ml) ground cinnamon
2 tbs (30 ml) butter

Preheat oven to 400°F (205°C). Grease 12-cup muffin pan or line with paper baking cups.

Combine buttermilk baking mix, wheat germ, sugar, cinnamon and raisins, if desired, in large bowl. Beat pumpkin pie mix and eggs in medium bowl. Add to dry ingredients; stir just until moistened.

Spoon into muffin cups. Sprinkle with Streusel Topping. Bake for 14-16 minutes or until wooden pick inserted in center comes out clean. Remove to wire rack; cool slightly. Serve warm. Yields 2 dozen.

Streusel Topping: Combine flour, granulated sugar and ground cinnamon in small bowl. Cut in butter with pastry blender or 2 knives until mixture is crumbly.

Sweet Corn Muffins

Quick Breads

Soda
Fruit
Vegetable
Milk
Seed
Nut
Corn
QUICK BREADS

Holiday Quick Breads

Basic Bread Batter:
1 cup (240 ml) sugar
¼ cup (60 ml) vegetable shortening
1 cup (240 ml) milk
1 egg, lightly beaten
1 tsp (5 ml) McCORMICK/SCHILLING Pure Vanilla Extract
2 cups (480 ml) all-purpose flour
3 tsp (15 ml) baking powder
1 tsp (5 ml) salt

Variations
Cranberry Bread:
1 tsp (5 ml) McCORMICK/SCHILLING Pure Orange Extract
1 tsp (5 ml) McCORMICK/SCHILLING Ground Cinnamon
1½ cups (355 ml) chopped cranberries

Fresh Apple Bread:
2 cups (480 ml) peeled, chopped apples
¼ cup (60 ml) sugar
1½ tsp (8 ml) McCORMICK/SCHILLING Apple Pie Spice

Pumpkin Bread:
¼ cup (60 ml) milk
1 tbs (15 ml) McCORMICK/SCHILLING Pumpkin Pie Spice
1 cup (240 ml) canned pumpkin

Preheat oven to 350°F (180°C). Lightly grease and flour 9x5x3-inch loaf pan and set aside.

Cream sugar and shortening in a large bowl. Add milk, egg and vanilla and beat well until combined. Combine flour, baking powder and salt in separate bowl. Stir into sugar mixture until well mixed.

Pour batter into prepared pan. Bake in preheated 350°F (180°C) oven to 45-50 minutes or until toothpick inserted in center comes out clean. Cool in pan on wire rack 10 minutes. Remove from pan and cool completely on rack. Serves 12.

Cranberry Bread: Add orange extract and cinnamon to egg batter. Stir cranberries into flour mixture. Bake as directed above.

Fresh Apple Bread: Combine apples with sugar and apple pie spice. Pour half of Basic Bread Batter into prepared pan and cover with half of apple mixture. Repeat layers and bake as directed above.

Pumpkin Bread: Add additional ¼ cup milk to first cup of milk. Add pumpkin pie spice to Basic Bread Batter. Stir in pumpkin. Bake as directed above.

Whole-Wheat, Carrot and Zucchini Mini-Loaves

1½ cups (355 ml) all-purpose flour
1½ cups (355 ml) sifted whole-wheat flour
1½ tsp (8 ml) baking powder
1 tsp (5 ml) McCORMICK/SCHILLING Ground Cinnamon
1 tsp (5 ml) McCORMICK/SCHILLING Ground Nutmeg
¼ tsp (1 ml) McCORMICK/SCHILLING Ground Cloves
1 cup (240 ml) sugar
1 cup (240 ml) shredded carrots
1 cup (240 ml) shredded zucchini
2 eggs, lightly beaten or 2 egg whites
1 cup (240 ml) water
⅓ cup (80 ml) corn oil
1 tsp (5 ml) McCORMICK/SCHILLING Pure Vanilla Extract

Preheat oven to 400°F (205°C). Lightly grease seven 4x2½-inch miniloaf pans and set aside.

Combine sifted flours, baking powder, baking soda, cinnamon, nutmeg and cloves. Sift into large bowl and set aside.

Combine sugar, carrots, zucchini, eggs, water, oil and vanilla in separate mixing bowl and beat with electric mixer at low speed 1 minute. Stir reserved flour mixture into carrot mixture with spoon just until dry ingredients are moistened.

Spoon into prepared pans. Bake for 25-30 minutes or until toothpick inserted in center comes out clean. Cool in pans on wire racks 10 minutes. Remove from pans and cool completely on racks. Yields 7 miniloaves.

Tip: If you don't own minipans, fill as many pans as you have and bake loaves in 2 or more batches.

Whole-Wheat, Carrot and Zucchini Mini-Loaves

Zucchini Sesame Bread

3 cups (720 ml) flour
1 tbs (15 ml) baking powder
1 tbs (15 ml) ground cinnamon
1 tsp (5 ml) baking soda
1 tsp (5 ml) salt
3 eggs
2 cups (480 ml) DOMINO BROWNULATED Sugar
2 cups (480 ml) shredded, unpeeled zucchini
¾ cup (180 ml) light olive or vegetable oil
1 tbs (15 ml) vanilla extract
2 tbs (30 ml) sesame seeds

Preheat oven to 350°F (180°C). Grease and flour 9x5-inch loaf pan or two 8x4-inch pans.

In bowl, combine first 5 ingredients. In separate bowl, beat together eggs and sugar. Stir in zucchini, oil and vanilla until smooth. Add dry ingredients to egg mixture, stirring just to thoroughly combine.

Spread into prepared pan and sprinkle top with sesame seeds. Bake 1 hour 10 minutes or until toothpick inserted in center comes out clean. If using 2 smaller loaf pans, bake for 45 minutes. Cool 10 minutes, then remove bread from pan and cool on a wire rack. Yields 1 large loaf or 2 small loaves.

Easy Buttermilk Nut Bread

2½ cups (590 ml) all-purpose flour
5 tbs (75 ml) SACO Buttermilk Blend
½ cup (120 ml) granulated sugar
½ cup (120 ml) brown sugar, packed
3 tsp (15 ml) baking powder
1 tsp (5 ml) salt
½ tsp (3 ml) baking soda
¼ cup (60 ml) shortening
2 eggs
1¼ cup (295 ml) water
1 cup (240 ml) chopped nuts

Preheat oven to 350°F (180°C). Grease and flour 9x5x 3-inch baking pan.

In a large mixing bowl, sift together flour, buttermilk blend, sugars, baking powder, salt and baking soda. Add remaining ingredients and beat on low speed 15 seconds. Beat on medium speed for 30 seconds, scraping bowl constantly.

Pour batter into prepared pan. Bake for 50-65 minutes or until loaf tests done in the center with a wooden toothpick. Cool in pan 10 minutes. Remove from pan and cool thoroughly. Wrap in foil; store overnight before slicing. Yields 1 loaf.

Zucchini Sesame Bread

Opposite: Easy Buttermilk Nut Bread

Buttermilk Zucchini Bread

3 cups (720 ml) all-purpose flour
¼ cup (60 ml) SACO Buttermilk Blend
1 tsp (5 ml) cinnamon
1 tsp (5 ml) salt
1 tsp (5 ml) baking soda
½ tsp (3 ml) baking powder
1 cup (240 ml) oil
2 cups (480 ml) sugar
3 eggs
1 tsp (5 ml) vanilla
2 cups (480 ml) shredded zucchini

Preheat oven to 325°F (165°C). Grease and flour two 8½x4½x2¼-inch loaf pans.

Sift the flour, buttermilk blend, cinnamon, salt, baking soda and baking powder together and set aside.

In a separate mixing bowl, add the oil and sugar and beat together until fluffy. Add eggs, one at a time, beating well after each addition. Add vanilla. Now add the dry ingredients and mix just until smooth. Do not overbeat. Mix in the shredded zucchini thoroughly.

Pour batter into prepared pans. Bake for 45-50 minutes or until tested done. Let cool for 10 minutes in pans. Remove from pans and cool on rack. Yields 2 loaves.

Buttermilk Zucchini Bread

Pumpkin Bread

1½ cups (355 ml) sugar
½ cup (120 ml) oil
1 egg
16-oz can pumpkin
2½ cups (590 ml) all-purpose flour
2 tsp (10 ml) baking soda
1 tsp (5 ml) cinnamon
¼ tsp (1 ml) nutmeg
¼ tsp (1 ml) cloves
1 cup (240 ml) chopped DIAMOND Walnuts
½ cup (120 ml) SUN•MAID Raisins

Preheat oven to 350°F (180°C). Grease 9x5-inch loaf pan.

Combine sugar, oil and egg; beat until light and fluffy. Blend in pumpkin. Combine flour, baking soda, cinnamon, nutmeg and cloves. Add to pumpkin mixture; beat until smooth. Fold in walnuts and raisins.

Spoon into greased pan. Bake for 60-70 minutes or until toothpick inserted in center comes out clean. Cool in pan 10 minutes. Remove from pan and cool on wire rack. Yields 1 loaf.

Quick Molasses Pumpkin Bread

1 pkg yellow cake mix
⅓ cup (80 ml) GRANDMA'S Molasses (gold label)
4 eggs
16-oz can (480 g) pumpkin
1 tsp (5 ml) cinnamon
1 tsp (5 ml) nutmeg
⅓ cup (80 ml) chopped nuts, optional
⅓ cup (80 ml) raisins, optional

Preheat oven to 350°F (180°C). Grease two 9x5-inch loaf pans.

Combine all ingredients in a large bowl and blend. Beat at medium speed for 2 minutes.

Pour into prepared pans. Bake in oven for 60 minutes or until toothpick inserted in center comes out clean. Yields 2 loaves.

Above: Pumpkin Bread

Cinnamon Raisin Coffee Bread

3 tbs (45 ml) butter-flavored shortening
1 cup (120 ml) sugar, divided
2¼ tsp (11 ml) cinnamon
2½ cups (590 ml) all-purpose flour
½ tsp (3 ml) salt
1¼ tsp (6 ml) ARM & HAMMER Baking Soda
2 eggs
5 tbs (75 ml) white distilled vinegar plus
 skim milk to make 1 cup (240 ml) liquid
¼ cup (60 ml) shortening, melted
½ cup (120 ml) raisins
¼ cup (60 ml) chopped nuts

Preheat oven to 350°F (180°C). Grease 8x8x2-inch baking pan

Combine butter-flavored shortening, ½ cup sugar and cinnamon. Set aside.

Sift flour, salt, baking soda and second ½ cup sugar into mixing bowl. Beat eggs, add liquid, blend well; then add shortening and raisins. Pour all at once into flour mixture; stir until flour is just dampened.

Spread half the batter into prepared baking pan; sprinkle with half the cinnamon mixture. Cover with remaining batter and draw knife through batter several times to distribute filling slightly. Sprinkle top with rest of cinnamon mixture and nuts.

Bake for 45 minutes. Serve warm, cutting into 12 squares. Yields 1 loaf.

Half Moon Bay Pumpkin Bread

4 eggs
3 cups (720 ml) sugar
1 cup (240 ml) oil
2 cups (480 ml) canned pumpkin
3 cups (720 ml) unsifted flour
2 tsp (10 ml) baking soda
1 tsp (5 ml) salt
1 tsp (5 ml) baking powder
1½ tsp (8 ml) cinnamon
¾ tsp (4 ml) nutmeg
¾ tsp (4 ml) allspice
½ tsp (3 ml) ginger
⅔ cup (160 ml) orange juice
1 cup (240 ml) finely chopped walnuts
4-oz bar GHIRARDELLI Semi-Sweet Chocolate, grated

White Chocolate Frosting:
3 cups (720 ml) powdered sugar, sifted
3-oz pkg (90 g) cream cheese, softened
3 tbs (45 ml) half and half
2 tsp (10 ml) vanilla
dash salt
4 oz (120 g) sweet white chocolate
2 tbs (30 ml) butter

Preheat oven to 350°F (180°C). Grease two 9x5-inch loaf pans.

In large mixing bowl, combine eggs, sugar and oil; cream on high speed for 5 minutes. On medium speed, blend in pumpkin. Sift flour with baking soda, salt, baking powder and spices. To pumpkin mixture add dry ingredients alternately with orange juice. Mix until smooth. Do not overmix. Fold nuts and grated chocolate into batter.

Spread into prepared loaf pans. Bake for 1-1¼ hours or until loaf shrinks away from sides of the pan. Bread will keep for several days or may be frozen. Serve plain or buttered. If desired, frost top and sides with White Chocolate Frosting. Yields 2 loaves.

White Chocolate Frosting: In mixer, blend sifted powdered sugar, cream cheese, half and half, vanilla and salt. In double boiler, melt white chocolate with butter over 1-inch simmering water. Add to creamed mixture. Beat until smooth. Refrigerate leftover frosting.

Opposite: Half Moon Bay Pumpkin Bread

Sweet Potato Breakfast Loaf

1½ cups (355 ml) all-purpose flour
2 tsp (10 ml) baking powder
1 tsp (5 ml) ground cinnamon
½ tsp (3 ml) ground cloves
½ tsp (3 ml) salt
¼ tsp (1 ml) ground nutmeg
2 eggs
1 cup (240 ml) DOMINO Light Brown Sugar, packed
½ cup (120 ml) vegetable oil
1 cup (240 ml) cooked, mashed sweet potato
½ cup (120 ml) currants

Preheat oven to 350°F (180°C). Lightly grease 9x5 or 8½x4½-inch loaf pan and set aside.

In a large mixing bowl, combine flour, baking powder, cinnamon, cloves, salt and nutmeg; whisk lightly to blend.

In a medium mixing bowl, beat together eggs, brown sugar and oil on medium speed until creamy. Beat in sweet potato until just combined.

Add sweet potato mixture to dry ingredients in two batches, beating on low speed for about 1 minute after each addition. Mix just until blended. Fold in currants.

Pour batter into prepared pan. Bake for about 1 hour or until tester inserted in center comes out clean. Cool cake in pan, on wire rack, for 15 minutes. Turn onto rack to finish cooling. Yields 1 loaf.

Whole Wheat Buttermilk Bread

¼ cup (60 ml) shortening
¼ cup (60 ml) sugar
2 eggs
1½ cups (355 ml) all-purpose flour
1 cup (240 ml) whole wheat flour
1 tbs (15 ml) baking powder
1 tsp (5 ml) salt
½ tsp (3 ml) baking soda
1½ tsp (8 ml) dill weed
1¼ cups (295 ml) buttermilk
1 cup (240 ml) chopped California almonds, toasted

Preheat oven to 350°F (180°C). Grease 9x5x2¾-inch loaf pan.

Cream shortening with sugar; beat in eggs. Combine flours, baking powder, salt, baking soda and dill weed. Stir into creamed mixture with buttermilk and almonds.

Spoon into prepared loaf pan. Bake for 1 hour and 10 minutes or until loaf tests done. Cool 10 minutes, then turn out of pan and cool on wire rack. Yields 1 loaf.

Courtesy of the Almond Board of California.

Dated-Up Walnut Loaf

8-oz pkg pitted dates
1¼ cups (295 ml) boiling water
6 tbs (90 ml) butter or margarine
1½ cups (355 ml) IMPERIAL Brown Sugar
1 egg, beaten
1 cup (240 ml) chopped walnuts
2¼ cups (540 ml) all-purpose flour
1½ tsp (8 ml) baking soda
1½ tsp (8 ml) salt

Preheat oven to 350°F (180°C). Grease 9x5x3-inch loaf pan and line bottom only with wax or parchment paper.

Cut dates into fine pieces and place in medium bowl; add boiling water and stir in butter or margarine and brown sugar. Let cool to room temperature. Stir in egg and nuts.

Combine dry ingredients; then stir quickly into date mixture just until blended.

Turn into prepared loaf pan; let rest 15 minutes. Bake for 70 minutes or until tester inserted in center comes out clean. Cool in pan 5 minutes, then turn out onto wire rack. Cool before slicing. Keeps for several days. Serves 16.

Sweet Potato Breakfast Loaf

Banana Date Bread

⅓ cup (80 ml) shortening
⅔ cup (160 ml) sugar
2 eggs
1 cup (240 ml) mashed bananas
1¾ cups (415 ml) sifted PRESTO
1 cup (240 ml) chopped dates
½ cup (120 ml) chopped nuts

Preheat oven to 350°F (180°C). Grease 9½x5½x3-inch loaf pan

Cream shortening, add sugar gradually. Add eggs one at a time, beating well after each addition. Add mashed banana alternately with sifted Presto. Fold in dates and nuts that have been dusted with Presto.

Put in prepared loaf pan. Bake for about 1 hour. Yields 1 loaf.

Oat Nut Bread

3 cups (720 ml) sifted PRESTO
¾ cup (180 ml) brown sugar
¼ cup (60 ml) shortening
1 cup (240 ml) oats
½ cup (120 ml) chopped nuts
1 egg, well beaten
1½ cups (355 ml) milk

Preheat oven to 350°F (180°C). Grease 9½x5½x3-inch loaf pan

Mix sifted Presto and brwon sugar. Cut in shortening with pastry blender or tips of fingers. Add oats and nuts and stir in well-beaten egg and milk. Do not overmix.

Turn into prepared pan. Bake for about 1 hour. Yields 1 loaf.

Banana Date Bread

Opposite: Oat Nut Bread

Lemon Bread

3 cups (720 ml) unsifted PRESTO
½ cup (120 ml) wheat germ
2½ tbs (38 ml) finely shredded lemon rind
⅓ cup (80 ml) lemon juice
⅔ cup (160 ml) water
½ cup (120 ml) margarine
1 cup (240 ml) sugar
2 eggs

Preheat oven to 350°F (180°C). Grease 9x5x3-inch baking pan.

Stir together Presto, wheat germ and lemon rind. Combine lemon juice and water in a small bowl. Mix together margarine and sugar until well blended; add eggs, one at a time, beat until mixture is light and creamy. Stir in flour mixture, alternately with lemon juice mixture, but beginning and ending with flour mixture.

Turn into prepared pan and bake for about 1 hour. Yields 1 loaf.

Orange Nut Bread

2 cups (480 ml) sifted PRESTO
¾ cup (180 ml) sugar
½ cup (120 ml) chopped walnuts
1 egg, beaten
¾ cup (180 ml) orange juice
grated rind of 1 orange
juice of ½ lemon
grated rind of ½ lemon
3 tbs (45 ml) butter, melted

Preheat oven to 350°F (180°C). Grease 9½x5½x3-inch loaf pan

Mix sifted Presto, sugar and nuts together. Add well-beaten egg. Fold in fruit juices mixed with grated rinds and melted butter. Mix well.

Turn into prepared loaf pan. Bake for 50-60 minutes. Yields 1 loaf.

Orange Nut Bread

Opposite: Lemon Bread

Orange Buttermilk Nut Bread

2 cups (480 ml) all-purpose flour
¾ cup (180 ml) sugar
¼ cup (60 ml) SACO Buttermilk Blend
½ tsp (3 ml) salt
½ tsp (3 ml) baking soda
1 beaten egg
1 tbs (15 ml) grated orange peel
¾ cup (180 ml) orange juice
2 tbs (30 ml) lemon juice
2 tbs (30 ml) cooking oil
½ cup (120 ml) coarsely chopped walnuts

Preheat oven to 350°F (180°C). Grease 8½x4½x2½-inch loaf pan

   Sift together flour, sugar, buttermilk blend, salt and baking soda; set aside. In a separate mixing bowl, combine beaten egg, orange peel, orange juice, lemon juice and oil. Add dry ingredients, stirring just until moistened. Fold in nuts.

   Pour batter into prepared pan. Bake for 50-60 minutes or until loaf tests done in the center with a wooden toothpick. Cool in pan 10 minutes. Remove from pan and cool thoroughly. Wrap in foil; store overnight before slicing. Yields 1 loaf.

Lemon Walnut Tea Loaf

2 cups (480 ml) all-purpose flour
1 tbs (15 ml) baking powder
1 tbs (15 ml) grated lemon peel
⅓ cup (80 ml) margarine, softened
½ cup (120 ml) sugar
¼ cup (60 ml) fresh-squeezed lemon juice
2 eggs
½ cup (120 ml) milk
1 cup (240 ml) PLANTERS Walnut Halves, chopped

Preheat oven to 350°F (180°C). Grease 8½x4½x2½-inch loaf pan.

   Combine flour, baking powder and lemon peel; set aside. In medium bowl, with mixer at medium speed, beat margarine and sugar until creamy; add lemon juice. Beat in eggs. On low speed, alternately add flour mixture and milk until blended; stir in chopped nuts.

   Spread into prepared loaf pan. Bake for 55-60 minutes or until toothpick comes out clean. Cool in pan for 10 minutes; remove from pan. Cool completely on wire rack. Yields 1 loaf.

Orange Buttermilk Nut Bread

Opposite: Lemon Walnut Tea Loaf

Banana Walnut Bread

2 cups (480 ml) all-purpose flour
30 NILLA Wafers, finely crushed
    (about 1½ cups [355 ml] crumbs)
2¼ tsp (11 ml) DAVIS Baking Powder
1 tsp (5 ml) salt
½ cup (120 ml) FLEISCHMANN'S Margarine, softened
¾ cup (180 ml) sugar
2 eggs
2 medium, ripe bananas, mashed
½ cup (120 ml) milk
¾ cup (180 ml) chopped PLANTERS Walnuts

Preheat oven to 350°F (180°C). Grease 9x5x3-inch loaf pan.

In medium bowl, combine flour, wafer crumbs, baking powder and salt; set aside.

In medium bowl, with electric mixer at high speed, beat margarine and sugar until creamy. Beat in eggs until light and fluffy. Stir in bananas. Alternately add flour mixture and milk, beating well after each addition. Stir in ½ cup walnuts.

Spread into prepared loaf pan. Sprinkle with remaining walnuts. Bake for 1 hour ane 10 minutes or until toothpick inserted comes out clean. Cool in pan on wire rack 10 minutes. Remove from pan; cool on wire racks. Yields 1 loaf.

Above: Banana Walnut Bread

Aloha Loaf

½ cup (120 ml) butter or margarine
1 cup (240 ml) sugar
2 eggs
½ cup (120 ml) mashed ripe banana
2 cups (480 ml) sifted flour
1 tsp (5 ml) baking powder
½ tsp (3 ml) baking soda
½ tsp (3 ml) salt
8-oz can DEL MONTE Crushed Pineapple in its Own Juice, undrained
½ cup (120 ml) shredded coconut

Preheat oven to 350°F (180°C). Grease and flour 9x5-inch loaf pan.

Cream butter and sugar until light and fluffy. Add eggs; mix well. Stir in banana. Sift together flour, baking powder, baking soda and salt. Add to creamed mixture; mix well. Fold in undrained pineapple and coconut.

Pour into prepared loaf pan. Bake for 1 hour and 10 minutes or until loaf tests done. Let stand 10 minutes. Remove from pan to cool. Yields 1 loaf.

Anza Vista Chocolate Banana Bread

½ cup (120 ml) butter or margarine
½ cup (120 ml) sugar
2 eggs
⅔ cup (160 ml) GHIRARDELLI Ground Chocolate
1½ cups (355 ml) mashed ripe bananas
½ cup (120 ml) chopped walnuts
1¾ cups (415 ml) unsifted flour
1 tsp (5 ml) baking powder
1 tsp (5 ml) baking soda
½ tsp (3 ml) salt

Chocolate Applesauce Bread:
1½ cups (355 ml) applesauce

Preheat oven to 350°F (180°C). Grease bottom only of 9x5-inch loaf pan.

Cream butter or margarine lightly with sugar; mix in eggs. Add ground chocolate, beating until smooth. Mix in bananas and nuts. Sift flour with baking powder, baking soda and salt. Mixing by hand, add dry ingredients all at once to banana mixture. Do not overmix.

Spread batter into pan and bake for 55-60 minutes. Cool 15 minutes; remove from pan. Yields 1 loaf.

Chocolate Applesauce Bread: Substitute applesauce for bananas.

Aloha Loaf

Following page:
Anza Vista Chocolate Banana Bread

Banana Cranberry Nut Bread

½ cup (120 ml) butter or margarine
¾ cup (180 ml) sugar
2 eggs
1½ cups (355 ml) CHIQUITA Bananas, mashed
1 tsp (5 ml) grated orange rind
½ tsp (3 ml) salt
4 tsp (20 ml) baking powder
1⅔ cups (400 ml) flour
½ cup (120 ml) coarsely chopped cranberries
⅓ cup (80 ml) chopped walnuts

Preheat oven to 375°F (190°C). Grease three 6x3x1¾-inch loaf pans.

In a large bowl, beat together butter and sugar until light and airy. Add eggs, bananas and orange rind. Combine salt, baking powder and flour; add to butter mixture. Mix well and stir in cranberries and walnuts.

Divide evenly into loaf pans. Bake for 45-55 minutes or until and inserted toothpick comes out clean. Remove from pans and cool on wire rack. Slice and enjoy warm or at room temperature. Yields 3 loaves.

Banana Cranberry Nut Bread

Classic Banana Bread

1 cup (240 ml) sugar
½ cup (120 ml) shortening
2 eggs
1 tsp (5 ml) vanilla
1 cup (240 ml) mashed ripe bananas
2 cups (480 ml) all-purpose flour
1 tbs (15 ml) baking powder
¼ tsp (1 ml) salt
1 cup (240 ml) chopped DIAMOND Walnuts

Preheat oven to 350°F (180°C). Grease 9x5-inch loaf pan.

Combine sugar, shortening, eggs and vanilla; beat until light and fluffy. Blend in banana. Combine flour, baking powder and salt. Add to banana mixture; stir just until dry ingredients are moistened. Fold in walnuts.

Spoon batter into greased pan. Bake for 60-70 minutes or until toothpick inserted in center comes out clean. Cool in pan 10 minutes. Remove from pan and cool on wire rack. Yields 1 loaf.

Grandma's Molasses Banana Bread

½ cup (120 ml) butter or margarine, softened
1 egg
1 cup (240 ml) GRANDMA'S Molasses (gold label)
3 large mashed bananas
1 cup (240 ml) whole wheat flour
¾ cup (180 ml) all-purpose flour
2 tsp (10 ml) baking soda
½ tsp (3 ml) salt
½ cup (120 ml) chopped walnuts
½ tsp (3 ml) finely grated orange rind, optional
½ tsp (3 ml) ground nutmeg, optional

Preheat oven to 350°F (180°C). Grease and flour 9x5-inch loaf pan.

Cream butter. Beat in egg, molasses and banana. Mix in remaining ingredients just until blended.

Pour into prepared loaf pan. Bake for 50-60 minutes. Cool on wire rack. Yields 1 loaf.

Aunt Lois' Buttermilk Banana Nut Bread

1½ cups (355 ml) MARTHA WHITE or PILLSBURY BEST
All Purpose Flour
¾ tsp (4 ml) baking soda
¼ tsp (1 ml) salt
1 cup (240 ml) sugar
¾ cup (180 ml) oil
2 eggs, beaten
3 tbs (45 ml) buttermilk
1 cup (240 ml) mashed bananas
½ cup (120 ml) chopped pecans

Preheat oven to 325°F (165°C). Grease and flour bottom only of 8x4 or 9x5-inch loaf pan.

Spoon flour into measuring cup; level off. In large bowl, stir together flour, baking soda and salt. Add sugar, oil and beaten eggs; stir well to blend. Stir in bananas and pecans until well mixed.

Pour into greased pan. Bake for 1 hour and 15 minutes to 1 hour and 30 minutes or until toothpick inserted in center comes out clean. Cool in pan for 15 minutes. Remove from pan and cool completely. Refrigerate leftovers. Yields 1 loaf.

Maple-Walnut Bread

Maple-Walnut Bread

¼ cup (60 ml) butter or margarine, softened
1¼ cups (295 ml) sugar
1 egg
1 tsp (5 ml) McCORMICK/SCHILLING Maple Flavor Extract
½ tsp (3 ml) McCORMICK/SCHILLING Pure Vanilla Extract
¼ tsp (1 ml) McCORMICK/SCHILLING Ground Cinnamon
1 cup (240 ml) mashed ripe bananas
¼ cup (60 ml) dairy sour cream
2 cups (480 ml) all-purpose flour
1 tsp (5 ml) baking powder
½ tsp (3 ml) baking soda
½ tsp (3 ml) salt
½ cup (120 ml) chopped walnuts

Preheat oven to 350°F (180°C). Lightly grease and flour 9x5x3-inch loaf pan and set aside.

Cream butter with sugar in large mixing bowl until smooth. Add egg, maple flavor extract, vanilla and cinnamon. Beat with electric mixer at medium speed 2 minutes. Add bananas and sour cream and mix well. Sift flour with baking powder, baking soda and salt. Add to banana mixture and mix well. Stir in walnuts and spoon into prepared pan.

Bake for 65-70 minutes or until toothpick inserted in center comes out clean. Cool in pan on wire rack 10 minutes. Remove from pan and cool completely on rack. Yields 1 loaf.

Country Bread

½ cup (120 ml) all-purpose flour
½ cup (120 ml) buckwheat flour
½ cup (120 ml) cornmeal
2½ tsp (13 ml) baking powder
1½ tsp (8 ml) salt
2 eggs
¼ cup (60 ml) GRANDMA'S Molasses
¼ cup (60 ml) vegetable oil
1 cup (240 ml) milk
¼ cup (60 ml) sunflower seeds, optional

Preheat oven to 450°F (230°C). Grease bread pan.

Mix dry ingredients together. Beat eggs, molasses, oil and milk together in large bowl. Mix in dry ingredients. Add sunflower seeds, if desired.

Pour batter into prepared bread pan. Bake for about 45 minutes. Yields 1 loaf.

Microwave instructions: Line bottom of bread pan with sheet of paper towel and pour batter into microwave-safe pan. Cook 6 minutes at maximum power. Let stand 2 minutes in microwave before checking to see whether bread is done.

Country Bread

Caraway Soda Bread

1 tbs (15 ml) McCORMICK/SCHILLING Instant Minced Onion
1 tbs (15 ml) warm water
4 cups (60 ml) unsifted flour
1 tsp (5 ml) salt
1 tbs (15 ml) baking powder
1 tsp (5 ml) baking soda
2 tbs (30 ml) sugar
¼ cup (60 ml) butter
1 egg
1¾ cups (420 ml) buttermilk
1 tsp (5 ml) McCORMICK/SCHILLING Caraway Seed, divided

Preheat oven to 375°F (190°C). Grease baking sheet.

Combine onion and water, let stand 5 minutes or until all water is absorbed. In a large bowl, combine flour, salt, baking powder, baking soda and sugar. Cut in butter using pastry blender or 2 knives. Beat egg with buttermilk; add onion mixture and ½ tsp caraway seed. Stir into flour mixture until well blended.

Turn out on floured board and knead 2-3 minutes or until dough is smooth and elastic. Divide dough in half. On a prepared baking sheet, form each half into a round about 8 inches in diameter and 1-inch thick. Slash the top of each loaf making two ½-inch deep cuts all the way across, dividing each loaf into 4 equal portions. Sprinkle each loaf with ¼ teaspoon of the remaining caraway seed.

Bake 35-40 minutes. Yields 2 loaves.

Hercules Loaf

1½ cups (355 ml) whole wheat flour
¼ cup (60 ml) soya flour (not soy bean flour) or additional whole wheat flour
¼ cup (60 ml) wheat germ
1 tsp (5 ml) baking soda
½ tsp (3 ml) salt
½ tsp (3 ml) nutmeg
½ tsp (3 ml) cinnamon
½ tsp (3 ml) ginger
1 cup (240 ml) sugar
½ cup (120 ml) brown sugar, packed
1 cup (240 ml) pumpkin purée, fresh or canned
½ cup (120 ml) vegetable oil
2 eggs
¾ cup (180 ml) very finely chopped almonds, toasted
⅓ cup (80 ml) apple jelly, optional
chopped almonds, for garnish

Preheat oven to 325°F (165°C). Grease and flour 8½x4½x2½-inch glass loaf pan.

Mix whole wheat and soya flours, wheat germ, baking soda, salt and spices. Combine sugars, pumpkin, oil, eggs and almonds in large mixing bowl until smooth; stir in dry ingredients until just mixed.

Turn into prepared loaf pan. Bake for 55-60 minutes or until toothpick inserted into center comes out dry. If you wish, melt ⅓ cup apple jelly or crab apples in saucepan, then spoon over baked bread and sprinkle with additional almonds. Yields 1 loaf.

Courtesy of the Almond Board of California.

Hercules Loaf

Irish Soda Bread

4 cups (960 ml) sifted all-purpose flour
1 tbs (15 ml) sugar
1½ tsp (5 ml) ARM & HAMMER Baking Soda
½ tsp (3 ml) salt
1 tsp (5 ml) baking powder
¼ cup (60 ml) unsalted margarine or butter-flavored hydrogenated shortening
1 cup (240 ml) seedless raisins
1½ cups (355 ml) buttermilk or mock buttermilk made with skim milk*

Preheat oven to 350°F (180°C). Grease baking sheet.

Sift together flour, sugar, baking soda, salt and baking powder into large bowl. Cut in margarine or shortening until crumbly. Stir in raisins. Add buttermilk or mock buttermilk and stir to make a soft dough.

Turn onto lightly floured board and knead to form a soft ball.

Pat by hand on baking sheet to 1¼-inch thickness. With sharp knife score into 4 sections. Bake 1 hour or until bread is browned and a toothpick inserted in center comes out clean. Serve warm with margarine. Yields 1 loaf.

* To make mock buttermilk add 1 tbs (15 ml) lemon juice or vinegar to a measuring cup and fill to 1-cup (240-ml) mark with milk. For 1½ cups (355 ml) mock buttermilk use an additional 1½ tsp (8 ml) vinegar or lemon juice and fill to 1½-cup (355-ml) mark or make ½ cup (120 ml) separately.

Opposite: Irish Soda Bread

Merry Christmas Irish Soda Bread

4 cups (960 ml) sifted all-purpose flour
1 tbs (15 ml) sugar
1½ tsp (8 ml) ARM & HAMMER Baking Soda
1 tsp (5 ml) baking powder
½ tsp (3 ml) salt
6 tbs (90 ml) cold butter
⅓ cup (80 ml) chopped red glacé cherries
⅓ cup (80 ml) chopped green glacé cherries
1½ cups (355 ml) buttermilk

Preheat oven to 350°F (180°C). Grease baking sheet.

Sift together flour, sugar, baking soda, baking powder and salt into a large bowl. Using a pastry blender, cut in the butter until the mixture is crumbly. Stir in glacé cherries. Add buttermilk and stir to make a soft dough.

Turn dough onto a lightly floured board and knead to form a soft ball. Pat by hand on baking sheet to a 1¼-inch thick circle. With a sharp knife score into 4 sections.

Bake for 1 hour or until bread is browned and a toothpick inserted in the center comes out clean. Cool on a rack. Yields 1 loaf.

Variation: Replace the glacé cherries with ½ cup (120 ml) each of dried cherries and unsalted pistachio nuts that have been shelled and coarsely chopped.

Irish Buttermilk Soda Bread

4½ cups (1.1 l) all-purpose flour
6 tbs (90 ml) SACO Buttermilk Blend
3 tbs (45 ml) sugar
1 tbs (15 ml) baking powder
1 tsp (5 ml) salt
1 tsp (5 ml) baking soda
¾ cup (180 ml) butter or margarine
2 eggs, beaten
1½ cups (355 ml) water

Preheat oven to 350°F (180°C). Grease well 1½-quart (1.4 l) round casserole dish.

Sift flour, buttermilk blend, sugar, baking powder, salt and baking soda into a large mixing bowl. Cut in butter or margarine until mixture resembles cornmeal.

Beat eggs. Remove 1 tablespoon and reserve. Stir remaining beaten eggs and water into flour mixture, just until flour is moistened. Do not overbeat. Dough should be sticky.

Turn dough out onto well-floured surface and knead lightly for about 15 seconds (10 times). Shape dough into a ball and place in greased casserole dish. In the center of the ball, cut a 4-inch cross about ¼-inch deep with a sharp knife. Brush dough with reserved egg.

Bake for 1 hour and 10 minutes or until tested done. Cool in casserole dish for about 10 minutes, then remove and cool completely on rack. Yields 1 loaf.

Almond Granola Soda Bread

4 cups (960 ml) flour
¼ cup (60 ml) sugar, plus 1 tbs (15 ml)
1 tbs (15 ml) baking powder
1 tsp (5 ml) baking soda
1 tsp (5 ml) salt
¼ cup (60 ml) butter
1 cup (240 ml) granola
1 cup (240 ml) roasted diced almonds
1½ cups (355 ml) buttermilk
1 egg, beaten
½ tsp (3 ml) almond extract
1 tbs (15 ml) melted butter

Preheat oven to 375°F (190°C). Grease baking stone or baking sheet.

Combine flour, sugar, baking powder, baking soda and salt; mix well. Cut in butter until crumbly. Stir in granola and almonds. Blend buttermilk with beaten egg and almond extract. Add to dry ingredients; stir until well blended.

Turn out onto floured board and knead until smooth, 2-3 minutes. Roll into ball and place on greased baking stone, following manufacturer's instructions, or place on greased baking sheet. Flatten into 7-inch circle. With a sharp knife, cut top into ¼-inch deep quarters. Brush top with melted butter and sprinkle with remaining 1 tablespoon sugar.

Bake for 1 hour. Serve warm or cool. Yields 1 loaf, serves 8.

Courtesy of the Almond Board of California.

Orange Cranberry Bread

2¼ cups (540 ml) all-purpose flour
2 tsp (10 ml) baking powder
1 tsp (5 ml) baking soda
¼ tsp (3 ml) salt
1¼ cups (295 ml) granulated sugar
3 egg whites
½ cup (120 ml) MOTT'S Natural Apple Sauce
2 tbs (30 ml) vegetable oil
1 tbs (15 ml) grated orange peel
¼ cup (60 ml) orange juice
1 tsp (5 ml) vanilla extract
1 cup (240 ml) chopped cranberries

Preheat oven to 350°F (180°C). Spray 8½x4⅓x3-inch loaf pan with nonstick cooking spray.

In a medium bowl, combine flour, baking powder, baking soda and salt. In a separate large bowl, mix together sugar, egg whites, applesauce, vegetable oil, grated orange peel, orange juice and vanilla extract. Add flour mixture to wet ingredients and stir gently until combined. Fold in chopped cranberries.

Pour batter into prepared loaf pan. Bake for 60 minutes or until toothpick inserted in center comes out clean. Yields 1 loaf.

Above: Orange Cranberry Bread

Apples and Oranges Nut Bread

1 cup (240 ml) brown sugar
1 cup (240 ml) orange juice
½ cup (120 ml) dried apples, cut into bits
¼ cup (60 ml) chopped walnuts
¼ cup (60 ml) MOTT'S Chunky Apple Sauce
½ tsp (3 ml) salt
1 tsp (45 ml) baking soda
1 egg, beaten
2 cups (480 ml) all-purpose flour

Preheat oven to 350°F (180°C). Spray 9x5x3-inch loaf pan with cooking spray.

In a saucepan, combine the first 6 ingredients. Stir over medium heat until warm and ingredients are blended. Set aside and cool. Stir in baking soda, beaten egg and flour.

Pour batter into prepared pan and bake for 55-60 minutes. Remove from oven and cool on rack.
Yields 1 loaf.

Variation: Lightly frost top with Mott's Natural Apple Sauce, and garnish with mandarin slices.

Apple-Nut Bread

Apple-Nut Bread

2 eggs
1 cup (240 ml) sugar
½ tsp (3 ml) McCORMICK/SCHILLING Pure Vanilla Extract
2 cups (480 ml) all-purpose flour
1 tsp (5 ml) baking soda
½ tsp (3 ml) salt
½ tsp (3 ml) McCORMICK/SCHILLING Ground Nutmeg
½ tsp (3 ml) McCORMICK/SCHILLING Ground Cinnamon
½ cup (120 ml) vegetable oil
2 tbs (30 ml) dairy sour cream
1 cup (240 ml) peeled, chopped apples
1 cup (240 ml) coarsely chopped walnuts

Preheat oven to 350°F (180°C). Lightly grease 9x5x3-inch loaf pan and set aside.

Beat eggs, sugar, and vanilla in large mixing bowl until light and fluffy. Sift flour with baking soda, salt, nutmeg and cinnamon. Add to egg mixture alternating with oil and sour cream and beating well after each addition. Stir in apples and nuts and spoon into prepared pan.

Bake for 1 hour. Cool in pan on wire rack 10 minutes. Remove from pan and cool completely on rack.
Yields 1 loaf.

Mott's Pear Bread

2½ cups (590 ml) all-purpose flour
1 tbs (15 ml) baking soda
½ tsp (3 ml) salt
¼ tsp (1 ml) ground cloves
¼ tsp (1 ml) ground nutmeg
¼ tsp (1 ml) allspice
3 egg whites
½ cup (120 ml) granulated sugar
½ cup (120 ml) MOTT'S Cinnamon Apple Sauce
2 tbs (30 ml) vegetable oil
16-oz can (480 ml) pears in juice, drained and chopped into small bits

Preheat oven to 350°F (180°C). Spray 9x5x3-inch loaf pan with cooking spray.

In a large bowl, combine flour, baking soda, salt and spices. In a separate bowl, blend egg whites, sugar, applesauce, oil and pears. Add flour mixture to wet ingredients and stir until well combined.

Pour into prepared pan. Bake 50-55 minutes or until an inserted toothpick comes out clean. Remove from oven and cool before serving. Yields 1 loaf.

Maple and Brown Sugar Bread

Maple and Brown Sugar Bread

2¼ cups (540 ml) all-purpose flour
⅓ cup (80 ml) wheat germ
1 tbs (15 ml) baking powder
½ tsp (3 ml) salt
1 tsp (5 ml) ground cinnamon
3 egg whites
1 tbs (15 ml) vegetable oil
½ cup (120 ml) dark brown sugar
⅓ cup (80 ml) maple syrup
½ cup (120 ml) MOTT'S Chunky Apple Sauce
½ cup (120 ml) skim milk

Preheat oven to 350°F (180°C). Spray 9x5x3-inch loaf pan with cooking spray.

In a large bowl, combine flour, wheat germ, baking powder, salt and cinnamon. In a separate bowl, gently whisk together egg whites, oil, brown sugar, maple syrup, applesauce and skim milk. Add wet ingredients to dry mixture and mix until combined.

Pour into prepared loaf pan and bake 50-55 minutes or until an inserted toothpick comes out clean. Cool before slicing. Yields 1 loaf.

Cranberry Graham Cracker Bread

2½ cups (590 ml) all-purpose flour
2 tsp (10 ml) baking powder
1 tsp (5 ml) baking soda
1 tsp (5 ml) salt
1 tbs (15 ml) lemon juice
½ cup (120 ml) skim milk
3 egg whites, beaten
½ cup (120 ml) granulated sugar
¼ cup (60 ml) honey
2 cups (480 ml) crushed graham crackers
1 cup (240 ml) cranberries or cranberry sauce
¾ cup (180 ml) MOTT'S Natural Apple Sauce
1 tsp (5 ml) vanilla extract

Preheat oven to 350°F (180°C). Spray the bottom of 9x5½-inch loaf pan with cooking spray.

Sift together flour, baking powder, baking soda and salt. Set aside.

In a large bowl, combine lemon juice and skim milk then whisk in egg whites, sugar, honey, graham crackers, cranberries or cranberry sauce, applesauce and vanilla extract. Stir in the dry ingredients until the flour disappears.

Pour the batter into prepared baking pan and bake for 1 hour or until cake tester inserted in center comes out clean. Remove from oven and cool completely on wire rack before removing from pan. Yields 1 loaf.

Almond Loaf

1 can SOLO Almond Paste
¾ cup (180 ml) butter or margarine, softened
¾ cup (180 ml) sugar
3 eggs
2 tsp (10 ml) baking powder
2 cups (480 ml) all-purpose flour
¼ cup (60 ml) milk
½ cup (120 ml) chopped nuts, raisins or candied cherries
⅓ cup (80 ml) SOLO Toasted Crunch Topping

Preheat oven to 350°F (180°C). Grease 9x5-inch loaf pan.

Break almond paste into small pieces and place in medium-size bowl or container of food processor. Add butter or margarine and beat with electric mixer or process until mixture is creamy and smooth. Add sugar and eggs and beat or process until thoroughly blended. If using food processor, transfer mixture to medium-size bowl.

Stir baking powder into flour. Add to almond mixture alternately with milk, beating until blended. Fold in chopped nuts. Pour into prepared pan and sprinkle toasted almond crunch topping over batter.

Bake 60-70 minutes or until cake tester inserted in center comes out clean. Cool in pan on wire rack 10 minutes. Remove from pan and cool completely on rack. Yields 1 loaf.

Opposite: Cranberry Graham Cracker Bread

Chocolate Nut Loaves

2¼ cups (540 ml) all-purpose flour
1 tsp (5 ml) baking soda
¼ tsp (1 ml) salt
1 cup (240 ml) margarine or butter, softened
2 cups (480 ml) sugar
5 eggs
3 squares BAKER'S Unsweetened Chocolate, melted, cooled slightly
1 cup (240 ml) buttermilk or sour milk*
2 tsp (10 ml) vanilla
1 cup (240 ml) finely chopped nuts
powdered sugar, optional
chopped nuts, optional

Preheat oven to 350°F (180°C). Grease and flour five
5x3-inch loaf pans

Mix flour, baking soda and salt; set aside. Beat margarine or butter and sugar in large bowl until light and fluffy.
Add eggs, one at a time, beating well after each addition.
Stir in chocolate. Add flour mixture alternately with
buttermilk or sour milk, beating after each addition until
smooth. Mix in vanilla and nuts.

Pour into prepared loaf pans. Bake about 50 minutes
or until toothpick inserted into centers comes out clean.
Cool in pans 10 minutes. Remove from pans to cool on
wire racks. Sprinkle with powdered sugar and garnish with
chopped nuts, if desired. Yields 5 loaves

Loaves may also be baked in two 9x5-inch loaf pans
for 1 hour.

* To make sour milk, add 1 tbs (15 ml) vinegar to
1 cup (240 ml) milk; let stand 5 minutes.

Chocolate Nut Loaves

Spicy Onion Bread

2 tbs (30 ml) instant minced onion
⅓ cup (80 ml) water
1½ cups (355 ml) biscuit mix
1 egg, slightly beaten
½ cup (120 ml) milk
½ tsp (3 ml) TABASCO Pepper Sauce
½ tsp (3 ml) caraway seeds, optional
2 tbs (30 ml) butter, melted

Preheat oven to 400°F (205°C). Grease 8-inch pie plate
Soak instant minced onion in water for 5 minutes.
Combine biscuit mix, beaten egg, milk and Tabasco Sauce
and stir until blended. Stir in onion.

Turn into pie plate. Sprinkle with caraway seeds, if
desired. Brush melted butter all over. Bake 20-25 minutes
or until bread is golden brown. Yields 1 loaf.

Opposite: **Spicy Onion Bread**

Sweet Potato Corn Bread

2 cups (480 ml) cooked, mashed sweet potatoes
½ cup (120 ml) butter or margarine, softened
½ cup (120 ml) light brown sugar, firmly packed
4 eggs
1 cup (240 ml) plain yogurt
1½ cups (355 ml) yellow cornmeal
¾ cup (180 ml) all-purpose flour
1 tsp (5 ml) McCORMICK/SCHILLING Ground Cinnamon
1 tsp (5 ml) McCORMICK/SCHILLING Ground Allspice
1 tsp (5 ml) salt
½ tsp (3 ml) baking soda

Preheat oven to 350°F (180°C). Lightly grease 9-inch square baking pan.

Place mashed sweet potatoes in mixing bowl. Add butter or margarine and sugar and beat with electric mixer until creamy. Add eggs, one at a time, beating after each addition. Blend in yogurt.

Place remaining ingredients in medium-size bowl and stir until well combined. Add to sweet potato mixture and stir with spoon just until dry ingredients are well moistened.

Pour batter into prepared pan and bake 45-50 minutes or until toothpick inserted in center comes out clean.

Cut into squares and serve immediately or cool uncut in pan on wire rack 10 minutes, remove from pan and cool completely on rack. Reheat before serving. Yields nine 3-inch squares.

Spicy Corn Bread

Spicy Corn Bread

2 tbs (30 ml) cooking oil or shortening
¾ cup (180 ml) yellow corn meal
1¼ cups (295 ml) all-purpose flour
¼ cup (60 ml) IMPERIAL Granulated Sugar
½ tsp (3 ml) salt
1 tbs (15 ml) baking powder
½ tsp (3 ml) red cayenne pepper
dash garlic powder
1 beaten egg or egg substitute
¾ cup (180 ml) milk
¼ cup (60 ml) cooking oil
1 tbs (15 ml) minced onion
2 tbs (30 ml) minced green pepper
2 tbs (30 ml) minced pimiento

Preheat oven to 425°F (220°C). Preheat heavy 8-inch dish (cast-iron skillet or thick pottery) with cooking oil or shortening.

Combine dry ingredients in large bowl and mix well with slotted spoon. Combine remaining ingredients and stir lightly into first mixture.

Empty into prepared baking dish. Bake 20-25 minutes. Preheating dish or pan produces brown crusty bread. Yields 9 squares.

Opposite: Sweet Potato Corn Bread

Southern Corn Bread, Corn Muffins or Corn Sticks

2 cups (480 ml) INDIAN HEAD Corn Meal
4 tsp (20 ml) baking powder
1½ tsp (8 ml) salt
1 egg
1½ cups (355 ml) milk

Preheat oven to 450°F (230°C).

Place first three ingredients in bowl. Stir to blend; set aside. Beat egg and milk together. Add to dry ingredients and stir until smooth.

Corn Bread: Put 2 tbs (30 ml) cooking oil in cast-iron skillet or 9-inch square pan. Place in oven until hot. Follow directions above and pour batter into skillet or pan. Bake 20-25 minutes. Serves 6-9.

Cracklin' Corn Bread: Add ½ cup (120 ml) cracklings to corn bread batter.

Corn Muffins or Corn Sticks: Put ½ tsp (3 ml) cooking oil into each cup of muffin pan or corn stick pan. Place in oven until hot. Follow directions above for batter and pour into pans. Bake 15-20 minutes. Yields 12 large muffins or corn sticks.

Egg Corn Bread

2 tbs (30 ml) cooking oil
1 cup (240 ml) INDIAN HEAD Corn Meal
½ tsp (3 ml) salt
2 tsp (10 ml) baking powder
1 egg, beaten
¼ tsp (1 ml) baking soda
¾ cup (180 ml) buttermilk

Preheat oven to 425°F (220°C).

Place oil in 8-inch square pan and heat in oven until hot.

Combine corn meal, salt and baking powder in bowl. Stir to blend; set aside. Blend together beaten egg, baking soda and buttermilk. Add to cornmeal mixture.

Pour into hot pan. Bake 20-25 minutes. Cut into squares and serve hot. Serves 6-9.

Opposite:
**Southern Corn Bread,
Corn Muffins or Corn Sticks**

Pie Pan Corn Bread

¾ cup (180 ml) INDIAN HEAD Corn Meal
1 egg, slightly beaten
½ tsp (3 ml) baking soda
½ tsp (3 ml) salt
1 cup (240 ml) buttermilk

Preheat oven to 450°F (230°C). Grease and preheat glass pie pan.

Combine cornmeal, egg, baking soda and salt in bowl. Stir in buttermilk until blended.

Pour into hot pie pan. Bake 15 minutes until golden. Cut in wedges and serve warm. Makes flat corn bread, crusty on the outside and soft on the inside. Serves 4.

Pie Pan Corn Bread

Corn Pone

2 cups (480 ml) INDIAN HEAD Corn Meal
1 tsp (5 ml) salt
1 tsp (5 ml) baking soda
2 eggs, beaten
1¾ cups (415 ml) buttermilk or sour milk
⅓ cup (80 ml) cooking oil

Preheat oven to 475°F (245°C). Grease and preheat 13x9x2-inch pan.

Stir together in large bowl corn meal, salt and baking soda. In a separate bowl, combine beaten eggs, buttermilk or sour milk and oil; mix well. Add cornmeal mixture and beat until smooth. Pour into hot pan. Bake 20-25 minutes. Serves 12.

Savory and Spicy Spoon Bread

1 cup (240 ml) yellow cornmeal
3¼ cups (780 ml) milk
16-oz can (480 g) whole-kernel corn, drained
¾ cup (180 ml) butter or margarine, melted
1¼ cups (295 ml) all-purpose flour
3 tbs (45 ml) sugar
1 tbs (15 ml) baking powder
1½ tsp (8 ml) McCORMICK/SCHILLING Bon Appétit
¼ tsp (1 ml) McCORMICK/SCHILLING Ground Nutmeg
¼ tsp (1 ml) McCORMICK/SCHILLING Ground Red Pepper
5 eggs, beaten

Preheat oven to 350°F (180°C). Lightly grease 13x9x2-inch baking pan.

Place cornmeal and milk in large stainless steel bowl set over (not in) saucepan containing 2 inches of boiling water. Stir until smooth and cook, stirring, 10 minutes. Stir in corn and butter or margarine. Remove from heat.

Place flour, sugar, baking powder, Bon Appétit, nutmeg and red pepper in bowl and mix well. Stir into cornmeal mixture. Add beaten eggs and stir until well combined.

Pour into prepared pan. Bake in preheated oven 40-45 minutes. Serve immediately, scooping out servings with large spoon. Serves 12.

Southern Spoon Bread

1 cup (240 ml) INDIAN HEAD Corn Meal
2 cups (480 ml) milk
2 tbs (30 ml) butter or margarine
3 eggs, well beaten
1 tsp (5 ml) salt
1 cup (240 ml) milk
3 tsp (15 ml) baking powder

Preheat oven to 450°F (230°C). Grease 2-quart casserole.

Combine first three ingredients in pan over medium heat. Bring to a boil, stirring constantly. Blend next three ingredients and add to cornmeal mixture. Mix well. Stir baking powder into cornmeal mixture.

Pour into casserole. Bake 20-25 minutes. Serve hot with butter. Serves 6-8.

Corn Pone

Yeast Breads

White
Whole Wheat
Rye
Pumpernickel
Seed
Nut
Spice
YEAST BREADS

Basic Rapid-Rise Refrigerated Yeast Bread

2 cups (480 ml) WASHINGTON All-Purpose Flour
2 pkgs active dry yeast, undissolved
2 tbs (30 ml) sugar
1 tbs (15 ml) salt
¼ cup (60 ml) margarine, at room temperature
2¼ cups (540 ml) very hot water
1 cup (240 ml) WASHINGTON All-Purpose Flour
2½-3½ cups (590-840 ml) WASHINGTON All-Purpose Flour

Preheat oven to 400°F (205°C) 10 minutes before baking. Grease two 8½x4½-inch loaf pans.

Place first three ingredients in large mixing bowl. Add salt and margarine. Add hot water all at once to ingredients in bowl. Beat with electric mixer at medium speed for 2 minutes. Scrape sides of bowl occasionally.

Add 1 cup flour. Beat with electric mixer at high speed for 1 minute or until thick and elastic. Scrape sides of bowl occasionally.

Gradually stir in remaining flour with wooden spoon to make a soft dough. Turn onto floured board. Round up into a ball.

Knead 8-10 minutes until dough is smooth and elastic. Cover with plastic wrap, then a towel. Let rest 15-20 minutes on board. Punch down. Divide dough in half. Shape each portion into a loaf and place in prepared pans. Brush surface of dough with oil. Cover pan loosely with wax paper then plastic wrap. Refrigerate 2-4 hours.

When ready to bake, remove from refrigerator. Uncover. Let stand 10 minutes. Bake 35-40 minutes until done. Remove from pan immediately. Brush top crust with margarine, if desired. Cool on rack. Yields 2 loaves.

Whole Wheat Bread: Add 2 tbs (30 ml) molasses. Substitute brown sugar for white sugar and 3 cups (720 ml) whole wheat flour for first 3 cups (720 ml) of the white flour. Proceed as in basic recipe.

Rye Bread: Substitute 3 cups (720 ml) rye flour for first 3 cups (720 ml) of the white flour. If desired, add 1-2 tbs (15-30 ml) caraway seeds while kneading the dough. Proceed as in basic recipe.

Potato Bread: Substitute potato cooking water for water or add 1 cup (240 ml) mashed potatoes to the hot water in the recipe. Proceed as in basic recipe.

Raisin Bread: Add 1 cup (240 ml) raisins to mixture when adding flour at end. If cinnamon is desired, flatten kneaded dough, sprinkle on 2 tsp (10 ml) cinnamon and roll dough to form loaf. Proceed as in basic recipe.

Wheat Germ Bread: Stir ½ cup (120 ml) wheat germ into the mixture just before adding the flour. The sugar and shortening may be increased, if desired. Proceed as in basic recipe.

Bubble Loaf: Form dough into small balls, 1-inch in diameter; pile double layer in greased loaf pan or 10-inch tube pan. Proceed as in basic recipe.

Braided Loaf: Divide dough into 4 equal parts. Shape 3 parts into long even rolls, about 15 inches. Place side by side on greased baking sheet; form into a braid beginning at center and working toward ends. Divide the remaining part into 3 pieces and form a smaller braid. Place it on top of the large braid and pinch ends together. Let rise to double in size. Bake as in basic recipe. When cool, frost with ¾ cup (180 ml) confectioners sugar combined with 1 tbs (15 ml) water.

Opposite:
Basic Rapid-Rise Refrigerated
Yeast Bread

One Big Beautiful Loaf

1 pkg active dry yeast or 1 cake compressed yeast
⅔ cup (160 ml) water
⅔ cup (160 ml) milk
2 tbs (30 ml) sugar
2 tbs (30 ml) shortening
1½ tsp (8 ml) salt
3½-4 cups (840-960 ml) HECKERS/CERESOTA
    Unbleached Flour

Preheat oven to 425°F (220°C) 10 minutes before baking. Grease 9x5x3-inch bread pan.

Dissolve active dry yeast in warm water (105°-115°F; 41°-46°C) or compressed yeast in lukewarm (80°-85°F; 27°-29°C) water. Scald milk; add sugar, shortening and salt. Cool to lukewarm, add to yeast. Add flour gradually, mixing with spoon, then with hands until well blended.

Place on lightly floured board; knead until smooth and elastic. Place in greased bowl; rub top with shortening; cover with damp cloth. Let rise in warm place (80°-85°F; 27°-29°C) until double in bulk (1½-2 hours). Punch down; cover; let rise again until almost double (30-40 minutes).

Form into loaf and place in prepared pan. Rub top with shortening; cover; let rise in warm place until sides of dough reach top of pan and center is well-rounded (about 50 minutes).

Bake about 30 minutes or until tests done. Remove from pan; cool on rack. If soft crust is desired, brush with butter before cooling. Yields 1 loaf.

Above: **One Big Beautiful Loaf**

Quick Buttermilk White Bread

2 pkgs active dry yeast
5½-6½ cups (1.3-1.6 l) all-purpose flour
6 tbs (90 ml) SACO Buttermilk Blend
2 tbs (30 ml) sugar
½ tsp (3 ml) baking soda
2 tsp (10 ml) salt
¼ cup (60 ml) soft shortening
2¼ cups (540 ml) water

Preheat oven to 400°F (205°C) 10 minutes before baking. Grease two 8½x4½x2½-inch pans.

Combine 2 packages active dry yeast, 2 cups flour, buttermilk blend, sugar, baking soda, salt and soft shortening. Mix well. Add very warm (120°-130°F; 49°-54°C) water to flour mixture. Blend at low speed until moistened; beat 3 minutes at medium speed. By hand, gradually stir in enough of remaining flour to make a soft dough.

Turn out on lightly floured board and knead until smooth and elastic (5-8 minutes). Place in greased bowl, turning to grease all sides. Cover; let rise in warm place, free from drafts, until doubled (about 20 minutes). Punch down.

Divide dough and shape into 2 loaves. Place in prepared pans. Let rise 20 minutes or until doubled. Bake for 30-35 minutes or until golden brown and loaves sound hollow when tapped. Remove the loaves from pans immediately and cool on racks. Yields 2 loaves.

Whole Wheat Bread

1 cup (240 ml) milk
2 pkgs active dry yeast or 2 small cakes compressed yeast
½ cup (120 ml) warm water
2 eggs
1 tbs (15 ml) sugar
¼ cup (60 ml) molasses
2 tsp (10 ml) salt
3 tbs (45 ml) melted shortening
2 cups (480 ml) HECKERS/CERESOTA Whole Wheat Flour
3-3½ cups (720-840 ml) sifted HECKERS/CERESOTA Unbleached Flour

Preheat oven to 400°F (205°C) 10 minutes before baking. Grease two 9x5x3-inch bread pans.

Scald milk; cool to lukewarm. Dissolve yeast in warm (105°-115°F; 41°-46°C) water [use lukewarm (80°-85°F; 27°-29°C) water for compressed yeast]. Combine milk, eggs, sugar, molasses, salt and shortening in large bowl; add yeast. Stir in whole wheat flour, then unbleached flour; mix well.

Turn out on floured board or pastry cloth and knead until smooth. Place in greased bowl. Cover and let rise in warm (80-85°F; 27°-29°C), draft-free place for one hour. Punch down and return to warm place for another 30 minutes.

Punch down; divide in half; round each dough piece into a ball and let rest 10 minutes. Shape into loaves and place in prepared bread pans. Cover and let rise until sides reach top of pan and top is well rounded. Bake for 30-40 minutes or until done. Yields 2 loaves.

If desired, knead 1 cup (240 ml) seedless raisins into the dough before dividing.

Whole Wheat Bread

Buttermilk Honey Whole Wheat Bread

2 pkgs active dry yeast
2¾ cups (650 ml) whole wheat flour
4-4½ cups (960-1,080 ml) all-purpose flour
1 tbs (15 ml) salt
¼ cup (60 ml) SACO Buttermilk Blend
⅓ cup (80 ml) soft margarine or other shortening
⅓ cup (80 ml) honey
2¼ cups (540 ml) warm water

Preheat oven to 400°F (205°C) 10 minutes before baking. Grease two 9x5x3-inch pans or two 8½x4½x2½-inch pans.

In large mixing bowl, combine 2 packages yeast, 1 cup of whole wheat flour and 1 cup of all-purpose flour, salt, buttermilk blend, soft margarine and honey. Add very warm (120°-130°F; 49°-54°C) water to flour mixture. Blend at low speed until moistened; beat 3 minutes at medium speed. By hand, gradually stir in remaining 1¾ cups whole wheat flour and enough of remaining white flour (3-3½ cups) to make a soft dough.

Turn out on lightly floured board and knead until smooth and elastic (8-10 minutes). Place in greased bowl, turning to grease all sides. Cover; let rise in warm place, free from drafts, until double in bulk (about 1 hour). Punch down. Divide dough into two parts; mold into balls. Allow to rest, covered with inverted bowl, 10 minutes.

Shape into loaves. Place in prepared pans. Let rise until doubled (about 1 hour). Bake for 25-30 minutes or until golden brown and loaves sound hollow when tapped. Remove from pans and cool on racks. Yields 2 loaves.

Honey Wheat Germ Bread

2 pkgs active dry yeast
1 cup (240 ml) warm water
2 cups (480 ml) very warm water
½ cup (120 ml) soft butter or margarine
¼ cup (60 ml) honey
1 tbs (15 ml) salt
½ cup (120 ml) instant potato flakes
½ tsp (3 ml) baking soda
1 cup (240 ml) plain wheat germ
½ cup (120 ml) SACO Buttermilk Blend
6-7½ cups (1.4-1.8 l) all-purpose flour

Preheat oven to 375°F (190°C) 10 minutes before baking. Grease three 8½x4½x2½-inch pans.

Sprinkle yeast over 1 cup warm (105°-115°F; 41°-46°C) water in a large bowl (warm water should feel comfortably warm on wrist). Stir until yeast dissolves. In another bowl, combine 2 cups very warm (120°-130°F; 49°-54°C) water with butter or margarine, honey and salt. Stir until butter or maragrine is melted; stir in potato flakes. Combine with yeast mixture in large bowl. Stir in baking soda, wheat germ, buttermilk blend and 3 cups flour until smooth. Beat in enough additional flour (3-4½ cups) to make a soft dough.

Turn out onto lightly-floured surface. Knead until smooth and elastic (8-10 minutes). Place in greased bowl, turning to grease all sides. Cover; let rise in warm place, free from drafts, until double (about 1-1½ hours). Punch down.

Turn out onto lightly-floured surface. Knead a few times. Allow to rest, covered with inverted bowl 10 minutes. Divide dough in thirds and shape into loaves. Place each loaf in prepared pan. Let rise 30 minutes or until double.

Bake for 45 minutes or until loaves sound hollow when tapped. Loosely cover tops with aluminum foil if tops are browning too fast. Remove from pans to racks; cool completely. Yields 3 loaves.

Opposite: Honey Wheat Germ Bread

Buttermilk Whole Wheat Bread

2 pkgs active dry yeast
4½ cups (1.1 l) whole wheat flour
2-3 cups (480-720 ml) all-purpose flour
3 tbs (45 ml) sugar
1 tbs (15 ml) salt
¼ cup (60 ml) SACO Buttermilk Blend
⅓ cup (80 ml) margarine, spftened
⅓ cup (80 ml) molasses
2¼ cups (540 ml) warm water

Preheat oven to 400°F (205°C) 10 minutes before baking. Grease two 9x5x3-inch pans or two 8½x4½x2½-inch pans .

In large mixing bowl, combine 2 packages yeast, 1 cup whole wheat flour, 1 cup of all-purpose flour, sugar, salt, buttermilk blend, soft margarine and molasses. Add very warm (120-130°F; 49°-54°C) water to flour mixture. Blend at low speed until moistened; beat 3 minutes at medium speed. By hand, gradually stir in remaining 3½ cups whole wheat flour and enough of remaining white flour (1-2 cups) to make a soft dough.

Turn out on lightly floured board and knead until smooth and elastic (8-10 minutes). Place in greased bowl, turning to grease all sides. Cover; let rise in warm place, free from drafts, until double in bulk (about 1 hour). Punch down. Divide dough into 2 parts; mold into balls. Allow to rest, covered with inverted bowl, 10 minutes.

Shape into loaves. Place in prepared pans. Let rise until doubled (about 1 hour). Bake for 25-30 minutes or until golden brown and loaves sound hollow when tapped. Remove from pans and cool on racks. This bread is denser and darker then the Honey Whole Wheat Bread. Yields 2 loaves.

Oatmeal Bread

2 pkgs active dry yeast
2½ tsp (13 ml) salt
6 tbs (90 ml) SACO Buttermilk Blend
4-4½ cups (960-1,080 ml) all-purpose flour
¼ cup (60 ml) soft shortening
⅓ cup (80 ml) molasses or honey
2 cups (480 ml) warm water (120°-130°F; 49°-54°C)
1½ cups (355 ml) quick-cooking oatmeal

Preheat oven to 375°F (190°C) 10 minutes before baking. Grease two 8½x4½-inch pans.

In a large mixing bowl combine yeast, salt, buttermilk blend and 2½ cups flour. Add soft shortening and molasses or honey. Add warm water and blend at low speed until moistened. Beat on medium speed for 3 minutes. By hand, stir in oatmeal and enough remaining flour (1½-2 cups) to make a soft dough.

Turn out on lightly floured board, cover and let rest 5 minutes. Knead until smooth and elastic (6-8 minutes). Place in greased bowl, turning to grease all sides. Cover, let rise in warm place, free from drafts, until double in bulk (about 1-1½ hours). Punch down. Cover and allow to rest 10 minutes. Shape into 2 loaves.

Place in prepared loaf pans. Let rise until doubled (45 minutes to 1 hour). Bake for 35-40 minutes or until golden brown and loaves sound hollow when tapped. Remove from pans and cool on racks. Yields 2 loaves.

Buttermilk Whole Wheat Bread

Health Loaf

1 pkg yeast
½ cup (120 ml) warm water
1 tsp (5 ml) sugar
1 orange or ¾ cup (180 ml) grated carrots
2 cups (480 ml) warm water
⅓ cup (80 ml) oil
¼ cup (60 ml) GRANDMA'S Molasses
½ tsp (3 ml) salt
3 cups (720 ml) whole wheat flour
¼ cup (60 ml) sunflower seeds
2 cups (480 ml) white flour

Preheat oven to 350°F (180°C) 10 minutes before baking. Butter and flour 2 bread pans.

In a very large bowl, mix first 3 ingredients and let stand 10 minutes. Add orange or carrots and the 2 cups warm water. Add remaining ingredients, except white flour, and let stand 1 hour. Mix and add enough of 2 cups white flour to make a dough that can be handled. Knead about 5 minutes folding the dough toward you every half turn.

Divide dough in half. Shape into loaves. Butter top of loaves and place in prepared bread pans. Cover with a towel and leave in a warm place until they have doubled in bulk. Bake 30-40 minutes. Yields 2 loaves.

Light Rye Bread

2 pkgs active dry yeast
1 cup (240 ml) rye flour
4½-5½ cups (1.1-1.3 l) all-purpose flour
6 tbs (90 ml) SACO Buttermilk Blend
1 tbs (15 ml) salt
¼ cup (60 ml) brown sugar
¼ cup (60 ml) oil or other soft shortening
2 cups (480 ml) water

Preheat oven to 400°F (205°C) 10 minutes before baking. Grease two 9x5x3-inch pans or two 8½x4½x2½-inch pans.

In large mixing bowl, combine 2 packages yeast, rye flour, 1 cup all-purpose flour, buttermilk blend, salt, sugar, and shortening. Add very warm (120°-130°F; 49°-54°C) water to flour mixture. Blend at low speed until moistened; beat 3 minutes at medium speed. By hand, gradually stir in enough of remaining all-purpose flour (3½-4½ cups) to make a soft dough.

Turn out on lightly floured board and knead until smooth and elastic (8-10 minutes). Place in greased bowl, turning to grease all sides. Cover; let rise in warm place, free from drafts, until double in bulk (about 1 hour). Punch down. Divide dough into 2 parts; mold into balls. Allow to rest, covered with inverted bowl, for 10 minutes.

Shape into loaves. Place in prepared pans. Let rise until doubled (about 1 hour). Bake for 25-30 minutes until brown and loaves sound hollow when tapped. Remove from pans and cool on racks. Yields 2 loaves.

Light Rye Bread

Opposite: Health Loaf

Dark Rye Bread

2 pkgs active dry yeast
1½ cups (355 ml) warm water
¼ cup (60 ml) molasses
⅓ cup (80 ml) sugar
1 tbs (15 ml) salt
2 tbs (30 ml) soft shortening
2 cups (480 ml) rye flour
¼ cup (60 ml) SACO Buttermilk Blend
3¼-3½ cups (780-840 ml) all-purpose flour

Preheat oven to 375°F (190°C) 10 minutes before baking. Lightly grease a cookie sheet.

Soften yeast in ½ cup of the warm water. To remaining 1 cup of water add molasses, sugar and salt. Stir in shortening, softened yeast, rye flour, and buttermilk blend. Gradually beat in enough white flour (3¼-3½ cups) to make a stiff dough.

Turn out onto floured surface and knead until smooth (8-10 minutes). Place in greased bowl, turning to grease all sides. Let rise in warm place, free from drafts, until doubled. Punch down. Divide dough into 2 parts; mold into balls. Allow to rest, covered with inverted bowl, for 10 minutes.

Shape into 2 round loaves. Place at opposite corners of prepared cookie sheet. Let rise until doubled. Bake for 30-40 minutes or until brown and loaves sound hollow when tapped. Yields 2 loaves.

Orange-Flavored Rye Bread: Add 2 tbs (30 ml) grated orange peel with molasses, sugar and salt.

Caraway-Flavored Rye Bread: Add 2 tbs (30 ml) caraway seeds with molasses, sugar and salt.

Anise-Flavored Rye Bread: Add 1 tsp (5 ml) anise seeds with molasses, sugar and salt.

Black Bread

½ cup (120 ml) cornmeal
2 cups (480 ml) water
¼ cup (60 ml) butter, cut in pieces
1 oz (30 g) unsweetened chocolate
½ cup (120 ml) dark molasses
1½ tsp (8 ml) salt
2 tbs (30 ml) McCORMICK/SCHILLING Caraway Seed
2 tsp (10 ml) instant coffee
¼ cup (60 ml) lukewarm water
1 pkg active dry yeast
5½ cups (1.3 l) flour

Preheat oven to 350°F (180°C) 10 minutes before baking. Butter two 2¼x3½x7½-inch loaf pans.

In saucepan, combine cornmeal and water. Cook, stirring over medium heat, until mixture comes to a boil. Simmer 1 minute. Remove from heat. Add next 6 ingredients. Stir well. Cool to lukewarm. Combine lukewarm water and yeast. Let stand 5 minutes. Stir into cornmeal mixture. Beat in 4½ cups flour, ½ cup at a time.

Place dough on well-floured surface and knead in remaining flour. Continue kneading until dough is smooth and elastic, about 5 minutes. Butter inside of large bowl. Place dough in bowl. Turn dough until entire surface is lightly buttered.

Cover with towel. Set in warm, draft-free place and let rise 1½ hours or until double in size. Punch dough down. Knead 2 minutes on floured surface. Divide dough in half and shape each half into small loaf. Place each in a prepared loaf pan. Cover with towel and let rise 40 minutes.

Bake 1 hour or until loaves shrink away from sides of pan. Cool on wire racks. Yields 2 loaves.

Opposite: **Black Bread**

Rye Bread with Poppy Seed and Caraway

2 pkgs active dry yeast
⅓ cup (80 ml) sugar
1 tbs (15 ml) salt
¼ cup (60 ml) SACO Buttermilk Blend
1 tbs (15 ml) caraway seeds
2 cup (480 ml) rye flour
¾ cup (180 ml) whole wheat flour
2 tbs (30 ml) soft shortening
¼ cup (60 ml) molasses
2 cups (480 ml) warm water (120°-130°F (49°-54°C))
2½-3 cups (590-720 ml) all-purpose flour
1 egg white, slightly beaten
poppy seeds

Preheat oven to 375°F (190°C) 10 minutes before baking.

In a large mixing bowl combine yeast, sugar, salt, buttermilk blend, caraway seeds, rye flour and whole wheat flour. Add soft shortening and molasses. Add warm water and beat at low speed until blended. Beat on medium speed for 2 minutes. Stir in enough all-purpose flour, one cup at a time, to make a stiff dough.

Turn out on floured board, cover and let rest 5 minutes. Knead until smooth and elastic (5-8 minutes). Place in a greased bowl, turning to grease all sides. Cover and let rise in warm place, free from drafts, until doubled, about 1 hour. Punch down and divide in half. Shape each half into a round ball and place on opposite corners of cookie sheet. Cover and let rise 45 minutes.

Just before baking, slash tops of loaves with a sharp knife about 3 times. Carefully brush loaves with egg white and sprinkle with poppy seeds. Bake 30-40 minutes or until brown and loaf sounds hollow when tapped. If loaves are browning too fast, cover with aluminum foil for last 10 minutes of baking. Yields 2 loaves.

French Bread

cornmeal
1 pkg RED STAR Active Dry Yeast or QUICK•RISE Yeast
1¼ cups (295 ml) warm water
2¾-3 cups (660-720 ml) all-purpose flour
1 tsp (5 ml) salt

Preheat oven to 425°F (220°C) 10 minutes before baking. Grease a cookie sheet and sprinkle with cornmeal.

Dissolve yeast in warm water (110°-115°F; 43°-46°C); let stand 5 minutes. By hand, stir in 1½ cups flour and salt. Gradually stir in just enough remaining flour to make a soft dough.

Knead on floured surface until smooth and elastic, about 10 minutes. Place in greased bowl, turning to grease tops. Cover; let rise at room temperature until double, 2½-3 hours (1¼-1½ hours for Quick•Rise Yeast).

Punch down dough. On lightly floured surface, roll or pat dough to a 12x6-inch rectangle. Starting with longer side, roll up tightly, pressing dough into roll with each turn. Pinch edges and ends to seal. Place on prepared cookie sheet. Cover; let rise at room temperature until more than doubled, 1-1½ hours (30-45 minutes for Quick•Rise Yeast). With very sharp knife, make 2 or 3 diagonal slashes across top of loaf. Spray or brush loaf with cold water.

Bake for 25-30 minutes until golden brown. Spray or brush loaf with water several times during baking for a crispier crust. Remove from cookie sheet; cool. Yields 1 loaf.

Rye Bread with Poppy Seed and Caraway

Buttermilk French Bread

cornmeal
4¼-4¾ cups (1-1.1 l) all-purpose flour
2 pkgs dry yeast
¼ cup (60 ml) SACO Buttermilk Blend
2 tbs (30 ml) sugar
2½ tsp (13 ml) salt
2 tbs (30 ml) shortening
1¾ cups (415 ml) warm water (120°-130°F; 49°-54°C)

Preheat oven to 400°F (205°C) 10 minutes before baking. Grease 15½x12-inch baking sheet and sprinkle with cornmeal.

In large mixing bowl, combine 1¾ cups flour, buttermilk blend, sugar, salt and shortening. Add warm water to flour mixture and beat at low speed for ½ minute, scraping bowl constantly. Beat 3 more minutes at high speed. By hand, stir in enough remaining flour (2½-3 cups) to form a soft dough.

Turn out on lightly floured board and knead 5-10 minutes until smooth. Cover dough. Let rest 20 minutes. Divide dough into two parts.

To shape loaf, roll out 1 part with floured rolling pin to rectangle, about 13x5 inches and ½-inch thick. Starting from long side, roll up as for jelly roll pan. Pinch edges and turn seam side down. Taper ends of loaf by shaping with hands. Repeat with remaining dough.

Place loaves a few inches apart on prepared baking sheet. Let rise in a warm place until almost doubled (about 45 minutes). Make 3 or 4 diagonal slashes, ¼-inch deep, on top of each loaf. Brush tops with warm water just before baking.

Bake 25-30 minutes. Remove from baking sheet and cool on racks. Yields 2 loaves.

Sourdough French Bread

cornmeal
1½ cups (355 ml) lukewarm water
1 cake compressed yeast
1 cup (240 ml) Sourdough Starter
2 tsp (10 ml) sugar
2 tsp (10 ml) salt
½ tsp (3 ml) soda
6-6½ cups (1.4-1.6 l) sifted HECKERS/CERESOTA
*   Unbleached Flour*

Preheat oven to 425°F (220°C) 10 minutes before baking. Sprinkle 3 baking sheets lightly with cornmeal.

Dissolve yeast in lukewarm water. Mix Soughdough Starter into yeast mixture. Combine sugar, salt and soda; add to yeast. Add 3 cups flour; mix well. Add remaining flour; mix thoroughly. Turn out onto floured board; knead until smooth and elastic. Place in greased bowl; cover and let rise in warm (80-85°F) draft-free place for about 1½ hours or until nearly doubled.

Divide dough into 3 pieces. Shape each into a ball; let rest 10 minutes. Shape into tapered loaves. Place loaves on prepared baking sheets, allowing room for dough to expand. Brush dough with water. Let rise again about 45 minutes; brushing dough with water about every 15 minutes. With a very sharp knife, make 3 diagonal slashes across loaves.

Bake for about 25 minutes or until tests done. If desired, brush tops with beaten egg white just before baking. Yields 3 loaves.

Sourdough Starter

1 cake compressed yeast or 1 pkg active dry yeast
2 cups (480 ml) lukewarm (80°-85°F; 27°-29°C) water
2 cups (480 ml) HECKERS/CERESOTA Unbleached Flour
1 tbs (15 ml) sugar
1 tsp (5 ml) salt

Dissolve yeast in water (use 105°-110°F; 41°-43°C for active dry yeast). Combine flour, sugar and salt. Add flour mixture to liquid; mix very well. Pour into 48-oz (1.4 kg) glass jar; seal tightly with lid. Let stand at room temperature for 2-3 days (to ferment). Starter should then be used; refrigerate if not used. Be sure to reserve 1 cup of starter, refrigerated, for future use.

To Increase Starter:
1 cup starter
½ cup (120 ml) HECKERS/CERESOTA Unbleached Flour
½ cup (120 ml) warm water
1 tsp (5 ml) sugar

Let ferment 2 days before turning into recipe or increasing again. Refrigerate if you don't use.

Pepper Baguettes

1 tbs (15 ml) cornmeal
1 cup (240 ml) lukewarm water
1 pkg yeast
1 tbs (15 ml) TABASCO Pepper Sauce
1 tsp (5 ml) sugar
2½ cups (590 ml) unbleached flour
½ tsp (3 ml) salt

Preheat oven to 400°F (205°C) 10 minutes before baking. Lightly oil a baking sheet and sprinkle it with cornmeal.

Place the water in the bowl of a food processor, sprinkle in the yeast, pepper sauce and sugar. Allow to sit for 5 minutes. Lightly oil a 4-5-quart (3.8-4.8 l) bowl. Set aside.

Add the flour and salt to the yeast mixture in the processor bowl and blend for 30 seconds to 1 minute or until the dough leaves the side of the bowl. Transfer the dough to an oiled bowl. Cover and allow to rise at room temperature for 1-1½ hours or until dough has doubled in size.

When the dough is ready, punch it down and form into a ball. Place the dough on a lightly floured surface. Divide the dough into 3 parts, shape each into a baguettes and place on prepared baking sheet. Cover with plastic wrap. Allow bread to rise 40 minutes.

While preheating the oven, place a small ovenproof pan on rack beneath rack to be used for the bread. After the second rise sprinkle the baguettes with flour and slash tops with a sharp knife or scissors.

Place baking sheet in the oven, then throw enough ice cubes into the hot pan underneath to fill to two-thirds. The ice will melt and create steam to crisp the crust. Bake for 30 minutes or until golden. Remove and cool on a rack. Yields 3 baguettes.

Onion Bread

7-7½ cups (1.7-1.8 l) all-purpose flour
2 pkgs RED STAR Active Dry Yeast or QUICK•RISE Yeast
½ cup (120 ml) finely chopped fresh onion
⅓ cup (80 ml) sugar
2 tsp (10 ml) salt
2 cups (40 ml) water
⅓ cup (80 ml) shortening
2 eggs
1 egg, slightly beaten
1 tbs (15 ml) water

Preheat oven to 375°F (190°C) 10 minutes before baking. Grease two 9x5-inch bread pans.

In large mixing bowl, combine 3 cups flour, yeast onion, sugar and salt; mix well. Heat the water and shortening until very warm (120°-130°F; 49°-54°C; shortening does not need to melt). Add to flour mixture. Add 2 eggs. Blend at low speed until moistened; beat 3 minutes at medium speed. By hand, gradually stir in enough remaining flour to make a firm dough.

Knead on floured surface, 5-8 minutes. Place in greased bowl, turning to grease top. Cover; let rise in warm place about 30 minutes (15 minutes for rapid-rise yeast). Punch down dough. Divide into 2 parts. On lightly floured surface, roll or pat each half to a 14x7-inch rectangle. Starting with shorter side, roll up tightly, pressing dough into roll with each turn. Pinch edges and ends to seal.

Place in prepared pans. Cover; let rise in warm place about 40 minutes (20 minutes for rapid-rise yeast). Combine the beaten egg and 1 tbs water; brush loaves. With sharp knife, carefully make a slash ½-inch deep lengthwise down center of each loaf.

Bake for 35-40 minutes until golden brown. Remove from pans; cool. Yields 2 loaves.

Onion Bread

Almond Onion Bread

5 cups (1.2 l) flour
2 pkgs rapid-rise dry yeast
2 tbs (30 ml) sugar
1 tbs (15 ml) salt
2 cups (480 ml) milk
½ cup (120 ml) almond or vegetable oil
2 tsp (10 ml) dried, sweet basil
¾ cup (180 ml) chopped almonds, toasted
¾ cup (180 ml) finely chopped onions

Preheat oven to 375°F (190°C) 10 minutes before baking. Grease a baking sheet.

In large mixing bowl, combine 4 cups flour, yeast, sugar and salt. Combine milk, oil and basil in saucepan; heat to 110°-120°F (43°-49°C) or until warm to touch. Stir warm liquids into dry ingredients.

Knead in remaining 1 cup flour. Knead until dough is smooth and elastic, about 3 minutes. Cover dough and let rise until doubled in bulk, about 1 hour. Punch dough down; knead in almonds and onions. Shape into two 7-inch rounds. Place on prepared baking sheet. Let rise until doubled in bulk.

Bake in center of oven, 45-55 minutes. If top is getting too dark, cover loosely with foil. Bake until loaves sound hollow when tapped on the bottom. Place on wire rack to cool. Yields 2 loaves.

Courtesy of the Almond Board of California.

Wisconsin-Cheddar Jalapeño Bread

2 pkgs active dry yeast
1 tsp (5 ml) granulated sugar
½ cup (120 ml) warm water (110°F; 43°C)
8¾ cups (2.1 l) all-purpose flour
3 cups (720 ml) shredded extra-sharp cheddar cheese
¼ cup (60 ml) minced jalapeño pepper
1 tbs (15 ml) salt
2 tsp (10 ml) TABASCO Pepper Sauce
2 cups (480 ml) milk
4 large eggs

Preheat oven to 375°F (190°C) 10 minutes before baking. Grease 2 large cookie sheets.

In a small bowl, stir yeast, sugar and warm water. Let stand 5 minutes until foamy.

Meanwhile, in a large bowl combine 8 cups flour, cheddar cheese, jalapeño pepper, salt and pepper sauce. In a small saucepan over low heat, heat the milk until warm (120°-130°F; 49°-54°C). Stir milk into flour mixture. In a medium bowl, lightly beat eggs. Set aside 1 tbs beaten egg to brush on dough later. Add remaining eggs to flour mixture; stir until the mixture makes a soft dough.

On a lightly floured surface, knead the dough 5 minutes or until smooth and elastic, kneading in the remaining ¾ cup flour. Shape the dough into a ball and place in a large, greased bowl, turning dough over to grease the top. Cover with a towel and let rise in a warm place until doubled, about 1½ hours.

Punch down dough and divide it in half. Shape each half of dough into a ball and place the balls on the cookie sheets. Cover with a towel and let rise in a warm place until doubled, about 1½ hours.

Brush the loaves with the reserved beaten egg. Bake loaves about 45 minutes or until loaves sound hollow when lightly tapped. Remove to wire racks to cool. Yields 2 loaves.

Opposite:
Wisconsin-Cheddar Jalapeño Bread

Spicy Cheese Bread

2 pkgs active dry yeast
1 tsp (5 ml) granulated sugar
½ cup (120 ml) warm water
8½ cups (2 l) all-purpose flour
3 cups (720 ml) shredded Jarlsberg or Swiss cheese
2 tbs (30 ml) fresh chopped rosemary or 2 tsp (10 ml)
    dried rosemary
1 tbs (15 ml) salt
1 tbs (15 ml) TABASCO Pepper Sauce
2 cups (480 ml) milk
4 large eggs

Preheat oven to 375°F (190°C) 10 minutes before baking. Grease 2 large cookie sheets.

In small bowl, stir yeast, sugar and warm water. Let stand 5 minutes until foamy.

Meanwhile, in large bowl combine 8 cups flour, cheese, rosemary, salt, and pepper sauce. In small saucepan over low heat, heat the milk until warm (120°-130°F; 49°-54°C). Stir into flour mixture. In medium bowl, lightly beat eggs; set aside 1 tablespoon beaten egg (to brush on dough later). Add eggs to flour mixture along with foamy yeast mixture; stir until the mixture makes a soft dough.

On lightly floured surface, knead the dough 5 minutes or until smooth and elastic, kneading in remaining ½ cup flour. Shape the dough into a ball and place in a large, greased bowl, turning dough over to grease the top. Cover with towel and let rise in warm place until almost doubled, about 1½ hours.

Punch down dough and divide it in half. Cut each half in three strips and braid. Place each braid on a prepared cookie sheet. Cover and let rise in warm place until almost doubled, 30 minutes to 1 hour.

Brush braids with reserved egg. Bake about 45 minutes or until braids sound hollow when lightly tapped. Remove to wire racks to cool. Yields 2 braids.

Bacon-Cheese Batter Bread

1 pkg active dry yeast
½ cup (120 ml) lukewarm water
2 tbs (30 ml) sugar
2 tbs (30 ml) light corn syrup
¼ cup (60 ml) butter, softened
1 tsp (5 ml) salt
3 eggs
3 cups (720 ml) flour
1 cup (240 ml) shredded sharp cheddar cheese
1 tbs (15 ml) McCORMICK/SCHILLING
    Instant Chopped Onion
¼ tsp (3 ml) McCORMICK/SCHILLING Instant Garlic Powder
⅓ cup (80 ml) McCORMICK/SCHILLING
    Imitation Bacon Chips

Preheat oven to 375°F (190°C) 10 minutes before baking. Grease a 9¼x5¼x2¾-inch metal loaf pan.

In a large bowl, dissolve yeast in water. Stir in sugar and corn syrup. Add butter, salt, eggs and 2 cups flour. Beat with mixer on low speed until blended. Scrape bowl. Beat 1 minute on high speed. With wooden spoon, stir in remaining flour. Add remaining ingredients, mix well. Cover and let rise in warm place until doubled in bulk, about 45 minutes. Punch batter down by stirring 30 strokes with wooden spoon.

Spoon into prepared loaf pan. Let rise, covered, in warm place 30-40 minutes or until batter rises to edge of pan (not over). Bake in preheated oven 30-35 minutes. Remove from pan. To determine doneness, tap bottom of loaf with fingertips. It should sound hollow. If not, return to pan and bake 5 more minutes. Cool on wire rack. Yields 1 loaf.

Opposite: Bacon-Cheese Batter Bread

Herbed Whole Wheat Batter Bread

1 pkg active dry yeast
1¼ cups (295 ml) lukewarm water
2 tbs (30 ml) sugar
2 tbs (30 ml) light corn syrup
¼ cup (60 ml) butter, softened
1 tsp (5 ml) salt
1½ cups (355 ml) all-purpose flour
1½ cups (355 ml) whole wheat flour
2 tbs (30 ml) McCORMICK/SCHILLING
    Instant Chopped Onion
½ tsp (3 ml) McCORMICK/SCHILLING Basil Leaves
½ tsp (3 ml) McCORMICK/SCHILLING Thyme Leaves
½ tsp (3 ml) McCORMICK/SCHILLING Marjoram Leaves
1 egg
1 tbs (15 ml) water

Preheat oven to 350°F (180°C) 10 minutes before baking. Grease a 1½-quart round glass baking dish.

In large bowl, dissolve yeast in warm water. Stir in sugar and corn syrup. Add butter, salt and all-purpose flour. Beat with mixer at low speed until blended. Add ½ cup whole wheat flour. Beat at low speed. Scrape bowl. Beat 1 minute at high speed. With wooden spoon, stir in remaining whole wheat flour, 1 tbs of the chopped onion and herbs. Cover and let rise in warm place until doubled in bulk, about 45 minutes. Punch batter down by stirring 30 strokes with wooden spoon.

Spoon batter into prepared baking dish. In small bowl, combine egg and water. Beat well with fork. Brush top of batter with egg mixture. Sprinkle remaining chopped onion evenly over batter. Let rise, covered, in warm place 30-40 minutes or until batter rises to edge of pan (not over).

Bake in preheated oven 35-40 minutes. Remove from dish. To determine doneness, tap bottom of loaf with fingertips. It should sound hollow. If not, return to pan and bake 5 more minutes. Cool on wire rack. Yields 1 loaf.

Pizza Dough

1 pkg dry active yeast or 1 small cake compressed yeast
1¼ cups (295 ml) lukewarm water
4 cups (960 ml) sifted HECKERS/CERESOTA
    Unbleached Flour
1 tsp (5 ml) salt
2 tbs (30 ml) shortening, melted

Preheat oven to 425°F (220°C) 10 minutes before baking.

Dissolve yeast in lukewarm water. Add flour, salt and shortening; mix thoroughly. Turn onto floured board and knead until smooth and elastic. Place in greased bowl, cover and let rise in warm place until double in bulk (about 1½ hours). Divide dough into 2 or 4 pieces.

Roll out thin to fit either 12-inch round pizza pans or 8-inch pie pans. Fit dough into pans; crimp edges. Brush with olive oil or salad oil. Top as desired. Bake for 12-15 minutes until crust is golden and topping is bubbling. Yields 2-4 crusts.

Soft Pretzels

1 cake compressed yeast or 1 pkg active dry yeast
1½ cups (355 ml) lukewarm (80°-85°F; 27°-29°C) water
¾ tsp (4 ml) salt
1½ tsp (8 ml) sugar
4 cups (960 ml) sifted HECKERS/CERESOTA
    Unbleached Flour
1 egg, beaten
coarse salt

Preheat oven to 425°F (220°C) 10 minutes before baking. Line 2 baking sheets with parchment paper.

Dissolve yeast in water (use 105°-115°F; 41°-46°C for active dry yeast). Add salt and sugar. Blend flour and knead until smooth and elastic. Cut into small pieces, and roll into ropes; twist. Place on prepared aking sheets. Brush with beaten egg; sprinkle with coarse salt. Bake 12-15 minutes or until browned. Serve immediately. Yields about 20 pretzels.

Braided Buttermilk Bread

2 pkgs active dry yeast
½ cup (120 ml) warm water (105°-115°F; 41°-46°C)
6 tbs (90 ml) shortening
2 tbs (30 ml) sugar
2 tsp (10 ml) salt
6 tbs (90 ml) SACO Buttermilk Blend
1½ cups (355 ml) water
3 eggs (reserving 1 yolk)
7 cups (1.7 l) all-purpose flour
poppy seeds, optional

Preheat oven to 375°F (190°C) 10 minutes before baking.

Have all ingredients except ½ cup warm water at room temperature. In a small bowl, dissolve the yeast in ½ cup warm water and add a pinch of sugar. Do not stir. Let stand for 10 minutes. Meanwhile, in a large mixing bowl, combine the shortening, sugar, salt, buttermilk blend, 1½ cups water, eggs (reserving one yolk) and 3½ cups of the flour. Then stir in the activated yeast and mix well. Add enough of the remaining flour to make the dough soft and easy to handle (dough should pull away from the sides of the bowl).

For kneading, turn dough onto a lightly floured board or countertop. Knead for 5-10 minutes or until the dough is smooth and elastic. Cover and set the dough in a warm place to rise. When the dough has doubled in bulk (about 1½ hours), punch it down and divide into 3 parts. Divide each part into 3 more parts, rolling each piece into a long strand. Braid into 3 loaves, pinching strands together at each end of loaf. Put each braided loaf into a greased 4½x8½-inch pan.

Mix the remaining egg yolk with 1 tbs of cold water and brush over the loaves. Sprinkle with poppy seeds. Cover and set in a warm place to rise until each loaf has doubled in bulk (about 1 hour).

Bake for 45-50 minutes or until golden brown. Yields 3 loaves.

Variation: Braid as directed but place braid on cookie sheet. Brush with egg yolk and water mixture. Sprinkle with poppy seeds. Cover and set in warm place to rise until doubled in bulk (about 1 hour). Bake at 375°F (190°C) for 40 minutes or until golden brown and loaves sound hollow when tapped. If bread is browning too fast, loosely cover with aluminum foil.

Easy Egg Braid

4-4½ cups (960-1080 ml) all-purpose flour
2 pkgs RED STAR Active Dry Yeast or QUICK•RISE Yeast
2 tbs (30 ml) sugar
2 tsp (10 ml) salt
½ cup (120 ml) water
½ cup (120 ml) milk
2 tbs (30 ml) shortening
3 eggs, slightly beaten (reserve 1 tbs; 5 ml)

Preheat oven to 400°F (205°C) 10 minutes before baking. Grease a cookie sheet.

In large mixing bowl, combine 2 cups flour, yeast, sugar and salt; mix well. In saucepan, heat water, milk and shortening until very warm (120°-130°F; 49°-54°C; shortening does not need to melt). Add to flour mixture. Reserving 1 tbs, add beaten eggs. Blend at low speed until moistened; beat 3 minutes at medium speed. By hand, gradually stir in enough remaining flour to make a firm dough. Knead on floured surface until smooth and elastic, 5-8 minutes. Place in greased bowl, turning to grease top. Cover; let rise in warm place until light and doubled, about 1 hour (30 minutes for rapid-rise yeast).

Punch down dough. Divide into 3 parts. On lightly floured surface, roll each third to a 15-inch rope. On greased cookie sheet loosely braid beginning with center-piece. Pinch ends and tuck under to seal. Cover; let rise in warm place until almost doubled, 30 minutes (15 minutes for rapid-rise yeast). Brush with reserved 1 tbs egg.

Bake for 25-30 minutes until golden brown. Remove from cookie sheet; cool. Yields 1 large braid.

Easy Egg Braid

Famous Bread Braid

¼ cup (60 ml) warm water
1 pkg active dry yeast
2 eggs
1½ cups (355 ml) scalded milk, cooled
2 tbs (30 ml) melted butter
2 tsp (10 ml) salt
2 tbs (30 ml) sugar
¼ tsp (1 ml) McCORMICK Coriander Seed
6-6½ cups (1.4-1.6 l) sifted flour
1 egg yolk
1 tbs (15 ml) milk
1 tsp (5 ml) McCORMICK Poppy Seed

Preheat oven to 375°F (190°C) 10 minutes before baking. Grease a baking sheet.

Combine warm water and yeast; stir to dissolve. Beat eggs in large bowl. Beat in scalded milk and melted butter a little at a time. Stir in yeast mixture. Add salt, sugar and coriander. Stir in 4 cups of the flour, one cup at a time. Beat mixture until dough is smooth and elastic. Mix in another cup of the flour. Knead dough on board adding more flour as needed until dough is no longer sticky, has a smooth feel and a satiny look (about 10 minutes).

Place in greased bowl, turn dough over so top is greased. Cover bowl with a towel and let stand in a warm place until double in bulk (1½-2 hours).

Punch dough down, squeeze to remove air bubbles. Divide dough in fourths. Roll each piece into a 15-inch long strip. Place on greased baking sheet and braid, starting at center and braiding to the end. Cover and let rise in warm place until double in bulk (about 1 hour). Beat egg yolk and milk together. Brush over surface of dough. Sprinkle with poppy seed.

Bake 1 hour. Yields 1 loaf.

Applesauce Bran Bread

½ cup (120 ml) all bran cereal
½ cup (120 ml) all-purpose enriched flour
¼ cup (60 ml) GRANDMA'S Molasses
pinch salt
1 pkg active dry yeast
1½ cups (355 ml) MOTT'S Unsweetened Apple Sauce
¼ cup (60 ml) milk
2 tbs (30 ml) margarine
2 eggs
3 cups all-purpose flour (720 ml), sifted

Preheat oven to 375°F (190°C) 10 minutes before baking. Grease 2 9x5x3-inch loaf pans.

Combine cereal, flour, molasses, salt and yeast in large mixing bowl.

Place applesauce, milk and margarine in large saucepan. Heat until temperature reaches 120°-130°F; 49°-54°C (margarine does not need to melt). Add to cereal mixture. Using the dough attachment of a mixer, mix at medium speed for 2 minutes, scraping bowl occasionally. Add eggs and about ¼ of the sifted flour. Mix on high speed for 2 minutes, scraping bowl occasionally. Add additional flour, mixing on low speed until dough is stiff and sticky.

Cover bowl loosely and let it rise in warm place until double in volume. Punch dough down. Shape dough into 2 loaves. Place loaves in prepared loaf pans. Cover and let rise in warm place until double in volume.

Bake for 25-30 minutes. To prevent overbrowning during last few minutes of baking, cover loosely with foil. Yields 2 loaves.

Opposite: Applesauce Bran Bread

Basic Rapid-Rise Refrigerator Sweet Dough

5½-6 cups (1.3-1.4 l) WASHINGTON All-Purpose Flour, divided
2 pkgs active dry yeast, undissolved
½ cup (120 ml) sugar
1½ tsp (8 ml) salt
½ cup (120 ml) margarine, room temperature
1½ cups (355 ml) very hot water
2 eggs, room temperature vegetable oil

Preheat oven to 375°F (190°C) 10 minutes before baking. Grease two 9-inch round pans.

Place 2 cups flour, yeast, sugar and salt in large mixing bowl. Stir well to blend. All at once add margarine and very hot water to ingredients in bowl. Beat with electric mixer at medium speed for 2 minutes. Scrape sides of bowl occasionally. Beat 2 eggs and 1 cup flour with mixer 1 minute or until thick and elastic. Scrape sides of bowl occasionally. Gradually stir in 2½-3 cups flour in with wooden spoon to make a soft dough that leaves sides of bowl. Turn onto floured board. Round up into a ball.

Knead 8-10 minutes or until dough is smooth and elastic. Cover with plastic wrap then a towel. Let rest for 15-20 minutes on board. Punch down. Divide dough in half.

Daisy Braid: Roll half the dough into a 6x18-inch rectangle on lightly floured board. Cut lengthwise into 3 equal strips. Roll each strip to make a round rope 18 inches long. Braid 3 ropes together. Begin at center and braid to each end. Place in prepared pan. Braid loose ends together to complete the circle. Repeat with other half of dough.

Brush surface of dough with oil. Cover loosely with plastic wrap. Refrigerate 2-4 hours.

When ready to bake, remove from refrigerator. Uncover. Let stand for 10 minutes. Puncture any surface bubbles with an oiled toothpick just before baking. Bake on a lower oven rack position for best results. Remove from pan immediately. Cool on rack. Brush with margarine while warm, if desired frost with Confectioners Sugar Frosting. Yields 2 loaves.

Confectioners Sugar Frosting: Combine ½ cup (120 ml) confectioners sugar with 2-3 tsp (10-15 ml) milk, coffee, fruit juice or water to bring to spreading consistency.

Honey-Wheat Twist

2 pkgs active dry yeast
1 cup (240 ml) warm water (105°-115°F; 41°-46°C)
¼ cup (60 ml) honey
3 tbs (45 ml) margarine or butter, melted
2 tsp (10 ml) salt
1 egg
2¾-3 cups (660-720 ml) GOLD MEDAL All-Purpose Flour*
¾-1 cup (180-240 ml) GOLD MEDAL Whole Wheat Flour

Honey-Almond Glaze:
¼ cup (60 ml) chopped almonds
1 tbs (15 ml) margarine or butter
¼ cup (60 ml) honey
2 tbs (30 ml) sugar

*if using self-rising flour, omit salt.

Preheat oven to 350°F (180°C) 10 minutes before baking. Grease cookie sheet.

Dissolve yeast in warm water in large bowl. Stir in honey, margarine or butter, salt, egg and 2 cups all-purpose flour. Beat until smooth. Divide dough in half. Stir in enough of the whole wheat flour into one half to form a soft dough. Stir in enough of the remaining all-purpose flour into the other half to form a soft dough.

Turn each half onto lightly floured surface; knead about 5 minutes or until smooth and elastic. Place in greased bowls; turn greased sides up. Cover; let rise in warm place about 1½ hours or until double. Dough is ready if indentation remains when touched.

Punch down dough; roll each half into rope, about 15 inches long. Place ropes side by side on prepared cookie sheet; twist together gently and loosely. Pinch ends to fasten. Let rise about 1 hour or until double.

Bake 30-35 minutes or until twist is golden brown and sounds hollow when tapped; remove from cookie sheet. Cool slightly on wire rack. Spread with Honey-Almond Glaze. Yields 1 loaf.

Honey-Almond Glaze: Cook almonds and margarine or butter, stirring frequently, until almonds are brown. Stir in honey and sugar. Heat to boiling, stirring constantly; cool.

Opposite: **Honey-Wheat Twist**

Panhandle Ghirardelli Chocolate Bread

1 cup (240 ml) milk
1¼ cups (295 ml) water
1 pkg active dry yeast
2 tbs (30 ml) oil
¼ cup (60 ml) sugar
½ tsp (3 ml) vanilla
6 cups (1.4 l) unsifted flour
1 cup (240 ml) GHIRARDELLI Ground Chocolate
2 tsp (10 ml) salt
1 tsp (5 ml) cinnamon
vegetable oil

Preheat oven to 425°F (220°C) 10 minutes before baking. Grease two 9x5-inch loaf pans.

Heat milk with water until lukewarm (105°-115°F; 41°-46°C). Soften yeast in warm liquid. Stir in oil, sugar and vanilla then transfer to large bowl. Sift flour with ground chocolate, salt and cinnamon. Using wooden spoon, add half the dry ingredients to liquid, add remaining dry ingredients 1 cup at a time, beating until dough leaves the side of the bowl.

Turn out on lightly floured board and let rest 10 minutes. Knead dough lightly about 10 minutes or until smooth and elastic; add flour to board as needed to keep dough from sticking. Place in greased bowl; turn over to grease top. Cover with damp cloth. Let rise in warm place (75°-80°F; 24°-27°C) for about 2 hours or until double in bulk. Knead lightly in bowl. Let rise a second time.

Divide dough and shape into 2 loaves. Place in prepared loaf pans. Grease tops lightly with vegetable oil. Cover and let rise until double in bulk.

Place on lower rack in preheated oven for 5 minutes. Reduce heat to 350°F (180°C) and bake about 30 minutes or until top is firm. Brush top crust with melted butter. Remove bread from pans and cool on rack away from drafts. Yields 2 loaves.

Opposite:
Panhandle Ghirardelli
Chocolate Bread

California Poppy Coffeecake

¾ cup (180 ml) sugar
½ cup (120 ml) milk, scalded
2 eggs
½ tsp (3 ml) salt
½ tsp (3 ml) ground cardamom
½ cup (120 ml) butter or margarine, softened
4½ cups (1.1 l) unsifted flour
2 pkgs active dry yeast
½ cup (120 ml) warm water

Chocolate Filling:
1 cup (240 ml) GHIRARDELLI Semi-Sweet Chocolate Chips
¼ cup (60 ml) milk
½ tsp (3 ml) cinnamon
⅓ cup (80 ml) poppy seeds

Crumb Topping:
¼ cup (60 ml) flour
¼ cup (60 ml) sugar
¼ cup (60 ml) butter or margarine
1 tsp (5 ml) cinnamon
⅓ cup (80 ml) sliced almonds

Preheat oven to 350°F (180°C) 10 minutes before baking. Grease a baking sheet.

In a large bowl, combine sugar, scalded milk, eggs, salt and cardamom; beat until smooth. Add butter or margarine and 2 cups flour; beat until smooth. Sprinkle yeast into warm water; stir until dissolved. Add yeast liquid and 1 cup flour to dough; beat 3 minutes. Work in remaining 1½ cups flour. Cover; let rise in warm place until doubled, about 1½ hours.

Punch down dough; turn out and knead lightly on floured board. Roll into rectangle. Spread dough with Chocolate Filling and sprinkle with poppy seeds. Roll up, as for jelly roll, starting with wide end. Place seam side down on prepared baking sheet. Shape into a ring and press ends together. Cut 2-inch slices and alternate slices to form a fan ring. Sprinkle with Crumb Topping. Cover and let rise about 1 hour or until doubled in bulk. Bake for 30-35 minutes. Serve warm or cold. Yields 1 cake.

Chocolate Filling: Melt chocolate chips with milk and cinnamon; stir until smooth. Reserve poppy seeds.

Crumb Topping: Combine flour, sugar, butter or margarine and cinnamon; mix with fork until crumbly and toss with nuts.

Christmas Cardamom Braid

¾ cup (180 ml) SUN•MAID Golden Raisins
½ cup (120 ml) diced candied fruits and peels
¼ cup (60 ml) brandy
2 tsp (10 ml) grated lemon peel
3½-4 cups (840-960 ml) all-purpose flour
¼ cup (60 ml) sugar
2 pkgs fast-rising active dry yeast
2 tsp (10 ml) ground cardamom
½ tsp (3 ml) salt
¾ cup (180 ml) milk
½ cup (120 ml) butter or margarine
2 eggs

Combine raisins, fruits and peels, brandy and lemon peel; set aside. In mixing bowl, combine 2½ cups of the flour, sugar, yeast, cardamom and salt. Heat milk and butter or margarine to 125°-130°F (52°-54°C); stir into dry mixture. Mix in one of the eggs and the raisin-brandy mixture. Stir in enough of the remaining flour to make a soft dough.

Knead on floured surface 8-10 minutes, until smooth and elastic. Cover; let rest 10 minutes. Form dough into three 18-inch ropes; braid together, tucking ends under. Place on greased baking sheet. Cover; let rise in warm place until almost doubled in size, 50-60 minutes. Brush with remaining egg, beaten.

Bake at 350°F (180°C) for 30-35 minutes or until golden. Cover with foil as needed during baking to prevent overbrowning. Cool. Decorate with additional candied fruits and raisins, if desired; drizzle with Icing.
Yields 1 braid.

Icing: Whisk smooth 1 cup (240 ml) sifted powdered sugar and 2 tbs (30 ml) milk.

Christmas Cardamom Braid

Walnut-Filled Coffeecake

2 pkgs active dry yeast
½ cup (120 ml) warm water
1½ cups (355 ml) milk, scalded and cooled to lukewarm
¾ cup (180 ml) melted, unsalted butter
½ cup (120 ml) sugar
2 tsp (10 ml) salt
2 tsp (10 ml) grated lemon rind
2 eggs
5 cups (1.2 l) flour

Filling:
2¾ cups (650 ml) finely chopped walnuts or pecans
⅓ cup (80 ml) light cream
¼ cup (60 ml) sugar
2 tsp (10 ml) McCORMICK/SCHILLING Cinnamon
1 tbs (15 ml) McCORMICK/SCHILLING Pure Vanilla Extract
½ cup (120 ml) honey
1 egg, separated

Preheat oven to 350°F (180°C) 10 minutes before baking. Grease a cookie sheet.

In large mixing bowl blend yeast and water. Let stand 5 minutes. Add next 6 ingredients. Mix on low speed. Gradually beat in 3 cups flour. Beat 2 minutes. Beat in remaining 2 cups flour using wooden spoon. Beat until dough is very elastic. Cover. Let stand until double. Punch down.

Divide into 3 equal portions. Roll out each portion into a rectangle about 14x17 inches. Spread ⅓ of the Filling on each piece of the dough. Roll up as jelly roll on greased cookie sheet. Cut diagonal slits in top layer of dough. Let rise 30 minutes.

Bake 35-40 minutes.

Filling: Combine walnuts, light cream, sugar, cinnamon, vanilla, honey and egg yolk. Mix well. Beat egg white and fold in. Yields 3 loaves.

Crunch Cinnamon Coffeecake

3 cups (720 ml) all-purpose flour
2 pkgs RED STAR Active Dry Yeast or QUICK•RISE Yeast
⅓ cup (80 ml) sugar
½ tsp (3 ml) salt
½ cup (120 ml) milk
½ cup (120 ml) water
¼ cup (60 ml) butter or margarine
1 egg

Topping:
½ cup (120 ml) sugar
½ cup (120 ml) all-purpose flour
½ cup (120 ml) nuts
1 tsp (5 ml) cinnamon
½ cup (120 ml) firm butter

Preheat oven to 375°F (190°C) 10 minutes before baking. Grease a 13x9-inch cake pan.

In large mixing bowl, combine 1½ cups flour, yeast, sugar and salt; mix well. In saucepan, heat milk, water and butter or margarine until very warm (120°-130°F; 49°-54°C; butter does not need to melt). Add to flour mixture. Add egg. Blend at low speed until moistened; beat 3 minutes at medium speed. By hand, gradually stir in remaining 1½ cups flour to make a stiff batter. Spread in well-greased cake pan. Cover; let rise in warm* oven for 25 minutes (15 minutes for rapid-rise yeast). Sprinkle on the Topping.

Topping: Combine sugar flour, nuts and cinnamon. Cut in butter with pastry blender until particles are the size of small peas. Sprinkle over batter. With back of spoon, make random indentations in batter.

Bake for 20-25 minutes. Serve warm or cold. Yields 1 cake.

*Turn oven to lowest setting for 1 minute, then turn it off.

Praline Pecan Loaf

2 tbs (30 ml) butter or margarine
¾ cup (180 ml) IMPERIAL Brown Sugar
1 tsp (5 ml) cinnamon
1 cup (240 ml) pecan halves
2 tbs (30 ml) honey
2 tbs (30 ml) water

Streusel:
½ cup (120 ml) chopped pecans
3 tbs (45 ml) melted butter or margarine
½ cup (120 ml) all-purpose flour
½ cup (120 ml) IMPERIAL Brown Sugar
½ tsp (3 ml) cinnamon

Loaf:
1 pkg active dry yeast
¼ cup (60 ml) warm water
2¼ cups (540 ml) all-purpose flour
2 tbs (30 ml) IMPERIAL Granulated Sugar
1¼ tsp (6 ml) cinnamon
2 tsp (10 ml) baking powder
½ tsp (3 ml) salt
⅓ cup (80 ml) butter or margarine
⅓ cup (80 ml) milk, scalded, cooled
1 egg, beaten

Preheat oven to 350°F (180°C) 10 minutes before baking.

Melt butter or margarine, spread on bottom of 9x5x3-inch loaf pan. Sprinkle with brown sugar and cinnamon. Toast pecans in oven and spread over cinnamon mixture. Combine honey with water and drizzle over pecans. Set pan aside.

Streusel: Mix all ingredients in bowl. Mixture should be very crumbly. Set aside.

Loaf: Dissolve yeast in warm water; set aside. Combine flour, granulated sugar, cinnamon, baking powder and salt in mixing bowl; cut in butter or margarine until mixture resembles fine crumbs. Combine dissolved yeast with milk, beaten eggs and stir into crumb mixture and beat well.

Knead about 5 minutes on floured surface until dough is no longer sticky. Roll out to 15x10-inch rectangle. Sprinkle with Streusel mixture and roll up from shorter side (like a jelly roll). Cut into three equal pieces and place in loaf pan (cut sides up); press lightly. Cover with oiled plastic wrap and let rise in warm place 1½-2 hours or until even with top of pan.

Bake in preheated oven in middle rack about 30 minutes. Remove from pan onto rack to cool. Yields 1 loaf, serves 8-10.

Cinnamon Loaf Coffeecake

1¼ cups (295 ml) milk
½ cup (120 ml) sugar
2 pkgs active dry yeast
5 cups (1.2 l) sifted HECKERS/CERESOTA Unbleached Flour
1½ tsp (8 ml) salt
2 eggs
¼ cup (60 ml) melted butter or margarine
2 tbs (30 ml) melted butter
1 tbs (15 ml) cinnamon mixed with
¼ cup (60 ml) sugar

Powdered Sugar Icing:
1 tbs (15 ml) boiling water
¾ cup (180 ml) confectioners sugar
½ tsp (3 ml) lemon juice, optional

Preheat oven to 375°F (190°C) 10 minutes before baking. Grease 2 bread pans.

Scald milk, add sugar; cool to lukewarm. Dissolve yeast in the milk-sugar mixture. Mix in 3 cups flour; beat well. Add salt and eggs; beat well. Blend in melted butter or margarine; gradually add remaining 2 cups of flour; mix well. Turn onto floured board; knead until smooth. Place in greased bowl, cover, let rise in warm place (80°-85°F; 27°-29°C) until doubled in bulk. Punch down, let rise again. When light, place on floured board; roll out into rectangle ½-inch thick.

Brush lightly with melted butter, sprinkle with cinnamon-sugar mixture; roll up tightly like a jelly roll. Cut roll into 2 parts, seal ends, place each in a well-greased bread pan. Cover, set in warm place; let rise until doubled in bulk.

Bake for about 40-45 minutes. Brush with melted butter on removal from oven. When cool, frost with Powdered Sugar Icing. Yields 2 loaves.

Powdered Sugar Icing: Combine all ingredients in a small bowl.

Opposite: Praline Pecan Loaf

Filled Cardamom Crescent

Cardamom Fruit Filling:
1 cup (240 ml) chopped dates
⅓ cup (80 ml) orange juice
¼ cup (60 ml) granulated sugar
¼ tsp (1 ml) McCORMICK/SCHILLING Ground Cardamom
pinch salt
¼ cup (60 ml) chopped walnuts or pecans
1 tbs (15 ml) butter or margarine

Dough:
½ cup (120 ml) milk
1 pkg active dry yeast
1 egg, beaten
3 tbs (45 ml) granulated sugar
1 tsp (5 ml) salt
1 tsp (5 ml) McCORMICK/SCHILLING Lemon Peel
½ tsp (3 ml) McCORMICK/SCHILLING Ground Cardamom
2-2¼ cups (480-590 ml) all-purpose flour
6 tbs (90 ml) butter or margarine, softened, divided

Glaze:
1 cup (240 ml) confectioners sugar
4 tsp (20 ml) milk or water

Preheat oven to 350°F (180°C).

Cardamom Fruit Filling: Place dates, orange juice, granulated sugar, cardamom and salt in small saucepan. Cook, stirring, over medium heat until mixture thickens. Remove from heat and stir in nuts and butter or margarine. Set aside.

Dough: Scald milk and place in large bowl. Set aside to cool to lukewarm. Add yeast to warm milk and stir to dissolve. Add beaten egg, 3 granulated sugar, salt, lemon peel and cardamom to milk mixture. Stir to mix well. Gradually beat in 2 cups flour, mixing to moderately stiff dough. If dough is soft, add up to ¼ cup additional flour.

Turn out onto lightly floured surface, flour hands and knead just until smooth. Place in lightly greased bowl and turn to coat entire surface of dough. Cover with damp towel and let rise in warm, draft-free place until dough doubles in size, about 1½ hours.

Turn out onto lightly floured surface and roll out to 15x12-inch rectangle. Spread 4 tbs softened butter or margarine over dough. Fold 1 short end of dough in to middle of dough and fold other short end over to opposite edge of dough to make 3 even layers. Roll out again to 15x12-inch rectangle. Spread remaining 2 tbs softened butter over dough. Fold as before, cover with damp towel and let stand 15 minutes.

Lightly grease cookie sheet and set aside.

Roll out dough to 16x10-inch rectangle and spread with reserved Cardamom Fruit Filling. Roll up dough, from 1 long side and pinch seam and ends to seal.

Place, seam-side down, on prepared cookie sheet and shape into crescent. Cut two-thirds of the way through top of crescent at about 1-inch intervals using scissors or razor blade. Cover with damp towel and let rise in warm, draft-free place until dough doubles in size, about 1 hour.

Bake for 25-30 minutes. Remove from cookie sheet and cool on wire rack.

Glaze: Place confectioners sugar and milk in small bowl and stir to combine. Drizzle over top of cooled crescent. Yields 1 cake, serves 12.

Biscuits
Scones
Rolls

Cheese

Fruit

Nut

Corn

Seed

Spice

BISCUITS,
ROLLS & SCONES

Biscuits

2 cups (480 ml) sifted WASHINGTON Self-Rising Flour or
2 cups (480 ml) sifted WASHINGTON All-Purpose Flour plus
3 tsp (15 ml) baking powder plus
1 tsp (5 ml) salt, sifted together
¼ cup (60 ml) shortening
scant ⅔ cup (160 ml) milk

Preheat oven to 450°F (230°C). Use ungreased baking sheet or pan.

Place flour in medium bowl. Cut in shortening until mixture is like coarse crumbs. Add milk gradually; stir to make a soft dough. Turn onto lightly floured surface. Knead gently 6-8 strokes.

Roll or pat to one-half thickness in baked biscuits. Cut with floured cutter. Place on baking sheet. Bake 12-15 minutes, or until golden. Yields 12-14 biscuits.

Cheese Biscuits

3 tbs (45 ml) shortening
2 cups (480 ml) sifted PRESTO
¾ cup (180 ml) sharp cheese, grated
⅔ cup (160 ml) milk and water in equal parts

Preheat oven to 475°F (246°C). Grease baking sheet.

Work shortening into sifted flour with tips of fingers or pastry blender, add grated cheese and liquids, slowly mixing to a soft dough.

Place on board sprinkled with flour, pat or roll to about ¾-inch thickness. Cut rounds and place on baking sheet Bake 10-12 minutes. Yields 12-14 biscuits.

Quick Biscuits (with cooking oil)

2 cups (480 ml) sifted WASHINGTON Self-Rising Flour
½ cup (120 ml) milk
¼ cup (60 ml) cooking oil

Preheat oven to 450°F (230°C). Use ungreased baking sheet or pan.

Place flour in medium bowl; gradually add liquids. Stir just to make a soft dough. Turn onto floured surface. Knead gently 6-8 strokes.

Roll or pat one-half thickness desired in baked biscuits. Cut with floured cutter. Place on baking sheet. Bake 12-15 minutes, or until golden. Yields 12-14 biscuits.

Drop Biscuits: Increase milk to ¾ cup (180 ml) ; drop from spoon onto greased baking sheet or into greased muffin cups.

Square Biscuits: Pat dough into an 8-inch square. With long blade knife, cut into 2-inch squares. Separate on baking sheet.

Buttermilk Biscuits: Buttermilk or sour milk may be substituted for the sweet milk. Add ¼ tsp (1 ml) baking soda to the flour.

Bacon Biscuits: Crumble 4 strips cooked bacon; add to flour mixture before adding milk.

Ham Biscuits: Add ½ cup (120 ml) chopped cooked ham to flour mixture before adding milk.

Chive Biscuits: Add 3 to 4 tbs (45-60 ml) minced chives to flour mixture before adding milk.

Opposite: Biscuits

Orange-Cream Cheese Biscuits

3 cups (720 ml) BISQUICK Original Baking Mix
2 tsp (10 ml) grated orange peel
¾ cup (180 ml) orange juice
1 3-oz pkg (90 g) cream cheese, softened
2 tbs (30 ml) orange marmalade
sugar

Preheat oven to 450°F (230°C). Use ungreased cookie sheet.

Mix baking mix, orange peel and orange juice until soft dough forms; beat vigorously 30 seconds.

Turn dough onto surface generously dusted with baking mix; roll in baking mix to coat. Shape into ball; knead 10 times. Roll ½-inch thick. Cut with 2½-inch cutter dipped in baking mix.

Place on cookie sheet. Mix cream cheese and marmalade. Spoon about 1 teaspoon cream cheese mixture onto center of each circle; sprinkle with sugar. Bake 8-10 minutes or until golden brown. Yields 15 biscuits.

Cloverleaf Biscuits

2 cups (480 ml) sifted PRESTO
3 tbs (45 ml) shortening
3 tbs (45 ml) maple syrup
⅓ cup (80 ml) milk
¼ cup (60 ml) finely chopped walnuts

Preheat oven to 400°F (205°C). Grease muffin pan. Work the shortening into the sifted flour with fingertips. Add maple syrup and stir in with knife. Cut in milk with knife. Add chopped nuts lightly sprinkled with flour. Mix well and shape into 36 small balls, placing 3 together to make 1 biscuit.

Place in muffin pan and bake in oven for 12-15 minutes. Yields 1 dozen biscuits.

Opposite: **Orange-Cream Cheese Biscuits**

Cloverleaf Biscuits

Butter Flake Biscuits

2 cups (480 ml) all-purpose flour
1 tbs (15 ml) baking powder
¾ tsp (4 ml) salt
1 tbs (15 ml) IMPERIAL Granulated Sugar
½ cup (120 ml) plus 2 tbs (30 ml) butter or margarine
2 eggs, well beaten
⅓ cup (80 ml) cold milk

Preheat oven to 475°F (246°C). Use ungreased baking pan.

Combine dry ingredients; cut butter or margarine into mixture with pastry blender. Mix well beaten eggs and milk, add to mixture and mix lightly with fork.

Shape dough into ball and turn out on lightly floured surface. With rolling pin, lightly roll dough into rectangle about ½-inch thick. Fold dough in thirds then roll into a rectangle and fold into thirds two more times. With dough ½-inch thick, cut into 2-inch diameter biscuits.

Bake until biscuits are puffed and golden brown. Yields 12-16 biscuits.

Cinnamon Raisin Scones

2 cups (480 ml) all-purpose flour
⅓ cup (80 ml) sugar
1 tbs (15 ml) baking powder
1 tsp (5 ml) cinnamon
¼ tsp (1 ml) salt
½ cup (120 ml) butter or margarine
⅔ cup (160 ml) milk
1 egg, beaten
1 tsp (5 ml) vanilla
1 cup (240 ml) SUN•MAID Raisins

Preheat oven to 400°F (205°C). Use ungreased cookie sheet.

Combine flour, sugar, baking powder, cinnamon and salt. Using pastry blender or fork, cut in butter or margarine until mixture resembles coarse crumbs. Combine milk, egg and vanilla. Add to flour mixture; stir just until dry ingredients are moistened. Stir in raisins.

With floured hands, shape dough into 8-inch round on cookie sheet. Sprinkle with additional sugar, if desired. Cut dough into 8 wedges; slightly separate wedges. Bake for 15-20 minutes. Serve warm. Yields 8 scones.

Orange Cinnamon Scones: Add 1 tbs (15 ml) grated orange peel to dry ingredients.

Gingerbread Scones: Add 1 tsp (5 ml) ginger to dry ingredients and 2 tbs (30 ml) molasses to liquid ingredients.

Herb Biscuits

2 cups (480 ml) biscuit mix
½ tsp (3 ml) McCORMICK/SCHILLING Thyme Leaves
¼ tsp (1 ml) McCORMICK/SCHILLING Marjoram Leaves
¼ tsp (1 ml) McCORMICK/SCHILLING Oregano Leaves
¼ tsp (1 ml) McCORMICK/SCHILLING Onion Powder
1 cup (240 ml) milk

Preheat oven to 425°F (220°C). Lightly grease cookie sheet.

Place biscuit mix in large bowl and stir in seasonings. Add milk and stir with spoon just until biscuit mix is moistened.

Drop 10 equal-size biscuits from spoon onto prepared cookie sheet. Bake in preheated oven 12-15 minutes or until biscuits are lightly browned. Serve hot. Yields 10 biscuits.

Cinnamon Raisin Scones

Blueberry-Oat Bran Scones

1½ cups (355 ml) oat bran
1½ cups (355 ml) flour
¼ cup (60 ml) light brown sugar
1 tsp (5 ml) baking soda
4 oz (120 g) margarine or butter
2 eggs or egg whites
¼ cup (60 ml) honey
⅓ cup (80 ml) buttermilk
½ tsp (3 ml) McCORMICK/SCHILLING Imitation
    Rum Extract
½ tsp (3 ml) McCORMICK/SCHILLING Pure Vanilla Extract
1 pint (480 ml) fresh blueberries

Preheat oven to 400°F (205°C). Lightly grease cookie sheet.

In a separate bowl, mix oat bran, flour, brown sugar and baking soda. Cut in margarine or butter. Beat eggs and beat in honey. Add buttermilk and flavor extracts to egg mixture. Pour into oat bran mixture and stir only until moistened. Stir in blueberries.

Turn out dough on greased cookie sheet. Using spatula, shape dough into an 8-inch round, about 1½ inches thick. Level top. Using a floured sharp knife, cut through the dough to make 16 even wedges.

Bake 25-30 minutes. Serve hot. Garnish with Johnny-jump-up flowers and a small blueberry spray. Yields 10 scones.

Cheese Scones

2 cups (480 ml) all-purpose flour
¾ cup (180 ml) sharp cheddar cheese, grated
2 tsp (10 ml) baking powder
¼ tsp (1 ml) salt
¼ cup (60 ml) butter, chilled, cut in pieces
½ cup (120 ml) milk
2 large eggs
¾ tsp (4 ml) TABASCO Pepper Sauce

Preheat oven to 400°F (205°C). Lightly butter a baking sheet.

In a large bowl or a food processor mix flour, cheese, baking powder and salt. Cut in the butter, using a pastry blender, two knives or the pulsing motion in the food processor, until the mixture resembles coarse crumbs. If blended in the food processor, transfer the mixture to a large bowl.

In a small bowl, stir together milk, eggs and pepper sauce. Make a well in the center of the dry ingredients and add the milk mixture, stirring to combine. The dough will be sticky.

With lightly floured hands, pat dough into a 9-inch circle in the center of the prepared baking sheet. Cut the circle into 8 wedges. Bake the scones for 20-25 minutes or until lightly browned. Yields 8 scones.

Parmesan Cheese Scones: Substitute ¾ cup (180 ml) grated Parmesan cheese for sharp cheddar cheese and add 1 tsp (5 ml) dried oregano, crumbled, to dry ingredients.

Cheese Delights

½ cup (120 ml) INDIAN HEAD Corn Meal
1½ cups (355 ml) WASHINGTON All-Purpose Flour
1 tsp (5 ml) salt
⅔ cup (160 ml) shortening
½ cup (120 ml) water
2 tbs (30 ml) butter or margarine, melted
½ cup (120 ml) sharp cheese, grated

Preheat oven to 425°F (220°C). Use an ungreased baking sheet.

Combine first 3 ingredients in bowl. Cut in shortening until crumbly. Add a little water at a time until dough forms a ball. Let dough rest 5 minutes.

Divide into 8 parts. Roll each part on floured surface to form a rectangle 4x20 inches. Brush with melted butter or margarine and sprinkle with grated cheese. Starting with short side, roll as for jelly roll. Cut each roll cross-wise into 4 pieces.

Place on baking sheet. Bake 20 minutes. Yields 32 scones.

Cheese Scones

Chili-Corn Scones

2¼ cups (540 ml) all-purpose flour
2 tbs (30 ml) sugar
1 tbs (15 ml) baking powder
3 tbs (45 ml) FLEISCHMANN'S Margarine
¼ cup (60 ml) EGG BEATERS Real Egg Product
8-oz can (240 g) cream-style corn
¼ cup (60 ml) diced green chiles
1 tbs (15 ml) fresh cilantro or parsley, minced

Preheat oven to 400°F (205°C). Lightly grease bakng sheet.

In large bowl, combine flour, sugar and baking powder; cut in margarine until mixture resembles coarse crumbs. Stir in egg product, corn, chiles and cilantro or parsley just until mixture holds together.

On lightly floured surface, knead dough 10 times. Pat dough into 8-inch circle and place on baking sheet. Lightly score into 8 wedges.

Bake for 15-20 minutes or until golden brown. Cool slightly on wire rack. Cut on score lines; serve warm. Yields 8 scones.

Almond Crescents

10-oz pkg (300 g) BLUE DIAMOND Whole Natural Almonds
1¼ cups (295 ml) flour
¼ cup (60 ml) sugar
1 cup (240 ml) butter
1 tsp (5 ml) vanilla extract
1 cup (240 ml) powdered sugar, optional

Preheat oven to 350°F (180°C). Use ungreased cookie sheet.

Measure 1⅔ cups (400 ml) almonds. Whirl in blender or grind fine. Finely chop remaining almonds and set aside. Mix flour, sugar and ground almonds. With fingers work in butter and vanilla extract until mixture cleans bowl. Chill about 1 hour.

Roll dough into balls (about 1¼ inches), then into logs, 3½ inches long; turn points inward to form into crescents. Press tops into chopped almonds.

Bake on cookie sheet 12-15 minutes until lightly browned. Cool on pan about 10 minutes. While still warm, roll in powdered sugar, if desired. Yields 25-30 crescents.

Blueberry One-Pan Popover

½ cup (120 ml) milk
3 eggs
½ cup (120 ml) flour
2 tsp (10 ml) sugar
¼ tsp (1 ml) salt
4 strips bacon, cooked crisp and crumbled
2 tbs (30 ml) butter or margarine
21-oz can (630 g) COMSTOCK, THANK YOU
    or WILDERNESS Blueberry Pie Filling
⅓ cup (80 ml) maple syrup or pancake syrup
½ cup (120 ml) sour cream

Preheat oven to 425°F (220°C).

Beat milk and eggs in small bowl; beat in flour, sugar and salt (batter will not be completely smooth). Stir in bacon. Heat butter or margarine in 10-inch ovenproof skillet until bubbly; pour in batter. Bake 12 minutes.

Reduce heat to 350°F (180°C). Bake until golden brown, 10-15 minutes. Popover should puff up in pan and collapse slightly when removed from oven.

Heat blueberry filling and syrup in saucepan until hot. Cut popover into wedges; serve immediately with blueberry sauce and sour cream. Yields 4 popovers.

Opposite: Blueberry One-Pan Popover

Buttermilk Popovers

1 cup (240 ml) all-purpose flour
1 tbs (15 ml) SACO Buttermilk Blend
½ tsp (3 ml) salt
2 eggs
1 cup (240 ml) water

Preheat oven to 450°F (230°C). Grease very well 6 deep* custard cups or 12-cup muffin pan.

In a mixing bowl sift the flour, buttermilk blend and salt together. Beat the eggs with a hand beater until fluffy. Add water and eggs to the flour mixture. Beat just until smooth. Do not overbeat.

Pour batter into cups, filling only about ⅓ full. Bake for 20 minutes, then reduce heat to 350°F (180°C) and bake for 20 minutes more. Remove at once from pans. Serve hot and with butter. Yields 6-12 popovers.

* The deeper the cup the better. A shallow cup will not pop well. A 6-oz Pyrex custard cup works very well and cleans up easily too.

Angel Yeast Biscuits

1 pkg dry or compressed yeast
3 tbs (45 ml) warm water
5 cups (1.2 l) sifted WASHINGTON All-Purpose Flour
¼ cup (60 ml) sugar
5 tsp (25 ml) baking powder
1½ tsp (8 ml) salt
1 tsp (5 ml) baking soda
1 cup (240 ml) shortening
scant 2 cups (480 ml) buttermilk, room temperature

Preheat oven to 400°F (205°C). Grease baking sheet or pan.

Combine yeast and water. Set aside.

Place dry ingredients in bowl; stir to mix. Cut in shortening until mixture is like coarse crumbs. Add buttermilk and yeast mixture to dry ingredients. Stir well.

Turn onto floured surface. Knead a few strokes to get a smooth dough. Roll or pat to one-half thickness of desired biscuit. Cut with floured cutter.

Place on baking sheet. Brush tops with melted butter, if desired. Bake 15-18 minutes until golden. Yields 4-6 dozen biscuits.

Note: Dough will keep refrigerated up to one week. When ready to bake, allow biscuits to rise at room temperature before baking.

Angel Yeast Biscuits

Rich Parkerhouse Rolls

1 pkg dry yeast
1½ cups (355 ml) milk, scalded and cooled
⅓ cup (80 ml) IMPERIAL Granulated Sugar
2 eggs, beaten
1¼ tsp (6 ml) salt
4 cups (960 ml) all-purpose flour, divided
⅓ cup (80 ml) shortening, melted

Preheat oven to 425°F (220°C). Grease baking sheet.

Dissolve yeast in lukewarm milk and stir well; add sugar, beaten eggs, salt and half the flour. Combine well and add melted shortening. Beat and add balance of flour or enough to make a stiff dough.

Turn dough onto a floured surface, knead into a smooth dough, about 8 minutes. Transfer to large greased bowl and cover with plastic wrap or cloth; let rise in warm place until doubled in bulk, about 1 hour.

Turn dough out on floured surface, roll out ¼-inch thick and brush lightly with melted butter. Cut with biscuit cutter, dip blade of a knife in flour and using the dull side make a deep crease in center of each; fold one half over onto the other half of each roll.

Place close together on baking sheet and let rise about 15 minutes. Bake 15-20 minutes. Yields about 3 dozen hot rolls.

Note: these can be shaped into larger rolls such as hot dog or hamburger rolls. Shape them in 5-inch rounds or 5x2 inches, both about ½-inch thick. Bake as above.

Easy Yeast Rolls (standard method)

2 pkgs yeast
2 tbs (30 ml) sugar
2 tsp (10 ml) salt
1½ cups (355 ml) lukewarm milk
6 tbs (90 ml) soft shortening
approx. 5 cups (1.2 l) WASHINGTON All-Purpose Flour

Preheat oven to 400°F (205°C) 10 minutes before baking. Grease 9x13-inch baking pan.

Combine first 4 ingredients in large mixing bowl. Add shortening; let stand 5 minutes. Stir in flour, until dough leaves sides of bowl.

Turn dough onto lightly floured board. Knead until smooth and satiny (8-10 minutes). Place in greased bowl, turning to grease all sides. Cover with damp cloth and let rise in warm spot (80°-85°F; 27°-29°C) until dough doubles in volume, about 1 hour. Punch down. Let stand 10 minutes more. Shape rolls as desired. Brush tops with oil. Let rise until nearly double in volume (30 minutes).

Bake 15-18 minutes. Yields 1½ dozen rolls.

Rich Parkerhouse Rolls

English Muffins

1 pkg active dry yeast
6 tbs (90 ml) SACO Buttermilk Blend
1 tbs (15 ml) sugar
½ tsp (3 ml) baking soda
1½ tsp (8 ml) salt
3 tbs (45 ml) soft shortening
4½-5½ cups (1.1-1.3 l) all-purpose flour
2 cups (480 ml) warm water (120°-130°F; 49°-54°C)
cornmeal

Above: English Muffins

In large mixing bowl thoroughly mix yeast, buttermilk blend, sugar, baking soda, salt, shortening, and 2 cups all-purpose flour. Gradually blend in warm water and beat at low speed until moistened. Beat on medium speed for 2 minutes. By hand, add enough remaining flour (2½-3½ cups) to make a moderately stiff dough. Cover and let rise until double (about 1 hour).

Turn dough out on well-floured surface and knead 3 or 4 times. Let rest 5 minutes. Lightly roll about ½-inch thick. Cut into 3-inch rounds with floured cutter.

Carefully place on cookie sheet that is lightly covered with cornmeal. Cover and let rise 30 minutes.

Heat griddle over medium heat (electric griddle 350°F; 180°C). Sprinkle with cornmeal. Carefully transfer muffins to griddle. Bake 7-10 minutes. Turn, bake 7-10 minutes on second side. To serve, split horizontally with fork. Toast and serve with butter and jam. Yields 2-2½ dozen muffins.

Cornmeal Yeast Rolls

1 cup (240 ml) INDIAN HEAD Corn Meal
2 tsp (10 ml) salt
¼ cup (60 ml) margarine or butter
3 tbs (45 ml) sugar
1 cup (240 ml) milk, scalded
½ pkg yeast
¼ cup (60 ml) lukewarm water
1 egg, slightly beaten
3-4 cups (720-960 ml) WASHINGTON All-Purpose Flour

Preheat oven to 400°F (205°C). Grease 2 baking sheets.

Place first 4 ingredients in a large bowl. Pour milk over corn meal mixture, stirring until smooth. Set aside to cool.

Soften yeast in ¼ cup water. Add to corn meal mixture. Add egg to cornmeal mixture. Add 1 cup flour and beat well. Add more flour to make a medium-soft dough.

Turn onto a floured surface. Knead until smooth about 8-10 minutes. Place dough in greased bowl. Cover with damp tea towel. Let rise in warm place until double in bulk (1½ hours). Punch down. Let rest 10 minutes.

Shape into 2-inch rolls; place on baking sheets. Let rise until just double (45 minutes). Bake 15 minutes. Yields about 2½ dozen rolls.

Cornmeal Yeast Rolls

Quick One-Rise Orange Buttermilk Sweet Rolls

Orange Filling:
6 tbs (90 ml) butter or margarine, softened
2 tbs (30 ml) grated orange peel
¼ cup (60 ml) orange juice
3 cups (720 ml) confectioners sugar

2 pkgs dry yeast
½ cup (120 ml) sugar
½ tsp (3 ml) baking soda
2 tsp (10 ml) salt
5 tbs (75 ml) SACO Buttermilk Blend
5½-6 cups (1.3-1.4 l) all-purpose flour
½ cup (120 ml) soft butter or margarine
2 eggs, room temperature
1¾ cups (415 ml) warm water (120°-130°F; 49°-54°C)

Preheat oven to 375°F (190°C) 10 minutes before baking. Grease three 8 or 9-inch round cake pans.

Orange Filling: Combine butter or margarine, orange peel, orange juice and confectioners sugar and beat until smooth and creamy. Set aside.

In large mixer bowl combine yeast, sugar, baking soda, salt, buttermilk blend, and 2½ cups flour. Add soft butter and eggs. Add warm water and beat on low speed until moistened. Beat on medium speed for 2 minutes. By hand, add enough remaining flour, one cup at a time, to make a soft dough.

Turn dough onto lightly-floured board, cover and let rest for 5 minutes. Knead until smooth and elastic, 5-8 minutes. Divide in thirds. Roll each third into a 12x7-inch rectangle. Spread each rectangle with an equal portion of the orange filling. Roll up, starting with wide side. Pinch long edge of dough into roll to seal well. Stretch rolls to make even. Cut each roll into 10 slices.

Place slightly apart in cake pans (10 rolls per pan). Cover and let rise until doubled, about 1 hour. Bake 20-25 minutes. While warm, frost the rolls in each pan with remaining filling. Yields 30 rolls.

Whole Wheat Bran Hamburger Buns

2½-3 cups (590-720 ml) all-purpose flour
1 cup (240 ml) whole bran cereal
2 pkgs dry yeast
¼ cup (60 ml) brown sugar, packed
1 tsp (5 ml) salt
6 tbs (90 ml) SACO Buttermilk Blend
2 tbs (30 ml) soft shortening
1 egg
1¾ cups (180 ml) warm water (120°-130°F; 49°-54°C)
1½ cups (355 ml) whole wheat flour
1 egg white, slightly beaten
1 tbs (15 ml) water
1-1½ tbs (15-25 ml) sesame seeds

Preheat oven to 375°F (190°C). Grease 2 cookie sheets.

In large mixing bowl, combine 1½ cups all-purpose flour, cereal, yeast, brown sugar, salt and buttermilk blend. Add shortening and egg. Blend in 1¾ cup warm water at low speed until moistened. Beat 3 minutes on medium speed. By hand, stir in 1½ cups whole wheat flour and enough remaining all-purpose flour to make a stiff dough.

Knead on floured surface about 5 minutes. Place in greased bowl, turning to grease top. Cover, let rise in warm place until doubled, about 1-1½ hours. Punch down dough. Divide dough into 4 parts. Divide each fourth into 4 pieces. Shape each piece into a smooth ball. Place on cookie sheets. Flatten to 4-inch diameter. Cover. Let rise in warm place until almost doubled, about 20 minutes.

Combine egg white and 1 tbs water. Brush tops of buns. Sprinkle with sesame seeds.

Bake 15-18 minutes until golden brown. Remove from cookie sheets and cool. Make buns larger for steak sandwiches or smaller for snack buns. Yields 16 buns.

Opposite:
Whole Wheat Bran Hamburger Buns

Beer Rye Dinner Rolls

3-3½ cups (720-840 ml) all-purpose flour
2 pkgs RED STAR Active Dry Yeast or QUICK•RISE Yeast
¼ cup (60 ml) sugar
1 tbs (15 ml) salt
1½ cups (355 ml) beer
½ cup (120 ml) water
¼ cup (60 ml) dark molasses
3 tbs (45 ml) shortening
3 cups (720 ml) medium rye flour
melted butter

Preheat oven to 375°F (190°C). Grease cookie sheet.

In large mixing bowl, combine 2½ cups all-purpose flour, yeast, sugar and salt; mix well. Heat beer, water, molasses and shortening until very warm (120°-130°F; 49°-54°C); shortening does not need melt. Add to flour mixture. Blend at low speed until moistened; beat 3 minutes at medium speed. By hand, gradually stir in all the rye flour and enough remaining all-purpose flour to make a firm dough.

Knead on floured surface until smooth and elastic, about 5 minutes. (Dough will be slightly sticky.) Place in greased bowl, turning to grease top. Cover; let rise in warm place until double, about 1 hour (30 minutes for rapid-rise yeast). Punch down dough. Divide into 4 parts. Divide each fourth into 6 pieces. Shape each piece into a smooth ball.

Place on cookie sheet. Cover; let rise in warm place until almost doubled, about 15 minutes. Bake for 15-20 minutes until rolls sound hollow when tapped. Remove from cookie sheets; brush with butter. Serve warm or cool. Yields 2 dozen rolls.

Pan Roll Variation: Place 12 balls in greased 9-inch square cake pan. Cover; let rise until almost doubled, about 30 minutes (15 minutes for rapid rise yeast). Bake 20-25 minutes. Remove from pans; brush with butter. Serve warm or cold.

Beer Rye Dinner Rolls

Whole Wheat Cottage Cheese Rolls

1½-2 cups (355-480 ml) all-purpose flour
2 cups (480 ml) whole wheat flour
2 pkgs RED STAR Active Dry Yeast or QUICK•RISE Yeast
¼ cup (60 ml) packed brown sugar
2 tsp (10 ml) salt
½ tsp (3 ml) baking soda
½ cup (120 ml) water
1½ cups (355 ml) small curd creamed cottage cheese
2 tbs (30 ml) butter or margarine
2 eggs
melted butter or margarine

Preheat oven to 375°F (190°C). Grease two 12-cup muffin pans.

In large mixing bowl, combine ¾ cup all-purpose flour, ¾ cup whole wheat flour, yeast, brown sugar, salt and baking soda; mix well. Heat water, cottage cheese and butter until very warm (120-130°F; 49-54°C), butter does not need to melt. Add to flour mixture. Add eggs. Blend at low speed until moistened; beat 3 minutes at medium speed. By hand, gradually stir in remaining whole wheat flour and enough all-purpose flour to make a firm dough.

Knead on floured surface until smooth and elastic, 5-8 minutes. Place in greased bowl, turning to grease top. Cover; let rise in warm place until double, about 1 hour (30 minutes for rapid-rise yeast).

Punch down dough. Divide into 4 equal parts. Divide each part into 6 pieces. Shape each piece into a smooth ball. Place in muffin cups. Cover and let rise in warm place until double, about 45 minutes (20-25 minutes for rapid rise yeast).

Bake 12-15 minutes. Brush with butter or margarine. Remove from pans; cool. Yields 2 dozen rolls.

Whole Wheat Cottage Cheese Rolls

Sunflower Nut Crescents

4 cups (960 ml) all-purpose flour
2 pkgs RED STAR Active Dry Yeast or QUICK•RISE Yeast
2 tbs (30 ml) sugar
2 tsp (10 ml) salt
1 cup (240 ml) milk
½ cup (120 ml) water
¼ cup (60 ml) shortening
1 egg
½ cup (120 ml) salted sunflower nuts, chopped
1 egg, slightly beaten
3 tbs (45 ml) salted sunflower nuts, chopped

Preheat oven to 400°F (205°C). Grease 2 cookie sheets.

In large mixing bowl, combine 2 cups flour, yeast, sugar and salt; mix well. In saucepan, heat milk, water and shortening until very warm (120°-130°F; 49°-54°C); shortening does not need to melt. Add to flour mixture. Add egg. Blend at low speed until moistened; beat 3 minutes at medium speed. By hand, gradually stir in ⅛ cup sunflower nuts and remaining flour to make a soft dough. Cover; let rise in warm place until double, 20-30 minutes (10-15 minutes for rapid rise yeast).

Stir down dough. On well-floured surface turn dough to coat with flour. Divide into 3 parts. Roll each third to a 10-inch circle. Cut into 10 wedges. Starting with wide end of wedge, roll toward point.

Place point side down on cookie sheets. Curve to form crescent. Brush with egg; sprinkle sunflower nuts over top of rolls. Cover; let rise in warm place until almost doubled, about 20 minutes (10 minutes for rapid-rise yeast).

Bake 10-12 minutes until golden brown. Remove from cookie sheets; cool. Yields 30 crescents.

Quick Whole Wheat Buttermilk Rolls

1 cup (240 ml) whole wheat flour
3-3½ cups (720-840 ml) all-purpose flour
2 pkgs dry yeast
3 tbs (45 ml) brown sugar
1 tsp (5 ml) salt
5 tbs (75 ml) SACO Buttermilk Blend
½ tsp (3 ml) baking soda
½ cup (120 ml) shortening
1¾ cup (415 ml) very warm water

Preheat oven to 400°F (205°C) 10 minutes befroe cooking. Grease cookie sheet or 15½x10½x1½-inch pan.

In large mixing bowl combine 1 cup whole wheat flour, 1 cup all-purpose flour, yeast, brown sugar, salt, buttermilk blend, baking soda, and shortening; mix well. Add very warm tap water (120°-130°F; 49°-54°C) to flour mixture. Blend at low speed until moistened. Beat 3 minutes at medium speed. By hand, gradually stir in enough of remaining flour to make a firm dough.

Knead on floured surface until smooth and elastic, about 5 minutes. Place in greased bowl, turning to grease all sides. Cover; let rise in warm place until doubled, about 20 minutes. Punch down.

Divide dough into two balls. Shape each ball into a 12-inch rope and cut into 12 pieces. Form into balls.

Place balls about ½ inch apart on cookie sheet or pan. Cover; let rise in warm place until almost doubled, about 20 minutes.

Bake at for 15-20 minutes until golden brown. Remove from pan; brush with butter, if desired. Cool on racks. Yields 2 dozen rolls.

Opposite: **Sunflower Nut Crescents**

Classic Sweet Dough

8½-9½ cups (2-2.3 l) all-purpose flour
½ cup (120 ml) SACO Buttermilk Blend
½ cup (120 ml) sugar
2 tsp (10 ml) salt
2 pkgs active dry yeast
½ cup (120 ml) butter or margarine, softened
2 eggs, room temperature
2½ cups (590 ml) warm water (120°-130°F; 49°-54°C)

Cinnamon Rolls or Cinnamon Bread:
⅓ of the Classic Sweet Dough
¼ cup (60 ml) sugar
1½ tsp (8 ml) cinnamon
soft butter

Confectioners Icing:
milk or cream
1 cup (240 ml) confectioners sugar
½ tsp (3 ml) vanilla

Pecan Rolls:
½ cup (120 ml) butter or margarine
½ cup (120 ml) brown sugar, packed
½ cup (120 ml) pecan halves
⅓ cup (80 ml) of the Classic Sweet Dough
¼ cup (60 ml) sugar
1½ tsp (8 ml) cinnamon
soft butter

Preheat oven to 375°F (190°C) 10 minutes before baking.

In large mixing bowl, combine 3 cups all-purpose flour, buttermilk blend, sugar, salt and yeast. Add soft butter and eggs. Add 2½ cups warm water and beat at low speed until blended. Beat on medium speed for 2 minutes. By hand, add enough remaining flour, one cup at a time, to make a slightly stiff dough.

Turn dough onto lightly floured board, cover and let rest 5 minutes. Knead until smooth and elastic (5-8 minutes). Put in greased bowl, turn to grease all sides. Cover and let rise in warm place until doubled (about 1 hour). Punch down. Turn onto board and divide into thirds.

Cinnamon Rolls: Roll dough into 15x9-inch rectangle. Mix sugar and cinnamon together. Spread rectangle with soft butter and sprinkle with cinnamon-sugar mixture. Roll up, starting at wide side. Pinch long edge of dough into roll to seal well. Stretch roll to make even. Cut roll into 15 slices. Place slightly apart in greased 13x9x2-inch pan or in greased muffin cups. Cover and let rise until doubled (about 45 minutes). Bake 25-30 minutes (15-20 minutes in muffin cups). While warm, frost with Confectioners Icing.

Confectioners Icing: Add enough milk or cream to confectioners' sugar to make an icing of spreading consistency. Stir in vanilla.

Cinnamon Bread: Roll dough into a 12x7-inch rectangle. Mix sugar and cinnamon together. Spread rectangle with soft butter and sprinkle with cinnamon-sugar mixture, saving 1 tbs for topping. Roll up, starting at narrow end. Pinch long edge of dough into roll to seal well. Tuck ends under. Place sealed edge down in greased 8½x4½-inch loaf pan. Brush with soft butter and sprinkle with remaining 1 tbs cinnamon-sugar mixture. Cover and let rise until almost doubled (about 45 minutes). Bake 30-35 minutes. Cover top of loaf with aluminum foil if browning too fast.

Pecan Rolls: Melt ½ cup butter or margarine in 9x13x2-inch pan. Sprinkle brown sugar and pecan halves over melted butter. Roll dough into 15x9-inch rectangle. Mix sugar and cinnamon together. Spread rectangle with soft butter and sprinkle with cinnamon-sugar mixture. Roll up, starting at wide side. Pinch long edge of dough into roll and seal well. Stretch roll to make even. Cut roll into 15 slices. Place slightly apart in prepared pan. Cover and let rise until doubled (about 45 minutes). Bake 25-30 minutes. Immediately turn pan upside down on wire rack over cookie sheet. Let pan remain a minute so pecan topping drizzles down over rolls.

Opposite: Classic Sweet Dough

Brioche

1 pkg active dry yeast
¼ cup (60 ml) warm water (105°-110°F; 41°-43°C)
1 cup (240 ml) butter, softened
5 eggs
2 tbs (30 ml) sugar
¾ tsp (4 ml) salt
3 cups (720 ml) all-purpose flour, divided
1 egg
2 tsp (10 ml) water

On day of baking preheat oven to 375°F (190°C) 10 minutes before baking and grease two 12-cup 2½-inch muffin pans or 24 individual brioche pans.

In large mixing bowl, soften yeast in warm water. Add butter, 5 eggs, sugar, salt and 2 cups of the flour. Beat at medium speed until smooth, about 4 minutes. Add remaining flour and beat until smooth, about 1 minute. Cover and let rise in warm place until doubled in size, 1½-2 hours. Using spoon or rubber spatula, beat down dough. Cover and refrigerate overnight. Beat dough down again. Turn out onto lightly floured surface.

For Individual Rolls: Divide dough in half. Cover and refrigerate one half. Dough becomes soft and sticky when warm. Cut ¼ of the remaining dough into 12 equal pieces. With lightly floured hands, roll each piece into a small ball. Set aside.

Cut remaining ¾ of dough into 12 equal pieces. Roll each piece into a large ball. Place each large ball in muffin cup or individual brioche pan.

With lightly floured finger, make a deep indentation (about ½ inch in diameter and ½-inch deep) straight down in center of dough in each cup.

Place one of the reserved small balls in each indentation. Repeat with remaining refrigerated dough. Cover and let rise until large balls almost reach tops of muffin cups, 30-60 minutes.

Beat 1 egg with 2 tsp water. Gently brush tops of rolls with egg mixture. Bake until firm and lightly browned, 15-17 minutes. Remove from pans. Cool on wire rack or serve immediately. Yields 2 dozen rolls.

For Large Loaf: With lightly floured hands, roll ¾ of the dough into a large ball. Place in lightly greased 5-cup brioche pan. With lightly floured fingers, make a deep indentation (about 2 inches in diameter and 2 inches deep) straight down in center of dough in pan.

Roll remaining ¼ of dough into a small ball and place in indentation. Cover and let rise until dough almost reaches top of pan, 1½-2 hours. Beat 1 egg with 2 tsp water. Gently brush top of loaf with egg mixture. Bake at 375°F (190°C) until firm and lightly browned, 35-45 minutes. Cool on wire rack 10 minutes. Gently loosen at sides with narrow spatula and remove from pan. Yields 1 large loaf.

Courtesy of the American Egg Board.

Apple-Cinnamon Puffs

2 cups (480 ml) all-purpose flour
1 pkg RED STAR QUICK•RISE Yeast
2 tbs (30 ml) sugar
½ tsp (3 ml) salt
¾ cup (180 ml) warm water (120°-130°F; 49°-54°C)
¼ cup (60 ml) oil
1 egg
1 cup (240 ml) chopped apples
3 tbs (45 ml) butter, melted
¼ cup (60 ml) sugar
¼ cup (60 ml) finely chopped peanuts
1 tsp (5 ml) cinnamon

Preheat oven to 375°F (190°C). Grease 12-cup muffin pan.

In large mixing bowl, combine 1 cup flour, yeast, 2 tbs sugar and salt; mix well. Add very warm water and oil to flour mixture. Add egg. Blend at low speed until moistened; beat 3 minutes at medium speed. By hand, gradually stir in apples and remaining flour to make a soft batter.

Spoon into muffin cups. Cover; let rise in warm place until double, 30 minutes. Bake for 15-20 minutes until golden brown. Combine ¼ cup sugar, peanuts, and cinnamon. Dip tops of hot rolls into melted butter, then into sugar-cinnamon mixture. Serve warm. Yields 1 dozen rolls.

Opposite: Brioche

Hot Cross Buns

1 pkg dry yeast
¼ cup (60 ml) warm water
¾ cup (180 ml) milk, warmed
¼ cup (60 ml) GRANDMA'S Molasses
1½ tsp (8 ml) salt
¼ cup (60 ml) butter, softened
2 eggs
3½ cups (840 ml) all-purpose flour, approximately
1 tsp (5 ml) cinnamon
½ tsp (3 ml) nutmeg
¼ tsp (1 ml) allspice
½ cup (120 ml) currants or raisins
2 tbs (30 ml) chopped candied citron

Preheat oven to 375°F (190°C) 10 minutes before baking. Grease 2 baking sheets.

Stir the yeast into the water and let stand a few minutes to dissolve. Combine the milk, molasses, salt, butter and eggs in a large bowl, and beat well. Add the dissolved yeast and mix thoroughly. Beat in 1½ cups of the flour, the cinnamon, nutmeg and allspice. Cover the bowl, and let rise for about 1 hour, until the batter is bubbly and double in bulk.

Add remaining flour and blend well, adding more flour if necessary to make the dough firm enough to handle. Turn out onto a floured surface and knead until smooth and elastic; knead in the raisins and citron during the last minute or so. Put the dough in a greased bowl, cover and let rise until double in bulk.

Punch the dough down and turn it out onto a lightly floured surface. Roll out into a rectangle about 14x10 inches and ½-inch thick. Cut the buns with a round cutter about 2½-3 inches in diameter, and place about 1 inch apart on baking sheets. Gather up the scraps, reroll them, and continue cutting until you have used all the dough. Let rise, uncovered, until double in bulk.

Just before baking, use floured scissors to snip a cross in the top of each bun, cutting about ½-inch deep. Bake about 15 minutes, until the tops are golden brown. Remove from the oven and transfer to a rack. Yields 1½-2 dozen buns.

Hot Cross Buns

Caramel Apple Buns

3¼-3½ cups (780-840 ml) all-purpose flour
2 pkgs RED STAR QUICK•RISE Yeast
1 tbs (15 ml) sugar
1 tbs (15 ml) cinnamon
1 tsp (5 ml) salt
¾ cup(180 ml) apple juice
½ cup (120 ml) water
¼ cup (60 ml) butter
1 egg

Topping:
¾ cup (180 ml) brown sugar, packed
¼ cup (60 ml) butter
2 tbs (30 ml) light corn syrup
¾ cup (180 ml) chopped nuts

Preheat oven to 375°F (190°C) 10 minutes before baking. Grease two 12-cup muffin pans.

In large mixing bowl, combine 1¼ cups flour, yeast, sugar, cinnamon and salt; mix well. In saucepan, heat apple juice, water and butter until very warm (120°-130°F; 49°-54°C), butter does not need to melt. Add to flour mixture. Add egg. Blend at low speed until moistened; beat 3 minutes at medium speed. By hand, gradually stir in enough remaining flour to make a stiff batter.

Topping: In saucepan, combine brown sugar, butter and corn syrup; heat and stir until blended. Add nuts. Spoon topping into muffin cups.

Spoon batter over topping. Cover; let rise in warm place until double, about 25 minutes. Bake 15-20 minutes until golden brown. Cover pans with foil and invert onto rack sitting on cookie sheet. Cool 1 minute; remove from pans. Cool. Yields 2 dozen buns.

Philadelphia Sticky Buns

Dough:
1 cup (240 ml) milk
1 pkg active dry yeast
¼ cup (60 ml) warm water (110°F; 43°C)
3-4½ cups (720-1080 ml) sifted all-purpose flour, divided
¼ cup (60 ml) butter or margarine
⅓ cup (80 ml) granulated sugar
1 egg, well beaten
1 tsp (5 ml) salt
¼ tsp (1 ml) McCORMICK/SCHILLING Ground Nutmeg

Syrup:
1 cup (240 ml) dark corn syrup
½ cup (120 ml) honey
½ cup (120 ml) dark brown sugar, firmly packed
⅓ cup (80 ml) butter or margarine

Filling:
½ cup (120 ml) dark brown sugar, firmly packed
dash McCORMICK/SCHILLING Ground Ginger
¼ cup (60 ml) butter or margarine, softened
½ cup (120 ml) raisins

Preheat oven to 350°F (180°C) 10 minutes before baking. Use 13x9x2-inch baking pan.

Scald milk in small saucepan and cool to lukewarm. Pour into large bowl. Dissolve yeast in warm water and add to cooled milk. Add 1½ cups flour to milk mixture and mix until smooth. Cover with damp towel and let rise in warm, draft-free place until top is bubbly, about 30 minutes.

Cream butter or margarine with ⅓ cup granulated sugar in small bowl. Add egg, salt and nutmeg. Mix until smooth and add to dough. Add additional flour, mixing well until mixing becomes difficult.

Turn out onto floured work surface and knead in as much remaining flour as necessary to make soft dough that is easy to handle. Place in lightly greased bowl and turn to coat entire surface of dough. Cover with damp towel and let rise in warm, draft-free place until dough doubles in size, 1-2 hours.

Syrup: While dough is rising, prepare Syrup by combining all its ingredients in small saucepan. Heat over medium heat until butter has melted and sugar has dissolved. Set aside to cool slightly.

Roll out dough on lightly floured surface to 12x8-inch rectangle, ¾-inch thick.

Filling: Combine brown sugar with cinnamon and ginger in a small bowl. Spread ¼ cup softened butter or margarine over rolled-out dough and sprinkle sugar-spice mixture over butter. Scatter raisins over all.

Roll up filled dough from one long side jelly-roll style. Pinch edge of dough to seal and cut into 12 slices. Pour half of prepared syrup into baking pan. Place buns, cut side down, on syrup and pour remaining syrup over. Cover with damp towel and let rise in warm, draft-free place 30 minutes. Bake 45 minutes or until golden brown. Yields 1 dozen sticky buns.

Cakes

Coffee
Pound
Chiffon & Sponge
Yellow & White
Fruit
Cheese
Chocolate
Spice
Gingerbread
Carrot
Roll & Cup
CAKES

Coffeecake

2 cups (480 ml) WASHINGTON Self-Rising Flour or
    2 cups (480 ml) WASHINGTON All-Purpose Flour
3 tsp (15 ml) baking powder
½ tsp (3 ml) salt
½ cup (120 ml) sugar
1 egg, beaten
½ cup (120 ml) milk
⅓ cup (80 ml) cooking oil
1 tsp (5 ml) vanilla, optional

Preheat oven to 375°F (190°C). Grease bottom of 9-inch round or square pan. Prepare topping of your choice (below).

Place flour and sugar in medium bowl. Stir to blend. In a separate bowl, combine beaten egg, milk, oil and vanilla. Add to flour mixture. Stir to moisten (batter will be lumpy). Spoon into pan; spread on topping.

Bake 25-30 minutes or until done. Let stand 5 minutes. Remove from pan. Serves 9-12.

Cinnamon Butter Topping: Combine ⅓ cup (80 ml) soft butter or margarine, ⅔ cup (160 ml) sugar, ⅓ cup (80 ml) flour and 1 tsp (5 ml) cinnamon.

Rich Pecan Topping: Mix to crumbly consistency: 1 cup (240 ml) chopped pecans, ½ cup (120 ml) brown sugar, 1 tbs (15 ml) cinnamon, ½ cup (120 ml) flour and ½ cup (120 ml) butter or margarine.

Pineapple Topping: Combine 2 tbs soft butter or margarine, 2 tbs (30 ml) honey and ½ cup (120 ml) drained, crushed pineapple.

Marmalade Topping: Combine ½ cup (120 ml) flour, ½ cup (120 ml) brown sugar, 3 tbs (45 ml) soft butter or margarine, 1 tbs (15 ml) milk and ½ cup (120 ml) orange marmalade.

Honey Bee Topping: Combine ¼ cup (60 ml) sugar, ¼ cup (60 ml) soft butter or margarine, 1 egg white, ¼ cup (60 ml) honey, ½ tsp (3 ml) nutmeg and ½ cup (120 ml) chopped nuts.

Peach Topping: Arrange (over top of batter) 1 cup (240 ml) well-drained sliced peaches. combine 2 tbs (30 ml) sugar and 1 tsp (5 ml) cinnamon; sprinkle over peaches.

Instant Coffee Topping: Combine 2 tbs (30 ml) soft butter or margarine, ½ cup (120 ml) sugar and 1 tbs (15 ml) instant coffee.

Toffee Topping: Melt over hot water, one 6-oz pkg (180 g) chocolate chips; stir in ¾ cup (180 ml) nuts and 1½ tsp (8 ml) instant coffee.

Orange Coffeecake: Substitute orange juice for half of milk; add 1½ tsp (8 ml) grated orange peel to Cinnamon Butter Topping and sprinkle over cake batter before baking.

Fresh Fruit Coffeecake: Fold 1 cup (240 ml) fresh diced fruit into cake batter before baking (apple, pear, banana, peach, etc.). Add your favorite topping.

Buttermilk Coffeecake

Topping:
⅓ cup (80 ml) brown sugar
½ tsp (3 ml) cinnamon
3 tbs (45 ml) soft butter or margarine
¼ cup (60 ml) flour

1½ cups (355 ml) all-purpose flour
2 tbs (30 ml) SACO Buttermilk Blend
1 tsp (5 ml) baking powder
¼ tsp (1 ml) baking soda
½ tsp (3 ml) salt
¾ cup (180 ml) sugar
¼ cup (60 ml) soft shortening
1 egg
¾ cup (180 ml) water

Preheat oven to 350°F (180°C). Grease 9x9-inch pan.

Mix all ingredients for Topping and set aside.

Place remaining ingredients in large mixing bowl. Beat on low 30 seconds. Scrape bowl and beat 1½ minutes more on medium speed, scraping bowl occasionally. Do not overbeat.

Spread half batter in pan and sprinkle with half the Topping. Pour in remaining batter; sprinkle with remaining Topping. Bake 30-35 minutes or until tested done. Serves 9-12.

Opposite: Coffeecake

Rhubarb-Strawberry Coffeecake

Rhubarb-Strawberry Filling:
3 cups (720 ml) fresh rhubarb, cut in 1-inch pieces or 13-oz pkg
(390 g) frozen unsweetened rhubarb, cut in 1-inch pieces
16-oz pkg (480 g) frozen sliced sweetened strawberries, thawed
2 tbs (30 ml) lemon juice
1 cup (240 ml) sugar, or to taste
⅓ cup (80 ml) cornstarch

Batter:
3 cups (720 ml) all-purpose flour
1 cup (240 ml) sugar
½ tsp (3 ml) baking soda
1 tsp (5 ml) baking powder
¼ cup (60 ml) SACO Buttermilk Blend
1 tsp (5 ml) salt
1 cup (240 ml) margarine
1 cup (240 ml) water
2 eggs
1 tsp (5 ml) vanilla

Topping:
¾ cup (180 ml) sugar
½ cup (120 ml) flour
¼ cup (60 ml) margarine

Preheat oven to 350°F (180°C).

Prepare and cool Rhubarb-Strawberry Filling.

Rhubarb-Strawberry Filling: In saucepan, combine rhubarb and strawberries. Cook fruit, covered, 5 minutes. Add lemon juice. Combine sugar and cornstarch; add to rhubarb mixture. Cook and stir 4-5 minutes or until thick and bubbly. Cool before spreading on cake.

Batter: In a large bowl, sift together flour, sugar, baking soda, baking powder, buttermilk blend and salt. Cut in margarine until mixture resembles fine crumbs. Beat together water, eggs and vanilla and add to dry ingredients. Stir to moisten. Do not overbeat.

Spread half the batter in a greased 13x9x2-inch pan. Spread cooled Filling over the batter in the pan. Spoon remaining batter in small mounds atop Filling.

Topping: Mix ingredients until they resemble fine crumbs. Sprinkle over batter.

Bake 45-50 minutes. Serves 12-15.

Rhubarb-Strawberry
Coffeecake

Whole Wheat Crumb Coffeecake

1½ cups (355 ml) all-purpose flour
½ tsp (3 ml) cinnamon
½ tsp (3 ml) nutmeg
¼ tsp (1 ml) cloves, optional
¼ cup (60 ml) SACO Buttermilk Blend
½ tsp (3 ml) baking soda
¾ tsp (180 ml) salt
1 cup (240 ml) whole wheat flour
1 cup (240 ml) packed brown sugar
¾ cup (180 ml) shortening
1 cup (240 ml) raisins
1 egg
1 cup (240 ml) water
1 tsp (5 ml) vanilla

In a large bowl, sift together all-purpose flour, cinnamon, nutmeg, cloves if desired, buttermilk blend, baking soda and salt. Stir in whole wheat flour and brown sugar. Cut in shortening with pastry blender (or with a knife or fork) until mixture resembles coarse bread crumbs. Reserve 1 cup of this crumble mixture and set aside for topping.

To remainder, add raisins. Beat together egg, water and vanilla and stir into flour mixture until just blended. Do not overbeat.

Spread in greased 9-inch square pan and sprinkle with reserved crumbs. Bake at 375°F (190°C) 30-35 minutes or until done when tested with a toothpick. Serve warm. Serves 9-12.

Above: Whole Wheat Crumb Coffeecake

Earthquake Coffeecake

⅓ cup (80 ml) *GHIRARDELLI Ground Chocolate*
¼ cup (60 ml) sugar
½ tsp (3 ml) instant coffee
2 cups (480 ml) buttermilk baking mix
1 egg
½ cup (120 ml) sour cream
½ cup (120 ml) half and half

Topping:
⅓ cup (80 ml) buttermilk baking mix
2 tbs (30 ml) *GHIRARDELLI Ground Chocolate*
3 tbs (45 ml) brown sugar, packed
½ tsp (3 ml) cinnamon
2 tbs (30 ml) butter or margarine
2 tbs (30 ml) sliced almonds

Preheat oven to 400°F (205°C).

In bowl, blend together chocolate, sugar and coffee. Stir in buttermilk baking mix. Beat egg with sour cream and half and half; add to dry ingredients. Stir lightly to combine ingredients.
Do not overmix. Spread into greased 9x1½-inch round cake pan.

Topping: Combine buttermilk baking mix, chocolate, brown sugar and cinnamon. With pastry blender, cut in butter or margarine. Sprinkle over top of cake batter. Run knife through topping and batter in a swirl pattern for earthquake marbling. Sprinkle with nuts.

Bake 25 minutes. Cut into wedges. Serves 8.

Walnut Streusel Coffeecake

Walnut Streusel:
½ cup (120 ml) all-purpose flour
½ cup (120 ml) brown sugar, firmly packed
½ tsp (3 ml) cinnamon
¼ cup (60 ml) butter or margarine
½ cup (120 ml) chopped *DIAMOND Walnuts*

Coffeecake:
8-oz pkg (240 g) cream cheese, softened
½ cup (120 ml) butter or margarine
1¼ cups (295 ml) sugar
2 eggs
1 tsp (5 ml) vanilla
1¾ cups (415 ml) all-purpose flour
1 tsp (5 ml) baking powder
1 tsp (5 ml) cinnamon
½ tsp (3 ml) baking soda
¼ cup (60 ml) milk
1 cup (240 ml) *DIAMOND Walnuts*

Preheat oven to 350°F (180°C). Grease and flour a 13x9-inch pan.

Walnut Streusel: Combine flour, brown sugar and cinnamon. Cut in butter or margarine until mixture resembles coarse crumbs; stir in walnuts. Set aside.

Coffeecake: Combine cream cheese, butter or margarine and sugar; blend well. Add eggs and vanilla; beat until light and fluffy. Combine flour, baking powder, cinnamon and baking soda; stir into cream cheese mixture alternately with milk. Fold in walnuts.

Pour into prepared pan. Sprinkle with Walnut Streusel. Bake for 35-40 minutes. Serve warm. Serves 12.

Earthquake Coffeecake

Chocolate Chunk Coffeecake

Nut Layer:
1 4-oz pkg BAKER'S German Sweet Chocolate, chopped
½ cup (120 ml) chopped nuts
¼ cup (60 ml) sugar
1 tsp (5 ml) cinnamon

Cake:
1¾ cups (415 ml) all-purpose flour
½ tsp (3 ml) CALUMET Baking Powder
¼ tsp (1 ml) salt
1 cup (240 ml) sour cream or plain yogurt
1 tsp (5 ml) baking soda
½ cup (120 ml) margarine or butter, softened
1 cup (240 ml) sugar
2 eggs
½ tsp (3 ml) vanilla

Preheat oven to 350°F (180°C).

Nut Layer: Mix chocolate, nuts, sugar and cinnamon; set aside.

Cake: Mix flour, baking powder and salt; set aside. Combine sour creamor yogurt and baking soda; set aside.

Beat margarine or butter and 1 cup sugar in large bowl until light and fluffy. Add eggs, one at a time, beating well after each addition. Add vanilla. Add flour mixture alternately with sour cream mixture, beginning and ending with flour mixture. Spoon half the batter into greased 9-inch square pan. Top with half the Nut Layer, spreading carefully with spatula. Repeat layers.

Bake 30-35 minutes or until cake begins to pull away from sides of pan. Cool in pan; cut into squares. Serves 9-12.

Coffee Ring

3 cups (720 ml) sifted PRESTO
⅓ cup (80 ml) sugar
¼ cup (60 ml) shortening
1 egg, beaten
¾ cup (180 ml) milk
2 tbs (30 ml) melted butter
2 tbs (30 ml) brown sugar
¾ cup (180 ml) raisins
½ cup (120 ml) chopped citron
½ cup (120 ml) chopped walnuts

Sift flour and sugar and work in shortening with tips of fingers or pastry blender. Add beaten egg to milk and stir into flour mixture. Roll or pat to ¼-inch thickness into oblong shape. Spread with melted butter, sprinkle with brown sugar, raisins, citron and nuts. Roll as for jelly roll, bringing ends together to make a circle.

Put on greased baking sheet and cut gashes around outside, 2 inches apart, with scissors. Bake in 350°F (180°C) oven 25-30 minutes. Serves 9-12.

Chocolate Chunk Coffeecake

Rich Chocolate Walnut Coffee Ring

1½ cups (355 ml) butter or margarine, at room temperature
1½ cups (355 ml) sugar
4 eggs
2 tsp (10 ml) vanilla
4 cups (960 ml) flour
4 tsp (20 ml) baking powder
½ tsp (3 ml) salt
1 cup (240 ml) chopped walnuts
1½ cups (355 ml) milk
2 cups (480 ml) GHIRARDELLI Semi-Sweet Chocolate Chips

Preheat oven to 350°F (180°C). Generously grease and lightly flour 9½-inch bundt or other deep tube pan or mold that holds 14 cups (3.4 l).

Beat butter or margarine with sugar until creamy. Beat in eggs and vanilla until smooth and creamy. Mix flour, baking powder, salt and walnuts; stir into creamy mixture alternately with milk, mixing just until combined.

Spoon ⅓ batter (about 2½ cups) into pan. Layer with 1 cup chocolate chips. Portion another ⅓ batter in spoonfuls on top of chips, smoothing out to make an even layer of batter. Sprinkle evenly with remaining 1 cup chips. Spoon remaining batter in layer on top.

Bake in center of oven 60-70 minutes or until cake tester comes out clean. There may be melted chocolate on the pick. Cool 20 minutes, then gently invert from pan. Dust with powdered sugar, if desired. Serve cool or warm. This is wonderful with fruit, for brunch or a dessert table. May be frozen, if desired. Serves 16.

Above: Rich Chocolate Walnut Coffee Ring

Chocolate Pecan Coffeecake

4 oz (120 g) SACO Chocolate Chunks
1 cup (240 ml) small pecan pieces
1½ cups (360 ml) sugar, divided
1 tsp (5 ml) ground cinnamon
1 cup (240 ml) unsalted butter, softened
1 tsp (5 ml) vanilla extract
3 eggs
2 cups (480 ml) cake flour
⅓ cup (80 ml) SACO Baking Cocoa
1½ tsp (8 ml) baking powder
¾ tsp (4 ml) baking soda
½ tsp (3 ml) salt
1 cup (240 ml) sour cream

Syrup (optional):
¼ cup (60 ml) sugar
6 tbs (90 ml) water

Preheat oven to 350°F (180°C). Grease and flour a 12-cup (2.9 l) bundt cake pan, tapping out any excess flour.

Coarsely chop the chocolate (easily done in food processor, being careful not to overprocess). Combine chocolate with pecan pieces, ¼ cup sugar and cinnamon; set aside.

Cream butter and 1¼ cups sugar until light and fluffy. Add vanilla and eggs, mixing well. Scrape sides of the bowl down. Sift flour, cocoa, baking powder, baking soda and salt together. Add dry ingredients, in thirds, to butter mixture, alternately with sour cream, beginning and ending with dry ingredients.

Place half the batter into prepared pan, spreading level. Top with half the pecan mixture. Repeat with the rest of the batter and pecan mixture. Bake for 50-60 minutes, or until it tests done with a toothpick. Cake will start to pull away from pan sides. Cool 10 minutes then unmold onto cooling rack. Brush with Syrup, if desired. Serves 14.

Syrup: Combine sugar and water to dissolve. Brush outer surface of cake with all the syrup. This will make cake more moist and will extend the shelf life. Cake is best eaten at room temperature.

Tips and Hints: Sift cocoa before adding to recipes to prevent lumps from forming. If using salted butter in recipes, decrease or omit salt as taste dictates.

Pineapple Coffeecake

Pineapple Coffeecake

1½ cups (355 ml) sifted flour
⅓ cup (80 ml) sugar
1 tsp (5 ml) baking powder
½ tsp (3 ml) salt
8¼-oz can (248 g) DEL MONTE Crushed Pineapple
¼ cup (60 ml) butter or margarine, melted
1 egg, beaten
¼ cup (60 ml) sugar
1 tsp (5 ml) cinnamon
1 tbs (15 ml) butter or margarine, softened

Preheat oven to at 350°F (180°C).

Sift together flour, ⅓ cup sugar, baking powder and salt. Drain pineapple reserving syrup; set pineapple aside. Add enough water to reserved syrup to measure ½ cup. Combine syrup mixture with butter or margarine and egg. Mix with dry ingredients ; beat until smooth.

Spread in greased 9-inch pan. Combine reserved pineapple, remaining ¼ cup sugar, cinnamon and 1 tbs butter or margarine. Spoon mixture over top.

Bake 30-35 minutes. Serve warm. Serves 9.

Citrus Cream Cheese Coffeecake

2½ cups (590 ml) all-purpose flour
½ cup (120 ml) JACK FROST Light Brown Sugar, packed
½ cup (120 ml) JACK FROST Granulated Sugar
¾ cup (180 ml) butter or margarine
½ tsp (3 ml) baking powder
½ tsp (3 ml) baking soda
¼ tsp (1 ml) salt
1 cup (240 ml) lemon or orange yogurt
1 tsp (5 ml) lemon or orange rind
1 tsp (5 ml) vanilla
2 large eggs
2 3-oz pkgs (90 g each) cream cheese, softened
½ cup (120 ml) JACK FROST Granulated Sugar
½ cup (120 ml) orange marmalade
½ cup (120 ml) chopped walnuts

Preheat oven to 350°F (180°C).

In a large bowl, combine flour and sugars. Using a pastry blender or fork, cut in butter or margarine until mixture resembles coarse crumbs. Reserve 1 cup of crumb mixture. To remaining mixture, add baking powder, baking soda, salt, yogurt, lemon or orange rind, vanilla and 1 egg; blend well.

Spread batter over bottom and 2 inches up sides of a greased and floured 9- or 10-inch springform pan. Batter should be about ¼-inch thick on sides.

In small bowl, combine cream cheese, sugar and the other egg; blend well. Pour into batter-lined pan. Carefully spoon marmalade over cream cheese mixture. In small bowl, combine reserved crumb mixture and chopped walnuts. Sprinkle over preserves.

Bake for 50-60 minutes or until golden brown. Cool 15 minutes. Remove from sides of pan. Serve warm or cool. Cut into wedges. Refrigerate leftovers. Serves 16.

Banana Tea Ring

⅓ cup (80 ml) butter or margarine
¼ cup (60 ml) sugar
¾ cup (180 ml) brown sugar
2 eggs
1 tsp (5 ml) vanilla
1 cup (240 ml) ripe bananas, mashed (2 or 3)
¼ cup (60 ml) milk
2 cups (480 ml) WASHINGTON Self-Rising Flour
½ cup (120 ml) nuts, chopped

Glaze:
1 cup (240 ml) confectioners sugar
2 tbs (30 ml) milk
¼ tsp (1 ml) vanilla
dash salt
chopped nuts, optional

Preheat oven to 350°F (180°C). Grease 9-inch ring mold or 8-inch square pan.

Place butter or margarine and sugars in bowl. Cream until well blended. Add eggs and vanilla. In a separate bowl blend milk with bananas. Add alternately, with flour, to above mixture, beginning and ending with flour. Mix well after each addition. Stir in nuts.

Pour into pan. Bake 30-35 minutes. Cool 5 minutes; turn out of pan. Glaze. Serves 16.

Glaze: Combine all ingredients in bowl. Beat until smooth. Pour over warm tea ring. Sprinkle nuts on top, if desired.

Opposite: **Citrus Cream Cheese Coffeecake**

Orange Blueberry Brunch Cake

½ cup (120 ml) MOTT'S Natural Apple Sauce
1 cup (355 ml) granulated sugar
1 whole egg, beaten
1 egg white, beaten
2 tbs (30 ml) grated orange peel from large orange, divided
2 cups (480 ml) all-purpose flour
1 tsp (5 ml) baking soda
½ tsp (3 ml) salt
⅔ cups (160 ml) buttermilk
1 cup (240 ml) fresh blueberries or frozen blueberries, thawed

Topping:
½ cup (120 ml) orange juice from 2 large oranges
½ cup granulated sugar

Preheat oven to 375°F (190°C). Spray 9x5x3-inch loaf pan with cooking spray.

In a large bowl, combine applesauce, 1 cup granulated sugar, 1 beaten whole egg, egg white and 1 tbs orange peel. In a medium bowl, sift together flour, baking soda and salt. Add to liquid mixture alternately with buttermilk. Stir until combined. Fold in blueberries. Pour batter into prepared loaf pan. Bake 60-70 minutes or until an inserted toothpick comes out clean. Remove cake from oven and cool 10 minutes.

Topping: In a small bowl combine orange juice, ½ cup granulated sugar and remaining 1 tbs orange peel from batter recipe above. Remove cake from pan and prick the top of cake with fork. Carefully spoon topping over hot cake allowing the syrup to be absorbed. Cool completely and serve. Serves 9.

Orange
Blueberry
Brunch Cake

Fruit Swirl Coffeecake

1½ cups (355 ml) sugar
½ cup (120 ml) margarine or butter, softened
½ cup (120 ml) shortening
1½ tsp (8 ml) baking powder
1 tsp (5 ml) vanilla
1 tsp (5 ml) almond extract
4 eggs
3 cups (720 ml) GOLD MEDAL All-Purpose Flour*
21-oz can (630 g) apricot, blueberry or cherry pie filling

Glaze:
1 cup (240 ml) confectioners sugar
1-2 tbs (15-30 ml) milk

Preheat oven to 350°F (180°C). Generously grease 15½x10½x1-inch jelly roll pan.

Beat sugar, margarine or butter, shortening, baking powder, vanilla, almond extract and eggs in large bowl on low speed 30 seconds, scraping bowl constantly. Beat on high speed 3 minutes, scraping bowl occasionally. Stir in flour.

Spread ⅔ of the batter in pan. Spread pie filling over batter. Drop remaining batter by tablespoonfuls onto pie filling. Bake about 45 minutes or until cake springs back when touched lightly. While warm, drizzle with Glaze. Serves 18.

Glaze: Mix confectioners sugar and milk thoroughly.
*If using self-rising flour, omit baking powder.

Above: Fruit Swirl Coffeecake

Classic Pound Cake I

3 cups (720 ml) sifted SWANS DOWN Cake Flour
2 tsp (10 ml) baking powder
½ tsp (3 ml) salt
1 cup (240 ml) butter or margarine, softened
2 cups (480 ml) sugar
4 eggs
¾ cup (180 ml) milk
1 tsp (5 ml) vanilla
½ tsp (3 ml) almond extract

Preheat oven to 325°F (165°C).

Sift flour with baking powder and salt. Cream butter or margarine and sugar until light and fluffy. Beat on medium speed 10 minutes. Add eggs, 1 at a time, beating after each addition. Add flour mixture alternately with milk and flavorings, creaming until smooth after each addition.

Spread batter into prepared 10-inch bundt pan. Bake until tester inserted into cake comes out clean, about 1 hour and 25 minutes. Cool in pan 15 minutes. Remove from pan; cool on rack. Glaze with Old-Fashioned Bourbon Glaze.. Serves 16.

Old-Fashioned Bourbon Glaze

1 cup (240 ml) confectioners sugar
1 tbs (15 ml) bourbon
1 tsp (5 ml) grated orange zest
1-2 tbs (15-30 ml) thawed orange juice concentrate

Combine sugar, bourbon, zest and enough orange juice concentrate to make a thin glaze. Drizzle onto cake.

Classic Pound Cake II

1 cup (240 ml) butter, softened
1 cup (240 ml) granulated sugar
4 eggs
1 tsp (5 ml) vanilla
½ tsp (3 ml) salt
dash ground nutmeg
1½ cups (355 ml) all-purpose flour

Preheat oven to 325°F (165°C).

In large mixing bowl, beat together butter and sugar at medium speed until light and fluffy. Add remaining ingredients except flour. Beat until thoroughly blended. Reduce mixer speed to low and add flour, ½ cup at a time, beating just until blended.

Spread evenly in greased and floured 9x5x3-inch loaf pan. Bake until cake tester inserted near center comes out clean, about 60-70 minutes. Cool on wire rack 10 minutes. Remove from pan and cool completely. Serves 8.

Blueberry: Fold 1 cup (240 ml) blueberries and ¼ cup (60 ml) chopped almonds into prepared batter. Bake as above.

Butter Pecan: Substitute firmly packed brown sugar for granulated sugar. Fold ⅓ cup (80 ml) chopped pecans into prepared batter. Bake as above.

Cherry Pecan: Add ½ tsp (3 ml) almond extract to batter. Fold one 6-oz jar (180 g) maraschino cherries, drained and chopped and ¼ cup (60 ml) chopped pecans into prepared batter. Bake as above.

Lemon: Add 1 tsp (5 ml) lemon extract to batter. Bake as above.

Classic Pound Cake I

Opposite: **Classic Pound Cake II**
(Cherry Pecan)

160

Cream Cheese Pound Cake

1½ cups (355 ml) butter or margarine, softened
8-oz pkg (240 g) cream cheese, softened
3 cups (720 ml) sugar
6 eggs
1½ tsp (8 ml) vanilla
3 cups (720 ml) MARTHA WHITE All-Purpose Flour or
 PILLSBURY BEST All-Purpose Flour
¼ tsp (1 ml) salt
confectioners sugar

Preheat oven to 325°F (165°C). Grease and flour bottom and sides of 10-inch tube pan or 12-cup bundt pan.

In large bowl, beat butter or margarine and cream cheese on medium speed until well mixed. Add sugar; beat until light and fluffy. Add eggs, 1 at a time, beating well after each addition. Beat in vanilla. Spoon flour into measuring cup; level off. Add flour and salt. Beat just until mixed.

Spoon batter into pan. Bake for 1 hour 35 minutes-1 hour 45 minutes or until toothpick inserted 1 inch from edge comes out clean. Cool in pan 5 minutes. Turn out onto wire rack and cool completely. Sift with confectioners sugar. Serve with fresh fruit, if desired. Serves 16-20.

Cream Cheese Pound Cake

Buttermilk Pound Cake

3 cups (720 ml) sifted all-purpose flour
½ tsp (3 ml) baking soda
½ tsp (3 ml) baking powder
¾ tsp (4 ml) salt
¼ cup (60 ml) SACO Buttermilk Blend
1 cup (240 ml) butter
2 cups (480 ml) sugar
4 eggs
1 tsp (5 ml) vanilla
1 tsp (5 ml) lemon extract
1 cup (240 ml) water

Preheat oven to 350°F (180°C).

Sift together flour, baking soda, baking powder, salt and buttermilk blend. Set aside. In a separate mixing bowl, cream together butter and sugar thoroughly. Add eggs, 1 at a time. Beat at medium speed with electric mixer 2½ minutes. Add vanilla and lemon extract. Add dry ingredients to creamed mixture alternately with water, beginning and ending with dry ingredients. Do not overbeat.

Place in greased and floured bundt pan. Bake for 50-60 minutes or until cake tests done with a wooden toothpick. Let cake cool in pan 10 minutes, then turn it out on a rack and cool completely. Serve unfrosted or sift a little confectioners sugar over the top of the cake before serving. Serves 16.

Aunt Lottie's Chocolate Pound Cake

4-oz bar (120 g) GHIRARDELLI Semi-Sweet Chocolate
1 cup (240 ml) butter, softened
1 cup (240 ml) sugar
5 eggs
1 tsp (10 ml) vanilla
1⅓ cups (320 ml) sifted flour
½ tsp (3 ml) baking powder

Preheat oven to 350°F (180°C).

In double boiler, melt chocolate over 1 inch of simmering water. Cream butter until light. Gradually add sugar, creaming until fluffy. Add eggs, 1 at a time, beating well after each addition. Blend in vanilla and melted chocolate. Sift flour with baking powder. Gradually mix in dry ingredients.

Pour into greased 9x5-inch loaf pan. Bake for 50-60 minutes. Serves 8.

Aunt Lottie's Chocolate Pound Cake

Poppy Seed Pound Cake

⅓ cup (80 ml) poppy seeds
1 cup (240 ml) low-fat buttermilk
¾ cup (180 ml) EGG BEATERS Real Egg Product
1 tsp (5 ml) vanilla extract
⅔ cup (160 ml) FLEISCHMANN'S Margarine, softened
1¼ cups (295 ml) sugar
2½ cups (590 ml) all-purpose flour
2 tsp (10 ml) baking powder
1 tsp (5 ml) baking soda
confectioners sugar glaze, optional

Preheat oven to 350°F (180°C).

In small bowl, stir poppy seeds into buttermilk; let stand 5 minutes. Stir in egg product and vanilla. In large bowl, with electric mixer at high speed, beat margarine and sugar until creamy. Combine flour, baking powder and baking soda. Alternately blend buttermilk mixture and flour mixture into margarine mixture until smooth.

Pour batter into a greased 12-cup fluted tube pan. Bake for 40-45 minutes until toothpick inserted in center comes out clean. Cool on wire rack 10 minutes; remove from pan. Cool completely on wire rack. Drizzle with glaze, if desired. Serves 15.

Almond Lemon Pound Cake

2 cups (480 ml) cake flour
½ tsp (3 ml) cream of tartar
½ tsp (3 ml) salt
1 cup (240 ml) butter
1 cup (240 ml) sugar
4 eggs
5 tbs (75 ml) lemon juice, divided
1¼ cups (295 ml) BLUE DIAMOND Chopped Natural Almonds,
    toasted, divided
½ cup (120 ml) confectioners sugar
½ tsp (3 ml) vanilla extract

Preheat oven to 325°F (165°C).

Sift cake flour with cream of tartar and salt; reserve. Cream butter and sugar. Add eggs, 1 at a time, mixing well. Add 2 tbs lemon juice. Gradually add sifted ingredients; mix thoroughly. Fold in 1 cup almonds.

Pour batter into a greased 9x5x3-inch loaf pan. Sprinkle top with remaining ¼ cup almonds. Bake for 1 hour or until toothpick inserted in center comes out clean.

While cake is baking, combine confectioners sugar, remaining 3 tbs lemon juice and vanilla; heat, stirring to dissolve sugar. When cake is done, drizzle top with hot glaze. Let cake cool, then remove from pan. Serves 8-10.

Almond Lemon Pound Cake

Opposite: Poppy Seed Pound Cake

Walnut Pound Cake

3 cups (720 ml) all-purpose flour
½ tsp (3 ml) baking powder
1½ cups (355 ml) butter or margarine
1-lb box (455 g) DOMINO Light Brown Sugar
¼ cup (60 ml) DOMINO Granulated Sugar
6 eggs
1 tsp (5 ml) vanilla
1 cup (240 ml) milk
1 cup (240 ml) chopped walnuts

Preheat oven to 350°F (180°C).

Combine flour and baking powder; set aside. Cream butter and sugars until fluffy. Add 1 egg at a time, stirring well after each addition. Stir in vanilla. Alternately add flour mixture, then milk, beating well until blended. Stir in walnuts.

Pour batter into 2 well-greased and floured 9x5-inch loaf pans. Bake 55-60 minutes or until tester inserted in center comes out clean. Cool 15 minutes in pan. Remove from pan and cool completely. Yields 2 loaves, serves 8-10 each.

Pineapple Pound Cake

8-oz can (240 g) DEL MONTE Crushed Pineapple
    in its Own Juice
½ lb (230 g) butter
½ cup (120 ml) shortening
3 cups (720 ml) sugar
5 eggs
3 cups (720 ml) sifted flour
½ tsp (3 ml) baking powder
½ tsp (3 ml) salt
1 cup (240 ml) milk, room temperature
1 tbs (15 ml) vanilla extract
1 tsp (5 ml) lemon extract

Preheat oven to 350°F (180°C).

Thoroughly drain pineapple (reserve juice for other recipes). Cream together butter, shortening and sugar until light and fluffy. Add eggs, 1 at a time, beating well after each addition. Sift together flour, baking powder and salt; add to creamed mixture alternately with milk. Mix until well blended. Add vanilla and lemon extract. Fold in fruit.

Pour batter into greased and floured 9- or 10-inch tube pan. Place in cold oven and bake 1 hour 25 minutes or until tests done. Cool on rack 25 minutes; remove from pan. Serve plain or iced with thin icing. Serves 12.

Walnut Pound Cake

Opposite: Pineapple Pound Cake

Apricot Brandy Pound Cake

Apricot Brandy Pound Cake

3½ cups (840 ml) SOFTASILK Cake Flour
3 cups (720 ml) sugar
1 cup (240 ml) margarine or butter, softened
½ cup (120 ml) sour cream
½ cup (120 ml) apricot brandy or apricot nectar
6 eggs
1 tsp (5 ml) orange extract
1 tsp (5 ml) lemon extract
1 tsp (5 ml) almond extract
½ tsp (3 ml) salt
¼ tsp (1 ml) baking soda

Preheat oven to 325°F (165°C). Grease and flour 12-cup bundt cake pan, 10x4-inch tube pan or two 8½x4½x2½-inch loaf pans.

Beat all ingredients in large bowl on low speed 30 seconds, scraping bowl constantly. Beat on medium speed 2 minutes, scraping bowl occasionally.

Pour into pan(s). Bake about 1 hour 20 minutes or until toothpick inserted in center comes out clean. Cool 20 minutes; remove from pan(s) and cool completely on wire rack. Serves 15.

Vineyard Pound Cake

½ cup (120 ml) butter
1⅓ cups (320 ml) sugar
2 eggs
1 tsp (5 ml) vanilla
½ tsp (3 ml) almond extract
2 cups (480 ml) all-purpose flour
½ tsp (3 ml) baking powder
¼ tsp (1 ml) salt
⅓ cup (80 ml) dairy sour cream
1 cup (240 ml) SUN•MAID Raisins

Preheat oven to 325°F (165°C). Grease and flour 6-cup fluted tube pan.*

In large bowl, combine butter, sugar, eggs, vanilla and almond extract; beat until light and fluffy. Combine flour, baking powder and salt; stir into butter mixture alternately with sour cream. Stir in raisins.

Spoon batter into pan. Bake in center of oven for about 60-65 minutes or until toothpick inserted in center comes out clean. Cool 15 minutes. Remove from pan and cool on wire rack. Serves 10.

* To make a loaf cake, use 8½x4½-inch loaf pan. Bake about 1 hour 30 minutes.

Coconut Tea Cakes

17-oz pkg (510 g) pound cake mix
pinch McCORMICK/SCHILLING Ground Mace

Icing:
¼ cup (60 ml) butter or margarine, softened
¼ cup (60 ml) dairy sour cream
½ tsp (3 ml) McCORMICK/SCHILLING Pure Vanilla Extract
¼ tsp (1 ml) McCORMICK/SCHILLING Ground Cinnamon
¼ tsp (1 ml) McCORMICK/SCHILLING Coconut Extract
2½ cups (590 ml) confectioners sugar
3½-oz can (105 g) flaked coconut

Prepare pound cake according to package directions, adding mace with dry ingredients. Bake as directed and cool on wire rack. Cut cake into 3x1x1-inch rectangles.

Preheat broiler.

Place all Icing ingredients except coconut in small mixing bowl and mix well. Spread thin layer of icing on tops, sides, and ends of cake pieces. Do not spread icing on bottom of pieces. Pour coconut into shallow dish and roll iced sides of cake pieces in coconut.

Arrange on cookie sheet, iced sides up. Broil 6-8 inches from source of heat, just until coconut is lightly browned. Cool on cookie sheet. Yields 24 tea cakes.

Ukrainian Spiced Honey Cake

3 eggs
¾ cup (180 ml) brown sugar, packed
¼ cup (60 ml) melted butter or margarine
¾ cup (180 ml) honey, additional for glazing
2¼ cups (540 ml) all-purpose flour
¾ tsp (4 ml) baking powder
¾ tsp (4 ml) baking soda
½ tsp (3 ml) salt
1 tsp (5 ml) cinnamon
½ tsp (3 ml) nutmeg
½ tsp (3 ml) cloves
½ cup (120 ml) SUN•MAID Raisins
½ cups (120 ml) SUN•MAID Zante Currants
½ cup (120 ml) DIAMOND Chopped Walnuts
¾ cup (180 ml) milk

Preheat oven to 325°F (165°C).

In mixing bowl, beat eggs and brown sugar just to blend. Mix in butter or margarine and honey. Sift together flour, baking powder, baking soda, salt and spices. Toss raisins, currants and walnuts with a tbs of the flour mixture; set aside. Add dry ingredients to batter alternately with milk, beating just until smooth after each addition. Stir in raisin mixture.

Pour batter into greased and floured 9x5-inch loaf pan. Bake for 60-70 minutes or until toothpick inserted into center comes out clean. Cool in pan 10 minutes; loosen edges and remove to wire rack. Brush warm loaf with additional honey; cool. Wrap in plastic wrap and let stand 24 hours. Glaze with honey again before slicing and serving. Serves 8-10.

Greek Honey Cake

½ cup (120 ml) butter or margarine, softened
1 cup (240 ml) sugar
2 eggs
1¼ cups (295 ml) all-purpose flour
1 cup (240 ml) finely chopped DIAMOND Walnuts
1½ tsp (8 ml) baking powder
¼ tsp (1 ml) salt
¼ cup (60 ml) milk
1 tbs (15 ml) grated orange peel
¼ cup (60 ml) orange juice
¼ cup (60 ml) honey
DIAMOND Walnuts, for garnish
orange slices or figs, for garnish

Preheat oven to 350°F (180°C). Grease a 9-inch round cake pan. Line bottom of pan with waxed paper circle. Lightly grease paper; dust entire pan with flour.

In large bowl, combine butter or margarine and sugar; beat until light and fluffy. Beat in eggs, 1 at a time. Combine flour, 1 cup walnuts, baking powder and salt; stir into butter mixture alternately with milk. Stir in orange peel; pour into prepared pan.

Bake at 350°F (180°C) for about 40 minutes or until toothpick inserted in center comes out clean. Cool in pan 10 minutes. Run knife around edge of pan; invert cake on plate. Peel off waxed paper; invert onto wire rack.

Stir together orange juice and honey until smooth; spoon over warm cake. Cool completely. Garnish with walnuts and orange slices or figs. Serves 8.

Greek Honey Cake

Honey Walnut Cake

Honey Walnut Cake

½ cup (120 ml) FLEISCHMANN'S Margarine
½ cup (120 ml) light brown sugar, firmly packed
½ cup (120 ml) honey
¼ cup (60 ml) EGG BEATERS Real Egg Product
1 cup (240 ml) all-purpose flour
1 tsp (5 ml) instant coffee powder
¼ tsp (1 ml) baking powder
¼ tsp (1 ml) ground cinnamon
¼ tsp (1 ml) ground allspice
¼ tsp (1 ml) ground cloves
¼ cup (60 ml) skim milk
¼ cup (60 ml) PLANTERS Walnuts, chopped

Preheat oven to 375°F (190°C).

In bowl, with electric mixer at high speed, beat margarine, brown sugar and honey until creamy. Add egg product; beat until mixture is light and fluffy. Blend in flour, instant coffee, baking powder, cinnamon, allspice, cloves, skim milk and walnuts.

Spread batter in greased 8x8x2-inch baking pan. Bake for 30 minutes or until toothpick inserted comes out clean. Cool in pan on wire rack. Wrap in plastic wrap and store refrigerated for up to 1 week. Cake can be frozen for up to 1 month. Serves 9.

Six Egg Chiffon Cake

2¼ cups (540 ml) sifted PRESTO
1½ cups (355 ml) sugar
½ cup (120 ml) corn oil
6 egg, separated
¾ cup (180 ml) water
1 tsp (5 ml) grated lemon rind
2 tsp (10 ml) vanilla
½ tsp (3 ml) cream of tartar

Preheat oven to 325°F (165°C).
Sift flour and sugar together into mixing bowl. Make well in center and add corn oil, egg yolks, water, lemon rind and vanilla in order given. Beat with spoon until smooth.

Beat egg whites and cream of tartar in large bowl until mixture forms very stiff peaks when beater is raised. Gently fold first mixture into egg whites, blending well. Fold; do not stir.

Pour batter into ungreased 10-inch tube pan. Bake 70-75 minutes or until cake springs back when touched lightly with finger. Immediately invert pan over bottle to allow to cool. When cold, remove from pan. Serves 16.

Mocha Chiffon Cake: Follow above recipe, sifting 2 tbs (30 ml) instant coffee with dry ingredients, omitting lemon rind, decreasing vanilla to 1 tsp (5 ml) and stirring ½ cup (120 ml) semisweet chocolate pieces, melted, into batter before folding it into beaten egg whites.

Orange Chiffon Cake: Follow above recipe, substituting ¾ cup (180 ml) orange juice for water and, if desired, 1 tsp (5 ml) grated orange rind for lemon rind.

Two-Egg Yellow Chiffon Cake

2 eggs, separated
1½ cups (355 ml) sugar
2¼ cups (540 ml) sifted cake flour or 2 cups (480 ml) sifted
* all-purpose flour*
½ tsp (3 ml) baking powder
½ tsp (3 ml) baking soda
1 tsp (5 ml) salt
¼ cup (60 ml) SACO Buttermilk Blend
⅓ cup (80 ml) vegetable oil
1 cup (240 ml) water
1½ tsp (8 ml) vanilla

Have ingredients at room temperature.

Preheat oven to 350°F (180°C). Grease and flour a 13x9x2-inch baking pan or 2 round layer cake pans.

In a small mixing bowl, beat egg whites until foamy. Beat in ½ cup of the sugar, 1 tbs at a time. Continue beating until very stiff and glossy. Set meringue aside.

Sift remaining sugar, the flour, baking powder, baking soda, salt and buttermilk blend into large bowl. Add oil, ½ cup water and the vanilla. Beat 1 minute on high speed, scraping bowl constantly. Add remaining water and the egg yolks. Beat 1 minute, scraping bowl occasionally. Fold in meringue.

Pour into pan(s). Bake oblong pan for 40-50 minutes, layer pans for 30-35 minutes, or until wooden toothpick, inserted in center, comes out clean. Cool. Frost as desired or with French Silk Frosting. Serves 8-12.

French Silk Frosting

2⅔ cups (640 ml) confectioners sugar
1 tbs (15 ml) SACO Buttermilk Blend
⅔ cup (160 ml) butter, softened
2 oz (60 g) unsweetened chocolate, melted and cooled
¾ tsp (4 ml) vanilla
2 tbs (30 ml) milk

In small mixing bowl, blend confectioners sugar, buttermilk blend, butter, chocolate and vanilla on low speed. Gradually add milk; beat until smooth and fluffy. Makes enough to fill and frost two 9-inch layers or one 13x9-inch cake.

Opposite: **Six Egg Chiffon Cake**

Two-Egg Chocolate Chiffon Cake

2 eggs, separated
1½ cups (355 ml) sugar
1¾ cup (415 ml) sifted cake flour or 1½ cups (355 ml)
    sifted all-purpose flour
1 tsp (5 ml) salt
¾ tsp (4 ml) baking soda
¼ cup (60 ml) SACO Buttermilk Blend
⅓ cup (80 ml) vegetable oil
1 cup (240 ml) water
2 oz (60 g) unsweetened chocolate, melted and cooled

Have ingredients at room temperature.

Preheat oven to 350°F (180°C). Grease and flour a
13x9x2-inch baking pan, or 2 round layer cake pans.

In a small mixing bowl, beat egg whites until foamy.
Beat in ½ cup of the sugar, 1 tbs at a time. Continue
beating until stiff and glossy. Set meringue aside.

Sift remaining sugar, flour, salt, baking soda and
buttermilk blend into a large mixer bowl. Add oil and
½ cup water. Beat 1 minute on high speed, scraping bowl
constantly. Add remaining water, the egg yolks and the
chocolate. Beat 1 minute, scraping bowl occasionally.
Fold in meringue.

Pour into pan(s). Bake oblong pan for 40-50 minutes,
layer pans for 30-35 minutes, or until wooden toothpick
inserted in center comes out clean. Cool. Frost as desired
or use to make Saco Bavarian Torte (below). Serves 8-12.

Saco Bavarian Torte: Bake above cake in 2 round layer
cake pans, 8 or 9 inches. Cool and split to make 4 layers.
Fill layers and frost with Creme Filling, sprinkling each
layer with 1-2 tbs (15-30 ml) grated unsweetened chocolate. Refrigerate at least 8 hours.

Creme Filling

1½ cups (355 ml) chilled whipping cream
8-oz pkg (240 g) cream cheese, softened
⅔ cup (160 ml) brown sugar, packed
1 tsp (5 ml) vanilla
dash salt

In a chilled bowl, beat cream until stiff. Set aside. In a
separate bwl, blend cream cheese, sugar, vanilla and salt.
Fold into whipped cream.

Two-Egg Chocolate Chiffon Cake

Gingerbread Chiffon Cake

2 tsp (10 ml) baking soda
1 tsp (5 ml) salt
2 tsp (10 ml) McCORMICK/SCHILLING Ground Ginger
2 tsp (10 ml) McCORMICK/SCHILLING Ground Cinnamon
½ tsp (3 ml) McCORMICK/SCHILLING Ground Cardamom
2¼ cups (540 ml) sifted all-purpose flour
1½ cups (355 ml) dark brown sugar, firmly packed
¾ cup (180 ml) buttermilk
½ cup (120 ml) molasses
½ cup (120 ml) canola or other vegetable oil
4 egg yolks
8 egg whites, room temperature
½ tsp (3 ml) McCORMICK/SCHILLING Cream of Tartar

Preheat oven to 325°F (165°C).

Add baking soda, salt and spices to sifted flour and sift
again. Place brown sugar, buttermilk, molasses, oil and egg
yolks in large mixing bowl and beat with electric mixer
until well combined. Add dry ingredients and mix until
smooth. Place egg whites in large mixing bowl with cream
of tartar and beat with electric mixer until stiff peaks form
when beaters are lifted. Fold into batter until blended.

Pour into ungreased 10-inch bundt pan or tube pan.
Bake 1 hour and 10 minutes. Cool in pan on wire rack 10
minutes. Remove from pan and cool completely on rack.
Serves 16.

Black Forest Chiffon Cake

10-oz jar (300 g) maraschino cherries
1¾ cups (415 ml) SOFTASILK Cake Flour
3 tsp (15 ml) baking powder
½ tsp (3 ml) salt
1¾ cups (415 ml) sugar
½ cup (120 ml) baking cocoa
1 tsp (5 ml) vanilla
½ tsp (3 ml) almond extract
7 egs, separated
½ cup (120 ml) vegetable oil
½ cup (120 ml) cold water
¼ cup (60 ml) cherry liqueur
½ cup (120 ml) finely chopped, toasted, slivered almonds*
½ tsp (3 ml) cream of tartar
Cherry Glaze, if desired

Drain cherries, reserving juice for Cherry Glaze, if desired. Reserve 10 whole cherries; chop remaining cherries.

Move oven rack to lowest position. Preheat oven to 325°F (165°C).

Mix cake flour, baking powder, salt, 1 cup of the sugar and the cocoa in medium bowl. Beat in vanilla, almond extract, egg yolks, oil, water and liqueur on low speed 30 seconds. Stir in chopped cherries and almonds.

Beat egg whites and cream of tartar in large bowl on medium speed until frothy. Gradually beat in remaining ¾ cup sugar until blended. Beat on high speed about 2 minutes or until stiff peaks form. Gradually pour egg yolk mixture over beaten whites, folding just until blended.

Pour batter into ungreased tube pan, 10x4 inches. Cut through batter with metal spatula.

Bake 55-60 minutes or until top springs back when touched lightly. Turn pan upside down on heatproof funnel or bottle until completely cool. Remove from pan. Drizzle with Cherry Glaze, if desired; garnish with reserved whole cherries. Serves 16.

*To toast almonds, heat oven to 350°F (180°C). Bake in ungreased pan about 10 minutes, stirring occasionally, until golden.

Cherry Glaze

reserved cherry juice
2 tsp (10 ml) cornstarch
2 tbs (30 ml) light corn syrup
red food color, if desired

Add enough water to reserved cherry juice to measure ⅓ cup. Mix cornstarch, cherry juice and corn syrup in 1-quart saucepan until cornstarch is dissolved. Heat to boiling over medium heat; boil 2 minutes or until glossy and thickened. Remove from heat; stir in 3 or 4 drops food color.

Black Forest Chiffon Cake

Sponge Cake

3 eggs, separated
1 cup (240 ml) sugar
⅓ cup (80 ml) cold water
1 tsp (5 ml) vanilla or grated lemon rind
1 cup (240 ml) sifted PRESTO

Preheat oven to 300°F (150°C).

Beat egg whites until foamy. Gradually add ½ cup sugar, beating until mixture forms soft peaks when beater is raised. Set aside.

Beat egg yolks, gradually add remaining ½ cup sugar; beat until mixture is thick and lemon colored. Add water and flavoring, then flour, stirring until batter is smooth. Fold in egg white mixture.

Pour into ungreased 9x3½-inch tube pan. Bake about 60 minutes or until cake springs back when touched lightly with finger. Immediately invert pan over funnel or bottle. When cake is cool, remove from pan. Serves 16.

Sponge Cake

Delicate Sponge Cake

6 eggs, room temperature
1 tbs (15 ml) lemon juice
1 tsp (5 ml) grated lemon or orange rind
1 cup (240 ml) cake flour
¾ tsp (4 ml) salt
1 cup (240 ml) IMPERIAL Granulated sugar

Preheat oven to 325°F (165°C). Lightly grease and flour only the bottom of 10-inch tube pan.

Break eggs into large bowl of electric mixer. Add lemon juice and grated rind. Beat at highest speed until soft peaks form (12-16 minutes). Sift flour and salt while eggs beat. Continue beating eggs at highest speed, adding granulated sugar in fine stream, for about 2 minutes. Change to lowest speed and slowly add flour/salt mixture. Scrape sides and beat at lowest speed ½ minute.

Pour batter into pan and bake 50 minutes, or until toothpick comes out clean. Invert pan onto rack. Let cool before removing pan. Serve with your favorite topping. Serves 12.

Opposite: Delicate Sponge Cake

Banana Chiffon Cake

2¼ cups (540 ml) SOFTASILK Cake Flour
1½ cups (355 ml) sugar
3 tsp (15 ml) baking powder
1 tsp (5 ml) salt
½ cup (120 ml) vegetable oil
5 egg yolks
¾ cup (180 ml) mashed bananas
1 tbs (15 ml) lemon juice
1 tsp (5 ml) banana extract
1 cup (240 ml) egg whites (about 8)
½ tsp (3 ml) cream of tartar
Chocolate Glaze

Move oven rack to lowest position. Preheat oven to 325°F (165°C).

Mix cake flour, sugar, baking powder and salt in medium bowl. Beat in oil, egg yolks, bananas, lemon juice and banana extract on low speed 1 minutes. Beat egg whites and cream of tartar in large bowl on high speed until stiff peaks form. Gradually pour egg yolk mixture over beaten whites, folding just until blended.

Pour batter unto ungreased tube pan, 10x4 inches. Cut through batter with metal spatula.

Bake 55-60 minutes or until top springs back when touched lightly. Turn pan upside down onto heat proof funnel or bottle until completely cool. Remove from pan. Drizzle with Chocolate Glaze; decorate with sliced bananas if desired. Serves 16.

Chocolate Glaze

½ cup (120 ml) semisweet chocolate chips
2 tbs (30 ml) margarine or butter
2 tbs (30 ml) corn syrup
1-2 tsp (5-10 ml) hot water

Heat chocolate chips, margarine or butter and corn syrup over low heat. Stir constantly, until chocolate chips are melted; cool slightly. Stir in water, 1 tsp at a time, until spreading consistency.

Hot Milk Sponge Cake

4 eggs
2 cups (480 ml) sugar
1 cup (240 ml) milk
2 tbs (30 ml) butter or margarine
2 cups (480 ml) sifted WASHINGTON Self-Rising Flour
2 tsp (10 ml) vanilla

Preheat oven to 350°F (180°C). Use ungreased 10-inch tube pan, or two 9-inch layer pans, or one 13x9-inch pan.

Beat eggs in large mixing bowl at high speed, about 5 minutes, until thick and lemon colored. Gradually beat in sugar. Heat milk and butter to boiling. Add all at once to egg-sugar mixture. Blend in at low speed.

Pour into pan. Bake 45 minutes for tube pan, 25-30 minutes for layer pans or 13x9-inch pan. Invert pan and cool. Serve with whipped cream and fresh fruit. Serves 10-16.

Hot Milk Sponge Cake

Passover Orange Sponge Cake

⅓ cup (80 ml) matzo cake meal
½ cup (120 ml) potato starch
pinch salt
10 eggs, separated
1 cup (240 ml) DOMINO Pure Granulated Sugar
juice of 1 lemon
grated rind of 1 orange

Preheat oven to 350°F (180°C).

Sift together matzo cake meal, potato starch and salt 3 times; set aside.

Beat egg yolks until thick. Add ½ cup sugar, lemon juice and orange rind. Continue beating until thick and fluffy. Fold in sifted dry ingredients.

In a separate bowl, beat egg whites until foamy. Add ½ cup sugar gradually. Beat until stiff peaks form. Fold egg yolk mixture into egg whites.

Turn into ungreased 10-inch spring form tube pan. Bake for 45-50 minutes. Invert pan until cake is cool. Serves 10.

Passover Orange Sponge Cake

Party Chocolate Sponge Cake

6 eggs, separated
2 tsp (10 ml) vanilla
1 cup (240 ml) sugar
⅔ cup (160 ml) GHIRARDELLI Ground Chocolate
½ cup (120 ml) boiling water
1½ cups (355 ml) unsifted cake flour
1 tsp (5 ml) baking powder
¼ tsp (1 ml) salt

Preheat oven to 325°F (165°C.

In a large bowl, beat egg yolks with vanilla; gradually add sugar, beating until light and thick.

Mix ground chocolate with boiling water; cool. Beat into creamed mixture.

Sift flour with baking powder. Gradually add dry ingredients to batter, mixing until smooth.

Beat egg whites with salt until stiff peaks form. With metal spatula, carefully fold egg whites into chocolate mixture.

Pour batter into ungreased 10-inch tube pan. Bake for 50 minutes. Invert pan to cool cake completely. Remove cake from pan by running metal spatula around edge. Cake may be dusted with sifted confectioners sugar or frosted. Serves 16.

Millionaire Chocolate Truffle Cake

12-oz pkg (360 g) GHIRARDELLI Semi-Sweet Chocolate Chips
6 tbs (90 ml) butter
2 tbs (30 ml) sugar
2 tsp (10 ml) flour
1 tsp (5 ml) hot water
2 tsp (10 ml) vanilla
3 eggs, separated
pinch salt

Topping:
3-oz pkg (90 g) cream cheese, softened
½ pint (240 ml) whipping cream
3 tbs (45 ml) confectioners sugar
½ tsp (3 ml) vanilla

Preheat oven to 425°F (220°C). Butter an 8-inch springform pan.

In double boiler, melt chocolate chips with butter over 1 inch of simmering water. Mix in sugar, flour, hot water and vanilla. Remove from heat, let cool and stir in egg yolks, 1 at a time; cool. Beat egg whites with salt until stiff but not dry. Fold in chocolate mixture.

Spread into pan. Bake for 15 minutes. The cake will be soft in the center. Cool.

Topping: Beat cream cheese until smooth. Gradually add whipping cream, confectioners sugar and vanilla. Whip until thick enough to spread over top of cake. Chill several hours. Serves 12.

Cherry-Chocolate Shortcake

1¼ cups (295 ml) SOFTASILK Cake Flour
1 cup (240 ml) sugar
⅓ cup (80 ml) baking cocoa
½ tsp (3 ml) baking soda
½ tsp (3 ml) salt
¾ cup (180 ml) buttermilk
⅓ cup (80 ml) shortening
½ tsp (3 tsp) vanilla
1 egg
2 21-oz cans (630 g each) cherry pie filling

Preheat oven to 350°F (180°C). Grease and flour round pan, 9x1½ inches.

Beat all ingredients except pie filling in medium bowl on low speed 30 seconds, scraping bowl constantly. Beat on high speed 3 minutes, scraping bowl occasionally.

Pour into pan. Bake 35-40 minutes or until toothpick inserted in center comes out clean. Cool 10 minutes; remove from pan. Cool completely.

Split layer horizontally in half. Fill the layer and top cake with pie filling. Serve with whipped topping and chocolate chips if, desired. Serves 8.

Opposite: Millionaire Chocolate Truffle Cake

Strawberry Shortcake

4 cups (960 ml) sliced strawberries
½ cup (120 ml) sugar
3 eggs
¾ cup (180 ml) sugar
1¼ cups (295 ml) SOFTASILK Cake Flour
1½ tsp (8 ml) baking powder
½ tsp (3 ml) salt
⅓ cup (80 ml) hot water
1 tsp (5 ml) vanilla

Mix strawberries and ½ cup sugar. Let stand 1 hour.

Preheat oven to 350°F (180°C). Grease and flour round pan, 9x1½ inches.

Beat eggs in large bowl on high speed until very thick and lemon colored. Add sugar, cake flour, baking soda and salt. Gradually beat in water and vanilla.

Pour into pan. Bake 25-30 minutes or until toothpick inserted in center comes out clean. Cool 10 minutes; remove from pan. Cool completely. Split layer horizontally; fill and top with strawberries. Serve with whipped topping, if desired. Serves 8.

Chocolate Strawberry Shortcake

2 pints (960 g) strawberries, cut in half
2 tbs (30 ml) sugar
1 tsp (5 ml) vanilla

2 9-inch layers One-Bowl Chocolate Cake

Semisweet Chocolate Glaze

3½ cups (840 ml) COOL WHIP Whipped Topping, thawed chocolate dipped strawberries, optional

Mix strawberries, sugar and vanilla. Spoon ½ of the strawberries on 1 cake layer. Drizzle with ½ the Semisweet Chocolate Glaze; top with ½ the whipped topping. Repeat layers. Garnish with chocolate-dipped strawberries, if desired. Refrigerate. Serves 12.

One-Bowl Chocolate Cake

6 squares BAKER'S Semi-Sweet Chocolate
¾ cup (180 ml) margarine or butter
1½ cups (355 ml) sugar
3 eggs
2 tsp (10 ml) vanilla
2½ cups (590 ml) all-purpose flour
1 tsp (5 ml) baking soda
¼ tsp (1 ml) salt
1½ cups (355 ml) water

Preheat oven to 350°F (180°C).

Microwave chocolate and margarine or butter in large bowl on high 2 minutes or until margarine is melted. Stir until chocolate is completely melted.

Stir sugar into melted chocolate mixture until well blended. Beat in eggs, 1 at a time, with electric mixer until completely mixed. Add vanilla. Add ½ cup of the flour, the baking soda and salt; mix well. Beat in the remaining 2 cups flour alternately with the water until smooth.

Pour into 2 greased and floured 9-inch layer pans. Bake for 35 minutes or until toothpick inserted in center comes out clean. Cool in pans 10 minutes. Remove from pans to cool on wire racks. Fill and frost as desired.

Semisweet Chocolate Glaze

3 squares BAKER'S Semi-Sweet Chocolate
3 tbs (45 ml) water
1 tbs (15 ml) margarine or butter
1 cup (240 ml) confectioners sugar
½ tsp (3 ml) vanilla

Microwave chocolate, water and margarine or butter in large microwave-safe bowl on high 1-2 minutes or until chocolate is almost melted, stirring once. Stir until chocolate is completely melted. Stir in confectioners sugar and vanilla until smooth. For thinner glaze, add ½-1 tsp additional water. Yields ¾ cup.

Opposite: **Strawberry Shortcake**

Heavenly Strawberry Angel Food Cake

1¼ cups (295 ml) DOMINO Strawberry Flavored
    Confectioners Sugar
1 cup (240 ml) cake flour
1½ cups (355 ml) egg whites (12-14 egg whites)
1½ tsp (8 ml) cream of tartar
1½ tsp (8 ml) vanilla extract
¼ tsp (1 ml) salt
¼ tsp (1 ml) almond extract
1 cup (240 ml) DOMINO Pure Granulated Sugar

Preheat oven to 375°F (190°C). In small bowl, stir strawberry-flavored confectioners sugar and flour; set aside.

In large bowl, add egg whites, cream of tartar, vanilla, salt and almond extract and, with mixer at high speed, beat until well mixed. Beating at high speed, sprinkle in granulated sugar, 2 tbs at a time; beat just until sugar dissolves and whites form stiff peaks. Do not scrape bowl during beating.

With rubber spatula, fold in flour mixture, about ¼ cup at a time, just until flour disappears.

Pour mixture into ungreased 10-inch tube pan and with spatula, cut through batter to break any large air bubbles. Bake 35 minutes or until top of cake springs back when lightly touched with finger. Any cracks on surface should look dry.

Invert cake in pan on funnel, cool completely. With spatula, loosen cake from pan and remove to plate. Frost with Strawberry Whipped Cream. Serves 16.

Strawberry Whipped Cream

1 cup (240 ml) heavy cream, well chilled
⅓ cup (80 ml) DOMINO Strawberry Flavored Confectioners Sugar
red food coloring, optional

In small bowl, with mixer at medium speed, beat cream and strawberry-flavored confectioners sugar. If desired, add red food coloring, a drop at a time. Continue beating until stiff peaks form. Yields 2 cups.

Heavenly Strawberry
Angel Food Cake

Happy Day Cake
(Quick Method Yellow Cake)

2½ cups (590 ml) sifted SWAN'S DOWN Cake Flour
1 tbs (15 ml) baking powder
1 tsp (5 ml) salt
1½ cups (355 ml) sugar
½ cup (120 ml) butter, softened
1 cup (240 ml) milk
1 tsp (5 ml) vanilla
2 eggs

Preheat oven to 375°F (190°C).

Sift together flour, baking powder, salt and sugar. Combine butter, dry ingredients, ¾ cup of the milk and the vanilla in large bowl. Mix on low speed until moistened. Beat on low speed 2 minutes. Add eggs and remaining milk. Beat 1 minute longer.

Spread batter into 2 prepared 9-inch layer pans. Bake until tester inserted in center comes out clean, 20-25 minutes. Cool cakes in pan 10 minutes. Invert onto cooling racks. Frost with Chocolate Butter Frosting. Serves 8.

Chocolate Butter Frosting

½ cup (120 ml) butter, softened
4 cups (960 ml) confectioners sugar
1 tsp (5 ml) vanilla
3 oz (90 g) unsweetened chocolate, melted
1-2 tbs (15-30 ml) milk

Cream butter and 2 cups confectioners sugar in small bowl. Beat in vanilla and melted chocolate. Add remaining confectioners sugar gradually, beating well after each addition. Thin with milk to reach desired consistency.

Grandma's Yellow Cake
(Conventional)

½ cup (120 ml) shortening
1 cup (240 ml) sugar
1 tsp (5 ml) vanilla
2 eggs
2 cups (480 ml) sifted WASHINGTON Self-Rising Flour
¾ cup (180 ml) milk

Preheat oven to 350°F (180°C). Grease bottoms only of two 8-inch layer pans.

Cream together shortening, sugar and vanilla in large mixing bowl until fluffy. Beat in eggs one at a time. Mix flour into creamed mixture alternately with milk, beginning and ending with flour. Blend well.

Pour into pans. Bake 25-35 minutes. Cool in pans 10 minutes; remove from pans. Frost. Serves 8-10.

Grandma's Yellow Cake

Three-Layer Cake

⅔ cup (160 ml) shortening
1¼ cups (295 ml) sugar
3 eggs
1 egg yolk
3 cups (720 ml) sifted PRESTO
1 cup (240 ml) milk
1 tsp (5 ml) vanilla
½ tsp (3 ml) almond flavoring

Preheat oven to 350°F (180°C).

Cream shortening, add sugar gradually. Add eggs and egg yolk, one at a time, beating well after each addition. Add sifted flour alternately with milk to which flavorings have been added.

Put in 3 greased layer cake pans, 8 inches in diameter, and bake 25-30 minutes. Frost as desired. Serves 8-10.

Buttermilk Golden Layer Cake

Buttermilk Golden Layer Cake

2¼ cup (540 ml) sifted cake flour or 2 cups (480 ml)
*   sifted all-purpose flour*
1½ cups (355 ml) sugar
1 tsp (5 ml) baking powder
½ tsp (3 ml) baking soda
¼ cup (60 ml) SACO Buttermilk Blend
1 tsp (5 ml) salt
½ cup (120 ml) shortening
1 cup (240 ml) water
1½ tsp (8 ml) vanilla
2 eggs

Have ingredients at room temperature.

Preheat oven to 350°F (180°C). Grease and flour a 13x9x2-inch baking pan, or 2 round layer pans, 8 or 9x1½ inches.

Sift all dry ingredients together into large mixing bowl. Add remaining ingredients and blend ½ minute on low speed, scraping bowl constantly. Beat 3 minutes on high speed, scraping bowl occasionally.

Pour into pan(s). Bake oblong pan 40-45 minutes, layer pans 30-35 minutes or until wooden toothpick, inserted in center, comes out clean. Cool. Frost as desired or with Fudge Frosting. Serves 12-16.

Fudge Frosting

½ cup (120 ml) shortening
2 cups (480 ml) sugar
3 oz (90 g) unsweetened chocolate
⅔ cup (160 ml) milk
½ tsp (3 ml) salt
3 tbs (45 ml) SACO Buttermilk Blend
2 tsp (10 ml) vanilla

Mix all ingredients, except vanilla, in 2½-quart saucepan. Heat to rolling boil, stirring occasionally. Boil 1 minute without stirring. Place pan of frosting in bowl of ice and water. Beat frosting until smooth and of spreading consistency. Stir in vanilla. Makes enough to fill and frost two 9-inch layers or one 13x9-inch cake.

Opposite: Three-Layer Cake

Raisin Layer Cake

⅔ cup (160 ml) shortening
1¼ cups (295 ml) sugar
3 eggs
2¾ cups (660 ml) sifted PRESTO
1 tsp (5 ml) cinnamon
½ tsp (3 ml) nutmeg
½ tsp (3 ml) cloves
1 cup (240 ml) milk
1 tsp (5 ml) vanilla
1 cup (240 ml) raisins

Preheat oven to 350°F (180°C).

Cream shortening, add sugar gradually. Add eggs one at a time, beating well after each addition. Add flour sifted with spices alternately with milk to which vanilla has been added. Fold in raisins sprinkled with flour.

Bake in 3 greased 8-inch layer cake pans 25-35 minutes. When cold, frost. Serves 8-10.

Raisin Layer Cake

Golden Saffron Cake with Sour Cream Frosting

½ cup (120 ml) butter or margarine, softened
pinch crushed McCORMICK/SCHILLING Saffron Threads*
1 cup (240 ml) granulated sugar
2 eggs
1 tsp (5 ml) McCORMICK/SCHILLING Pure Vanilla Extract
2½ cups (590 ml) sifted cake flour
1 tbs (15 ml) baking powder
¼ tsp (1 ml) salt
1 cup (240 ml) milk

Sour Cream Frosting:
2 16-oz boxes (480 g each) confectioners sugar
2 egg whites
¼ cup (60 ml) white vegetable shortening
¼ cup (60 ml) dairy sour cream
1 tsp (5 ml) McCORMICK/SCHILLING Pure Vanilla Extract

Preheat oven to 375°F (190°C). Lightly grease and flour two 9-inch round cake pans.

Place butter and saffron in large mixing bowl and cream with electric mixer at medium speed 2 minutes. Add granulated sugar and beat until light and fluffy. Add eggs, 1 at a time, beating well after each addition. Stir in vanilla. Sift flour with baking powder and salt. Add dry ingredients to batter alternating with milk, mixing at low speed.

Divide batter evenly in prepared pans. Bake 25-30 minutes. Remove cake from oven and cool in pans on wire racks 5-10 minutes. Remove from pans and cool completely on racks.

Sour Cream Frosting: Sift all of the confectioners sugar into large bowl. Set 2 cups aside. Place egg whites in small bowl and beat until stiff peaks form when beaters are lifted. Place shortening in separate large mixing bowl and beat with electric mixer until fluffy. Add beaten egg whites, sour cream, vanilla and remaining 6 cups of confectioners sugar. Mix well. Beat in as much of the reserved 2 cups confectioners' sugar as necessary to make frosting of desired consistency.

Place 1 cake layer on serving plate bottom side up. Spread with frosting and add second layer top side up. Spread remaining frosting on top sides of cake. Serves 8.

*Crush saffron with fingers to break into ⅛-inch-long pieces.

Opposite: Golden Saffron Cake
with Sour Cream Frosting

Burned Sugar Cake

½ cup (120 ml) shortening
1½ cups (355 ml) IMPERIAL Granulated Sugar
2 eggs, beaten
1 tsp (5 ml) vanilla
2½ cups (590 ml) all-purpose flour
2½ tsp (13 ml) baking powder
½ tsp (3 ml) salt
1 cup (240 ml) water or milk
3 tbs (45 ml) Burned Sugar Syrup (below) or dark molasses

Preheat oven to 350°F (180°C).

Cream shortening and granulated sugar until light and fluffy in large bowl. Add beaten eggs and beat until thoroughly blended. Add vanilla. Combine dry ingredients and add alternately with milk or water, stirring well after each addition. Stir in Burned Sugar Syrup or dark molasses.

Pour batter into two 9-inch layer pans lined bottom with greased waxed paper or use non-stick pans. Bake about 30 minutes or until done when tested with a wooden toothpick.

Frosting: When cool, fill and frost with powdered sugar icing. Use 1 tbs burned sugar syrup and 3 tbs (45 ml) milk with 2 cups (480 ml) Imperial 10X Powdered Sugar (measure unsifted). Sprinkle frosting with chopped nuts. Serves 12.

Burned Sugar Syrup: Place 1 cup (240 ml) Imperial Granulated Sugar in large, heavy skillet and heat over medium heat, stirring constantly, until sugar melts and browns; it will begin to smoke. Remove from heat and add 1 cup (240 ml) boiling water very carefully; it will foam up. Return to heat, stirring until sugar is dissolved and makes a thick syrup. This may take 10-15 minutes. Set aside to cool.

Burned Sugar Cake

Opposite: Orange Cake

Orange Cake (Quick-n-Easy)

2½ cups (590 ml) sifted WASHINGTON Self-Rising Flour
1½ cups (355 ml) sugar
⅔ cup (160 ml) shortening
¾ cup (180 ml) orange juice
2 tsp (10 ml) grated orange peel
¼ cup (60 ml) milk
3 eggs

Preheat oven to 350°F (180°C). Grease bottoms only of two 9-inch layer pans.

Place flour and sugar in large mixing bowl. Blend on low speed. Add shortening, orange juice and grated orange peel; blend to moisten flour. Beat 2 minutes on medium speed. Blend in milk and eggs. Beat 2 minutes at medium speed.

Pour into pans. Bake 30-35 minutes. Cool 10 minutes; remove from pans. Cool, then frost. Serves 8-10.

White Layer Cake

½ cup (120 ml) shortening
1¼ cups (295 ml) sugar
4 egg whites
3 cups (720 ml) sifted PRESTO
1 cup (240 ml) milk
½ tsp (3 ml) lemon flavoring

Preheat oven to 350°F (180°C).

Cream shortening, add sugar gradually. Add egg whites, one at a time, beating well after each addition. Add sifted flour alternately with milk to which flavoring has been added.

Bake in 3 well-greased layer cake pans, 8 inches for 25-35 minutes. Frost and fill as desired. Serves 8-10.

White Layer Cake (Quick-n-Easy)

3 cups (720 ml) sifted WASHINGTON Self-Rising Flour
2 cups (480 ml) sugar
⅔ cup (160 ml) shortening
1 cup (240 ml) milk
2 tsp (10 ml) vanilla
5 egg whites
¼ cup (60 ml) water

Preheat oven to 350°F (180°C). Grease bottoms only of two 9-inch layer pans.

Place flour and sugar in large mixing bowl. Blend on low speed. Add shortening, milk and vanilla; blend to moisten flour. Beat 2 minutes on medium speed. Blend in egg whites and water. Beat 2 minutes on medium speed.

Pour into pans. Bake 30-35 minutes. Cool 10 minutes; remove from pans. Cool. Frost with Seven Minute Frosting sprinkled with flaked coconut. Serves 8-10.

White and Tan Cake

½ cup (120 ml) shortening
1 cup (240 ml) sugar
2 whole eggs
1 eg, separated
1¾ cups (420 ml) sifted PRESTO
⅔ cup (160 ml) milk
1 tsp (5 ml) vanilla
1 tbs (15 ml) molasses
¼ tsp (1 ml) cloves
¼ tsp (1 ml) nutmeg
½ tsp (3 ml) cinnamon
grated rind of a small orange
½ cup (120 ml) raisins

Preheat oven to 350°F (180°C).

Cream shortening, add sugar gradually. Add eggs and the egg white, one at a time, beating well after each addition. Add sifted flour alternately with milk to which vanilla has been added.

Pour ¾ of the batter in greased square pan, 8½x8½x8½ inches.

To the remaining batter add the egg yolk, molasses, spices, grated orange rind and raisins that have been sprinkled with flour. Mix well and spread over batter in pan.

Bake 35-40 minutes. Frost if desired. Serves 12-16.

White Marble Cake

¾ cup (180 ml) shortening
1½ cups (355 ml) sugar
4 egg whites
3 cups (720 ml) sifted PRESTO
1 cup (240 ml) milk
1 tsp (5 ml) vanilla
2 squares melted chocolate

Preheat oven to 350°F (180°C).

Cream shortening, add sugar gradually. Add egg whites, one at a time, beating well after each addition. Add sifted flour alternately with milk to which vanilla has been added. To half of the batter, add the chocolate that has been melted and cooled.

Drop batters alternately by tablespoonfuls into large, greased tube pan, 9 inches in diameter 3½ inched deep, and bake 50-60 minutes. Frost as desired. Serves 16.

Opposite: White Layer Cake

Almond Pear Cake

½ cup (120 ml) plus 2 tbs (30 ml) butter, softened, divided
2 cups (480 ml) plus 2 tbs (30 ml) sugar, divided
1¾ cups (415 ml) BLUE DIAMOND Chopped Natural Almonds,
    divided
2 cups (480 ml) flour
2 tsp (10 ml) baking soda
¼ tsp (1 ml) salt
2 eggs, beaten
½ cup (120 ml) vegetable oil
3 tsp (15 ml) vanilla extract, divided
1¾ tsp (9 ml) almond extract, divided
4 cups (60 ml) fresh pears (about 2 lbs; 910 g), peeled,
    cored and diced
12 oz (360 g) cream cheese, softened
1 cup (240 ml) confectioners sugar, sifted
2 tbs (30 ml) honey

Preheat oven to 350°F (180°C).

Melt 2 tbs butter and stir in 2 tbs sugar. Cook and stir over medium heat until sugar begins to bubble, about 30 seconds. Add 1½ cups almonds and cook and stir over medium heat until golden and well-coated with butter-sugar mixture. Cool and reserve.

Combine flour, baking soda and salt; reserve. In large bowl, beat together eggs, remaining 2 cups sugar, oil, 1 tsp vanilla and ¾ tsp almond extract. Add dry ingredients, mixing until well-blended (batter will be stiff). Stir in pears and butter-sugar coated almonds.

Spread batter into a greased and floured 9x13-inch pan. Bake 40 minutes or until toothpick inserted in center comes out clean. Cool.

Meanwhile, blend cream cheese and remaining ½ cup butter 1 minute. Add confectioners sugar. Add honey, remaining 2 tsp vanilla and remaining 1 tsp almond extract; beat until smooth. Frost top of cake. Toast and finely chop remaining ¼ cup almonds; sprinkle over frosting. Serves 15.

Almond Sherry Cake

Streusel Filling:
⅓ cup (80 ml) brown sugar, firmly packed
¼ cup (60 ml) flour
3 tbs (45 ml) firm butter
½ tsp (3 ml) cinnamon
¾ cup (180 ml) BLUE DIAMOND Sliced Natural Almonds,
    toasted

Sherry Cake:
18½-oz pkg (555 g) yellow cake mix (not pudding type)
4 large eggs
¾ cups (180 ml) cream sherry
¾ cup (180 ml) vegetable oil
3¾-oz pkg (113 g) instant vanilla pudding mix
½ tsp (3 ml) nutmeg

Sherry Glaze:
2 cups (480 ml) sifted confectioners sugar
⅓ cup (80 ml) melted butter
1 tbs (15 ml) cream sherry
1-2 tsp (5-10 ml) hot water
¾ cup (180 ml) BLUE DIAMOND Sliced Natural Almonds,
    toasted, for garnish

Preheat oven to 375°F (190°C).

Streusel Filling: Combine brown sugar, flour, butter and cinnamon until crumbly. Stir in almonds; reserve.

Sherry Cake: Combine cake mix, eggs, sherry, oil, pudding mix and nutmeg. Mix at low speed 1 minute, scraping bowl constantly. Mix at medium speed 3 minutes, scraping bowl occasionally (or beat by hand 5 minutes).

Pour ½ of the batter into a greased and floured 10-inch bundt pan. Sprinkle Streusel Filling evenly over batter in pan. Pour in remaining cake batter. Bake 45-50 minutes or until cake springs back when touched lightly in the center. Cool on wire rack 15 minutes. Unmold from pan; cool completely on rack.

Sherry Glaze: Combine confectioners sugar, melted butter and sherry. Stir in enough water to make glaze of desired consistency. Glaze top of cake and garnish with almonds. Serves 16.

Opposite: **Almond Sherry Cake**

Frontier Pecan Cake

2 cups (480 ml) butter or margarine
4½ cups (1.1 l) all-purpose flour
¼ tsp (1 ml) salt
1 tsp (5 ml) baking powder
2⅓ cups (560 ml) IMPERIAL Brown Sugar
6 eggs, separated
½ cup (120 ml) milk
1 tsp (5 ml) vanilla
3 tbs (45 ml) instant coffee, dissolved in
3 tbs (45 ml) hot water, optional
4 cups (60 ml) chopped pecans

Set out butter or margarine to soften. Combine flour, salt baking powder. Set aside.

In large mixing bowl, cream butter and brown sugar. Beat egg yolks until thick and yellow and add to creamy mixture combining well. Combine milk, vanilla and dissolved coffee. Add alternately to batter with dry ingredients. Fold in pecans. Beat egg whites until stiff, but not dry and fold in batter.

Pour into greased (bottom only) 10-inch tube pan. Bake in preheated oven at 325°F (165°C) 1½ hours or until done. Let cool in pan on rack. Remove from pan. Keeps well when tightly wrapped. Serve with Whipped Cream Imperial, if desired. Serves 16.

Whipped Cream Imperial

1 cup (240 ml) whipping cream
pinch salt
½ tsp (3 ml) vanilla
¼ cup (60 ml) IMPERIAL Brown Sugar, packed

Combine whipping cream, salt, vanilla and sieved brown sugar. Chill 1 hour. Beat until stiff.

Lady Baltimore Cake

2½ cups (590 ml) sifted SWAN'S DOWN Cake Flour
2½ tsp (13 ml) baking powder
¼ tsp (1 ml) cream of tartar
½ cup (120 ml) butter, softened
1½ cups (355 ml) sugar
½ cup (120 ml) milk
1 tsp (5 ml) vanilla
6 egg whites
whole dried apricots
pecan halves

Preheat oven to 350°F (180°C).

Sift flour, baking powder and cream of tartar. Cream butter in large bowl, gradually add sugar, beating until light and fluffy. Add dry ingredients, alternately with milk, beating well after each addition. Add vanilla. Beat egg whites until stiff. Fold into cake mixture.

Spread batter into 2 prepared 9-inch layer pans. Bake until tester inserted in center comes out clean, 25-30 minutes. Cool in pans 10 minutes. Remove from pans and cool thoroughly. Spread Lady Baltimore Filling between layers and Frosting on top and sides of cake. Garnish with dried apricots and pecan halves. Serves 8-10.

Lady Baltimore Filling* and Frosting

2 egg whites
1½ cups (355 ml) sugar
pinch salt
⅓ cup (80 ml) light corn syrup
1 tsp (5 ml) vanilla
½ cup (120 ml) chopped dried apricots
½ cup (120 ml) raisins
½ cup (120 ml) chopped pecans

Combine egg whites, sugar, salt, water and corn syrup in top of double boiler. Beat 1 minute. Place over rapidly boiling water. Beat constantly on high 7 minutes or until frosting stands in peaks. Remove from boiling water. Transfer to large bowl; add vanilla. Beat 1 minute.
    * For Filling, add fruits and nuts to ⅓ of the Frosting.

Frontier Pecan Cake

Walnut Cake

¾ cup (180 ml) shortening
1¼ cup (295 ml) sugar
2 whole eggs
1 egg yolk
2 cups (480 ml) sifted PRESTO
¾ cup (180 ml) milk
2 tbs (30 ml) sherry
1 tsp (5 ml) vanilla
1 cup (240 ml) chopped walnuts

Preheat oven to 350°F (180°C).

Cream shortening, add sugar gradually. Add eggs and egg yolk, 1 at a time, beating well after each addition. Add flour alternately with milk to which sherry and vanilla have been added. Fold in walnuts.

Put in well greased 9x3½-inch tube pan and bake about 1 hour. Frost and decorate with walnut halves. Serves 16.

Banana Walnut Cake

2¼ cups (540 ml) all-purpose flour
2 tsp (10 ml) baking powder
1 tsp (5 ml) baking soda
⅓ cup (80 ml) FLEISCHMANN'S Margarine, softened
1¼ cups (295 ml) sugar
8-oz carton (240 ml) EGG BEATERS Real Egg Product
1¼ cups (295 ml) mashed ripe bananas (about 2 large)
⅔ cup (160 ml) plain nonfat yogurt
½ cup (120 ml) PLANTERS Black Walnuts, chopped
confectioners sugar

Preheat oven to 350°F (180°C).

Mix flour, baking powder and baking soda; set aside.

With mixer, beat margarine and sugar until creamy in large bowl; blend in egg product and bananas. Add flour mixture alternately with yogurt, blending until smooth. Stir in walnuts.

Spread batter in greased and floured 13x9x2-inch baking pan. Bake 45 minutes or until toothpick inserted comes out clean. Cool in pan on wire rack. Dust with confectioners sugar; cut into squares. Serves 24.

Golden Carrot Pecan Cake

2½ cups (590 ml) all-purpose flour
2 tsp (10 ml) baking powder
2 tsp (10 ml) pumpkin pie spice
½ tsp (3 ml) baking soda
1 cup (240 ml) pecan halves
8-oz can (240 g) crushed pineapple
2 cups (480 ml) grated carrots
1 cup (240 ml) light brown sugar, firmly packed
¾ cup (180 ml) EGG BEATERS Real Egg Product
¾ cup (180 ml) nonfat plain yogurt
⅓ cup (80 ml) raisins
3 tbs (45 ml) margarine, melted
2 tsp (10 ml) vanilla extract
1½ cups (355 ml) confectioners sugar
pecan halves, for decoration

Preheat oven to 350°F (180°C).

In medium bowl, combine flour, baking powder, pumpkin pie spice and baking soda; chop pecan halves.

Drain pineapple; reserve juice. In large bowl, with spoon, mix pineapple, chopped pecans, carrots, brown sugar, egg product, yogurt, raisins, margarine and vanilla until well blended. Stir in dry ingredients until well combined.

Spread batter in 2 greased and floured 9-inch round cake pans. Bake for 25-30 minutes or until toothpick inserted in center comes out clean. Cool in pan on wire racks for 10 minutes. Remove from pan and cool completely on wire racks.

In small bowl, blend confectioners sugar and 2-3 tbs reserved pineapple juice to make frosting spreading consistency. Place 1 cake layer on serving plate. Spread frosting on top layer; top with remaining cake layer. Dust with additional confectioners sugar and garnish with reserved pecan halves. Serves 12.

Opposite: Banana Walnut Cake

Pumpkin Walnut Cake

2 cups (480 ml) all-purpose flour
2 tsp (10 ml) DAVIS Baking Powder
1 tsp (5 ml) baking soda
½ tsp (3 ml) salt
1 tsp (5 ml) ground cinnamon
¼ tsp (1 ml) ground cloves
¼ tsp (1 ml) ground allspice
¼ tsp (1 ml) ground ginger
½ cup (120 ml) EGG BEATERS Real Egg Product
16-oz can (480 g) pumpkin
1 cup (240 ml) sweetened applesauce
1½ cups (355 ml) sugar
1 cup (240 ml) 100% bran cereal
1 cup (240 ml) seedless raisins
1 cup (240 ml) PLANTERS Walnuts, chopped

Preheat oven to 350°F (180°C).

In medium bowl, mix flour, baking powder, baking soda, salt, cinnamon, cloves, allspice and ginger; set aside.

In large bowl, blend egg product, pumpkin, applesauce, sugar and bran cereal. Gradually blend in flour mixture. Fold in raisins and walnuts.

Spoon batter in greased 12-cup fluted tube pan. Bake 50-55 minutes or until toothpick inserted comes out clean. Cool 10 minutes on wire rack. Remove from pan; cool completely on wire rack. Serves 16.

Pumpkin Walnut Cake

Apple Nut Cake

2 cups (480 ml) sifted PRESTO
1½ cups (355 ml) sugar
½ cup (120 ml) margarine
4 eggs
½ cup (120 ml) evaporated milk
1 tsp (5 ml) vanilla
½ cup (120 ml) raisins
½ cup (120 ml) chopped walnuts
6-8 apples, cored, pared and sliced
2 tbs (30 ml) sugar
1 tbs (15 ml) lemon juice
½ tsp (3 ml) cinnamon

Preheat oven to 350°F (180°C). Grease and flour 13x9x2-inch pan.

Beat together flour, sugar, margarine, eggs, evaporated milk and vanilla in large mixing bowl on medium speed of electric mixer, until batter is light and creamy.

Turn into prepared pan, sprinkle with raisins and nuts. Toss together apples, sugar, lemon juice and cinnamon. Arrange over batter.

Bake oven 50-55 minutes or until cake tester inserted in center comes out clean. Serves 12-16.

Apple Ginger Cake

2 eggs
1½ cups (355 ml) granulated sugar
½ cup (120 ml) vegetable oil
2 tsp (10 ml) vanilla
1 can SOLO Apple Filling or 1 jar BAKER Apple Filling
2 cups (480 ml) all-purpose flour
2 tsp (5 ml) baking powder
2 tsp (10 ml) ground ginger
1 tsp (5 ml) cinnamon
1 tsp (5 ml) salt
1 tsp (5 ml) nutmeg
½ cup (120 ml) chopped walnuts or pecans

Preheat oven to 350°F (180°C). Grease 10-inch tube pan or fluted cake pan and set aside.

Beat eggs, granulated sugar, oil and vanilla in large bowl with electric mixer until blended. Stir in apple filling. Sift flour, baking soda, ginger, cinnamon, salt and nutmeg. Add to apple mixture and stir until blended. Fold in nuts and spread batter evenly in prepared pan.

Bake 60-65 minutes or until cake tester inserted in center comes out clean. Cool in pan on wire rack 15 minutes. Remove from pan and cool completely on wire rack. Spread Cream Cheese Frosting over top and around side of cake. Refrigerate 1 hour before serving. Serves 10-12.

Cream Cheese Frosting

2 3-oz pkgs (90 g each) cream cheese, softened
1 tsp (5 ml) vanilla
4 cups (60 ml) sifted confectioners sugar
2-3 tbs (30-45 ml) milk or half and half
1-2 tsp (5-10 ml) cinnamon, optional

Beat cream cheese in medium-size bowl with electric mixer until creamy. Add vanilla, confectioners sugar, and 2 tbs milk or half and half. Beat until frosting is fluffy and of good spreading consistency, adding more only if necessary. Beat in cinnamon, if desired. Spread frosting on cake and refrigerate 1 hour before serving.

Apple Cake

4 cups (960 ml) chopped apples
2 cups (480 ml) DOMINO Granulated Sugar
1 cup (240 ml) raisins
¼ cup (60 ml) apple juice
½ cup (120 ml) vegetable oil
2 eggs
2 tsp (10 ml) vanilla extract
2 cups (480 ml) all-purpose flour
1½ tsp (8 ml) baking soda
1 tsp (5 ml) salt
1 tsp (5 ml) ground cinnamon
1 tsp (5 ml) ground nutmeg·
1 tsp (5 ml) ground cloves
1 cup (40 ml) nuts

Preheat oven to 350°F (180°C). Grease and flour 13x9-inch baking pan.

In large bowl, combine apples and sugar. Set aside 1 hour. In small bowl, combine raisins and apple juice; set aside.

In 1-cup glass measure, measure oil; add eggs and vanilla and beat with fork until combined. Stir into apple mixture. Sift flour, baking soda, salt, cinnamon, nutmeg and cloves into apple mixture; add juice-raisin mixture and gently stir together. Fold in nuts.

Pour into prepared pan, spreading evenly. Bake 40-45 minutes or until pick inserted in center of cake comes out clean. Remove pan to wire rack to cool. Cut into squares to serve. Serves 12.

Apple Almond Cake

3 large apples, peeled and sliced
4 tbs (30 ml) almond liqueur
1½ cups (355 ml) BLUE DIAMOND Diced or Slivered Almonds, toasted
2 cups (480 ml) all-purpose flour
1 ½ cups (360 ml) granulated sugar
4 tsp (20 ml) baking powder
1 tbs (15 ml) grated lemon peel
1 tsp (5 ml) salt
1 cup (240 ml) butter or margarine, melted
1 cup (240 ml) milk
2 extra large eggs
2 tbs (30 ml) almond liqueur
whipped cream

Preheat oven to 350°F (180°C). Grease and flour two 9-inch spring form pans

In bowl, toss apple slices with 2 tbs almond liqueur; set aside.

In food processor, grind 1 cup of the almonds and the 1 cup of sugar until fine. Set remaining almonds aside. In mixing bowl, stir together ground almond and sugar mixture, flour, baking powder, lemon peel and salt. Stir in melted butter or margarine, milk, eggs and remaining almond liqueur.

Pour batter evenly into pans.

Drain apple slices; arrange in concentric rows on top of batter in pans. Sprinkle with remaining sugar and reserved almonds.

Bake for 35-45 minutes or until golden brown on top and cake springs back lightly when touched. Cool; remove pan sides. Cut each cake into 6-8 wedges. For each portion, serve a cool or warmed wedge topped with whipped cream. Serves 12-16.

Apple Almond Cake

Apple Butter Bundt Cake

¾ cup (180 ml) whole wheat flour
1½ cups (355 ml) unbleached flour
2 tsp (10 ml) baking soda
2 cups (480 ml) MUSSELMAN'S Apple Butter
2 egg whites
½ cup (120 ml) dark raisins
1½ tbs (25 ml) confectioners sugar

Preheat oven to 350°F (180°C).

Coat a 12-cup bundt pan with nonstick cooking spray.

Combine the flours and baking soda and stir to mix well. Add the apple butter and egg whites and stir again. Stir in the raisins.

Spread batter evenly in the pan and bake for 30-35 minutes or just until a wooden toothpick inserted in the center of the cake comes out clean. Cool the cake in the pan for 20 minutes. Then invert onto a wire rack and cool to room temperature.

Transfer to a serving plate, sift the confectioners sugar over the top, slice and serve. Serves 16.

Applesauce Cake

½ cup (120 ml) butter or margarine, softened
1½ cups (355 ml) sugar
2 eggs, beaten
1 tsp (5 ml) baking powder
½ tsp (3 ml) baking soda
1 tsp (5 ml) McCORMICK/SCHILLING Ground Cinnamon
½ tsp (3 ml) McCORMICK/SCHILLING Ground Nutmeg
½ tsp (3 ml) McCORMICK/SCHILLING Ground Cloves
¼ tsp (1 ml) salt
2 cups (480 ml) sifted all-purpose flour
1 cup (240 ml) applesauce
1 cup (240 ml) chopped, golden seedless raisins
1 tbs (15 ml) all-purpose flour
1 cup (240 ml) chopped pecans

Preheat oven to 350°F (180°C). Lightly grease and flour 9x5x3-inch loaf pan.

Place butter or margarine and sugar in large mixing bowl and cream with electric mixer until light and fluffy. Add eggs and beat well. Add baking powder, baking soda, spices and salt to sifted flour and sift again. Add to butter or margarine mixture, alternating with applesauce. Coat raisins with 1 tbs flour and stir into batter with pecans.

Pour into prepared pan. Bake 1 hour. Cool cake in pan on wire rack 5-10 minutes. Remove from pan and cool completely on rack. Serves 12.

Apple Butter Bundt Cake

Apple
Upside-Down
Cake

Apple Upside-Down Cake

2 tbs (30 ml) butter or margarine
½ cup (120 ml) IMPERIAL Brown Sugar
½ cup (120 ml) chopped pecans
3 medium cooking apples, pared, sliced
2 tbs (30 ml) lemon juice
½ cup (120 ml) butter or margarine
⅔ cup (160 ml) IMPERIAL Granulated Sugar
1 egg
½ tsp (3 ml) vanilla
2 cups (480 ml) all-purpose flour
½ tsp (3 ml) baking soda
1 tsp (5 ml) baking powder
½ tsp (3 ml) cinnamon
½ tsp (3 ml) salt
¼ tsp (1 ml) nutmeg
½ cup (120 ml) buttermilk
whipped cream

Preheat oven to 375°F (190°C).

In 9x9-inch square pan, melt 2 tbs butter or margarine; spread brown sugar on bottom of pan. Sprinkle with pecans; arrange apple slices on top; cover with lemon juice and set aside.

Cream ½ cup butter or margarine and remaining sugars until fluffy and light. Beat in egg and vanilla thoroughly. Combine remaining dry ingredients; add alternately with buttermilk.

Spread batter over apple slices in pan. Bake 45 minutes or until done. Place on cooling rack 10 minutes, then turn upside down on plate. Serve warm. Cut into squares and top with whipped cream. Serves 9.

Quick-n-Easy Pineapple Upside-Down Cake

1/4 cup (60 ml) butter
3/4 cup (180 ml) brown sugar
2 tbs (30 ml) pineapple juice from can
4 pineapple slices
4 maraschino cherries
1 1/2 cups (355 ml) sifted *WASHINGTON Self-Rising Flour*
3/4 cup (180 ml) sugar
3 tbs (45 ml) shortening
1/2 cup (120 ml) milk
1 egg
1 tsp (5 ml) vanilla

Preheat oven to 375°F (190°C). Grease 8-inch square pan.

Melt together butter, brown sugar and pineapple juice in baking pan. Arrange pineapple over mixture. Place cherry in center of each slice. Set aside.

Place flour and sugar in bowl. Stir to blend. Add shortening and milk ; blend to moisten. Beat 2 minutes at medium speed. Add egg and vanilla. Beat 2 more minutes at medium speed.

Pour over fruit in pan. Bake 30-35 minutes. Cool in pan 5 minutes. Invert on serving plate; let stand 1 minute; remove pan. Serve warm with whipped cream. Serves 9.

Apricot Upside-Down Cake: Substitute canned apricot halves and juice for the pineapple.

Apple Upside-Down Cake: Add 1/2 tsp (3 ml) cinnamon or nutmeg to brown sugar mixture. Substitute slices from 2 large apples for pineapple slices.

Quick-n-Easy Pineapple Upside-Down Cake

Cheesecake Elegante

Crust:
1½ cups (355 ml) graham cracker crumbs
¼ cup (60 ml) sugar
¼ cup (60 ml) butter or margarine, softened
½ tsp (3 ml) McCORMICK/SCHILLING Ground Cinnamon

Filling:
4 8-oz pkgs (240 g each) cream cheese, room temperature
4 eggs, beaten
1⅓ cups (320 ml) sugar
1 tbs (15 ml) McCORMICK/SCHILLING Pure Vanilla Extract

Topping:
2 cups (480 ml) dairy sour cream
⅓ cup (80 ml) sugar
1 tbs (15 ml) McCORMICK/SCHILLING Pure Vanilla Extract
¼ tsp (1 ml) McCORMICK/SCHILLING Rum Extract

Preheat oven to 325°F (165°C).

To make Crust, place all crust ingredients in medium-size bowl and mix thoroughly. Spoon into 9-inch springform pan and spread evenly on bottom of pan. Press firmly onto bottom and 1 inch up sides of pan with bottom of small, straight-sided glass.

To make Filling, place cream cheese in mixing bowl and beat with electric mixer until soft and creamy. Add beaten eggs, sugar and vanilla and beat until very smooth. Pour into crust. Bake 1 hour 15 minutes. Remove from oven and increase temperature to 450°F (230°C).

To make Topping, place all topping ingredients in bowl and stir to mix well. Spoon over hot cheesecake and smooth top. Return cake to oven and bake 7 minutes. Remove from oven and cool to room temperature in pan on wire rack. Cover and refrigerate 4 hours or overnight. Run knife around inside edge of springform pan and release sides of pan. Place on serving plate. Serves 12.

Preceding page:
Philly Free 3-Step Cheesecake

Philly Free 3-Step Cheesecake

3 8-oz pkgs (240 g each) PHILADELPHIA BRAND FREE Fat Free Cream Cheese, softened
¾ cup (180 ml) sugar
1 tsp (5 ml) vanilla
3 eggs
⅓ cup (80 ml) graham cracker crumbs

Preheat oven to 325°F (165°C). Spray 9-inch pie plate with nonstick cooking spray.

Mix cream cheese, sugar and vanilla with electric mixer on medium speed until well blended. Add eggs; mix just until blended. Do not overbeat after adding eggs.

Sprinkle bottom of pie plate with crumbs. Pour cream cheese mixture into prepared pie plate.

Bake for 45 minutes or until center is almost set. Cool. Refrigerate 3 hours or overnight. Garnish with strawberry slices, blueberries and mint leaves to form flowers. Serves 10.

Blueberry Variation: Stir ½ cup (120 ml) blueberries into batter. Sprinkle with additional ½ cup (120 ml) blueberries before baking.

Almond Variation: Substitute ¾ tsp (4 ml) almond extract for vanilla.

Cherry Berry Cheesecake

½ cup (120 ml) chocolate wafer crumbs
1 cup (240 ml) part skim or low-fat ricotta cheese
2 8-oz pkgs (240 g each) nonfat cream cheese, softened
1 cup (240 ml) sugar
½ cup (120 ml) low-fat egg substitute
2 tsp (10 ml) almond extract
2 egg whites
pinch cream of tartar
1 cup (240 ml) fresh or frozen sweet cherries, pitted
1 cup (240 ml) fresh or frozen blueberries
2 tsp 910 ml) lemon juice
½ tsp (3 ml) grated lemon peel

Preheat oven to 325°F (165°C).

Spray bottom of 9-inch springform pan with cooking spray; sprinkle chocolate wafer crumbs evenly over bottom of pan; set aside.

Reserve 1 tbs sugar. Beat ricotta cheese, cream cheese, remaining sugar, egg substitute and almond extract in mixing bowl until blended. In small mixing bowl, beat egg whites and cream of tartar until stiff peaks form. Fold egg white mixture into cheese mixture.

Spoon mixture into prepared pan. Bake about 70-90 minutes or until browned and firm. If top is completely browned before end of cook time, cover with foil.

Toss cherries and blueberries with reserved tablespoon sugar, lemon juice and lemon peel; spoon on top of cheesecake. Increase heat to 375°F (190°C); bake cheesecake 5 minutes or until fruit appears to be glazed. Cool on wire rack. Cover with foil and refrigerate until chilled. Serves 16.

Courtesy of North American Blueberry Council.

Peach Blueberry Cheesecake

Crust:
2 cups (480 ml) crushed gingersnap cookies
¼ cup (60 ml) margarine or butter, melted

Filling:
3 8-oz pkgs (240 g each) cream cheese, softened
½ cup (120 ml) brown sugar, firmly packed
½ cup (120 ml) GRANDMA'S Molasses Unsulphured
3 eggs
1 cup (240 ml) plain yogurt
1 tbs (15 ml) lemon juice

Topping:
2 tbs (30 ml) peach or apricot preserves, melted
16-oz can (480 g) peach slices, drained
fresh blueberries

Preheat oven to 350°F (180°C). Lightly grease 9-inch springform pan.

Crust: In small bowl, combine Crust ingredients; press bottom and up sides of prepared pan. Refrigerate.

Filling: In large bowl, beat cream cheese until fluffy. Gradually beat in brown sugar and molasses until smooth. Add eggs, one at a time, beating well after each addition. Add yogurt and lemon juice; blend well.

Pour into prepared crust. Place shallow pan ½ full of water on lower oven rack. Place cheesecake on middle oven rack. Bake at 350°F (180°C) for 1 hour or until set.

Turn oven off; let cake stand in oven with door open at least 8 inches for 30 minutes. Remove from oven; cool to room temperature on wire rack. Remove sides of pan. Refrigerate overnight. Just before serving, brush top with melted preserves. Top with peach slices and blueberries. Store in refrigerator. Serves 16.

Opposite: Peach Blueberry Cheesecake

Pear Cheesecake

Cookie Crumb Pastry:
1H cups (355 ml) vanilla wafers
3 tbs (45 ml) melted butter or margarine
2 tbs (30 ml) finely chopped almonds
2 tbs (30 ml sugar

3 8-oz pkgs (240 g each) low calorie cream cheese, softened
1¼ cups (295 ml) sugar, divided
4 eggs, room temperature
2½ tsp (13 ml) vanilla, divided
1½ tsp (8 ml) grated lemon peel
¾ cup (180 ml) low-fat dairy sour cream
2 USA pears, pared, cored, sliced and poached*

Preheat oven to 350°F (180°C).

Cookie Crumb Pastry: Crush vanilla wafers equal to 1½ cups (355 ml). Combine with 3 tbs (45 ml) melted butter or margarine and 2 tbs (30 ml) each finely chopped almonds and sugar; mix well. Press into bottom of 9-inch springform pan. Yields one 9-inch pastry for cheesecake.

Beat cream cheese and 1 cup sugar until light and fluffy. Add eggs, one at a time; mix well after each. Add 1½ tsp vanilla and lemon peel.

Pour cream cheese mixture into Cookie Crumb Pastry. Bake 40-50 minutes; cool on rack 20 minutes.

Combine sour cream, ¼ cup sugar and 1 tsp vanilla. Spread over top of cheesecake. Bake 15 minutes longer. Cool 2 hours on rack. Refrigerate at least 8 hours. Remove from springform pan. Arrange poached pear slices on top in spoke-fashion. Serves 16.

*Poach pears in 4 cups (960 ml) water, ½ cup (120 ml) lemon juice and ½ cup (120 ml) sugar until slices are fork-tender.

Courtesy of Oregon Washington California Pear Bureau.

Baileys Cheesecake

1½ cups (355 ml) coarse graham cracker crumbs
½ stick butter, melted
15 oz (450 g) ricotta cheese
8-oz pkg (240 g) cream cheese
4 eggs, lightly beaten
½ cup (120 ml) sugar
⅓ cup (80 ml) BAILEYS Original Irish Cream
1 tsp (5 ml) vanilla
¼ tsp (1 ml) salt

Preheat oven to 325°F (165°C).

Combine crumbs and butter; press over bottom and sides of greased 9-inch springform pan. Chill.

Beat together ricotta and cream cheese until smooth. Add remaining ingredients; beat until smooth.

Pour mixture into pan. Bake 1 hour and 15 minutes or until firm in middle. Cool 20-30 minutes in pan before removing. Cool completely before serving. Serves 10-12.

•

Opposite: **Pear Cheesecake**

Banana Dream Cheesecake

⅔ cup (160 ml) graham cracker crumbs
1 tbs (15 ml) sugar
1 tbs (15 ml) butter, melted
3 8-oz pkgs (720 g) cream cheese, softened
¾ cup (180 ml) sugar
4 eggs
1 cup (240 ml) puréed CHIQUITA Bananas (about 2 large)
2 tsp (10 ml) lemon juice
1 tsp (5 ml) vanilla
1 pint (480 ml) strawberries

Preheat oven to 350°F (180°C).

Mix together graham cracker crumbs, 1 tbs each sugar and butter; press mixture into an 8 or 9-inch spring form pan.

Beat together cream cheese and sugar until smooth and creamy. Add eggs, bananas, lemon juice and vanilla. Mix well, scraping sides of bowl often.

Pour over graham cracker crust. Bake for 1 hour or until cheesecake is firm in the center.

Remove outer ring from spring form pan. Cool on wire rack for 1 hour. Refrigerate 3 hours before serving. Slice or halve strawberries and arrange in a circular pattern on top of cheesecake. Glaze with 1 tbs melted fruit jelly, if desired. Serves 16.

For a lower cholesterol version, use 12 oz (360 g) cream cheese and ¾ cup (180 ml) puréed tofu (soy bean curd).

Almond Butter Cheesecake

4 3 oz pkgs (360 g) cream cheese, softened
1 cup (240 ml) sugar
½ cup (120 ml) almond butter
3 eggs
¾ cup (180 ml) sour cream
1½ tbs (25 ml) honey

Preheat oven to 400°F (205°C). Butter and flour an 8-inch springform pan
Blend together first 3 ingredients. Add eggs, one at a time, beating well after each addition.

Pour into pan. Bake for 5 minutes. Reduce heat to 325°F (165°C) and bake 30 minutes longer.

While cheesecake is baking, combine sour cream and honey until smooth. Remove cheesecake from oven and spread sour cream mixture evenly over cheesecake.

Return to oven for about 10 minutes, until sour cream is set. Cool to room temperature and chill. Serves 8-10.

Opposite: Banana Dream Cheesecake

Nestlé Brands Pumpkin Cheesecake with Topping

Crust:

1½ cups (355 ml) graham cracker crumbs
¼ cup (60 ml) granulated sugar
⅓ cup (80 ml) butter or margarine, melted

Cheesecake:

3 8-oz pkgs (240g each) cream cheese, softened
1 cup (240 ml) granulated sugar
¼ cup (60 ml) light brown sugar, packed
15-oz can (450 g) LIBBY'S Solid Pack Pumpkin
2 eggs
5-fl-oz can (150 ml) CARNATION Evaporated Milk
2 tbs (30 ml) cornstarch
1¼ tsp (6 ml) ground cinnamon
½ tsp (3 ml) ground nutmeg

Topping:

16-oz carton (480 g) sour cream, at room temperature
¼-⅓ cup (60-80 ml) granulated sugar
1 tsp (5 ml) vanilla extract

Preheat oven to 350°F (180°C).

Crust: Combine graham cracker crumbs, sugar and butter in medium bowl. Press onto bottom and 1 inch up side of 9-inch springform pan. Bake for 6-8 minutes. Do not allow to brown. Remove from oven; cool.

Cheesecake: Beat cream cheese, granulated sugar and brown sugar in large mixing bowl until fluffy. Beat in pumpkin, eggs and evaporated milk. Add cornstarch, cinnamon and nutmeg; beat well.

Pour into crust. Bake at 350°F (180°C) 55-60 minutes or until edge is set.

Topping: Combine sour cream, sugar and vanilla in small bowl. Spread over surface of warm cheesecake. Bake at 350°F (180°C) for 5 minutes. Cool on wire rack. Remove from sides of pan; chill for several hours or overnight. Serves 16.

Nestlé Brands Pumpkin Cheesecake with Topping

Easy Raspberry Swirl Cheesecake

Easy Raspberry Swirl Cheesecake

Crust:
1 cup (240 ml) graham cracker crumbs or chocolate wafer crumbs
3 tbs (45 ml) sugar
¼ cup (60 ml) butter, melted and cooled

Filling:
3 8-oz pkgs (240 g each) cream cheese, softened
½ cup (120 ml) sugar
3 tbs (45 ml) all-purpose flour
3 eggs
1 tsp (5 ml) vanilla
1 can SOLO Raspberry, Blueberry, Apricot, or Pineapple Filling or
1 jar BAKER Raspberry, Blueberry, Apricot, or Pineapple Filling
confectioners sugar, optional

Preheat oven to 350°F (180°C). Grease bottom of 9-inch springform pan.

Crust: Combine crumbs and sugar in small bowl. Add melted butter and stir until blended. Press crumbs onto bottom of prepared pan. Bake 10 minutes. Cool completely on wire rack.

Filling: Beat cream cheese and sugar in medium-size bowl with electric mixer until light and fluffy. Beat in flour. Add eggs and vanilla and beat until thoroughly blended.

Carefully grease inside edge of pan above crust. Spoon half of batter over cooled crust. Spoon raspberry filling over batter and top with remaining batter. Cut through batter and filling with flat-bladed knife to create swirled effect.

Bake 60-65 minutes or until center is set and top is golden. Cool completely in pan on wire rack. Refrigerate until ready to serve.

To serve, run tip of sharp knife around inside edge of pan and release side of pan. Place cheesecake on serving plate. Dust top with confectioners sugar, if desired. Serves 12-14.

Three-Step Fat-Free Pumpkin Cheesecake

3 8-oz pkgs (240 g each) PHILADELPHIA BRAND Fat Free
    Cream Cheese, softened
¾ cup (180 ml) canned pumpkin
¾ cup (180 ml) sugar
1 tsp (5 ml) vanilla
¾ tsp (4 ml) ground cinnamon
pinch ground cloves
pinch nutmeg
3 eggs
⅓ cup (80 ml) graham cracker crumbs

Preheat oven to 325°F (165°C).

Mix cream cheese, pumpkin, sugar, vanilla and spices with electric mixer on medium speed until well blended. Add eggs; mix just until blended. Do not overbeat after adding eggs.

Spray 9-inch pie plate with nonstick cooking spray; sprinkle bottom with crumbs. Pour cream cheese mixture into prepared pie plate.

Bake 45 minutes or until center is almost set. Cool. Refrigerate 3 hours or overnight. Garnish with Cool Whip Lite Whipped Topping. Serves 10.

Heath Bits Cheesecake

Crust:
1¾ cups (415 ml) vanilla wafer crumbs
2 tbs (30 ml) sugar
⅓ cup (80 ml) butter or margarine, melted

Filling:
3 8-oz pkgs (240 g each) cream cheese, softened
1 cup (240 ml) sugar
3 eggs
1 cup (240 ml) sour cream
½ tsp (3 ml) vanilla
6-oz pkg (180 g) HEATH BITS

Preheat oven to 350°F (180°C).

Crust: Combine crumbs, sugar and butter or margarine; press mixture into bottom and up sides 1 inch of a 9-inch springform pan. Refrigerate.

Filling: In a large mixing bowl, beat the cream cheese with the sugar until fluffy. Add eggs, one at a time, beating well after each addition. Blend in the sour cream and vanilla until smooth.

Pour ½ of the cream cheese mixture into the crust; sprinkle with 1 cup Heath Bits. Top with remaining cream cheese mixture. Bake 1 hour or until the filling is just firm when the pan is tapped. Remove from the oven and let cool 10-15 minutes. Sprinkle remaining Heath Bits over top. Cool on wire rack. Refrigerate until ready to serve. Serves 12.

Opposite:
Three-Step Fat-Free
Pumpkin Cheesecake

Easy Chocolate Cheesecake

Crust:
1¾ cups (415 ml) chocolate cookie or graham cracker crumbs
2 tbs (30 ml) sugar
⅓ cup (80 ml) margarine or butter, melted

Filling:
2 4-oz pkgs (120 g each) BAKER'S German Sweet Chocolate
2 eggs
⅔ cup (160 ml) corn syrup
⅓ cup (80 ml) heavy cream
1½ tsp (8 ml) vanilla
2 8-oz pkgs (240 g) PHILADELPHIA BRAND Cream Cheese,
*   cubed and softened*

Preheat oven to 325°F (165°C).

Crust: Combine cookie crumbs, sugar and margarine or butter in 9-inch pie plate or spring form pan until well mixed. Press into pie plate or onto bottom and 1¼ inches up sides of pan. Filling: Microwave 1½ pkgs of the chocolate in microwave-safe bowl on high 1½-2 minutes or until almost melted, stirring after 1 minute. Stir until completely melted.

Blend eggs, corn syrup, cream and vanilla in electric blender until smooth. With blender running, gradually add cream cheese, blending until smooth. Blend in melted chocolate. Pour into crust.

Bake 50-55 minutes or until firm. Cool on wire rack. Cover; refrigerate. Just before serving, melt the remaining half pkg chocolate and drizzle over top. Serves 8.

Easy Chocolate Cheesecake

Three-Layer Chocolate Cheesecake

Crust:
1 cup (240 ml) chocolate cookie or graham cracker crumbs
3 tbs (45 ml) butter or margarine, melted

Filling:
1 envelope unflavored gelatin
¼ cup (60 ml) cold water
2 8-oz pkgs (240 g each) cream cheese, softened
1 cup (240 ml) DOMINO Chocolate Flavored Confectioners Sugar
1 tsp (5 ml) vanilla extract
8-oz container (240 g) frozen whipped topping, thawed
½ cup (120 ml) DOMINO Confectioners 10-X Sugar
¼ cup (60 ml) cold strong coffee
chocolate-covered coffee beans, chocolate shavings, or semisweet
*   chocolate chips, optional*

Crust: In medium bowl, mix crumbs and butter or margarine until well blended. Press mixture evenly onto bottom of 8- or 9-inch springform pan. Place pan in freezer while preparing Filling.

Filling: In small saucepan, mix gelatin with cold water; let stand 1 minute to soften. Cook over medium heat until gelatin completely dissolves, stirring frequently. Remove from heat.

In large bowl, with mixer at low speed, beat 1 pkg cream cheese, chocolate confectioners sugar, vanilla and 2 tbs gelatin mixture until well blended. Add 1¼ cups whipped topping; continue mixing until well blended. Spoon mixture over crust in pan; return to freezer while preparing second layer.

In same bowl, beat remaining cream cheese until fluffy; gradually add confectioners sugar, cold coffee and remaining gelatin mixture until well-blended. Add 1¼ cups whipped topping; continue mixing until blended. Remove pan from freezer; spoon mixture carefully over chocolate layer, spreading evenly. Cover and refrigerate at least 3 hours or until firm.

To serve, spread remaining whipped topping over cake. Carefully remove cheesecake from pan. Sprinkle with chocolate-covered coffee beans, chocolate chips or chocolate shavings, if desired. Serves 10.

Marbled White Chocolate Cheesecake

1½ cups (355 ml) crushed chocolate wafer cookies
3 tbs (45 ml) margarine or butter, melted
3 8-oz pkgs (240 g each) PHILADELPHIA BRAND
    Cream Cheese, softened
½ cup (120 ml) sugar
½ tsp (3 ml) vanilla
3 eggs
2 squares BAKER'S Semi-Sweet Chocolate, melted
1 pkg (6 squares) BAKER'S Premium White Chocolate, melted

Preheat oven to 350°F (180°C).

Mix crushed cookies and margarine or butter in medium bowl. Press into bottom of 9-inch springform pan. Bake 10 minutes.

Beat cream cheese, sugar and vanilla in large bowl with electric mixer on medium speed until well blended. Add eggs, one at a time, beating well after each addition. Mix 1 cup of the cream cheese mixture and melted semisweet chocolate in small bowl until well blended. Mix remaining cream cheese mixture and melted white chocolate until well blended.

Spoon semisweet and white chocolate mixtures alternately into prepared pan. Swirl with knife to marble-ize. Bake 40 minutes or until center is almost set. Cool on wire rack.

Refrigerate 4 hours or overnight until firm. Run a small knife or spatula around sides of pan to loosen crust; remove sides of pan. Store leftover cheesecake in refrigerator. Serves 12.

Note: Cheesecake can also be baked in 13x9-inch baking pan. Bake 30 minutes or until center is almost set.

Blueberry Cream Cheese Tartlets

8 17x12-inch sheets filo dough, divided
3 tbs (45 ml) butter or margarine, melted
2 3-oz pkgs (90 g each) cream cheese, softened
¼ cup (60 ml) sugar
1 egg
2 tbs (30 ml) almond-flavored liqueur, divided
2 cups (480 ml) fresh or frozen North American blueberries
¼-½ cup (60-120 ml) sugar
2 tbs (30 ml) orange juice
2 tsp (10 ml) cornstarch

Stack 4 sheets of filo dough and cut into five 4-inch circles. Repeat with remaining 4 sheets. For each tart shell, layer 4 circles of fillo, brushing the second and fourth layers with melted butter or margarine. Carefully press stack of circles into buttered 3-inch tart pan. Repeat for remaining tart shells. Cover with wet towel and set aside.

Combine cream cheese, sugar, egg and 1 tbs liqueur; beat until well blended.

Spoon 3 tablespoons into each filo shell. Bake at 375°F (190°C) 4-6 minutes or until filling is set and shell is golden. Cool.

Combine blueberries, sugar, orange juice, remaining liqueur and cornstarch. Cook and stir over medium-high heat until thickened. Cool. Spoon 2 tablespoons blueberry topping in each tart. Serves 10.

Courtesy of the North American Blueberry Council.

Blueberry Cream Cheese Tartlets

Miniature Cheesecakes

12 cupcake liners
12 vanilla wafers
2 8-oz pkgs (240 g each) cream cheese, softened
¾ cup (180 ml) sugar
2 eggs
1 tbs (15 ml) lemon juice
1 tsp (5 ml) vanilla extract
21-oz can (630 g) COMSTOCK, THANK YOU or
    WILDERNESS Cherry, Strawberry or Blueberry Pie Filling

Preheat oven to 375°F (190°C). Line cupcake pans with liners. Place a vanilla wafer in bottom of each.

In a small mixing bowl, beat cream cheese, sugar, eggs, lemon juice and vanilla until light and fluffy.

Fill the liners ⅔ full with cheese mixture. Bake 15-20 minutes. Remove from oven and top each with cherry, strawberry or blueberry filling. Chill. Yields 12 cheesecakes.

Almond Chocolate Torte
with Raspberry Sauce

2½ cups (590 ml) BLUE DIAMOND Blanched Whole Almonds,
     toasted, divided
9 oz (270 g) semisweet chocolate
¼ cup (60 ml) butter
6 eggs, beaten
¾ cup (180 ml) sugar
2 tbs (30 ml) flour
¼ cup (60 ml) brandy or 2 tsp (10 ml) brandy extract

Chocolate Glaze:
6 tbs (90 ml) water
3 tbs (45 ml) sugar
3 oz (90 g) semi-sweet chocolate
1 tbs (15 ml) brandy or 1 tsp (5 ml) brandy extract

Raspberry Sauce:
2 10-oz pkgs (300 g each) frozen raspberries, thawed
sugar

In food processor or blender, finely grind 1 cup almonds. Generously grease 9-inch round cake pan; sprinkle sides and bottom with 2 tbs ground almonds; reserve. Preheat oven to 350°F (180°C).

Melt chocolate and butter in top of double boiler over simmering water. In large bowl, beat eggs with sugar. Beat in chocolate mixture. Beat in flour, remaining ground almonds and brandy.

Pour into prepared pan. Bake about 25 minutes or until toothpick inserted in center comes out clean. Cool 10 minutes.

Invert torte onto wire rack; remove pan. Cool completely.

Chocolate Glaze: In small saucepan, simmer water and sugar together until sugar dissolves. Add chocolate and brandy. Simmer a few minutes until chocolate melts and glaze coats back of spoon.

Pour glaze over torte, spreading over top and sides with spatula. Transfer torte to serving plate. Allow glaze to set.

Raspberry Sauce: Purée raspberries and strain through fine sieve. Add sugar to taste.

To garnish torte, arrange remaining 1½ cups whole almonds, points toward center, in circle around outer edge. Working towards center, repeat circles, overlapping almonds slightly.

To serve, pour small amount of Raspberry Sauce on each plate and top with a slice of torte. Serves 10-12.

Coffee Torte

Meringue:
6 egg whites, room temperature
¼ tsp (1 ml) McCORMICK/SCHILLING Cream of Tartar
1½ cups (355 ml) sifted confectioners sugar
1 cup (240 ml) granulated sugar
1 tsp (5 ml) McCORMICK/SCHILLING Pure Almond Extract
pinch McCORMICK/SCHILLING Ground Allspice
pinch McCORMICK/SCHILLING Ground Mace

Filling:
6 egg yolks, beaten
½ cup (120 ml) granulated sugar
½ cup (120 ml) cold strong coffee
1 tbs (15 ml) all-purpose flour
½ cup (120 ml) butter or margarine, softened

Topping:
1 cup (240 ml) heavy cream
⅓ cup (80 ml) confectioners sugar
1 tsp (5 ml) McCORMICK/SCHILLING Pure Vanilla Extract

Preheat oven to 250°F (121°C). Chill small mixing bowl.

Place egg whites in large mixing bowl and beat with electric mixer until foamy. Add cream of tartar and beat until stiff peaks form when beaters are lifted. Add confectioners sugar and granulated sugar, 1 tablespoon at a time, beating well after each addition. Add almond extract, allspice and mace. Beat 2 minutes.

Cut four 8-inch circles out of heavy brown paper and place circles on cookie sheets. Divide meringue into 4 equal parts and spread evenly over each circle of paper with back of large spoon.

Bake 1 hour 15 minutes. Remove from oven and set aside to cool. When cool, carefully peel paper off bottoms of meringue layers.

Filling: Place egg yolks, granulated sugar, coffee and flour in top of double boiler over (not in) simmering water. Cook, stirring constantly, until mixture thickens. Set aside to cool to lukewarm. Add butter or margarine and stir until well blended.

Place 1 meringue layer on flat cake plate. Spread ¼ of Filling over layer. Top with second layer and spread with ¼ Filling. Continue until all layers are stacked, ending with Filling.

Topping: Place cream, confectioners' sugar, and vanilla in chilled bowl and beat with electric mixer until stiff. Decorate top of torte with whipped cream. Serves 10-12.

Summer Berry Brownie Torte

¾ cup (180 ml) granulated sugar

6 tbs (90 ml) butter or margarine

1 tbs (15 ml) water

9 oz (270) *NESTLÉ TOLL HOUSE Semi-Sweet*
 Chocolate Morsels, divided

½ tsp (3 ml) vanilla extract

2 eggs

⅔ cup (160 ml) all-purpose flour

¼ tsp (1 ml) baking soda

¼ tsp (1 ml) salt

Filling:

½ cup (120 ml) whipping cream

¼ cup (60 ml) granulated sugar

2 cups sliced strawberries and blueberries

Preheat oven to 350°F (180°C).

Combine sugar, butter or margarine and water in small, heavy-duty saucepan. Bring to a boil, stirring constantly; remove from heat. Add ¾ cup morsels; stir until smooth. Stir in vanilla. Add eggs one at a time, stirring well after each addition. Add flour, baking soda and salt; stir until well-blended. Stir in remaining morsels.

Pour into waxed paper-lined and greased 9-inch round cake pan. Bake for 20-25 minutes or until wooden toothpick inserted in center comes out slightly sticky. Cool for 15 minutes in pan. Invert onto wire rack; remove waxed paper. Turn right side up; cool completely.

Spread Filling over brownie; top with berries. Chill until serving time. Serves 8-10.

Filling: Beat whipping cream and sugar in small mixing bowl until stiff peaks form.

Summer Berry Brownie Torte

Chocolate Walnut Torte

1 cup (240 ml) butter, softened
1⅓ cups (320 ml) sugar
1 tbs (15 ml) bourbon whiskey
½ cup (120 ml) GHIRARDELLI Unsweetened Cocoa
6 eggs, separated
1 cup (240 ml) finely ground walnuts

Preheat oven to 325°F (165°C).

Cream butter with sugar. Mix in bourbon and cocoa. Beat egg yolks until fluffy; add to cocoa mixture and beat 2 minutes on medium. Mix in walnuts. Beat egg whites until soft peaks form. Stir ⅓ beaten egg whites into chocolate mixture to lighten; fold in remainder.

Spread into buttered 8-inch springform pan. Bake for about 1 hour or until cooked in the center. Cool in pan before removing. Cake will sink in the center. Spread Cocoa Whipped Cream into indentation in center of cake. Top with Dark Cocoa Sauce. Serves 10-12.

Cocoa Whipped Cream

¼ cup (60 ml) confectioners sugar
3 tbs (45 ml) GHIRARDELLI Unsweetened Cocoa
1 cup (240 ml) whipping cream
½ tsp (3 ml) instant coffee, optional
½ tsp (3 ml) vanilla

Sift confectioners sugar with cocoa into bowl. Gradually stir in whipping cream and instant coffee. Chill for at least 1 hour. Whip cream mixture with vanilla. This cream may also be used to fill or frost your favorite chocolate cake or to top many other desserts.

Dark Cocoa Sauce

1 cup (240 ml) GHIRARDELLI Unsweetened Cocoa
1¾ cups (415 ml) sugar
½ cup (120 ml) hot water
½ cup (120 ml) milk
pinch salt
1 tsp (5 ml) vanilla

In saucepan, blend cocoa with sugar. Stir in hot water and mix until smooth. Add milk and salt. Heat to boiling; cook 2 minutes. Cool. Stir in vanilla. Serve over ice cream, cake or other desserts. Yields 2 cups sauce.

Chocolate Walnut Torte

Old World Raisin Torte

⅔ cup (160 ml) butter or margarine, softened
⅔ cup (160 ml) sugar
1 tbs (15 ml) grated lemon peel
1 tsp (5 ml) vanilla
1 egg
2¼ cups (540 ml) all-purpose flour
½ tsp (3 ml) baking powder
¼ tsp (1 ml) salt

Raisin Apricot Filling:
½ cup (120 ml) apricot jam
¼ cup (60 ml) sugar
1 tsp (5 ml) cinnamon
1½ cups (355 ml) SUN•MAID Raisins
1 cup (240 ml) flaked coconut
1 cup (240 ml) DIAMOND Chopped Walnuts

Preheat oven to 350°F (180°C). Grease an 8-inch square pan.

Combine butter or margarine, sugar, lemon peel and vanilla; beat until light and fluffy. Beat in egg. Combine flour, baking powder and salt. Stir into butter mixture; mix well. Divide dough into 3 portions. Wrap dough; refrigerate until firm.

Raisin-Apricot Filling: Combine jam, sugar and cinnamon. Stir in raisins, coconut and walnuts; set aside.

Press 1 portion of dough into greased pan. Spread with ½ the filling.

On floured surface, roll second portion of dough into 8-inch square; place on filling.

On floured surface, roll out remaining portion of dough into 8x6-inch rectangle. Cut dough into strips; arrange on top of filling in lattice pattern.

Bake 35 minutes or until brown. Cool completely; cut into squares. Yields 16 squares.

Venetian Creme Torte

½ cup (120 ml) butter
1⅔ cups (400 ml) sugar
3 eggs
1 tsp (5 ml) vanilla
dash salt
2 cups (480 ml) sifted HECKERS/CERESOTA
    Unbleached Flour
½ cup (120 ml) sifted cocoa
½ tsp (3 ml) baking soda
1 cup (240 ml) buttermilk

Preheat oven to 350°F (180°C). Grease and lightly flour three 9-inch round cake pans.

Cream butter and sugar until light. Add eggs, 1 at a time, beating thoroughly after each addition. Add vanilla and salt. Sift dry ingredients together and add alternately with buttermilk.

Pour into pans and bake 18-20 minutes or until tests done.

Cool on rack. When cool, slice each layer in half, forming 6 thin layers. Spread Butter Cream Icing between layers and on top and side of cake. These layers are not as high as a regular cake layer. Serves 10-12.

Butter Cream Icing

½ cup (120 ml) HECKERS/CERESOTA Unbleached Flour
1½ cups (355 ml) milk
1¼ cups (295 ml) butter, softened
1½ cups (355 ml) granulated sugar
1¼ tsp (6 ml) vanilla

Measure flour in small saucepan, add milk gradually mixing until smooth. Cook and stir continually until thickened. Cool thoroughly. Cream butter at high speed until smooth. Add granulated sugar; beat 5 minutes at high speed. Add cold, thickened milk mixture and favoring. Beat at high speed until well blended.

Opposite: Venetian Creme Torte

Linzer Torte

10 tbs (150 ml) butter or margarine, softened
¾ cup (180 ml) sugar
1 egg
2 cups (480 ml) sifted all-purpose flour
1 tsp (5 ml) cinnamon
½ tsp (3 ml) baking powder
½ tsp (3 ml) salt
¼ tsp (1 ml) ground cloves
½ cup (120 ml) ground almonds
1 tbs (15 ml) milk
1 can SOLO Raspberry Filling or 1 jar BAKER Raspberry Filling
1 egg beaten with
1 tbs (15 ml) water for brushing
confectioners sugar, optional

Preheat oven to 350°F (180°C).

Beat butter or margarine and sugar in large bowl with electric mixer until light and fluffy. Add egg and beat until blended. Combine flour, cinnamon, baking powder, salt and cloves, and add to butter mixture. Stir until blended. Stir in ground almonds and milk.

Shape dough into slightly flattened ball, wrap in plastic wrap or waxed paper and refrigerate 1 hour.

Press or pat out ⅔ of dough in bottom of ungreased 10-inch springform pan, pressing dough about ¾ inch upside of pan. Spread raspberry filling on dough.

Divide remaining dough into 10 equal-size pieces. Dust hands with flour and roll each piece into thin 10-inch rope. Arrange ropes in lattice pattern over raspberry filling, trimming ends to fit. Brush pastry with beaten egg mixture.

Bake 40-45 minutes or until crust is golden brown. Cool completely in pan on wire rack. Run tip of sharp knife around inside edge of pan and remove side of pan. Dust with confectioners sugar, if desired. Serves 10-12.

Red Letter Torte

1⅓ cups (320 ml) all-purpose flour
1½ tsp (8 ml) DAVIS Baking Powder
½ cup (120 ml) EGG BEATERS Real Egg Product
3 tbs (45 ml) skim milk
¼ tsp (1 ml) almond extract
¼ cup (60 ml) FLEISCHMANN'S Margarine, softened
½ cup (120 ml) sugar
21-oz can (630 g) light cherry pie filling and topping

Streusel Topping:
¼ cup (60 ml) all-purpose flour,
3 tbs (45 ml) confectioners sugar
2 tbs (30 ml) toasted, chopped, sliced almonds
¼ tsp (1 ml) cinnamon
1 tbs (15 ml) FLEISCHMANN'S Margarine

Confectioners Sugar Glaze, optional

Combine flour and baking powder; set aside. Combine egg product, milk and almond extract; set aside. In mixing bowl, with electric mixer at medium speed, beat margarine and sugar until creamy. Alternately add flour mixture and egg mixture, blending well after each addition.

Spread batter in greased 9-inch springform pan. Bake at 350°F (180°C) 40 minutes.

Spoon cherry pie filling over batter; sprinkle Streusel Topping over filling around outside edge of pan. Bake 10-15 minutes more or until toothpick inserted in center comes out clean. Cool in pan on wire rack for 25 minutes. Remove outside ring of pan; cool completely on wire rack. Drizzle with Confectioners' Sugar Glaze, if desired. Serves 8.

Streusel Topping: Mix flour, confectioners sugar, almonds, cinnamon and margarine until crumbly.

Opposite: **Linzer Torte**

Bonanza King Devil's Food Cake

Strike-It-Rich Chocolate Butter Cream Frosting

2 cups (480 ml) sifted cake flour
1½ cups (355 ml) GHIRARDELLI Ground Chocolate
1 cup (240 ml) sugar
2 tsp (10 ml) baking soda
½ tsp (3 ml) cream of tartar
½ tsp (3 ml) salt
1 cup (240 ml) shortening
1½ cups (355 ml) buttermilk
3 eggs
1½ tsp (8 ml) vanilla

Preheat oven to 350°F (180°C).

Into a mixing bowl, sift flour with ground chocolate, sugar, baking soda, cream of tartar and salt. Add shortening and 1 cup buttermilk. Beat on medium speed for 2 minutes. Scrape bowl down. Add ½ cup buttermilk, eggs and vanilla. Beat additional 2 minutes on medium speed.

Grease bottoms of two 9x1½-inch round cake pans. Line with waxed paper.

Spread batter into pans. Bake for 30-35 minutes. Cool on racks 10-15 minutes; remove from pans. Frost. Serves 10.

4-oz bar (120 g) GHIRARDELLI Semi-Sweet Chocolate
¼ cup (60 ml) water
¼ tsp (1 ml) instant coffee, optional
2½ cups (590 ml) sifted confectioners sugar
2 egg yolks
½ tsp (3 ml) vanilla
6 tbs (90 ml) butter, very soft

In medium-size heavy saucepan, melt broken chocolate with water and coffee. Stir constantly until mixture is very smooth. Remove from heat. Mix in confectioners sugar and beat in until smooth. Beat in egg yolks and vanilla. Place pan in bowl of ice and water. Add butter, in 4 additions, beating until frosting is very light in color and thick enough to spread. Chill cake to set frosting.

Bonanza King Devil's Food Cake

Devil's Food Cake

2 cups (480 ml) sifted SWANS DOWN Cake Flour
1 tsp (5 ml) baking soda
½ cup (120 ml) butter, softened
1¼ cups (295 ml) light brown sugar, packed
2 eggs
6 squares unsweetened chocolate, melted, cooled
1 tsp (5 ml) vanilla
1¼ cups (295 ml) milk

Preheat oven to 350°F (180°C).

Sift flour and baking soda. In large bowl, cream butter, gradually add brown sugar until light and fluffy. Add eggs; beat well. Beat in chocolate and vanilla. Add dry ingredients alternately with milk, beating well after each addition.

Spread batter in 2 prepared 9-inch layer pans. Bake until tester inserted in center comes out clean, 25-30 minutes. Cool in pans 10 minutes. Remove from pans; cool thoroughly. Frost with Orange Cream Cheese Frosting. Serves 8.

Orange Cream Cheese Frosting

2 3-oz pkgs (90 g each) cream cheese, softened
¼ cup (60 ml) butter, softened
5 cups (1.2 l) confectioners sugar
1 tsp (5 ml) grated orange zest
2-3 tbs (30-45 ml) orange juice

Beat cream cheese and butter until light and creamy. Gradually add confectioners sugar. Add orange zest and enough orange juice to reach desired spreading consistency.

Ghirardelli Square Cake

1 cup (240 ml) butter or margarine, softened
½ cup (120 ml) sugar
½ cup (120 ml) brown sugar, packed
2 eggs, well beaten
2 tsp (10 ml) vanilla
2½ cups (590 ml) sifted cake flour
1½ cups (355 ml) GHIRARDELLI Ground Chocolate
½ tsp (3 ml) salt
1 tsp (5 ml) baking powder
1 tsp (5 ml) baking soda
1 cup (240 ml) milk

Preeat oven to 350°F (180°C).

Cream butter or margarine with sugar and brown sugar until fluffy; beat in eggs and vanilla. Sift flour with ground chocolate, salt, baking powder and baking soda. Add dry ingredients alternately with milk, ending with dry ingredients.

Grease bottoms of two 8-inch square cake pans, or two 9-inch round cake pans. Line with waxed paper.

Spread batter into cake pans. Bake for 30-35 minutes. Cool on racks 10-15 minutes; remove from pans. Frost with Pink Brick Frosting. Yields 2 cakes, each serves 16.

Pink Brick Frosting

2 egg whites
1½ cups (355 ml) sugar
pinch salt
⅓ cup (80 ml) cold water
2 tsp (10 ml) light corn syrup
2 tsp (10 ml) vanilla
few drops red food coloring

Combine all ingredients in double boiler over 1 inch of simmering water. Beat with electric mixer 7-8 minutes, until frosting forms peaks. Spread frosting on Ghirardelli Square Cake. Sprinkle with crushed peppermint sticks, if desired.

Ghirardelli Square Cake

Muir Woods Chocolate Cherry Cake

Muir Woods Cherry Cream Filling

6 oz (180 g) GHIRARDELLI Semi-Sweet Chocolate Chips
¼ cup (60 ml) water
¾ cup (180 ml) butter or margarine, softened
1¾ cups (415 ml) sugar
1½ tsp (8 ml) vanilla
3 eggs
2¼ cups (540 ml) unsifted cake flour
1 tsp (5 ml) baking powder
1 tsp (5 ml) baking soda
½ tsp (3 ml) salt
1 cup (240 ml) buttermilk

1-lb can (455 g) sour pitted cherries, drained
2 tbs (30 ml) sugar
¼ cup (60 ml) Kirsch (cherry liqueur)
1 tsp (5 ml) unflavored gelatin
½ pint (240 ml) whipping cream
3 tbs (45 ml) confectioners sugar

Preheat oven to 375°F (190°C).

In heavy saucepan, melt chocolate chips with water, stirring constantly; cool. Cream butter or margarine, gradually adding sugar and vanilla in large bowl. Add eggs, 1 at a time, beating well after each addition. Blend in chocolate. Sift flour with baking powder, baking soda and salt. Add dry ingredients alternately with buttermilk, beating until blended.

Spread batter into 3 waxed paper-lined 9-inch round cake pans. Bake for about 25 minutes. Cool on rack for 10 minutes. Remove cake and waxed paper; cool.

Fill with Muir Woods Cherry Cream Filling. Frost top and sides with Chocolate Sour Cream Frosting. Serves 12.

Marinate cherries with sugar and Kirsch for at least 2 hours; drain liquid. Add 1 tbs Kirsch liquid to the gelatin. Melt gelatin over hot water; add remaining Kirsch liquid. Whip cream until thick. Slowly add gelatin mixture and confectioners' sugar. Beat until stiff. Combine with cherries. Spread as filling between layers of Muir Woods Chocolate Cherry Cake. Chill to firm filling.

Chocolate Sour Cream Frosting for Cherry Cake

½ cup (120 ml) sour cream
1 tsp (5 ml) vanilla
2 cups (480 ml) confectioners sugar
1 cup (240 ml) GHIRARDELLI Semi-Sweet Chocolate Chips

Beat sour cream and vanilla with confectioners sugar until creamy. In double boiler, melt chocolate chips over 1 inch of simmering water. Let cool slightly. Mix chocolate into sour cream mixture, whipping until smooth and thick. Frost top and sides of Muir Woods Chocolate Cherry Cake (above). Decorate top with stemmed cherries marinated in Kirsch, if desired.

Muir Woods Chocolate
Cherry Cake

Telegraph Hill Chocolate Cake

1 cup (240 ml) milk
2 tbs (30 ml) red wine vinegar
4-oz bar (120 g) GHIRARDELLI Unsweetened Baking Chocolate
1 cup (240 ml) shortening
2 cups (480 ml) sugar
2 tsp (10 ml) vanilla
5 eggs
2 cups (480 ml) sifted cake flour
1 tsp (5 ml) baking soda
½ tsp (3 ml) salt

Preheat oven to 350°F (180°C).

Combine milk with vinegar; let stand to thicken.

Melt chocolate according to package directions.

Cream shortening with sugar and vanilla in large bowl. Add eggs 1 at a time, beating well after each addition. Mix in melted chocolate. Sift flour with baking soda and salt. Add dry ingredients alternately with milk, mixing well after each addition.

Line three 9x1½-inch round cake pans with waxed paper.

Divide batter into pans. Bake for 25-30 minutes. Cool on racks 10 minutes. Run knife around edge of pan. Remove cake from pans; peel off waxed paper. Cool on racks.

Spread layers with Velvet Coffee Cream Filling. Frost top and sides with Princess Chocolate Frosting. Serves 16.

Velvet Coffee Cream Filling

3-oz pkg (90 g) cream cheese, softened
⅓ cup (80 ml) confectioners sugar
2 tbs (30 ml) coffee liqueur
½ pint (240 ml) whipping cream

Beat cream cheese with confectioners sugar and liqueur. Gradually add whipping cream, beating until thick enough to hold a shape. Spread between layers of cake.

Princess Chocolate Frosting

½ cup (120 ml) butter, softened
2 cup (480 ml) confectioners sugar
1 tsp (5 ml) vanilla
3 egg yolks
2 oz (60 g) GHIRARDELLI Unsweetened Baking Chocolate

Cream butter with confectioners sugar and vanilla. Add egg yolks 1 at a time, beating well after each addition. Beat until very fluffy. Melt chocolate according to package directions. Add to creamed mixture; beat on high speed until very thick. Spread over top and sides of cake. Chill to firm frosting.

Telegraph Hill Chocolate Cake

A Lighter Black Forest Cake

2 cups (480 ml) pastry or cake flour
1 cup (240 ml) unsweetened cocoa powder
1 tsp (5 ml) baking powder
½ tsp (3 ml) salt
1½ cups (355 ml) maple or brown sugar
2 eggs
1 egg white
1 cup (240 ml) prune purée*
¾ cup (180 ml) nonfat milk
4 tsp (20 ml) vanilla
1 cup (240 ml) boiling water
2 tbs (30 ml) espresso powder
2 tsp (10 ml) baking soda
2 cups (480 ml) frozen dark sweet cherries, pitted, coarsely chopped,
    thawed and well drained
½ cup (120 ml) chopped, toasted walnuts
confectioners sugar, optional
additional frozen cherries, for garnish
mint sprig, for garnish

Preheat oven to 350°F (180°C). Coat a 3-4-quart bundt or other tube pan with vegetable cooking spray.

Into large bowl sift together flour, cocoa, baking powder and salt; mix in maple sugar or brown sugar, and reserve. In another bowl, whisk eggs with the purée, milk and vanilla; set aside.

Pour boiling water into measuring cup; stir in espresso powder and baking soda. Stir egg and water mixtures into flour mixture; mix just until blended.

Pour ½ the batter into prepared pan; sprinkle cherries and walnuts evenly over batter. Evenly pour in remaining batter. Bake about 45 minutes until toothpick inserted into cake comes out clean. Cool in pan on rack 15 minutes; invert onto rack, remove pan and cool completely.

Dust with confectioners sugar, if desired; place on serving plate. Fill cake center with additional cherries and garnish with mint. Serves 16.

*Prune Purée: Combine 1⅓ cups (320 ml) pitted prunes and 6 tbs (90 ml) hot water in container of food processor or blender. Pulse on and off until prunes are finely chopped and smooth. Store leftovers in a covered container in the refrigerator for up to 2 months. Yields 1 cup.

Courtesy of the California Prune Commission.

Opposite:
A Lighter Black Forest Cake

A Lighter Chocolate Decadence

1¼ cups (295 ml) sugar, divided
⅔ cup (160 ml) unsweetened coca powder
2 tbs (30 ml) flour
¾ cup (180 ml) nonfat milk
¾ cup (180 ml) semisweet chocolate chips
¼ cup (60 ml) prune purée*
1 whole egg
1 egg yolk
1 tsp (5 ml) vanilla
2 egg whites
pinch cream of tartar
12-oz pkg (360 g) frozen red raspberries
sugar, to taste
1½ cups (355 ml) light whipped topping
fresh raspberries, for garnish, optional

Preheat oven to 350°F (180°C). Line bottom of 9-inch round layer cake pan or 9-inch springform pan with baking parchment and coat pan with vegetable cooking spray.

In saucepan, combine 1 cup of the sugar, the cocoa powder and flour. Gradually whisk in milk to blend. Bring to simmer over low heat, stirring.

Place chocolate in large bowl; pour hot milk mixture over chocolate, stirring to melt. Whisk prune purée, whole egg, egg yolk and vanilla to blend; set aside to cool.

In mixing bowl, beat egg whites with cream of tartar until foamy. Gradually beat in remaining sugar until mixture is stiff but not dry. With rubber spatula fold ½ the egg white mixture into cooled chocolate mixture, then fold in remaining egg white mixture.

Pour into pan. Bake in center of oven 30-35 minutes until puffy and center is set but still moist. Do not over-bake. Cool completely on rack. Loosen edges and invert onto plastic wrap or aluminum foil; wrap and invert again or remove sides of springform pan. Chill 24 hours before serving. Cake can be frozen for longer storage.

Cut into wedges and serve with Raspberry Sauce and whipped topping. Garnish with fresh raspberries. Serves 12.

Raspberry Sauce: Thaw frozen raspberries. Purée in electric blender, then strain to remove seeds. Sweeten to taste with sugar. Yields 1 cup.

*Prune Purée: Combine 1⅓ cups (320 ml) pitted prunes and 6 tbs (90 ml) hot water in container of food processor or blender. Pulse on and off until prunes are finely chopped and smooth. Store leftovers in a covered container in the refrigerator for up to 2 months. Yields 1 cup.

Courtesy of the California Prune Commission.

Opposite:
A Lighter Chocolate Decadence

Chocolate Layer Cake

2¾ cups (650 ml) sifted PRESTO
2 cups (480 ml) sugar
½ cup (120 ml) cocoa
¼ tsp (1 ml) baking soda
2 cups (480 ml) buttermilk
¾ cup (180 ml) corn oil
2 eggs
2 tsp (10 ml) vanilla

Preheat oven to 350°F (180°C). Grease two 9-inch cake pans. Line bottoms with waxed paper.

Sift flour, sugar, cocoa and baking soda together. In another bowl, combine buttermilk, corn oil, eggs and vanilla. Blend half the liquid mixture into dry ingredients. Beat 2 minutes on medium speed of electric mixer or 300 strokes by hand. Add remaining mixture. Beat 1 minute or 150 strokes by hand.

Pour into prepared pans. Bake about 35 minutes or until cake springs back when touched lightly with finger. Frost as desired. Serves 8.

Quick Chocolate Cake

2¼ cups (540 ml) sifted PRESTO
1¼ cups (295 ml) sugar
½ cup (120 ml) cocoa
½ tsp (3 ml) baking soda
⅔ cup (160 ml) margarine
1 cup (240 ml) milk
1½ tsp (8 ml) vanilla
2 eggs

Preheat oven to 350°F (180°C). Grease two 8-inch layer cake pans and line bottom with waxed paper.

Sift flour, sugar, coca and baking soda together. Stir margarine to soften. Sift dry ingredients over margarine. Add milk and vanilla. Stir until dry ingredients are completely moistened, then beat 1 minute on medium speed of electric mixer or about 150 vigorous strokes by hand, scraping bowl and beaters often. Add eggs. Beat 1½ minutes on medium speed of electric mixer or 225 vigorous strokes by hand.

Pour into prepared pans. Bake for 40-45 minutes or until cake springs back when touched lightly with finger. Serves 8.

Quick Chocolate Cake

Chocolate Buttermilk Cake

2 cups (480 ml) all-purpose flour
2 cups (480 ml) sugar
2 eggs
1 tsp (5 ml) baking soda
½ tsp (3 ml) salt
½ cup (120 ml) water
2 tbs (30 ml) SACO Buttermilk Blend
1 cup (240 ml) butter or margarine
4 tbs (60 ml) SACO Baking Cocoa
1 cup (240 ml) water
1 tsp (5 ml) vanilla extract

Preheat oven to 350°F (180°C). Grease 9x13x2-inch pan or two 8 or 9-inch layer pans.

In large mixing bowl, combine flour, sugar, eggs, soda, salt, ½ cup water and buttermilk blend; set aside.

In medium saucepan, melt butter or margarine and stir in cocoa until well-blended. Add 1 cup water and vanilla extract to cocoa mixture and bring to a boil. Combine the cocoa mixture with the flour mixture and beat just until well-blended.

Pour into pan and bake 30 minutes or until toothpick inserted in center comes out clean. (25-30 minutes for layer pans.) Cool thoroughly and frost with Cocoa Butter Frosting. Serves 12-14.

Cocoa Butter Frosting

⅓ cup (80 ml) butter or margarine
⅓ cup (80 ml) SACO Baking Cocoa
1½ tsp (8 ml) vanilla extract
2 cup (480 ml) confectioners sugar
2 tbs (30 ml) milk, or more, if necessary

In medium saucepan melt butter or margarine over low heat (melt in microwave in a 1-quart container). Remove from heat, add cocoa, and stir until well-blended. Add vanilla. Beat in confectioners sugar and milk until smooth and of spreading consistency. Add additional milk, if necessary. Makes enough to fill and frost two 8- or 9-inch layers, or one 13x9-inch cake.

Chocolate Buttermilk Cake

German Sweet Chocolate Cake I

4-oz pkg (120 g) BAKER'S German Sweet Chocolate
½ cup (120 ml) water
2 cups (480 ml) flour
1 tsp (5 ml) baking soda
¼ tsp (1 ml) salt
1 cup (240 ml) margarine or butter, softened
2 cups (480 ml) sugar
4 eggs, separated
1 tsp (5 ml) vanilla
1 cup (240 ml) buttermilk

Preheat oven to 350°F (180°C). Line bottoms of three 9-inch round cake pans with wax paper.

Microwave chocolate and water in large microwave-safe bowl on high 1½-2 minutes or until chocolate is almost melted, stirring halfway through heating time. Stir until chocolate is completely melted*.

Mix flour, baking soda and salt; set aside. Beat margarine or butter and sugar in large bowl with electric mixer on medium speed until light and fluffy. Add egg yolks, 1 at a time, beating well after each addition. Stir in chocolate mixture and vanilla. Add flour mixture alternately with buttermilk, beating after each addition until smooth.

Beat egg whites in another large bowl with electric mixer on high speed until stiff peaks form. Gently stir into batter.

Pour into prepared pans. Bake 30 minutes or until cake springs back when lightly touched in center. Immediately run spatula between cakes and sides of pans. Cool 15 minutes; remove from pans. Remove wax paper. Cool completely on wire racks. Spread Coconut-Pecan Frosting between layers and over top of cake. Serves 12.

*Top of Stove Preparation: Heat chocolate and water in heavy 1-quart saucepan on very low heat, stirring constantly until chocolate is melted and mixture is smooth. Remove from heat. Continue as above.

Coconut-Pecan Frosting I

12-oz can (360 ml) evaporated milk
1½ cups (355 ml) sugar
¾ cup (180 ml) margarine or butter
4 egg yolks, slightly beaten
1½ tsp (8 ml) vanilla
7-oz pkg (210 g) BAKER'S Angel Flake Coconut
1½ cups (355 ml) chopped pecans

Mix evaporated milk, sugar, margarine or butter, beaten egg yolks and vanilla in large saucepan. Stirring constantly, cook on medium heat 12 minutes or until thickened and golden brown. Remove from heat. Stir in coconut and pecans. Cool to room temperature and desired spreading consistency. Yields 4½ cups.

One-Layer Chocolate Sour Cream Cake

2-oz (60 g) GHIRARDELLI Semi-Sweet Chocolate
¼ cup (60 ml) water
⅓ cup (80 ml) sugar
⅓ cup (80 ml) brown sugar, packed
1 tsp (5 ml) vanilla
1 egg plus 1 egg yolk, beaten
½ cup (120 ml) sour cream
1 cup (240 ml) unsifted cake flour
¾ tsp (4 ml) baking powder
½ tsp (3 ml) baking soda
¼ tsp (1 ml) salt

Preheat oven to 350°F (180°C).

In heavy saucepan, melt chocolate with water over low heat, stirring constantly. In a large bowl, cream butter with sugar and brown sugar; add vanilla and beaten eggs, beating until fluffy. Mix in sour cream. Sift flour with baking powder, baking soda and salt. Add dry ingredients alternately to chocolate liquid, mixing well after each addition. Fold in sour cream.

Spread batter into a waxed paper-lined 9x1½-inch round cake pan. Bake for 30 minutes. Cool on rack for 10-15 minutes. Remove cake and waxed paper. Serves 8.

Opposite:
One-Layer Chocolate Sour Cream Cake

German Chocolate Cake II

¼ cup (60 ml) SACO Baking Cocoa
3 tbs (45 ml) unsalted butter or margarine
¼ cup (60 ml) plus 1 tbs (15 ml) sugar
⅓ cup (80 ml) boiling water
1¾ cups (415 ml) cake flour
¾ tsp (4 ml) baking soda
½ tsp (3 ml) salt
¼ cup (60 ml) SACO Buttermilk Blend
⅔ cup (160 ml) unsalted butter or margarine, softened
¾ cup (180 ml) plus 2 tbs (30 ml) sugar
3 eggs, separated
1 tsp (5 ml) vanilla extract
⅔ cup (160 ml) water
¼ cup (60 ml) sugar

Preheat oven to 350°F (180°C). Grease and flour pans (one 13x9x2-inch, two 9-inch round or three 8-inch round).

Place cocoa, 3 tbs butter and ¼ cup plus 1 tbs sugar in small bowl. Add boiling water; stir until smooth and set aside to cool.

Sift flour, baking soda, salt and buttermilk blend together; set aside.

In medium mixing, bowl cream ⅔ cup butter or margarine and ¾ cup plus 2 tbs sugar until fluffy. Add egg yolks and vanilla, mixing well, then scrape the bowl sides. Add cocoa mixture and combine. Add dry ingredients alternately with water, beginning and ending with dry ingredients. Beat egg whites until soft peaks form. Continue to beat and gradually sprinkle in the ¼ cup sugar. Beat until soft peaks form. Gently fold egg whites into batter and spread evenly into pan(s).

Bake until a toothpick, inserted in center, comes out clean (40-45 minutes for 13x9x2-inch pan, 30-35 minutes for two 9-inch round pans, 25-30 minutes for three 8-inch round pans). Cool and unmold round cakes. Fill and frost top with Coconut-Pecan Frosting. Serves 8-14.

Coconut-Pecan Frosting II

½ cup (120 ml) unsalted butter or margarine
¾ cup (180 ml) heavy or whipping cream
½ cup (120 ml) sugar
½ cup (120 ml) brown sugar
pinch salt
1 tsp (5 ml) vanilla extract
3 egg yolks
1 cup (240 ml) shredded coconut
¾ cup (180 ml) pecan pieces

Place butter or margarine, cream, sugar, brown sugar, salt and vanilla in a small saucepan. Bring to a boil, stirring to dissolve sugars. Put egg yolks into a small mixing bowl and gradually add a few tablespoons of hot cream mixture, stirring well. Repeat until approximately half the cream mixture is mixed into yolks. Add yolk mixture back into saucepan with remaining cream. Return to a boil and cook for 2 minutes, stirring constantly. Remove from heat. Add coconut and pecans. Cool and spread.

Mt. Shasta Baked Alaska

One Layer Chocolate Sour Cream Cake (below)
1 pint (480 ml) ice cream
½ cup (120 ml) egg whites
¼ tsp (1 ml) cream of tartar
½ cup (120 ml) sugar
pinch salt
1 tsp (5 ml) vanilla
sliced almonds, if desired

Preheat oven 450°F (230°C).

To assemble dessert, spread slightly softened ice cream over cake, leaving 1-inch margin around edge. For color contrast, 2 flavors of ice cream may be combined. Place in freezer until ready to serve.

Beat egg whites until foamy; add cream of tartar, sugar, salt and vanilla. On high speed, beat until soft peaks form.

Spread meringue over ice cream and cake. Sprinkle with sliced almonds, if desired.

Place dessert on piece of heavy brown paper on baking sheet. Bake for 5 minutes. Serve immediately with Chocolate Zabaglione Sauce. Serves 8.

Chocolate Zabaglione Sauce

2 oz (60 g) GHIRARDELLI Semi-Sweet Chocolate, chopped
½ cup (120 ml) Marsala wine
⅓ cup (80 ml) sugar
2 egg yolks, well beaten

In heavy saucepan, combine broken chocolate, wine and sugar; heat, stirring until blended. Heat to boiling; cook 1 minute. Remove from heat. With wire whip, quickly stir in beaten egg yolks. Return saucepan to low heat, stir until thickened. Serve sauce warm or cold over Mt. Shasta Baked Alaska, strawberries or other fresh fruit.

Occidental Chocolate Rum Ring

3 cups (720 ml) unsifted flour
2 cups (480 ml) GHIRARDELLI Ground Chocolate
2 cups (480 ml) sugar
1 tbs (15 ml) baking powder
1 tsp (5 ml) salt
1 cup (240 ml) butter, softened
1½ cups (355 ml) half and half
1 tbs (15 ml) vanilla
3 eggs
¼ cup (60 ml) rum

Preheat oven to 325°F (165°C).

Into large mixing bowl, sift flour with ground chocolate, sugar, baking powder and salt. Add butter, half and half and vanilla to center of dry ingredients. Mix together and beat on high speed 5 minutes. Add eggs, 1 at a time, beating well after each addition. Mix in rum.

Pour into well-greased 10-inch angel food cake pan. Bake for approximately 1½ hours. Slices of cake may be served with vanilla ice cream and chocolate sauce or simply dusted with sifted confectioners sugar. Serves 16.

Quick Method Sour Cream Chocolate Cake

2¼ cup (540 ml) SOFTASILK Cake Flour
2 cups (480 ml) sugar
1 cup (240 ml) water
¾ cup (180 ml) sour cream
¼ cup (60 ml) shortening
1¼ tsp (6 ml) baking soda
1 tsp (5 ml) salt
½ tsp (3 ml) baking powder
2 eggs
1 tsp (5 ml) vanilla
4 oz (120 g) unsweetened baking chocolate, melted and cooled

Preheat oven to 350°F (180°C). Grease and flour 2 round pans, 9x1½ inches, 3 round pans, 8x1½ inches, or rectangular pan, 13x9x2 inches.

Beat all ingredients in large bowl on low speed 30 seconds, scraping bowl constantly. Beat on high speed 3 minutes, scraping bowl occasionally.

Pour into pan(s). Bake round pans 30-35 minutes, rectangular pan 40-45 minutes or until top springs back when touched lightly. Cool layers 10 minutes; remove from pans. Cool completely. Fill and frost layers, or frost rectangle, with Chocolate Frosting. Serves 12.

Chocolate Frosting

⅓ cup (80 ml) margarine or butter, softened
2 oz (60 g) unsweetened baking chocolate, melted and cooled
2 cups (480 ml) confectioners sugar
1½ tsp (8 ml) vanilla
2 tbs (30 ml) milk, approximately

Mix margarine or butter and chocolate in medium bowl. Stir in confectioners sugar. Beat in vanilla and milk until smooth enough to spread.

Quick Method Sour Cream Chocolate Cake

White Chocolate Fudge Cake

Frosting:
1 can PILLSBURY CREAMY SUPREME *Vanilla Frosting*
3 oz (90 g) *white chocolate baking bar or vanilla-flavored candy coating, melted*
1 tsp (5 ml) *vanilla*
8-oz *container frozen whipped topping, thawed*

Cake:
1 pkg PILLSBURY MOIST SUPREME *White Cake Mix*
1¼ cups (295 ml) *water*
⅓ cup (80 ml) *oil*
1 tsp (5 ml) *vanilla*
2 *eggs*
3 oz (90 g) *white chocolate baking bar or vanilla-flavored candy coating, melted*

Fudge Filling:
¼ cup (60 ml) *confectioners sugar*
6-oz pkg (180 g) *semisweet chocolate chips*
3 tbs (45 ml) *margarine or butter*
2 tbs (30 ml) *light corn syrup*

Garnish:
chocolate curls, if desired

Frosting: In large bowl, beat vanilla frosting at medium speed, gradually adding white chocolate baking bar. Beat at high speed 30 seconds or until smooth and well blended. Fold in vanilla and whipped topping. Refrigerate.

Preheat oven to 350°F (180°C). Grease and flour 13x9-inch pan.

Cake: In large bowl, combine all cake ingredients except white chocolate baking bar at low speed until moistened; beat 2 minutes at high speed. Gradually beat in melted white chocolate baking bar until well blended.

Pour batter into greased and floured pan. Bake 30-40 minutes or until toothpick inserted in center comes out clean. Cool 10 minutes.

Filling: In small saucepan over low heat, heat all Filling ingredients until melted and well blended, stirring constantly. Spread fudge filling over warm cake. Cool completely.

Frost cake. Garnish with chocolate curls. Store in refrigerator. Let stand at room temperature 10 minutes before cutting. Serves 12-14.

White Chocolate Fudge Cake

Mocha Fudge Cake

1½ cups (355 ml) SUN•MAID Raisins
⅓ cup (80 ml) coffee liqueur
¾ cup (180 ml) shortening
1 cup (240 ml) brown sugar, firmly packed
½ cup (120 ml) sugar
2 eggs
2 cups (480 ml) all-purpose flour
½ cup (120 ml) unsweetened cocoa
1 tsp (5 ml) baking soda
¼ tsp (1 ml) salt
1½ cups (355 ml) cold coffee

Soak raisins in coffee liqueur.

Preheat oven to 350°F (180°C). Grease 13x9-inch pan.

Combine shortening, brown sugar, sugar and eggs in large bowl; beat until light and fluffy. Combine flour, cocoa, baking soda and salt; add to shortening mixture alternately with coffee. Stir in raisins and coffee liqueur.

Pour batter in pan. Bake 40-45 minutes or until toothpick inserted in center comes out clean. Cool in pan on wire rack. Frost with Mocha Frosting. Serves 12.

Mocha Frosting

¼ cup (60 ml) butter or margarine
¼ cup (60 ml) unsweetened cocoa
1 tsp (5 ml) instant coffee crystals
2 tbs (30 ml) light corn syrup
2 tbs (30 ml) milk
1 tsp (5 ml) vanilla
2 cups (480 ml) confectioners sugar

Melt butter or margarine in small saucepan; blend in cocoa and coffee crystals until dissolved. Stir in corn syrup, milk, vanilla and confectioners sugar; beat until smooth. Spread over cake.

Wellesley Fudge Cake

4 squares BAKER'S Unsweetened Chocolate
1¾ cups (415 ml) sugar, divided
½ cup (120 ml) water
1⅔ cups (400 ml) flour
1 tsp (5 ml) baking soda
¼ tsp (1 ml) salt
½ cup (120 ml) margarine or butter, softened
3 eggs
¾ cup (180 ml) milk
1 tsp (5 ml) vanilla

Preheat oven to 350°F (180°C).

Microwave chocolate, ½ cup of the sugar and water in large microwave-safe bowl on high 1-2 minutes or until chocolate is almost melted, stirring halfway through heating time. Stir until chocolate is completely melted. Cool to lukewarm*.

Mix flour, baking soda and salt; set aside. Beat margarine or butter and remaining 1¼ cups sugar in large bowl with electric mixer on medium speed until light and fluffy. Add eggs, 1 at a time, beating well after each addition. Add flour mixture alternately with milk, beating after each addition until smooth. Stir in chocolate mixture and vanilla.

Pour into 2 greased and floured 9-inch round cake pans. Bake 30-35 minutes or until cake springs back when lightly touched. Cool 10 minutes; remove from pans. Cool completely on wire racks. Frost with Easy Fudge Frosting. Serves 12.

* Top of Stove Preparation: Heat chocolate and water in heavy 1-quart saucepan on very low heat, stirring constantly until chocolate is melted and mixture is smooth. Add ½ cup of the sugar; cook and stir 2 minutes. Cool to lukewarm. Continue as above.

Easy Fudge Frosting

4 squares BAKER'S Unsweetened Chocolate
2 tbs (30 ml) margarine or butter
16-oz pkg (480 g) confectioners sugar
½ cup (120 ml) milk
1 tsp (5 ml) vanilla

Microwave chocolate and margarine in large microwave-safe bowl on high 2 minutes or until melted. Stir until chocolate is completely melted.

Beat in confectioners sugar, milk and vanilla with electric mixer on low speed until well blended and smooth. If necessary, let stand until spreading consistency is reached, stirring occasionally. Spread quickly. If frosting becomes too thick, stir in additional milk until spreading consistency is reached. Yields 2½ cups or enough to frost tops and sides of two 9-inch round cake layers.

Top of stove preparation: Melt chocolate and margarine in heavy 2-quart saucepan on very low heat, stirring constantly. Remove from heat. Continue as above.

Cocoa Fudge Cake

1⅔ cups (400 ml) all-purpose flour
1½ cups (355 ml) sugar
⅔ cup (160 ml) baking cocoa
1½ tsp (8 ml) baking soda
1 tsp (5 ml) salt
6 tbs (90 ml) SACO Buttermilk Blend
1½ cups (355 ml) water
½ cup (120 ml) shortening
2 eggs
1 tsp (5 ml) vanilla

Have ingredients at room temperature.

Preheat oven to 350°F (180°C). Grease and flour a 13x9x2-inch baking pan, or two 8- or 9-inch layer pans.

Sift together dry ingredients in large mixing bowl. Add remaining ingredients. Blend ½ minute on low speed, scraping bowl constantly. Beat 3 minutes on high speed, scraping bowl occasionally.

Pour into pan(s). Bake oblong pan 35-40 minutes, layer pans 30-35 minutes, or until wooden toothpick, inserted in center, comes out clean. Cool. This recipe will also make 24 cupcakes. Frost as desired or with Fudge Frosting. Serves 8-12.

Fudge Frosting

½ cup (120 ml) shortening
2 cups (480 ml) sugar
3 oz (90 g) unsweetened chocolate
⅔ cup (160 ml) milk
½ tsp (3 ml) salt
3 tbs (45 ml) SACO Buttermilk Blend
2 tsp (10 ml) vanilla

Mix all ingredients, except vanilla, in 2-quart saucepan. Heat to rolling boil, stirring occasionally. Boil 1 minute without stirring. Place pan of frosting in bowl of ice and water. Beat frosting until smooth and correct spreading consistency. Stir in vanilla. Makes enough to fill and frost two 9-inch layers or one 13x9x2-inch cake.

Cocoa Fudge Cake

Baileys Fudge Cake

½ cup (120 ml) butter, softened
1 cup (240 ml) brown sugar
4 large eggs
1 cup (240 ml) chocolate syrup
⅔ cup (160 ml) BAILEYS Original Irish Cream
1 tsp (5 ml) instant coffee crystals, optional
1 cup (240 ml) flour
½ cup (120 ml) chopped pecans
16 pecan halves

Glaze:
¾ cup semisweet chocolate morsels, melted
¼ cup (60 ml) sour cream, at room temperature
1 tbs (15 ml) BAILEYS Original Irish Cream

Preheat oven to 350°F (180°C). Grease 9-inch round cake pan.

With mixer, cream butter and brown sugar, blend in eggs. Add chocolate syrup, Baileys, coffee crystals and flour, mixing until well blended. Fold in chopped pecans.

Pour into prepared pan. Bake for 55-60 minutes, until center is firm and a toothpick inserted in center comes out clean. Remove from pan onto wire rack to cool.

Dip 1 end of pecan halves halfway into melted chocolate morsels to coat, place on waxed paper; chill to set chocolate.

Glaze: To remaining melted chocolate add sour cream, 1 tbs at a time, and Baileys. Spread over top of cooled cake that has been placed on a serving platter, letting some chocolate drizzle down side of cake.

Place 4 dipped pecans in center of cake; place remaining dipped pecans around edge of cake. Cool to set topping. Serves 10-12.

Baileys Fudge Cake

Chocolate Fudge Pudding Cake

⅔ cup (160 ml) sugar
5 tbs (75 ml) SACO Baking Cocoa
1 cup (240 ml) all-purpose flour
¾ cup (180 ml) sugar
3 tbs (45 ml) SACO Baking Cocoa
1 tsp (5 ml) baking powder
½ tsp (3 ml) salt
3 tbs (45 ml) unsalted butter, melted
1 egg
2 tbs (30 ml) milk
1 tsp (5 ml) vanilla extract
½ tsp (3 ml) almond extract
½ cup (120 ml) almonds, coarsely chopped
6 tbs (90 ml) unsalted butter, melted
1⅓ cups (320 ml) boiling water

Preheat oven to 350°F (180°C). Grease a 9-inch square pan.

Combine ⅔ cup sugar and 5 tbs cocoa; sprinkle evenly over bottom of prepared pan and set aside.

Mix flour, ¾ cup sugar, 3 tbs cocoa, baking powder and salt; set aside.

Mix 3 tbs butter, egg, milk and extracts; add to dry ingredients, stirring to combine. Stir in almonds. Combine 6 tbs butter and boiling water; pour over cocoa mixture in baking pan, without stirring. Drop batter by tablespoonful into pan.

Bake 35-40 minutes. Cool 15-20 minutes. Serves 16.

Chocolate Fudge Pudding Cake

Microwave Chocolate Banana Cake

2 squares BAKER'S Semi-Sweet Chocolate
⅓ cup (80 ml) margarine or butter
1¼ cups (295 ml) all-purpose flour
1 cup (240 ml) sugar
1 large ripe banana, mashed
¾ cup (180 ml) water
1 egg
1 tsp (5 ml) vanilla
½ tsp (3 ml) baking soda
¼ tsp (1 ml) salt
banana slices, optional

Microwave chocolate and margarine on large microwave-safe bowl on high 1-2 minutes or until margarine or butter is melted. Stir until chocolate is completely melted. Beat in flour, sugar, banana, water, egg, vanilla, baking soda and salt until smooth.

Pour into greased 8-inch square microwave-safe dish. Microwave on high 8 minutes or until toothpick inserted in center comes out clean, rotating dish ¼ turn every 2 minutes. Cool in dish on countertop. Frost cake. Garnish with banana slices, if desired. Serves 9.

Cinnamon Chocolate Cake
with Fudge Frosting

2¼ cups (540 ml) sugar
¾ cup (180 ml) butter or margarine, softened
2 tsp (10 ml) McCORMICK/SCHILLING Pure Vanilla Extract
1 tsp (5 ml) McCORMICK/SCHILLING Ground Cinnamon
6 eggs
4 oz (120 g) unsweetened baking chocolate, melted
3 cups (720 ml) sifted cake flour
2 tsp (10 ml) baking soda
1 tsp (5 ml) salt
1½ cups (355 ml) ice water, divided

Frosting:
2 12-oz pkgs (360 g each) semisweet chocolate morsels
14-oz can (420 ml) sweetened condensed milk
1 tsp (5 ml) McCORMICK/SCHILLING Pure Vanilla Extract
½ tsp (3 ml) McCORMICK/SCHILLING Ground Cinnamon
½ cup (120 ml) coffee-flavored liqueur

Preheat oven to 350°F (180°C). Lightly grease a 13x9x2-inch cake pan and line the pan with wax paper.

Place sugar, butter or margarine, vanilla, and cinnamon in large mixing bowl. Cream with electric mixer until light and fluffy. Beat in eggs and melted chocolate. Sift flour with baking soda and salt. Beat ⅓ of dry ingredients into chocolate mixture and stir in ¾ cup ice water. Repeat, using ⅓ of dry ingredients and remaining ¾ cup ice water. Stir in remaining dry ingredients.

Pour batter into prepared pan and smooth top. Bake 30-40 minutes. Do not overbake.

Frosting: Place about 1 inch water in bottom of double boiler and heat to boil. Place chocolate morsels, condensed milk, vanilla and cinnamon in top of double boiler. Cover and place over, not in, boiling water. Remove double boiler from heat. Let stand over water until chocolate has melted. Add liqueur and stir until smooth and glossy.

Remove cake from oven and cool in pan on wire rack 10 minutes. Remove from pan, peel off wax paper and place on serving plate bottom side up. Spread frosting over cake. Spread remaining frosting on sides of cake.
Serves 10.

Cinnamon Chocolate Cake with Fudge Frosting

Chocolate Chip Cake

2 cups (480 ml) plus 2 tbs (30 ml) sifted HECKERS/
*   CERESOTA Unbleached Flour*
1½ cups (355 ml) sugar
3½ tsp (18 ml) baking powder
1 tsp (5 ml) salt
½ cup (120 ml) softened shortening
1 cup (240 ml) milk
1 tsp (5 ml) vanilla
4 egg whites
½ cup (120 ml) finely chopped chocolate chips

Preheat oven to 350°F (180°C).

Sift dry ingredients into bowl. Add shortening, milk and vanilla; beat 2 minutes. Scrape bowl down. Add egg whites; beat 2 minutes, scraping bowl frequently. Fold in chocolate chips.

Pour into two well-greased and floured 8-inch layer pans (or one 13x9x2-inch baking pan). Bake 35-40 minutes for layers; 40-45 minutes for rectangle. Remove from oven; cool and frost with Cocoa Butter Frosting. Serves 10-12.

Cocoa Butter Frosting

½ cup (120 ml) softened butter
½ cup (120 ml) cocoa
3 cups (720 ml) sifted confectioners sugar
1 tsp (5 ml) vanilla
3-4 tbs (45-60 ml) evaporated milk

Cream butter and cocoa; add confectioners sugar gradually with vanilla and evaporated milk until smooth and thick.

Opposite: Chocolate Chip Cake

Chocolate Indulgence

4 eggs
½ cup (120 ml) sugar
⅓ cup (80 ml) light brown sugar, firmly packed
2 tbs (30 ml) water
1 tsp (5 ml) vanilla extract
9-oz pkg (270 g) NABISCO Famous Chocolate Wafers, finely
*   crushed, about 2 cups (480 ml) crumbs*
½ cup (120 ml) semisweet chocolate chips
¼ cup (60 ml) FLEISCHMANN'S Margarine, melted and cooled
½ cup (120 ml) PLANTERS Pecans or Walnuts, chopped
sweetened whipped cream, for garnish
hot fudge sauce, for garnish

Preheat oven to 350°F (180°C).

With mixer, beat eggs, sugars, water and vanilla until smooth; stir in crumbs, chips, margarine and nuts.

Spread in greased 8x8x2-inch baking pan. Bake for 40 minutes or until cake tests done. Cool in pan on wire rack 10 minutes; cut into squares. Serve warm topped with whipped cream and fudge sauce. Serves 9.

Chocolate Indulgence

Peanut Butter-n-Chocolate Cake

2 cups (480 ml) SOFTASILK Cake Flour
2 cups (480 ml) sugar
1 tsp (5 ml) baking soda
1 tsp (5 ml) salt
½ tsp (3 ml) baking powder
¾ cup (180 ml) water
¾ cup (180 ml) buttermilk
½ cup (120 ml) shortening
2 eggs
1 tsp (5 ml) vanilla
4 1-oz envelopes (30 g each) premelted unsweetened baking chocolate

Preheat oven to 350°F (180°C). Grease and flour two 9-inch round pans.

Beat all ingredients in large bowl on low speed 30 seconds, scraping bowl constantly. Beat on high speed 3 minutes, scraping bowl occasionally.

Pour into pans. Bake 30-35 minutes or until toothpick inserted in center comes out clean. Cool 10 minutes; remove from pans. Cool completely.

Fill layers and frost top of cake with Peanut Butter Frosting. Frost sides of cake with Chocolate Butter Frosting. Decorate cake as desired with any remaining frosting. Top cake with finely chopped peanuts, if desired. Serves 8.

Peanut Butter Frosting

¼ cup (60 ml) margarine or butter, softened
¼ cup (60 ml) peanut butter
3 cups (720 ml) confectioners sugar
1 tsp (5 ml) vanilla
2-3 tbs (30-45 ml) milk

Beat all ingredients in large bowl on low speed until smooth.

Chocolate Butter Frosting

½ cup (120 ml) margarine or butter, softened
3 cups (720 ml) confectioners sugar
2 1-oz envelopes (30 g each) premelted unsweetened baking chocolate
1½ tsp (8 ml) vanilla
2-3 tbs (30-45 ml) milk

Beat all ingredients in large bowl on low speed until smooth.

Peanut Butter-n-Chocolate Cake

Layered Spice Cake

2½ cups (590 ml) sifted cake flour
1 tsp (5 ml) baking powder
1 tsp (5 ml) baking soda
1 tsp (5 ml) salt
1 tsp (5 ml) McCORMICK/SCHILLING Ground Cinnamon
¼ tsp (1 ml) Ground Cloves
¼ tsp (1 ml) Ground Nutmeg
pinch McCORMICK/SCHILLING Ground Mace
pinch McCORMICK/SCHILLING Ground Allspice
½ cup (120 ml) soft butter
½ cup (120 ml) light brown sugar
1 cup (240 ml) granulated sugar
2 eggs
1 tsp (5 ml) McCORMICK/SCHILLING Pure Vanilla Extract
¼ tsp (1 ml) McCORMICK/SCHILLING Lemon Extract
1¼ cups (295 ml) buttermilk

Preheat oven to 350°F (180°C).

Sift together flour, baking powder, baking soda, salt, cinnamon, cloves, nutmeg, mace and allspice. Cream butter in large bowl. Add brown sugar, granulated sugar, eggs, vanilla extract and lemon extract. Beat at high speed 5 minutes or until light and fluffy. Scrape bowl often. Add sifted dry ingredients and buttermilk alternately, mixing at lowest speed just until smooth, about 1 minute.

Pour batter into 2 greased and floured 8-inch layer cake pans. Bake 30 minutes or until cake tests one. Cool 5 minutes, then turn layers out into wire racks. Cool thoroughly. Frost with Orange Cream Cheese Frosting. Serves 8.

Orange Cream Cheese Frosting

½ cup (120 ml) butter
2 8-oz pkgs (240 g each) cream cheese
1 navel orange, juice and peel
1 tsp (5 ml) McCORMICK/SCHILLING Pure Vanilla Extract
pinch salt
2 cups (480 ml) confectioners sugar

Allow butter and cream cheese to soften. Shred 1 tbs orange peel, set aside. Extract 2 tbs juice from orange. In large mixing, bowl combine butter, cream cheese, vanilla and salt. Beat well. Gradually add confectioners sugar, alternately with orange juice. Beat until smooth and creamy. Spread ½ of icing over bottom cake layer. Sprinkle 1 tsp orange peel over icing. Add top cake layer. Spread remaining icing over top. Sprinkle with remaining orange peel. Yields 3½ cups.

Layered Spice Cake

Gold Digger's Chocolate Spice Cake

1 cup (240 ml) GHIRARDELLI Ground Chocolate
1½ cups (355 ml) flour
1 cup (240 ml) sugar
1½ tsp (8 ml) pumpkin pie spice
1½ tsp (8 ml) baking powder
½ tsp (3 ml) salt
½ cup (120 ml) butter or margarine, softened
¾ cup (180 ml) milk
1½ tsp (8 ml) vanilla
2 eggs

Preheat oven to 350°F (180°C).

Into mixing bowl, sift together ground chocolate, flour, sugar, spice, baking powder and salt. Make a well in center; add butter or margarine, milk and vanilla. Mix to blend, then beat 5 minutes on high speed of mixer. Add eggs, 1 at a time, beating well after each addition.

Pour into greased 9x5-inch loaf pan. Bake 1 hour or until baked in center. Cool 15 minutes; remove from pan. Serve plain or frosted with Milk Chocolate Frosting. Serves 12-14.

Milk Chocolate Frosting

10-oz pkg (300 g) GHIRARDELLI Milk Chocolate Blocks
1 tsp (5 ml) butter
¼ cup (60 ml) milk
pinch salt
1 tsp (5 ml) vanilla

In double boiler, melt chocolate with butter over 1 inch of simmering water, stirring constantly. Stir in milk and salt. Remove from heat. Add vanilla and beat until thick and smooth. Makes enough frosting for 9x13-inch cake or 14 cupcakes.

Cocoa Spice Cakes

⅓ cup (80 ml) shortening
1 cup (240 ml) sugar
2 eggs
2 cups (480 ml) sifted PRESTO
3 tbs (45 ml) cocoa
1 tsp (5 ml) cinnamon
½ tsp (3 ml) cloves
¾ cup (180 ml) milk
1 tsp (5 ml) vanilla
½ cup (120 ml) raisins

Preheat oven to 350°F (180°C).

Cream shortening, add sugar gradually. Add eggs, 1 at a time, beating well after each addition. Add flour that has been sifted with cocoa and spices alternately with milk to which flavoring has been added. Fold in raisins sprinkled with flour.

Drop by tablespoonfuls into greased muffin pans and bake about 20-25 minutes. Frost.

Cocoa Spice Cakes

Opposite:
Gold Digger's Chocolate Spice Cake

Buttermilk Spice Cake

2½ cups (590 ml) all-purpose flour
1 cup (240 ml) granulated sugar
¾ cup (180 ml) brown sugar, packed
1 tsp (1 ml) baking powder
¾ tsp (4 ml) baking soda
5 tbs (75 ml) SACO Buttermilk Blend
1 tsp (5 ml) salt
¾ tsp (4 ml) cinnamon
¾ tsp (4 ml) allspice
½ tsp (3 ml) cloves
½ tsp (3 ml) nutmeg
1⅓ cups (320 ml) water
½ cup (120 ml) shortening
3 eggs

Have ingredients at room temperature.

Preheat oven to 350°F (180°C). Grease and flour a 13x9x2-inch baking pan or 2 round layer pans, 8 or 9x1½ inches.

Sift together dry ingredients into large mixing bowl. Add remaining ingredients and blend ½ minute on low speed, scraping bowl constantly. Beat 3 minutes in high speed, scraping bowl occasionally.

Pour into pan(s). Bake oblong pan 45 minutes, layer pans 40-45 minutes or until wooden toothpick inserted in center, comes out clean. Cool. Frost as desired or with Caramel Frosting. Serves 8-12.

Caramel Frosting

½ cup (120 ml) butter
1 cup (240 ml) dark brown sugar, firmly packed
¼ tsp (1 ml) salt
¼ cup (60 ml) milk
1 tbs (15 ml) SACO Buttermilk Blend
2 cups (480 ml) confectioners sugar

Melt butter in a saucepan over low heat, but do not let it brown. Stir in brown sugar and salt. Bring to a boil over medium heat and boil hard 2 minutes, stirring constantly. Remove from heat. Add milk and buttermilk blend, stir vigorously. Return pan to heat and bring mixture to a full boil again. Remove from heat at once and set aside to cool to lukewarm; it will take about 20 minutes.

Stir confectioners sugar into the lukewarm mixture and beat until smooth. If the frosting hardens too much to spread, beat in a few drops of milk. Makes enough to fill and frost two 9-inch layers.

Buttermilk Spice Cake

Moist and Spicy Prune Cake

2 cups (480 ml) all-purpose flour
1 tsp (5 ml) ground cinnamon
½ tsp (3 ml) ground cloves
½ tsp (3 ml) ground nutmeg
½ tsp (3 ml) ground allspice
¼ tsp (1 ml) salt
4 egg white
1½ cups (355 ml) granulated sugar
1 cup (240 ml) MOTT'S Natural Apple Sauce
2 tbs (30 ml) vegetable oil
½ cup (120 ml) non-ft buttermilk
1 cup (240 ml) stewed prunes, mashed

Lemon Almond Icing:
2 cups (480 ml) confectioners sugar
1½ tsp (8 ml) lemon juice
¼ tsp (1 ml) almond extract

Preheat oven to 350°F (180°C). Spray bundt pan with nonstick cooking pan.

In a medium bowl, sift together flour, baking soda, spices and salt. In a separate large bowl, whisk together egg whites, sugar, applesauce and vegetable oil. Add flour mixture alternating with buttermilk, mixing well between additions. Stir in prunes and mix well.

Pour batter into prepared pan and bake for 60 minutes or until toothpick inserted in center comes out clean. Drizzle Icing over cooled cake. Wrap cake loosely to store. Serves 14.

Lemon Almond Icing: Combine confectioners sugar, lemon juice and almond extract, plus enough water to make a thick glaze.

Moist and Spicy Prune Cake

Pumpkin Vermont Spice Cake

1½ cups (355 ml) granulated sugar
¾ cup (180 ml) butter, softened
3 eggs
1½ cups (355 ml) LIBBY'S Solid Pack Pumpkin
1½ tsp (8 ml) vanilla extract
½ cup (120 ml) CARNATION Evaporated Milk
¼ cup (60 ml) water
3 cups (720 ml) all-purpose flour
3½ tsp (18 ml) baking powder
1 tsp (5 ml) baking soda
½ tsp (3 ml) salt
1½ tsp (8 ml) ground cinnamon
¾ tsp (4 ml) ground nutmeg
¼ tsp (1 ml) ground cloves
¼ tsp (1 ml) ginger
chopped nuts and halves, optional

Preheat oven to 325°F (165°C).

Cream sugar and butter in large mixing bowl. Add eggs; beat for 2 minutes. Add pumpkin and vanilla; mix well. Beat in evaporated milk and water. Combine flour, baking powder, baking soda, salt and spices. Gradually beat into pumpkin mixture.

Spread evenly into 2 greased and floured 9-inch round cake pans. Bake for 35-40 minutes or until wooden toothpick inserted in center comes out clean. Cool in pans on wire racks for 15 minutes. Remove from pans; cool completely.

To assemble, cut each cake in half horizontally with long, serrated knife. Frost between layers and on top of cake. Garnish with nuts, if desired. Serves 12.

Maple Frosting

11 oz (330 g) cream cheese, softened
⅓ cup (80 ml) butter, softened
3½ cups (840 ml) sifted confectioners sugar
2-3 tsp (10-15 ml) maple flavoring

Beat cream cheese, butter and confectioners sugar in mixing bowl until fluffy. Add maple flavoring; mix well.

Pumpkin Vermont Spice Cake

Little Chocolate Spice Cakes with Strawberries and Mocha Sauce

⅓ cup (80 ml) semisweet chocolate pieces
3 tbs (45 ml) butter
¼ cup (60 ml) sifted flour
¼ tsp (1 ml) cinnamon
pinch ginger
pinch nutmeg
pinch cloves
pinch salt
2 egg whites
pinch cream of tartar
6 tbs sugar
½ cup (120 ml) whipping cream
1 lb (455 g) DRISCOLL Strawberries, rinsed, hulled and sliced

Preheat oven to 375°F (190°C).

Melt chocolate and butter over hot, not boiling, water or in microwave for about 60 seconds, checking after 30 seconds and stirring to melt evenly. Set aside.

Stir together flour and spices. Beat egg whites and cream of tartar until foamy. Add sugar, 1 tbs at a time, beating constantly, until whites are stiff and sugar is dissolved (rub between thumb and forefinger to test). Sprinkle flour mixture over egg whites and gently fold in. Gradually fold in slightly cooled melted chocolate.

Gently spoon batter in each of 8 buttered and floured nonstick 2¾-inch muffin cups. Bake just until top springs back when lightly touched, about 16 minutes. Let cakes cool in pan 5 minutes, then turn out onto rack to cool completely. Wrap tightly in plastic wrap or foil if not to be used immediately, or freeze for later use.

Whip cream until stiff. Split chocolate cakes crosswise and fill with some of the whipped cream and a few berry slices. Arrange each cake on dessert plate and surround with additional berry slices and more whipped cream. Drizzle with warm Mocha Sauce. Serves 8.

Mocha Sauce

⅓ cup (80 ml) milk
¼ cup (60 ml) sugar
1 tsp (5 ml) vanilla extract
½ tsp (3 ml) instant espresso powder
⅔ cup (160 ml) semi-sweet chocolate pieces

Combine all ingredients except chocolate in glass measuring cup or bowl and microwave on high for 1½-2 minutes or until milk is very hot. Add chocolate pieces and stir until chocolate is melted and mixture is smooth. Serve warm or cover and chill to reheat for service later.

Peppery Gingerbread

2 cups (480 ml) all-purpose flour
1 cup (240 ml) light molasses
¾ cup (180 ml) milk
½ cup (120 ml) sugar
½ cup (120 ml) butter or margarine, softened
1 tbs (15 ml) TABASCO Pepper Sauce
1½ tsp (8 ml) ground ginger
1 tsp (5 ml) ground cinnamon
1 tsp (5 ml) baking soda
1 large egg
confectioners sugar

Preheat oven to 325°F (165°C). Grease and flour 9x9-inch baking pan.

In large bowl with mixer at low speed, beat flour, molasses, milk, sugar, butter or margarine, pepper sauce, ginger, cinnamon, baking soda and egg until well blended and smooth. Increase speed to medium; beat 2 minutes, occasionally scraping bowl with rubber spatula.

Pour batter into pan; bake 1 hour or until toothpick inserted in center comes out clean. Cool in pan on wire rack. Sprinkle top of gingerbread with confectioners sugar. Serves 12.

Gingerbread

½ cup (120 ml) shortening
2 tbs (30 ml) sugar
1 egg
2½ cups (590 ml) sifted *WASHINGTON All-Purpose Flour*
1 tsp (5 ml) baking soda
½ tsp (3 ml) salt
1 tsp (5 ml ginger
1 tsp (5 ml) cinnamon
1 cup (240 ml) dark molasses
1 cup (240 ml) boiling water

Preheat oven to 325°F (165°C). Grease bottom of 9-inch square pan.

    Place first three ingredients in large mixing bowl. Beat together at medium speed until well blended. Sift next five ingredients together into creamed mixture. Blend thoroughly at medium speed. Add molasses and boiling water. Blend well at low speed.

    Pour into pan. Bake 45-50 minutes. Serve warm with apple sauce or whipped cream. Serves 16.

A Shade Lighter Gingerbread

½ cup (120 ml) shortening
½ cup (120 ml) sugar
2 eggs
½ cup (120 ml) corn syrup
1½ cups (355 ml) sifted *PRESTO*
1 tsp (5 ml) ginger
1 tsp (5 ml) cinnamon
½ cup (120 ml) water
1 tsp (5 ml) vanilla
½ cup (120 ml) nuts, chopped

Preheat oven to 350°F (180°C).

    Cream shortening, add sugar gradually. Add eggs 1 at a time, beating well after each addition. Mix in corn syrup. Add flour sifted with spices alternately with water to which vanilla has been added. Fold in chopped nuts.

    Put in well-greased square pan, 8½x8½x2½ inches and bake for 40-50 minutes. When cooled, frost with lemon or orange frosting. Serves 16.

A Shade Darker Gingerbread

½ cup (120 ml) boiling water
½ cup (120 ml) shortening
½ cup (120 ml) dark brown sugar
½ cup (120 ml) dark molasses
2 eggs, beaten
1½ cups (355 ml) sifted *WASHINGTON Self-Rising Flour*
pinch baking soda
¾ tsp (4 ml) ginger
¾ tsp (4 ml) cinnamon

Preheat oven to 350°F (180°C). Grease 8-inch square pan.

    Combine boiling water and shortening in large mixing bowl. Add brown sugar, molasses and eggs; beat 1 minute. Blend remaining ingredients into liquid mixture at low speed, then beat 2 minutes at medium speed.

    Pour into pan. Bake 35 minutes. Cool in pan. Serves 16.

Opposite: Gingerbread

Cranberry Christmas Gingerbread

1½ cups (355 ml) sifted all-purpose flour
1 tsp (5 ml) ARM & HAMMER Baking Soda
1 tsp (5 ml) ground ginger
¼ tsp (1 ml) salt
½ cup (120 ml) butter, softened
½ cup (120 ml) sugar
⅓ cup (80 ml) whole-berry cranberry sauce
1 egg
½ cup (120 ml) unsulphured molasses
½ cup (120 ml) boiling water
confectioners sugar, optional

Preheat oven to 350°F (180°C). Grease and flour 8x8x2-inch square baking pan.

Sift together flour, baking soda, ginger and salt; set aside.

Using an electric mixer in a large bowl, cream butter and sugar until light and fluffy. Beat in cranberry sauce and egg thoroughly; blend in molasses. Gradually stir in dry ingredients and beat thoroughly. Stir in boiling water.

Turn into the baking pan. Bake gingerbread for 45 minutes or until a toothpick inserted in center comes out clean. Cool in pan for 20 minutes; remove from pan and cool on rack. To create a floral design, sift confectioners sugar over a paper doily placed on gingerbread. Serves 16.

Opposite: Cranberry Christmas Gingerbread

Gingerbread with Fresh Fruit Sauce

2 cups (480 ml) all-purpose flour
1 tsp (5 ml) baking soda
1 tsp (5 ml) ginger
½ tsp (3 ml) cinnamon
¼ tsp (1 ml) salt
1 cup (240 ml) GRANDMA'S Molasses Unsulphured
½ cup (120 ml) margarine or butter, softened
2 eggs
½ cup (120 ml) milk

Fresh Fruit Sauce:
¼ cup (60 ml) GRANDMA'S Molasses Unsulphured
¼ cup (60 ml) brown sugar, firmly packed
1 tbs (15 ml) cornstarch
1 cup (240 ml) orange juice
2 tbs (30 ml) margarine or butter
1 tsp (5 ml) grated orange peel
11-oz can (330 g) mandarin orange segments, drained
8-oz can (240 g) pineapple chunks, drained
1 cup (240 ml) green grapes, halved

Preheat oven to 350°F (180°C). Grease 9-inch springform or square pan.

In medium bowl, combine flour, baking soda, ginger, cinnamon and salt. Set aside.

In large bowl, combine 1 cup molasses, ½ cup margarine or butter and eggs; mix well. Alternately add dry ingredients and milk, beginning and ending with dry ingredients; mix well.

Pour into prepared pan. Bake at 350°F (180°C) for 35-45 minutes or until toothpick inserted in center comes out clean. Cool 15 minutes. Remove sides of pan; cool on wire rack.

Fresh Fruit Sauce: In medium saucepan, combine ¼ cup molasses, brown sugar and cornstarch; mix well. Gradually stir in orange juice. Bring to a boil. Cook over medium heat for 5 minutes or until thickened, stirring constantly. Remove from heat. Add 2 tbs margarine or butter and orange peel; mix well. Carefully stir in fruit. Serve warm Fruit Sauce over slices of gingerbread. Serves 9.

Jeweled Fruitcake

1 cup (240 ml) dried apricots
boiling water
1½ cups (355 ml) SUN•MAID Raisins
1½ cups (355 ml) Brazil nuts
1 cup (240 ml) candied cherries
1 cup (240 ml) all-purpose flour
½ cup (120 ml) sugar
½ tsp (3 ml) baking powder
½ tsp (3 ml) pumpkin pie spice
¼ tsp (1 ml) salt
2 eggs, beaten

Preheat oven to 300°F (150°C). Grease 9x5-inch loaf pan.

Cut apricots in half; cover with boiling water and let stand 10 minutes. Drain well. Combine apricots, raisins, nuts and candied cherries in large bowl. Combine flour, sugar, baking powder, pumpkin pie spice and salt in separate bowl; fold into fruit mixture. Stir in eggs; mix well.

Spoon batter into greased pan; pack down. Garnish with additional candied fruits, if desired. Bake for 50-60 minutes. Cool in pan on wire rack. Cover; let stand overnight before slicing. Serves 12.

Note: Butter or shortening is not needed in this recipe. Cake can be made ahead and keeps well.

Jeweled Fruitcake

Sweet and Spicy Fruitcake

3 cups (720 ml) chopped walnuts
2 cups (480 ml) chopped dried figs
1 cup (240 ml) chopped dried apricots
1 cup (240 ml) chocolate chips
1½ cups (355 ml) all-purpose flour
¾ cup (180 ml) granulated sugar
4 large eggs
¼ cup (60 ml) butter or margarine, softened
⅓ cup (80 ml) apple jelly*
2 tbs (30 ml) orange-flavored liqueur
1 tbs (15 ml) grated orange peel
1 tbs (15 ml) vanilla extract
2 tsp (10 ml) TABASCO Pepper Sauce
1 tsp (5 ml) baking powder

Preheat oven to 325°F (165°C). Grease two 3-cup heat-proof bowls. Line bottom and sides of each with foil; grease foil.

In small mixing bowl, combine walnuts, figs, apricots, chocolate chips and ¼ cup of the flour to mix well.

In large mixing bowl, with mixer at low speed, beat sugar, eggs and butter or margarine until well blended. Add jelly, remaining ingredients and 1¼ cups flour. Beat at low speed until blended. Toss mixture with dried fruit in large bowl.

Spoon into prepared bowls. Cover bowls with greased foil. Bake 40 minutes; uncover and bake 40 minutes longer or until toothpick inserted in center comes out clean. Remove to wire racks to cool.

If desired, brush cooled fruitcakes with 1 tbs melted apple jelly and sprinkle each with 2 tbs finely chopped dried apricots. Store in cool place for up to 3 weeks. Yields 2 small fruitcakes.

* Or, substitute ⅓ cup McIlhenny Farms Pepper Jelly for apple jelly and omit Tabasco Pepper Sauce.

Opposite: Sweet and Spicy Fruitcake

Nutty Chip Fruitcake

2 cups (480 ml) all-purpose flour
2 tsp (10 ml) baking powder
¼ tsp (1 ml) salt
2 cups (480 ml) chopped pecans or almonds
1 cup (240 ml) chopped dates
1 cup (420 ml) red or green glacé cherries, halved
⅔ cup (160 ml) semisweet chocolate morsels
6 eggs
1 cup (240 ml) sugar
1 tsp (5 ml) vanilla
additional halved glacé cherries, optional

Preheat oven to 300°F (150°C).

In large bowl, stir together flour, baking powder and salt. Stir in nuts, fruits and chocolate morsels. Set aside.

In small mixing bowl at medium speed, beat together eggs, sugar and vanilla until well blended. Fold into reserved flour mixture.

Pour into greased and floured 9-cup fluted tube pan. Bake until lightly browned and cake tester inserted in center comes out clean, about 50-60 minutes. Cool on wire rack 10 minutes. Remove from pan and cool completely. Garnish with additional halved cherries, if desired. Serves 12.

Courtesy of the American Egg Board.

St. Francis Dark Fruitcake

1 lb (455 g) chopped mixed candied fruit
1 cup (240 ml) whole candied cherries
1 cup (240 ml) golden raisins
1 cup (240 ml) sweet sherry wine
1 cup (20 ml) butter, softened
1 cup (240 ml) brown sugar, packed
5 eggs
1 cup (240 ml) pecan halves
1 cup (240 ml) slivered almonds
2⅓ cups (560 ml) unsifted flour
1 cup (40 ml) GHIRARDELLI Ground Chocolate
1 tsp (5 ml) baking powder
1 tsp (5 ml) salt
2 tsp (10 ml) cinnamon
1 tsp (5 ml) allspice
½ tsp (3 ml) nutmeg
½ tsp (3 ml) ground cloves
2-4 tbs (30-60 ml) light corn syrup

Preheat oven to at 275°F (135°C).

Soak mixed fruit, cherries and raisins in the sherry overnight.

In a large bowl, cream butter, gradually adding brown sugar. Beat in eggs, 1 at a time. Stir in fruit and sherry mixture, pecans and almonds. Sift flour with ground chocolate, baking powder, salt and spices. Gradually stir dry ingredients into fruit mixture.

Line two 9x5-inch loaf pans with lightly greased waxed paper.

Divide batter into prepared pans. For miniature fruitcakes, fill greased muffin cups about ⅔ full. Decorate tops with additional candied cherry halves and nuts, as desired. Bake for about 2 hours for loaves and 1 hour for individual cakes or until dry when tested with a toothpick.

For surface glaze, brush with corn syrup immediately after removing from oven. Cool cakes on wire rack. Remove from pans. Wrap fruitcakes in cloth dampened with additional sherry. Overwrap with foil or place in tight metal container. Fruit cakes should age 1-4 weeks for mellow flavor. For best results, chill cakes before slicing. Yields 4½ lbs of fruit cake.

Opposite: **Nutty Chip Fruitcake**

Super Moist Carrot Cake

1 cup (240 ml) JACK FROST Granulated Sugar
1 cup (240 ml) JACK FROST Light Brown Sugar, packed
2 cups (480 ml) all-purpose flour
1 tsp (5 ml) baking powder
1 tsp (5 ml) baking soda
1 tsp (5 ml) salt
1 tsp (5 ml) cinnamon
3 cups (720 ml) finely shredded carrots
1½ cups (355 ml) vegetable oil
4 large eggs
2 tsp (10 ml) vanilla
½ cup (120 ml) chopped walnuts
½ cup (120 ml) raisins

Preheat oven to 325°F (165°C). Grease and flour a 13x9-inch* baking pan
In a large mixer bowl, combine first 7 ingredients. Add carrots, oil, eggs and vanilla, beating for 2-3 minutes on medium. Stir in nuts and raisins.

Pour into baking pan and bake 50-60 minutes. Cool on rack. Frost with Cream Cheese Frosting. Refrigerate until serving. Serves 12-16.

* Two 9-inch baking pans can be used. Reduce baking times to 40 minutes.

Cream Cheese Frosting

3-oz pkg (90 g) cream cheese, softened
¼ cup (60 ml) butter or margarine, softened
1 tsp (5 ml) vanilla
1½ cups (355 ml) JACK FROST Confectioners Sugar

In a large bowl, beat together cream cheese, butter or margarine and vanilla until light and fluffy. Gradually add confectioners sugar, beating until smooth. Spread over cooled 13x9-inch cake.

To frost two 9-inch cakes, double the frosting recipe.

Carrot Cake

2 cups (480 ml) flour
2 tsp (10 ml) baking powder
1½ tsp (8 ml) ARM & HAMMER Baking Soda
½ tsp (3 ml) cinnamon
2 cups (480 ml) sugar
1 cup (240 ml) oil
1 cup (240 ml) egg substitute or 4 eggs
2 cups (480 ml) grated carrots
8-oz can (240 g) crushed pineapple, drained
½ cup (120 ml) chopped nuts
3½-oz can (105 g) coconut

Preheat oven to 350°F (180°C). Grease and flour a 10-inch tube pan

Sift dry ingredients together in a large bowl. Add sugar, oil, egg substitute or eggs and mix well. Add carrots, nuts, coconut and pineapple and blend well. Pour into pan. Bake for 1 hour. Serves 16.

Opposite: **Super Moist Carrot Cake**

Low-Fat Applesauce Carrot Cake

2 cups (480 ml) LUCKY LEAF Regular, Natural or
   Chunky Apple Sauce
2 cups (480 ml) sugar
½ cup (120 ml) vegetable oil
3 egg whites, slightly beaten
2 tsp (10 ml) vanilla extract
2 cups (480 ml) unsifted all-purpose flour
2 tsp (10 ml) baking soda
2 tsp (10 ml) cinnamon
½ tsp (3 ml) salt
2 cups (480 ml) shredded carrots
1½ cups (355 ml) raisins
vegetable cooking spray

Light Apple-Cream Cheese Frosting:
3-oz pkg (90 g) light cream cheese (Neufchatel)
1 lb (455 g) confectioners sugar
2 tbs (30 ml) LUCKY LEAF Apple Juice
1 tsp (5 ml) vanilla extract

Preheat oven to 350°F (180°C). Grease a 13x9-inch pan lightly with vegetable cooking spray and flour it.
In large bowl, combine applesauce, sugar, oil, egg whites and vanilla, blending with spoon. In separate bowl, combine flour, baking soda, cinnamon and salt. Stir into applesauce mixture. Add carrots and raisins.

Spread in pan. Bake for 50-55 minutes or until cake is firm when touched lightly in center. Cool completely. Frost with Light Apple-Cream Cheese Frosting. Serves 12-16.

Light Apple-Cream Cheese Frosting: In large mixing bowl, beat cream cheese until soft and fluffy. Add confectioners sugar, apple juice and vanilla extract. Beat until smooth and spreading consistency.

Low-Fat Carrot Cake

2 cups (480 ml) granulated sugar
1½ cups (355 ml) prune purée*
4 large egg whites
2 tsp (10 ml) vanilla
2¼ cups (540 ml) all-purpose flour
2 tsp (10 ml) baking soda
2 tsp (10 ml) cinnamon
1 tsp (10 ml) nutmeg
½ tsp (3 ml) salt
3 cups (720 ml) grated carrots
1 cup (240 ml) SUN•MAID Raisins
½ cup (120 ml) DIAMOND Walnuts

Frosting:
6 oz (180 g) Neufchatel cheese
3 cups (720 ml) confectioners sugar, sifted
½ tsp (3 ml) vanilla

Preheat oven to 375°F (190°C). Coat a 13x9-inch baking pan with vegetable cooking spray.

Combine sugar, prune purée, egg whites and vanilla; mix until well blended. Combine flour, baking soda, cinnamon, nutmeg and salt. Stir into batter; mix well. Stir in carrots, raisins and walnuts. Spread batter in prepared pan. Bake 30-35 minutes, until toothpick inserted in center comes out clean. Cool on rack. Spread evenly with Frosting. Cut into squares. Serves 12.

Frosting: Beat together ingredients until smooth and creamy.

*Prune Purée: Combine 2 cups (480 ml) Sunsweet Pitted Prunes and 9 tbs (135 ml) water in container of food processor. Pulse on and off until prunes are finely chopped. Yields 1½ cups.

Low-Fat Carrot Cake

Opposite: Low-Fat Applesauce Carrot Cake

Orange Carrot Cake

1 cup (240 ml) margarine or butter, softened
1 cup (240 ml) GRANDMA'S Molasses Unsulphured
4 eggs
½ cup (120 ml) orange juice
1 cup (240 ml) all-purpose flour
1 cup (240 ml) whole wheat flour
2 tsp (10 ml) baking soda
1 tsp (5 ml) cinnamon
½ tsp (3 ml) salt
2 cups (480 ml) shredded carrots
½ cup (120 ml) chopped walnuts

Frosting:
3-oz pkg (90 g) cream cheese, softened
2 tbs (30 ml) margarine or butter, softened
1½ cups (355 ml) confectioners sugar
1 tsp (5 ml) grated orange peel

Preheat oven to 350°F (180°C). Grease two 8- or 9-inch round cake pans.

In large bowl, combine margarine or butter, molasses, eggs and orange juice; mix well. Stir in flours, baking soda, cinnamon and salt; mix well. Stir in carrots and walnuts.

Pour into prepared pans. Bake at 350°F (180°C) 30-35 minutes or until toothpick inserted in center comes out clean. Cool 15 minutes; remove from pans. Cool completely.

Frosting: In small bowl, combine all ingredients; beat until smooth. Place one cake layer on serving plate; spread with frosting. Top with second layer; spread with frosting. If desired, garnish with additional grated orange peel or walnuts. Serves 12.

Opposite:
Chocolate Carrot Cake
with Dark Chocolate Frosting

Chocolate Carrot Cake with Dark Chocolate Frosting

2 cups (480 ml) cake flour
2 cups (480 ml) granulated sugar
3 tbs (45 ml) unsweetened cocoa powder
1 tsp (5 ml) baking powder
1 tsp (5 ml) McCORMICK/SCHILLING Ground Cinnamon
¼ tsp (1 ml) McCORMICK/SCHILLING Ground Mace
pinch McCORMICK/SCHILLING Ground Nutmeg
1 cup (240 ml) butter or margarine, softened
4 eggs
1 tbs (15 ml) McCORMICK/SCHILLING Pure Vanilla Extract
3 cups (720 ml) shredded carrots
4 squares semisweet chocolate, cut into small pieces
1 cup (240 ml) finely chopped walnuts

Dark Chocolate Frosting:
4 squares semisweet chocolate
2 tbs (30 ml) light corn syrup
1 tsp (5 ml) McCORMICK/SCHILLING Pure Vanilla Extract
dash McCORMICK/SCHILLING Pure Almond Extract
pinch McCORMICK/SCHILLING Ground Cinnamon
1 cup (240 ml) confectioners' sugar
2 tbs (30 ml) hot water

Preheat oven to 350°F (180°C). Lightly grease and flour 13x9x2-inch baking pan.

Sift flour, granulated sugar, cocoa, baking powder, cinnamon, mace and nutmeg into bowl. Place butter or margarine in large mixing bowl and cream with electric mixer until fluffy. Add eggs and vanilla and beat until light and creamy. Add dry ingredients and carrots. Beat at medium speed 2 minutes. Stir in chocolate pieces and walnuts.

Pour into prepared pan. Bake 40-45 minutes.

Dark Chocolate Frosting: Melt chocolate in top of double boiler over (not in) simmering water. Add corn syrup, vanilla, almond extract and cinnamon and mix well with spoon. Stir in confectioners sugar. Add hot water gradually, mixing until smooth. Frost cake in pan while cake is still hot. Serves 12-16.

Gold Rush Carrot Cake

1½ cups (355 ml) oil
1⅔ cups (400 ml) sugar
4 eggs
2 cups (480 ml) flour
⅓ cup (80 ml) GHIRARDELLI Ground Chocolate
2 tsp (10 ml) baking soda
2 tsp (10 ml) cinnamon
1 tsp (5 ml) salt
3 cups (720 ml) shredded carrots, packed
¾ cup (180 ml) finely chopped walnuts

Preheat oven to 350°F (180°C). Grease bottom of 9x13-inch cake pan.

Mix oil with sugar; add eggs one at a time, beating well after each addition. Sift flour with ground chocolate, baking soda, cinnamon and salt. Add dry ingredients to creamed mixture. Mix in carrots and nuts.

Spread batter into pan. Bake 45-50 minutes. Cool 30 minutes. Frost warm cake. Sprinkle with additional chopped nuts or grated chocolate, if desired. Serves 12-16.

Cocoa Molasses Bundt Cake

2 tbs (30 ml) margarine, melted
½ cup (120 ml) MOTT'S Apple Sauce
1 cup (240 ml) granulated sugar
½ cup (120 ml) GRANDMA'S Molasses
1 whole egg
1½ cups (355 ml) nonfat buttermilk
1¾ cups (415 ml) all-purpose flour
3 tbs (45 ml) unsweetened cocoa
1½ tsp (8 ml) baking powder
1½ tsp (8 ml) baking soda
½ tsp (3 ml) salt
3 egg whites, beaten until stiff
confectioners sugar

Preheat oven to 350°F (180°C). Spray a bundt pan with nonstick cooking spray and dust with flour.

In a large bowl, mix melted margarine, applesauce, sugar, molasses, egg and buttermilk. In a separate bowl, mix flour, cocoa, baking powder, baking soda and salt. Using mixer on low speed, mix flour mixture and liquid mixture. When moistened, beat on high speed for 3 minutes. Gently fold in beaten egg whites.

Pour batter into prepared pan. Bake 5 minutes or until tester inserted in center of cake comes out clean. Remove from oven and cool on rack for 15 minutes before removing from pan. Cool completely and sift confectioners sugar on top of cake just before serving. Serves 12.

Poppy Seed Cake

4 eggs, room temperature
1½ cups (355 ml) sugar, divided
1 cup (240 ml) butter or margarine, softened
⅓ cup (80 ml) McCORMICK/SCHILLING Poppy Seeds
1 tsp (5 ml) baking soda
1 cup (240 ml) dairy sour cream, room temperature
2 cups (480 ml) sifted cake flour

Preheat oven to 350°F (180°C).

Separate eggs and set egg yolks aside. Place egg whites in mixing bowl and beat with electric mixer until almost stiff. Gradually beat in ½ cup sugar and continue beating until stiff peaks form when beaters are lifted. Set aside.

Place butter or margarine and remaining 1 cup sugar in large mixing bowl. Cream with electric mixer until light and fluffy. Add reserved egg yolks, 1 at a time, beating well after each addition. Stir in poppy seeds. Combine baking soda and sour cream. Add to batter alternating with flour, mixing after each addition just until smooth. Gently fold in beaten egg whites.

Spoon into ungreased 9-inch tube pan. Bake 1 hour. Cool cake in pan on wire rack 5-10 minutes. Loosen sides of pan and carefully turn out onto wire rack. Cool cake completely on rack. Serves 12.

Opposite: Cocoa Molasses Bundt Cake

Jelly Roll

4 eggs
1 cup (240 ml) sugar
1 cup (240 ml) sifted WASHINGTON Self-Rising Flour
1 tsp (5 ml) vanilla

Preheat oven to 375°F (190°C). Line 15x10x1-inch jelly roll pan with aluminum foil.

Beat eggs until very thick (high speed about 4 minutes). Gradually beat in sugar. Fold flour and vanilla into egg mixture.

Pour into pan. Bake about 12 minutes. Remove from pan with foil. Let cool 5 minutes.

Roll cake and foil together from narrow edge. When cool, unroll, remove foil. Spread jelly on cake; reroll. Sprinkle with confectioners sugar. Wrap in foil or wax paper. Serves 8-10.

Jelly Roll

Vanilla Cake Roll

5 egg yolks
1 cup (240 ml) sugar
pinch salt
2 tsp (10 ml) McCORMICK Pure Vanilla Extract
1 cup (240 ml) flour
1 tsp (5 ml) baking powder
5 egg whites
Vanilla Filling (below)
1 cup (240 ml) toasted, slivered almonds or pine nuts

Vanilla Filling:
2 3¹⁄₈-oz pkgs (94 g each) vanilla pudding mix
pinch McCORMICK Nutmeg
3¼ cups milk
1½ tsp (8 ml) McCORMICK Pure Vanilla Extract
¼ tsp (1 ml) McCORMICK Imitation Rum Extract

Preheat oven to 375°F (190°C).

Beat egg yolks until light. Gradually add sugar and salt. Beat until creamy. Stir in vanilla. Sift flour with baking powder. Add gradually to egg mixture. Beat until smooth. Whip egg whites until stiff but not dry. Fold in batter.

Spread in a greased and wax paper-lined 11x15x1-inch jelly roll pan. Bake 12-15 minutes.

Loosen edges of cake and turn out on clean kitchen towel. Trim off any hard edges. Roll cake in towel. Cool. Unroll cake. Reserve about ½ cup Filling for top. Spread remaining Filling over cake to within 1 inch of edges. Roll loosely. Spread reserved filling over cake and sprinkle generously with slivered almonds or pine nuts. Serves 8-10.

Vanilla Filling: In a large saucepan, combine pudding mix and nutmeg. Gradually stir in milk. Cook over medium heat, stirring constantly until mixture thickens. Remove from heat and stir in extracts. Chill.

Opposite: Vanilla Cake Roll

Mocha-Cream Roll

5 eggs, separated
1 cup (240 ml) DOMINO Chocolate Flavored Confectioners Sugar
pinch salt

Mocha-Cream Filling:
1½ cups (355 ml) heavy or whipping cream
¼ cup (60 ml) DOMINO Chocolate Flavored Confectioners Sugar
2 tbs (30 ml) cold strong coffee

Chocolate Glaze:
½ cup (120 ml) DOMINO Chocolate Flavored Confectioners Sugar
2-3 tsp (10-15 ml) water

Preheat oven to 400°F (205°C). Grease 15½x10½-inch jelly roll pan; line bottom of pan with waxed paper; grease and flour paper.

In large bowl with mixer at high speed, beat egg whites until soft peaks form. Beating at high speed, gradually sprinkle in ½ cup confectioners sugar, beating thoroughly after each addition. Continue beating until egg whites stand in stiff, glossy peaks. Set aside.

In small bowl with same beaters and with mixer at high speed, beat egg yolks until thick and lemon-colored. Reduce speed to low; beat in salt and ½ cup confectioners sugar until sugar is completely dissolved, occasionally scraping bowl with rubber spatula. With wire whisk or rubber spatula, gently fold yolk mixture into beaten whites just until mixture is blended.

Spread batter evenly in pan and bake 15 minutes or until top springs back when lightly touched with finger.

When cake is done, with small spatula, immediately loosen edges from side of pan; invert cake onto clean cloth towel. Gently peel waxed paper from bottom of cake. Roll towel with cake from narrow end, jelly-roll fashion. Cool completely, placing it seam side down, on wire rack. Meanwhile, prepare Mocha-Cream Filling.

When cake is cool, unroll from towel. Evenly spread Filling on cake almost to edges. Starting at same narrow end, roll up cake without towel. Place cake, seam side down, on platter.

Prepare Chocolate Glaze to drizzle over top of roll to make a decorative design. Keep roll in refrigerator until ready to serve. Serves 10-12.

Mocha-Cream Filling: In medium bowl combine all ingredients. With mixer at medium speed, beat until stiff peaks form.

Chocolate Glaze: In small bowl, stir together sugar and water until smooth.

Mocha-Cream Roll

Chocolate Cake Roll

¾ cup (180 ml) all-purpose flour
¼ cup (60 ml) SACO Baking Cocoa
1 tsp (5 ml) baking powder
¼ tsp (1 ml) salt
3 eggs
1 cup (240 ml) granulated sugar
⅓ cup (80 ml) water
1 tsp (5 ml) vanilla extract
confectioners sugar
1 cup (240 ml) heavy cream, whipped
crushed peppermint stick

Preheat oven to 375°F (190°C). Line 15½x10½x1-inch jelly roll pan with aluminum foil or waxed paper. Grease paper.

In a separate mixing bowl, sift together flour, cocoa, baking powder and salt; set aside.

In small mixing bowl, beat eggs about 5 minutes or until thick and lemon colored. Pour beaten eggs into large mixing bowl and gradually beat in sugar. By hand, blend in water and vanilla. Gradually stir in flour mixture, beating just until batter is smooth. Do not overbeat.

Pour into jelly roll pan, spreading batter into corners. Bake 12-15 minutes or until toothpick inserted in center comes out clean.

Loosen cake from edges of pan and invert on towel sprinkle with confectioners sugar. Carefully remove foil and trim off stiff edges if necessary. While hot, roll cake and towel starting at narrow end. Cool on wire rack. Unroll cake and remove towel.

Spread whipped cream over cake. Roll up. Sprinkle top of roll with confectioners sugar and crushed peppermint stick. Serve cold. Serves 10-12.

Chocolate Cake Roll

Almond Raspberry Cream Roll

¾ cup (180 ml) cake flour
1 tsp (5 ml) baking powder
¼ tsp (1 ml) salt
3 eggs
1 cup (40 ml) granulated sugar
⅓ cup (80 ml) water
1½ tsp (8 ml) vanilla extract, divided
1 tsp (5 ml) almond extract
confectioners sugar
2 cups (480 ml) heavy cream
¾ cup (180 ml) confectioners sugar
3 tbs (45 ml) amaretto liqueur or 1 tsp (5 ml) almond extract
1¼ cups (295 ml) BLUE DIAMOND Blanched Slivered Almonds, toasted, divided
⅔ cup (160 ml) seedless raspberry jam, stirred until smooth and spreadable

Preheat oven to 375°F (190°C). Line 15½x10½x1-inch jelly roll pan with foil or parchment paper; grease well with shortening.

Combine flour, baking powder and salt; reserve.

Beat eggs on high speed until foamy, about 3-5 minutes. Gradually beat in granulated sugar. On low speed, beat in water, ½ tsp vanilla and almond extract. Gradually beat in flour mixture until smooth.

Pour evenly into pan. Bake 12-15 minutes or until toothpick inserted in center comes out clean.

Meanwhile, sift confectioners sugar onto a towel until evenly coated. When cake is done, immediately reverse pan onto towel. Peel off foil. Roll up cake and towel together from narrow end; cool thoroughly on wire rack.

Meanwhile, whip heavy cream, ¾ cup confectioners' sugar, remaining 1 tsp vanilla and amaretto until stiff. Finely chop 1 cup almonds and fold into ½ of the whipped cream. Reserve remaining whipped cream in refrigerator.

Unroll cooled cake. Spread with raspberry jam. Spread whipped cream-almond mixture on top of jam, leaving a 1-inch border at one end. Carefully roll cake, starting from opposite end.

Place on serving plate, seam side down. Frost cake with remaining whipped cream. Stick tip of each remaining almond into cake in rows; about ¾-inch apart, until cake is covered and resembles a porcupine. Serves 8-10.

Forty-Niner Chocolate Roll

4 eggs, separated
1 tsp (5 ml) vanilla
½ cup (120 ml) GHIRARDELLI Ground Chocolate
¼ cup (60 ml) boiling water
¾ cup (180 ml) sifted cake flour
½ tsp (3 ml) baking powder
pinch salt
½ cup (120 ml) sugar
confectioners sugar

Filling:
½ pint (240 ml) whipping cream
3 tbs (45 ml) confectioners sugar
15¼-oz can (458 g) crushed pineapple, drained
3 tbs (45 ml) rum

Preheat oven to 325°F (165°C).

Beat egg yolks with vanilla. Blend ground chocolate with boiling water; beat into egg yolk mixture. Sift flour with baking powder. Gradually add dry ingredients to egg yolk mixture until smooth. Beat egg whites with salt until soft peaks form. Gradually add sugar, beating until stiff peaks. Using metal spatula, fold egg whites into chocolate mixture.

Pour batter into greased and floured waxed paper-lined 10x15-inch jelly roll pan. Bake 15 minutes.

Run knife around edge. Turn hot cake onto cloth heavily dusted with confectioners sugar. Remove waxed paper and, starting from narrow end, roll up cake with cloth; cool.

Filling: Whip cream with confectioners sugar until stiff. Stir in pineapple and rum. Unroll cake and spread with filling; reroll cake with filling. Chill until firm. Frost with Ghirardelli's Empress Frosting. Cut into slices. Serves 10-12.

Ice Cream Chocolate Roll: Prepare recipe above without the filling. Instead, spread cake with 1 quart (960 g) slightly softened chocolate ice cream, using same method for filling. Freeze until firm. Slice and serve frozen. If desired, serve with chocolate sauce.

Ghirardelli's Empress Frosting

⅓ cup (80 ml) half and half
½ cup (120 ml) butter, cut up
2 tbs (30 ml) sugar
1½ cups (355 ml) GHIRARDELLI Sweet Ground Chocolate
1 tsp (5 ml) vanilla

In 2-quart heavy saucepan, heat half and half with butter and sugar, stirring until blended. Add ground chocolate, mixing with wire whip until smooth. Heat on medium-low until mixture is thick and shiny and runs off spoon like syrup and the first bubble appears on the surface (160°F; 71°C). Do not boil or overcook frosting. Cool 5 minutes, add vanilla. Place pan of frosting in a bowl of ice and water. Beat slowly with spoon until frosting holds shape. Frost cake. Refrigerate to set frosting.

Opposite: Forty-Niner Chocolate Roll

Cupcakes

½ cup (120 ml) shortening
1 cup (240 ml) sugar
2 eggs
2 cups (480 ml) sifted PRESTO
¾ cup (180 ml) milk
1 tsp (5 ml) vanilla
½ cup (120 ml) raisins, optional

Preheat oven to 350°F (180°C).

Cream shortening, add sugar gradually. Add eggs 1 at a time, beating well after each addition. Add flour alternately with milk to which vanilla has been added.

Put in greased muffin pans and bake 20-25 minutes. Raisins may be added to batter before baking, if desired. Frost as desired. Yields 2 dozen cupcakes.

Velvety Cupcakes

¼ cup (60 ml) margarine
½ tsp (3 ml) lemon juice
1 cup (240 ml) sifted PRESTO
½ cup (120 ml) sugar
6 tbs (90 ml) milk
1 egg

Preheat oven to 350°F (180°C). Grease and flour muffin pans.

Blend margarine and lemon juice. Sift flour and sugar together over margarine mixture. Add 3 tbs milk and egg; stir until blended. Beat 2 minutes with medium speed of electric mixer. Add remaining 3 tbs of milk. Beat 1 minute with medium speed of electric mixer.

Pour into prepared pans, filling half full. Bake 20-25 minutes or until tops spring back when touched lightly with finger. Frost as desired. Yields 12 cupcakes.

Opposite: Cupcakes

Peanut Butter Brownie Cupcakes

4-oz pkg (120 g) BAKER'S German Sweet Chocolate
¼ cup (60 ml) margarine or butter
¾ cup (180 ml) sugar
2 eggs
1 tsp (5 ml) vanilla
½ cup (120 ml) all-purpose flour
¼ cup (60 ml) peanut butter
2 tbs (30 ml) confectioners sugar

Preheat oven to 350°F (180°C).

Microwave chocolate and margarine in large microwave-safe bowl on high 2 minutes or until melted. Stir sugar into melted chocolate mixture. Mix in eggs and vanilla until well blended. Stir in flour.

In a separate bowl, mix peanut butter and confectioners sugar until smooth.

Fill 12 paper-lined muffin cups half full with brownie batter. Place a teaspoonful of peanut butter mixture on top of each. Bake at 350°F (180°C) for 20 minutes or until toothpick inserted into brownie comes out with fudgy crumbs. Do not overbake. Remove from pan to cool on wire rack. Yields 12 cupcakes.

Peanut Butter Brownie Cupcakes

Upside-Down Pineapple Cupcakes

¼ cup (60 ml) IMPERIAL Brown Sugar
2 tbs (30 ml) butter or margarine
1 cup (240 ml) canned, sliced pineapple, cut into small wedges
6 maraschino cherries, cut in half
¼ cup (60 ml) butter or margarine
½ cup (120 ml) IMPERIAL Granulated Sugar
1 cup (240 ml) all-purpose flour
⅓ cup (80 ml) water
pinch salt
½ tsp (3 ml) baking powder
2 egg whites
whipping cream, optional

Preheat oven to 350°F (180°C).

Divide brown sugar and 2 tbs butter or margarine evenly among one dozen 2-inch muffin cups. Put in oven until butter melts and sugar dissolves. Remove from oven and arrange pineapple wedges in muffin cups with cherry half in center.

To make cake batter, cream ¼ cup butter or margarine until fluffy and gradually beat in granulated sugar. Add ⅓ of flour to mixture, then ½ of the water, beating well after each addition. Then add another ⅓ of flour and remaining water. Beat well. Add rest of flour along with salt and baking powder. Beat well. Beat egg whites until stiff and fold in until well mixed.

Distribute batter over ingredients in muffin cups. Bake 15-20 minutes or until cakes tests done. Cool 5 minutes, then invert onto baking sheet. Yields 12 cupcakes. If desired, serve with whipped cream.

Brownie Cupcakes

3 oz (90 g) unsweetened chocolate
½ cup (120 ml) butter or margarine
1½ cups (355 ml) sugar
3 eggs
1½ tsp (8 ml) vanilla
1 cup (240 ml) all-purpose flour
1 cup (240 ml) chopped walnuts
1 cup (240 ml) SUN•MAID Raisins

Preheat oven to 350°F (180°C). Grease or line one dozen 2¾-inch muffin cups with paper baking cups.

In large saucepan, over very low heat, combine chocolate and butter or margarine; heat just until melted, stirring occasionally. Remove from heat. Stir in sugar; blend well. Blend in eggs and vanilla. Stir in flour, walnuts and raisins.

Spoon batter into prepared muffin cups, filling almost full. Bake at 350°F (180°C) 30 minutes. Cool on wire rack. Yields 12 cupcakes.

Chocolate Surprise Cupcakes

Filling:
8-oz pkg (240 g) PHILADELPHIA BRAND Cream Cheese, softened
⅓ cup (80 ml) granulated sugar
1 egg
½ cup (120 ml) BAKER'S Semi-Sweet Real Chocolate Chips

Cupcakes:
2 squares BAKER'S Unsweetened Chocolate, melted
⅓ cup (80 ml) vegetable oil
1¼ cups (295 ml) all-purpose flour
1 cup (240 ml) granulated sugar
¾ cup (180 ml) water
1 egg
1 tsp (5 ml) vanilla
½ tsp (3 ml) baking soda
¼ tsp (1 ml) salt
confectioners sugar, optional

Preheat oven to 350°F (180°C).

Filling: Beat cream cheese, ⅓ cup granulated sugar and 1 egg until smooth. Stir in chips; set aside.

Cupcakes: Beat melted chocolate, oil, flour, 1 cup granulated sugar, water, 1 egg, vanilla, baking soda and salt in large bowl with wire whisk or fork until blended and smooth.

Spoon half the batter evenly into 18 greased or paper-lined muffin cups. Top each with 1 tbs of the cream cheese Filling. Spoon the remaining batter evenly over cream cheese Filling.

Bake 30-35 minutes or until toothpick inserted into center comes out clean. Remove from pans to cool on wire racks. Sprinkle with confectioners' sugar, if desired. Yields 18 cupcakes.

Pies &
Tarts

Crust
Fruit
Nut & Syrup
Pumpkin
Chocolate
Lemon
Cream
Cream Cheese
PIES & TARTS

Never-Fail Pie Crust

4-4¼ cups (960-1080 ml) sifted HECKERS/CERESOTA
Unbleached Flour
1 tbs (15 ml) sugar
3 tsp (15 ml) salt
1 egg
1 tbs (15 ml) vinegar
½ cup (120 ml) water
1¾ cups (415 ml) shortening

Sift the flour, sugar and salt into a large bowl. Beat the egg and combine with vinegar and water. Cut the shortening into the flour, sprinkle with the egg mixture and mix all together.

Gather the dough into a ball, wrap in wax paper and chill for about 30 minutes before using.

This dough can be kept in the refrigerator up to 1 week. Or you can divide it into 4 parts (1 pie shell each), wrap each securely and freeze until ready to use.

To make the shell: Turn ¼ of the dough on a floured board and roll to fit a 9-inch pie pan. Remember to allow for the sides and leave a little up over as well. Fold it in half, gently lift into pan, and with your fingers fit it to the pan without stretching it. Trim the edge slightly larger than the outer rim of the pan and flute. Yields four 9-inch pie crusts.

If the recipe calls for a baked shell: Prick the bottom and sides of the shell with a fork and bake for 12-15 minutes in a preheated 450°F (230°C) oven or until golden. Cool before adding the filling.

If the recipe calls for a partially baked shell: Bake the shell in a preheated 450°F (230°C) oven for 5 minutes; then cool.

And if you want to prevent a soggy bottom in a juicy pie: Chill the unbaked pie shell for 15 minutes before making the filling; add the filling just before baking. Or, bake the bottom crust for 10 minutes in a preheated 450°F (230°C) oven before adding the filling.

Double Crust Pie Crust

2 cups (480 ml) WASHINGTON All-Purpose Flour
1 tsp (5 ml) salt
⅔ cup (160 ml) shortening
4 tbs (60 ml) ice water

Use ungreased 8- or 9-inch pie pans.

Place flour and salt in bowl. Cut in shortening until mixture is like coarse crumbs. Sprinkle ice water over flour, while mixing with fork to make stiff dough. Flour hands; press dough into smooth ball. Place on lightly floured surface. Divide in half. Roll ⅛-inch thick into circles slightly larger than pans.

For baked pie shells: Preheat oven to 450°F (230°C). Fit dough into pan. Trim, leaving about ½-inch beyond rim of pan; turn under and flute edge. Prick through dough with fork on bottom and sides at about ½-inch intervals. Bake 8-10 minutes. Cool before filling.

For unbaked pie shells: Proceed as for baked shell, except do not prick dough. Add filling. Bake according to filling directions.

For 2-crust pies: Fit dough into pan. Trim even rim of pan. Add filling. Roll second part of dough 1 inch larger than pan; fold in half and cut several slits on folded edge. Moisten edge of lower crust with water. Place folded dough over filling; trim ½-inch beyond edge and fold under rim of bottom dough. Press edges together to seal, forming flutes with fingers or fork. Bake according to filling directions. Yields 2 pie shells or one 2-crust pie.

Rich Egg Pie Crust: Increase shortening to ¾ cup (180 ml). Combine 1 beaten egg with 1 tsp (5 ml) vinegar before adding to flour mixture.

Egg Yolk Pie Crust: Combine 1 beaten egg yolk with water before adding to flour mixture.

Lemon Pie Crust: Add 1-2 tsp (5-10 ml) grated lemon peel to flour-shortening mixture.

Orange Pie Crust: Substitute orange juice for water. Add 1-2 tsp (5-10 ml) grated orange peel to flour-shortening mixture.

Sesame Seed Pie Crust: Add 2-4 tbs (30-60 ml) toasted sesame seeds to flour-shortening mixture.

Nut Pie Crust: Add ½ cup (120 ml) finely chopped nuts to flour-shortening mixture.

Note: All pastry should be firm and crusty, but a light golden brown.

Pastry cloth will make rolling any dough almost foolproof.

Oil Pie Crust

2 cups (480 ml) WASHINGTON All-Purpose Flour
1 tsp (5 ml) salt
½ cup (120 ml) cooking oil
½ cup (120 ml) milk

Use ungreased 8- or 9-inch pie pans.

Mix flour and salt in bowl. Add oil and milk to flour mixture. Stir with fork to form dough. Divide in half.

Roll dough between 2 pieces of waxed paper into 12-inch circle. Wipe table with damp cloth to keep paper from slipping. Peel off top paper, place crust in pan with other paper side up. Peel off paper; fit pastry loosely into pan. Trim, leaving ½ inch overhanging edge.

For baked pie shells: Preheat oven to 450°F (230°C). Turn pastry edge under and flute. Prick with fork. Bake 8-10 minutes. Cool before filling.

For unbaked pie shells: Proceed as for baked shell, except do not prick dough. Add filling, bake according to directions.

For 2-crust pies: Add filling to dough in pan. Roll second part of dough 1 inch large than pan. Peel off top paper. Cut several slits near center. Moisten edge of lower crust with water. Place pastry, paper side up, over filling. Remove paper. Trim ½ inch beyond edge and fold under rim of bottom pastry. Press edges together to seal, forming flute with fingers or fork. Bake according to filling directions. Yields 2 pie shells or one 2-crust pie.

Hot Water Pastry

¼ cup (60 ml) boiling water
½ cup (120 ml) shortening, softened
1½ cups (355 ml) PRESTO

Gradually pour boiling water over slightly softened shortening and beat until creamy. Cool slightly and sift in flour. Mix to a soft dough with pastry blender or fork. Cover with wax paper and chill thoroughly.

Roll thin on slightly floured board. This pastry can be made a day ahead and kept in the refrigerator.

To prebake: Line an 8- or 9-inch pie plate with Hot Water Pastry. Prick with fork in center and lower edges. Flute upper edges and moisten with milk. Bake in 450°F (230°C) oven about 15 minutes or until lightly browned. Yields two 8- or 9-inch pie shells.

Cheese Cornmeal Crust

¾ cup (180 ml) WASHINGTON All-Purpose Flour
¼ cup (60 ml) INDIAN HEAD Corn Meal
½ tsp (3 ml) salt
¼ cup (60 ml) shortening
½ cup (120 ml) sharp cheese, grated
2-3 tbs (30-45 ml) cold water

Preheat oven to 450°F (230°C). Use one 9-inch pie pan.

Stir flour, cornmeal and salt together in bowl. Cut in shortening until mixture is crumbly. Stir in cheese. Add cold water gradually until pastry holds together.

Turn onto floured surface. Roll to fit pie pan. Bake 7 minutes.

Fill baked shell with chicken or ham and peas in a medium cream sauce for a main dish. May also be used for apple pie. Yields one 9-inch crust.

Homemade Peach Pie

4 cups (960 ml) sliced, peeled peaches
¾ cup (180 ml) sugar
¼ cup (60 ml) MINUTE Tapioca
1 tbs (15 ml) lemon juice
pastry for 2-crust 9-inch pie
1 tbs (15 ml) margarine or butter

Mix peaches, sugar, tapioca and lemon juice in large bowl. Let stand 15 minutes.

Preheat oven to 400°F (205°C).

Roll ½ of the pastry to 11-inch circle or 2 inches larger than pie plate, on lightly floured surface. Line 9-inch pie plate with pastry allowing ½-inch overhang.

Fill with peach mixture. Dot with margarine or butter. Roll remaining pastry to 12-inch circle. Cover pie with pastry; seal and flute edge. Cut several slits to permit steam to escape.

Bake 55-65 minutes or until juices form bubbles that burst slowly. Cool. Serves 8.

For lattice top crust: Roll remaining pastry to 12-inch circle. Cut into 10 ½-inch strips with pastry wheel or knife. Place 5 of the strips over filling. Weave lattice crust with remaining strips by folding back alternate strips as each cross strip is added. Fold trimmed edge of lower pastry over ends of strips; seal and flute edge. Bake as directed above.

Apple: Substitute 6 cups (1.4 l) sliced apples for peaches, reduce tapioca to 2 tbs (30 ml), omit lemon juice, add ½ tsp (3 ml) ground cinnamon and ¼ tsp (1 ml) ground nutmeg. Prepare as above.

Blueberry: Substitute 4 cups (960 ml) blueberries for peaches and add dash ground cinnamon, if desired. Prepare as above.

Cherry: Substitute 4 cups (960 ml) cherries for peaches, reduce tapioca to 3 tbs (45 ml) , increase sugar to 1⅓ cups (320 ml), omit lemon juice and add ¼ tsp (1 ml) almond extract. Prepare as above.

Plum: Substitute 3 cups (720 ml) sliced plums for peaches, decrease sugar to ¾ cup (180 ml), omit lemon juice and add dash ground cinnamon, if desired. Prepare as above.

Rhubarb: Substitute 4 cups (960 ml) rhubarb for peaches, decrease tapioca to 2 tbs (30 ml), increase sugar to 1 cup (240 ml), omit lemon juice and add 1 tsp (5 ml) grated orange peel. Prepare as above.

Opposite: **Springtime Rhubarb Pie**

Springtime Rhubarb Pie

HECKERS/CERESOTA Never Fail Pie Crust for 9-inch, 2-crust pie
4 cups (60 ml) rhubarb, cut in 1-inch pieces
1¾ cups (415 ml) sugar
dash salt
⅓ cup (80 ml) HECKERS/CERESOTA Unbleached Flour
2 tbs (30 ml) butter

Preheat oven to 425°F (220°C).

Roll out 1 piece pastry to ⅛-inch thickness. Line pie pan and trim edges to leave ½-inch overhang. Brush this bottom crust lightly with melted butter. Set aside while top crust is rolled and cut into 14 strips about ½-inch wide.

Place rhubarb in pastry-lined pan. Mix together sugar, salt ad flour; sprinkle evenly over rhubarb. Dot with butter.

Moisten pastry edge with water; arrange strips over filling in a criss-cross lattice design. Turn the overhanging pastry up over ends of strips; press firmly; flute edge. Brush strips and edge with melted butter.

Bake 40-50 minutes,or until crust is golden brown. Serves 8.

Homemade Peach Pie

Fresh Pear Pie

6 cups (1.4 l) thinly sliced, cored, peeled pears
½ cup (120 ml) brown sugar, firmly packed
3 tbs (45 ml) MINUTE Tapioca
1 tbs (15 ml) lemon juice
½ tsp (3 ml) ground ginger
¼ tsp (1 ml) ground cinnamon
15-oz pkg (450 g) refrigerated pie crust
1 tbs (15 ml) margarine or butter

Preheat oven to 400°F (205°C).

Mix pears, brown sugar, tapioca, lemon juice, ginger and cinnamon in large bowl. Let stand 15 minutes.

Prepare pie crusts as directed on package.

Line 9-inch pie plate with 1 of the pie crusts. Fill with fruit mixture. Dot with margarine or butter. Cover with second pie crust; seal and flute edge. Cut several slits to permit steam to escape.

Bake 60 minutes or until juices form bubbles that burst slowly. Cool. Serves 8.

Strawberry-Rhubarb Pie

2 cups (480 ml) sliced, fresh rhubarb
2 cups (480 ml) fresh strawberry halves
1¼ cups (295 ml) sugar
¼ cup (60 ml) MINUTE Tapioca
15-oz pkg (450 g) refrigerated pie crust
1 tbs (15 ml) margarine or butter

Mix rhubarb, strawberries, sugar and tapioca in large bowl. Let stand 15 minutes.

Preheat oven to 425°F (220°C).

Prepare pie crust as directed on package for 2-crust pie, using 9-inch pie plate.

Fill with fruit mixture. Dot with margarine or butter. Cover with second pie crust; seal and flute edge. Cut several slits to permit steam to escape. Bake 45 minutes or until juices form bubbles that burst slowly. Cool. Serves 8.

Fresh Pear Pie

Opposite: Strawberry-Rhubarb Pie

Caramelized Date and Apple Tart

16 California dates
4 Granny Smith apples, or other green baking apple
6 tbs (90 g) sugar
3 tbs (45 ml) butter
1 tsp (5 ml) lemon juice
½ tsp (3 ml) corn syrup
1 ready-made pie crust

Preheat oven to 400°F (205°C).

Combine sugar, butter, lemon juice and corn syrup in a 10-inch ovenproof skillet over medium high heat. Cook 4-5 minutes, stirring constantly until golden caramel brown. Remove from heat. Remember that the caramel will continue to darken even after it is removed from heat, so don't let it get too dark.

Peel, core, and quarter apples. Arrange quarters, rounded side down, around the edge of oven proof skillet. Fill in center with remaining apples. Place a date between each apple piece. Use extra dates to fill in empty spaces.

Measure pie crust dough. Roll it out to 11 inches if it is not already that size. Arrange the pie crust dough over the apples, folding it slightly, if necessary, and pushing it down between the fruit and side of the pan.

Bake for 25-30 minutes or until crust is golden brown. Remove from oven and allow to cool several minutes. Invert onto serving plate, slice and serve. Serves 6.

Courtesy of the California Date Administration Committee.

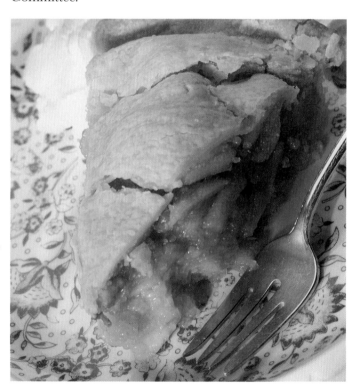

French Country Apple Pie

¾ cup (180 l) whole blanched California almonds
½ cup (120 ml) sugar
½ cup (120 ml) butter, softened
2 eggs
¼ tsp (1 ml) almond extract
2 tbs (30 ml) flour
9-inch unbaked pie shell
2 Granny Smith apples

Spread almonds in single layer in a shallow pan. Place in cold oven; toast 350°F (180°C), 5-10 minutes, stirring occasionally, until lightly toasted. Remove from pan to cool.

In food processor, with metal blade in place, grind almonds with sugar. Mix in butter, eggs and almond extract until thoroughly combined. Blend in flour.

Spoon mixture into unbaked pie shell.

Peel apples. Cut in half lengthwise and remove cores. Slice apple halves crosswise into ⅛-inch thick slices. Arrange over almond filling.

Bake pie at 375°F (190°C), 50 minutes to 1 hour, until center is set and crust is golden. Cool. Serves 8.

Pie Shell

1½ cups (355 ml) flour
½ tsp (3 ml) salt
½ cup (120 ml) shortening
¼ cups (60 ml) milk

Combine flour and salt. Cut in shortening until particles are size of peas. Stir in milk, blending just until mixture starts to form a ball. On floured surface, roll dough out to a 12-inch circle. Place into 9-inch pie plate. Turn edges under and flute. Yields one 9-inch pie shell.

Courtesy of the Almond Board of California.

Wonderful Apple Pie

pastry for 9- or 10-inch 1-crust pie
1 cup (240 ml) light brown sugar, firmly packed
½ cup (120 ml) all-purpose flour
½ cup (120 ml) butter or margarine, softened
1 tsp (5 ml) McCORMICK/SCHILLING Ground Cinnamon
½ tsp (3 ml) McCORMICK/SCHILLING Lemon Peel
pinch McCORMICK/SCHILLING Ground Allspice
pinch McCORMICK/SCHILLING Ground Cloves
pinch McCORMICK/SCHILLING Ground Nutmeg
6 medium-size apples, peeled, cored, and sliced

Preheat oven to 400°F (205°C). Line pie plate with pastry and set aside.

Place brown sugar, flour, butter or margarine, and spices in medium-size bowl and mix until crumbly.

Spread ⅓ of mixture over bottom of pastry-lined pie plate and arrange apples on top. Spoon remaining ⅔ of flour-sugar mixture evenly over apples.

Bake 50-55 minutes. Serves 8.

Opposite: French Country Apple Pie

Deep-Dish Apple Pie

10 cups (2.4 l) thinly sliced, peeled apples
¾ cup (180 ml) granulated sugar
⅓ cup (80 ml) firmly packed brown sugar
¼ cup (60 ml) MINUTE Tapioca
1 tsp (5 ml) ground cinnamon
¼ tsp (1 ml) ground nutmeg
⅓ cup (80 ml) raisins
½ cup (120 ml) water
2 tbs (30 ml) margarine or butter
15-oz pkg (450 g) refrigerated pie crust

Preheat oven to 425°F (220°C).

Mix apples, sugars, tapioca, cinnamon, nutmeg, raisins and water in large bowl. Let stand 15 minutes.

Fill 10-inch pie plate with apple mixture. Dot with margarine.

Roll 1 of the pie crusts to 12-inch circle on lightly floured surface. Cover apple mixture with pie crust; seal and flute edge. Cut several slits to permit steam to escape. Cut decorative shapes from remaining pie crust. Moisten with water; place on pie crust.

Bake 15 minutes. Decrease temperature to 350°F (180°C). Bake 45 minutes or until juices form bubbles that burst slowly. Serve warm. Serves 10.

Old-Fashioned Blueberry Pie

¾ -1 cup (180-240 ml) sugar, to taste
2½ tbs (38 ml) cornstarch
1 tsp (5 ml) grated lemon peel
pinch ground nutmeg
4 cups (960 ml) fresh or frozen North American blueberries
1-2 tbs (15-30 ml) butter or margarine
pastry for 2-crust pie

Combine sugar, cornstarch, lemon peel and nutmeg; toss with blueberries.

Pour into pastry-lined pie pan. Dot with butter or margarine. Arrange top crust over berries; cut slits in crust to vent.

Bake at 425°F (220°C) 10 minutes; reduce heat to 350°F (180°C) and bake 35-40 minutes or until fruit is bubbly and crust is golden brown. If necessary, cover edge of pie with aluminum foil to prevent excessive browning. Serves 8.

Courtesy of the North American Blueberry Council.

Washington Cherry Pie

pastry for 8-inch 2-crust pie
4 tbs (60 ml) WASHINGTON All-Purpose Flour
1 cup (240 ml) sugar
¼ tsp (1 ml) salt
2 1-lb cans (455 g each) red, tart, pitted cherries, drained
2 tbs (30 ml) butter or margarine
1 cup (240 ml) juice from cherries
½-1 tsp (3-5 ml) red food coloring

Preheat oven to 425°F (220°C).

Line pan with pastry for bottom crust.

Place flour, sugar and salt in bowl. Blend together. Sprinkle ¼ cup mixture over uncooked bottom crust. Add drained cherries. Dot with butter or margarine. Sprinkle remaining sugar mixture over cherries.

Combine juice from cherries and red food coloring and pour over cherries. Cover with top pastry; seal edges; cut slits for steam to escape.

Bake 50-55 minutes. Serves 6.

Blueberry Pie: Substitute drained canned blueberries and juice for cherries and juice. Add 2 tbs (30 ml) lemon juice before pouring mixture into pastry-lined pie pan.

Peach or Apricot Pie: Substitute canned sliced peaches or apricot halves and juice in place of cherries and juice.

Opposite: Old-Fashioned Blueberry Pie

Cranberry-Apple Pie

3 cups (720 ml) diced, peeled apples
1 cup (240 ml) cranberries
1½ cups (355 ml) sugar
3 tbs (345 ml) MINUTE Tapioca
¼ tsp (1 ml) salt
15-oz pkg (450 g) refrigerated pie crust
1 tbs (15 ml) margarine or butter

Preheat oven to 400°F (205 °C).

Mix fruit, sugar, tapioca and salt in large bowl. Let stand 15 minutes.

Prepare pie crusts as directed on package. Line 9-inch pie plate with 1 of the pie crusts.

Fill with fruit mixture. Dot with margarine. Cut second pie crust into ½-inch strips. Arrange in lattice design over fruit mixture. Seal and flute edge. Bake 60 minutes or until juices from bubbles that burst slowly. Cool. Serves 8.

Strawberry Crown Tart

pastry for single crust 9-inch pie
2 eggs
⅓ cup (80 ml) sugar
1 tbs (15 ml) lemon juice
1 tsp (5 ml) grated lemon peel
½ tsp (3 ml) vanilla
½ cup (120 ml) flour
3 tbs (45 ml) butter or margarine, melted and cooled
⅓ cup (80 ml) melted currant jelly
2 pint baskets (960 ml) fresh California strawberries, stemmed

Preheqat oven to 425°F (220°C).

Press pastry into 9-inch tart pan with removable bottom. Prick all over with fork; bake 10-12 minutes, just until pastry begins to brown. Remove to rack to cool.

In mixing bowl beat eggs, sugar, lemon juice, peel and vanilla until thick and pale, about 10 minutes. Gently fold in ⅓ of the flour, then ⅓ of the butter. Continue folding in, alternating flour and butter until all has been incorporated. Do not overmix.

Brush bottom of tart shell with some of the jelly. Slice about ½ basket of the strawberries and arrange over jelly.

Pour batter over strawberries, it will not quite cover. Bake in 375°F (190°C) oven 20-25 minutes until golden and filling is set. Cool on rack.

Arrange remaining whole strawberries, stem ends down, on top of tart. Brush with remaining melted jelly. Serves 8.

Courtesy of the California Strawberry Advisory Board.

Opposite: **Strawberry Crown Tart**

Cherry Crostada

3 cups (720 ml) Northwest fresh sweet cherries, pitted
2 tbs (30 ml) almond-flavored liqueur
pastry for single 9-inch pie
1 cup (240 ml) sugar
¾ cup (180 ml) butter or margarine
3 eggs
12½-oz can (375 g) almond filling
1¼ cups (295 ml) flour
1 tsp (5 ml) baking powder
¼ cup (60 ml) cherry or red currant jelly
whipped cream or topping

Preheat oven to 350°F (180°C).

Combine cherries and 1 tbs liqueur; set aside.

Line 9-inch springform pan with pastry; set aside.

Cream sugar and butter or margarine; beat in eggs and almond filling. Combine flour and baking powder; mix well. Stir into creamed mixture. Fold in cherry mixture.

Pour into pastry-lined pan. Gently pull crust edge to curve around filling. Bake 75-85 minutes or until wooden toothpick inserted in center comes out clean. Cover crostada with foil during last 30 minutes to prevent excessive browning. Cool.

Blend jelly with remaining liqueur; brush over warm crostada. Remove from pan. Serve warm with whipped cream. Serves 8-10.

Courtesy of the Northwest Cherry Growers.

Fruit Jewel Tart

2 CHIQUITA Bananas, 1 whole and 1 sliced
3 oz (90 g) cream cheese
2 tbs (30 ml) yogurt
1 large container (8 rolls) refrigerated crescent roll dough
⅔ cup (160 ml) strawberries, thinly sliced
2 kiwis, peeled, halved and thinly sliced
2 tbs (30 ml) brown sugar or melted jelly
4 tbs (60 ml) coconut

Preheat oven to 425°F (220°C).

Combine whole banana, cream cheese and yogurt in a food processor or blender; process until smooth.

Use 2 sections of crescent roll dough for each tart. Shape dough into 4 thin circles on cookie sheet, or use 4 small tart pans.

Divide cream cheese mixture evenly and spread on dough. Arrange strawberries, kiwis and sliced bananas in a circular pattern on dough. Sprinkle with brown sugar or glaze with melted jelly. Garnish with coconut. Bake 8-10 minutes or until crust is golden brown. Serves 4.

Fruit Jewel Tart

Opposite: Cherry Crostada

Impossible French Apple Pie

6 cups (1.4 l) sliced, peeled tart apples
1¼ tsp (6 ml) ground cinnamon
¼ tsp (1 ml) ground nutmeg
¾ cup (180 ml) milk
2 tbs (30 ml) margarine or butter, softened
2 eggs
1 cup (240 ml) granulated sugar
½ cup (120 ml) BISQUICK Original Baking Mix

Streusel:
3 tbs (45 ml) firm margarine or butter
1 cup (240 ml) BISQUICK Original Baking Mix
½ cup (120 ml) chopped nuts
⅓ cup (80 ml) brown sugar, packed

Preheat oven to 325°F (165°C). Grease pie plate, 10x1½ inches. Mix apples, cinnamon and nutmeg; turn into pie plate.

Beat milk, 2 tbs margarine or butter, the eggs, granulated sugar and ½ cup baking mix in blender on high speed about 15 seconds or with wire whisk or hand beater about 1 minute, until smooth.

Pour into plate. Prepare Streusel; sprinkle over top. Bake 55-65 minutes or until knife inserted in center comes out clean. Cool 5 minutes. Refrigerate any remaining pie. Serves 8.

Streusel: Cut margarine or butter into remaining ingredients until crumbly.

Fruit Empanadas

8-oz can (240 g) DEL MONTE Pineapple Tidbits
    in its Own Juice
1 17½-oz can (525 g) refried beans
1 medium banana, mashed
¾ cup (180 ml) brown sugar, firmly packed
⅓ cup (80 ml) DEL MONTE Seedless Raisins
⅓ cup (80 ml) chopped nuts
½ tsp (3 ml) cinnamon
4 pastry sticks or pastry for 2 double-crust pies
1 egg
1 tbs (15 ml) milk or cream

Preheat oven to 400°F (205°C).

Drain pineapple, reserving juice for other recipe uses. Combine beans, pineapple, banana, brown sugar, raisins, nuts and cinnamon in saucepan. Cook over low heat 10 minutes; cool.

Prepare pastry as package directs; roll out to ⅛-inch thick. Cut into 4-inch circles. Combine egg and milk in small bowl. For each empanada, place 2 tbs filling on each circle. Brush egg-milk mixture on edges; fold in half; crimp edges with fork to seal.

Place on baking sheet; coat each empanada with egg-milk mixture. Bake 15-20 minutes or until lightly brown. Serve warm or cold. Yields 3 dozen.

Opposite: Impossible French Apple Pie

Pecan Pie

Pastry for 9-inch 1-crust pie
4 eggs
1 cup (240 ml) sugar
1 cup (240 ml) dark corn syrup
¼ cup (60 ml) butter or margarine, melted
1 tbs (15 ml) cornstarch
1 tsp (5 ml) McCORMICK/SCHILLING Pure Vanilla Extract
½ tsp (3 ml) McCORMICK/SCHILLING Brandy Extract
pinvh salt
2 cups (480 ml) pecan halves

Preheat oven to 425°F (220°C). Line pie plate with pastry and set aside.

Place eggs in bowl and beat until lemon colored. Beat in sugar, corn syrup, melted butter or margarine, corn-starch, vanilla, brandy extract and salt.

Arrange pecan halves in single layer in bottom of pastry-lined pie plate and pour egg mixture over pecans. Bake 10 minutes. Reduce oven temperature to 325°F (165°C) and bake 50-55 minutes. Cool on wire rack. Serves 8.

Chocolate Pecan Pie

9-inch deep dish pie shell, prebaked
⅔ cup (160 ml) brown sugar
3 tbs (45 ml) SACO Baking Cocoa
2 tsp (10 ml) all-purpose flour
3 eggs
¾ cup (180 ml) corn syrup
¼ tsp (1 ml) salt
1½ tsp (8 ml) vanilla extract
3 tbs (45 ml) unsalted butter, melted
1¼ cups (295 ml) pecan pieces
2 oz (60 g) SACO Chocolate CHUNKS

Preheat oven to 350°F (180°C).

Combine brown sugar, cocoa, and flour. Stir in eggs, corn syrup, salt, vanilla and butter; mix well. Add pecans and chocolate, stirring to combine.

Pour into pie shell and bake 50-60 minutes, until set. Center will be soft, but will firm upon cooling. Serves 8-10.

Chocolate Pecan Pie

Opposite: Pecan Pie

Orange Pecan Pie

3 eggs
½ cup (120 ml) GRANDMA'S Molasses Unsulphured
½ cup (120 ml) light corn syrup
¼ cup (60 ml) orange juice
1 tsp (5 ml) grated orange peel
1 tsp (5 ml) vanilla
1½ cups (355 ml) whole pecans
9-inch unbaked pie shell
whipped cream

Preheat oven to 350°F (180°C).

In large bowl, beat eggs. Add molasses, corn syrup, orange juice, orange peel and vanilla; beat until well blended. Stir in pecans.

Pour into unbaked pie shell. Bake 40-50 minutes or until filling is set. Cool. Serve with whipped cream. Serves 8.

Decadent Pie

¾ cup (180 ml) brown sugar, firmly packed
¾ cup (180 ml) corn syrup
4 squares BAKER'S Semi-Sweet Chocolate
6 tbs (90 ml) margarine or butter
3 eggs
1⅓ cups (320 ml) BAKER'S ANGEL FLAKE Coconut
1 cup (240 ml) chopped pecans
1 unbaked 9-inch pie shell
1¾ cups (415 ml) COOL WHIP Whipped Topping, thawed
1 tbs (15 ml) bourbon, optional
chocolate shavings, optional

Preheat oven to 350°F (180°C).

Microwave brown sugar and corn syrup in large microwave-safe bowl on high 4 minutes or until boiling. Add chocolate and margarine or butter. Stir until chocolate is completely melted. Cool slightly. Add eggs, 1 at a time, beating well after each addition. Stir in coconut and pecans.

Pour into pie shell. Bake 1 hour or until knife inserted 1 inch from center comes out clean. Cool on wire rack. Combine whipped topping and bourbon, if desired; spoon or pipe onto pie. Garnish with chocolate shavings, if desired. Serves 8.

Heath Bar English Toffee Pecan Pie

9-inch unbaked pie shell
½ cup (120 ml) original HEATH BAR English Toffee Bits
4 eggs, slightly beaten
½ cup (120 ml) sugar
1 cup (240 ml) light corn syrup
4 tbs (60 ml) butter or margarine, melted
1 tbs (15 ml) vanilla
1 cup (240 ml) coarsely chopped pecans

Preheat oven to 350°F (180°C).

Cover the bottom of pie shell with broken Heat Bar bits.

In a mixing bowl combine beaten eggs, sugar, corn syrup, butter or margarine and vanilla, mix well and add pecans.

Pour mixture over the Heath Bar bits in the pie shell. Bake for 50-55 minutes, or until the pie is done. Serves 8-10.

Opposite: Orange Pecan Pie

Noreen's Favorite Walnut Pie

3 eggs, slightly beaten
1 cup (240 ml) sugar
2 tbs (30 ml) all-purpose flour
1 cup (240 ml) dark corn syrup
2 tbs (30 ml) butter, melted
1 tsp (5 ml) vanilla
1 9-inch unbaked pie shell
1½ cups (355 ml) large pieces DIAMOND Walnuts

Preheat oven to 400°F (205°C).

Combine eggs, sugar, flour, corn syrup, butter and vanilla; blend well.

Pour into unbaked pie shell; arrange walnuts on top. Bake in lower third of oven for 15 minutes. Reduce heat to 350°F (180°C); bake additional 35-45 minutes or until center appears set. Cool completely. Serves 8.

Walnut-Lemon Tart

1 cup (240 ml) plus 3 tbs (45 ml) all-purpose flour, divided
⅔ cup (160 ml) confectioners sugar
½ cup (120 ml) butter
3 eggs, lightly beaten
¾ cup (180 ml) sugar
½ tsp (3 ml) grated lemon peel
3 tbs (45 ml) lemon juice
1 cup (240 ml) coarsely chopped DIAMOND Walnuts

Preheat oven to 375°F (190°C).

Combine 1 cup flour and confectioners sugar; mix well. Using pastry blender or fork, cut in butter until mixture resembles fine meal; press into ungreased 9-inch tart pan with removable bottom. Line crust with heavy-duty foil to ensure uniform crust shape. Bake for 10 minutes. Carefully remove foil; bake additional 10 minutes. Set aside.

Stir together remaining 3 tbs flour, eggs, sugar, lemon peel and juice; pour into crust. Sprinkle with chopped walnuts.

Return to oven; bake additional 12-15 minutes or until set in center. Cool on wire rack. Serves 8-10.

Walnut-Lemon Tart

Opposite: Noreen's Favorite Walnut Pie

Chocolate Walnut Tart

1 refrigerated pie crust

¼ cup (60 ml) brown sugar, firmly packed
2 eggs
½ cup (120 ml) GRANDMA'S Molasses Unsulphured
1 cup (240 ml) chopped walnuts
2 tbs (30 ml) margarine or butter, melted
¼ cup (60 ml) semi-sweet chocolate chips, melted

Preheat oven to 450°F (230°C).

Prepare pie crust according to package directions in a 9-inch tart pan with removable bottom. Bake 9-11 minutes or until light brown. Cool.

Reduce oven temperature to 350°F (180°C).

In medium bowl, beat brown sugar and eggs until fluffy. Add remaining filling ingredients; mix well.

Pour into cooled, baked crust. Bake 35-45 minutes or until filling is set. Cool. Drizzle melted chocolate chips over top. Store in refrigerator. Serves 8.

Oatmeal Pie

3 eggs, well beaten
⅔ cup (160 ml) IMPERIAL Granulated Sugar
1 cup (240 ml) IMPERIAL Brown Sugar
⅔ cup (160 ml) quick-cooking oats, uncooked
2 tbs (30 ml) butter or margarine
⅔ cup (160 ml) coconut
½ cup (120 ml) milk
1 tsp (5 ml) vanilla
9-inch unbaked pie shell

Preheat oven to 375°F (190°C).

Combine all ingredients, mixing well.

Pour into unbaked pie shell. Bake for 45-50 minutes or until set. Cool completely before cutting. Serves 8.

Chess Pie

1 cup (240 ml) sugar
½ cup (120 ml) butter or margarine, softened
¼ cup (60 ml) sweetened condensed milk
2 eggs, beaten
1 tsp (5 ml) vanilla
1 cup (240 ml) DIAMOND Chopped Walnuts
1 cup (240 ml) SUN•MAID Raisins
9-inch unbaked pie shell

Preheat oven to 325°F (180°C).

Combine sugar, butter or margarine and sweetened condensed milk; blend well. Blend in beaten eggs and vanilla. Fold in walnuts and raisins; pour into pie shell.

Bake on lowest oven rack for 60 minutes. Cool before serving. Serves 8.

Chocolate Sweetheart Pie

8-oz pkg (240 g) BAKER'S Semi-Sweet Chocolate
⅔ cup (160 ml) corn syrup
1 cup (240 ml) heavy cream
3 eggs
9-inch unbaked pie shell
2 tbs (30 ml) sugar
½ tsp (3 ml) vanilla
1 pint strawberries, sliced

Preheat oven to 350°F (180°C).

Melt 6 squares of the chocolate. Stir in corn syrup and ½ cup of the cream. Add eggs, 1 at a time, beating well after each addition.

Pour into pie shell. Bake for 45 minutes or until knife inserted 1 inch from center comes out clean. Cool on wire rack. Center of pie will sink after cooling.

Whip the remaining ½ cup cream, the sugar and vanilla until soft peaks form; spoon into center of cooled pie. Top with strawberries. Melt the remaining 2 squares chocolate and drizzle over strawberries. Serves 8.

Opposite: **Chess Pie**

Mocha-Almond Pie

2 squares BAKER'S Unsweetened Chocolate
2 squares BAKER'S Semi-Sweet Chocolate
½ cup (120 ml) margarine or butter
1 tbs (15 ml) instant coffee
1 cup (240 ml) sugar
¼ cup (60 ml) corn syrup
3 eggs
2 tbs (30 ml) sour cream or plain yogurt
1 tsp (5 ml) vanilla
9-inch unbaked pie shell
½ cup (120 ml) sliced almonds

Preheat oven to 350°F (180°C).

Microwave chocolates, margarine or butter and instant coffee in large microwave-safe bowl on high 2 minutes or until melted. Stir until chocolate is completely melted.

Stir in sugar and corn syrup. Beat in eggs, sour cream and vanilla. Pour into pie shell; sprinkle with almonds. Bake for 45 minutes or until knife inserted 1 inch from center comes out clean. Cool on wire rack. Serves 8-10.

Saucepan preparation: Heat chocolates, margarine or butter and instant coffee in 2-quart saucepan over very low heat until just melted, stirring constantly. Remove from heat. Continue as above.

Opposite: Special Pumpkin Pie

Special Pumpkin Pie

2 eggs
16-oz can (480 ml) cooked pumpkin
½ cup (120 ml) brown sugar
1 tsp (5 ml) McCORMICK/SCHILLING Cinnamon
¼ tsp (1 ml) McCORMICK/SCHILLING Nutmeg
¼ tsp (1 ml) McCORMICK/SCHILLING Ginger
pinch McCORMICK/SCHILLING Cloves
½ tsp (3 ml) salt
13-oz can (390 ml) evaporated milk

Spiced Pecan Topping:
2 tbs (30 ml) brown sugar
2 tbs (30 ml) butter
pinch McCORMICK/SCHILLING Cinnamon
pinch McCORMICK/SCHILLING Nutmeg
pinch McCORMICK/SCHILLING Cloves
1 cup (240 ml) coarsely chopped pecans

Spiced Whipped Cream:
1 cup (240 ml) whipping cream
6 tbs (90 ml) confectioners sugar
¼ tsp (1 ml) McCORMICK/SCHILLING Cinnamon
pinch McCORMICK/SCHILLING Nutmeg
pinch McCORMICK/SCHILLING Cloves
1 tsp (5 ml) McCORMICK/SCHILLING Pure Vanilla Extract

Preheat oven to 450°F (230°C).

Line a 9-inch pie plate with pastry.

Beat eggs until light in large bowl. Stir in pumpkin. Combine brown sugar with spices and salt. Stir into pumpkin mixture. Gradually stir in evaporated milk.

Pour into pastry shell. Bake oven 15 minutes. Reduce temperature to 350°F (180°C) and bake 40 minutes longer. Cool. Sprinkle with Spiced Pecan Topping and decorate with spoonfuls of Spiced Whipped Cream. Serves 8.

Spiced Pecan Topping: In large heavy skillet, mix brown sugar and butter with cinnamon, nutmeg and cloves. Heat, stirring until sugar begins to melt. Quickly stir in pecans. Stir to coat nuts with sugar. Cool.

Spiced Whipped Cream: Combine cream with confectioners sugar. Beat, gradually adding spices, until stiff. Stir in vanilla.

Apple Butter Pumpkin Pie

Filling:
1 cup (240 ml) solid pack pumpkin
1 cup (240 ml) MUSSELMAN'S Apple Butter
¼ cup (60 ml) dark brown sugar, packed
½ tsp (3 ml) ground cinnamon
¼ tsp (1 ml) ground ginger
¼ tsp (1 ml) ground nutmeg
¼ tsp (1 ml) salt
3 eggs, lightly beaten
1 cup (240 ml) undiluted evaporated milk
9-inch deep-dished frozen pie shell, thawed

Streusel Topping:
3 tbs (45 ml) butter, softened
½ cup (120 ml) flour
⅓ cup (80 ml) dark brown sugar
⅓ cup (80 ml) chopped pecans

Preheat oven to 375°F (190°C).

   Combine filling ingredients in order given; pour into pie shell. Bake 50-60 minutes or until knife inserted 2 inches from center comes out clean.

   Combine all Streusel Topping ingredients and spread on pie. Bake additional 15 minutes. Serves 8-10.

Apple-Pumpkin Pie

Filling:
¾ cup (180 ml) granulated sugar
2 tbs (30 ml) all-purpose flour
pinch salt
1 cup (240 ml) canned pumpkin
1 large egg, lightly beaten
1 tbs (25 ml) McCORMICK/SCHILLING Pure Vanilla Extract
½ tsp (3 ml) McCORMICK/SCHILLING Ground Cinnamon
¼ tsp (1 ml) McCORMICK/SCHILLING Ground Nutmeg
¼ tsp (1 ml) McCORMICK/SCHILLING Ground Allspice
pinch McCORMICK/SCHILLING Ground Cloves
2 cups (480 ml) peeled, chopped, Granny Smith apples

pastry for 9-inch 1-crust pie

Crumb Topping:
⅓ cup (80 ml) all-purpose flour
⅓ cup (80 ml) brown sugar, firmly packed
¼ tsp (1 ml) McCORMICK/SCHILLING Ground Cinnamon
2 tbs (30 ml) butter or margarine, softened
whipped cream or ice cream to serve, if desired

Preheat oven to 375°F (190°C).

   Filling: Place granulated sugar, 2 tbs flour, and salt in large mixing bowl and stir to combine. Add pumpkin, egg and seasonings. Beat with electric mixer until smooth. Add apples and stir gently.

   Pour mixture into pie crust. Cover edges of crust with aluminum foil and bake 45 minutes.

   Crumb Topping: Place ⅓ cup flour, brown sugar, and cinnamon in small bowl and stir to combine. Add butter or margarine and stir with fork until mixture resembles coarse crumbs. Remove foil from edge of crust and sprinkle Topping over pie.

   Return pie to oven and bake 15 minutes. Serve warm with whipped cream or ice cream, if desired. Serves 8.

Apple Butter Pumpkin Pie

Opposite: Apple-Pumpkin Pie

Walnut Crunch Pumpkin Pie

1¼ cups (295 ml) coarsely chopped walnuts
¾ cup (180 ml) light brown sugar, packed
9-inch unbaked pie shell
2 eggs
15-oz can (450 g) LIBBY'S Sold Pack Pumpkin
¾ cup (180 ml) granulated sugar
1 tsp (5 ml) ground cinnamon
½ tsp (3 ml) ground ginger
¼ tsp (1 ml) ground cloves
¼ tsp (1 ml) salt
12-fl oz can (360 ml) CARNATION Evaporated Milk
3 tbs (45 ml) butter, melted

Preheat oven to 425°F (220°C).

Mix walnuts and brown sugar in small bowl; place ¾ cup in bottom of pie shell. Reserve remaining mixture for topping.

Combine eggs, pumpkin, sugar, cinnamon, ginger, cloves, salt and evaporated milk in bowl; mix well.

Pour into pie shell. Bake for 15 minutes. Reduce temperature to 350°F (180°C); bake for 40-50 minutes or until knife inserted near center comes out clean. Cool on wire rack.

Add melted butter to remaining nut-sugar mixture; stir until moistened. Sprinkle over cooled pie.

Broil about 5 inches from heat for 2-3 minutes or until bubbly. Cool before serving. Serves 8.

Walnut Crunch Pumpkin Pie

Di Saronno Sweet Potato Pie

40-oz can (1.2 kg) sweet potatoes or yams, in light syrup, drained
½ cup (120 ml) sweet butter, room temperature
⅔ cup (160 ml) DI SARONNO Amaretto
⅓ cup (80 ml) sugar
1 tbs (15 ml) flour
½ tsp (3 ml) ground cinnamon
¼ tsp (1 ml) nutmeg
¼ tsp (1 ml) salt
1 tsp (5 ml) vanilla extract
3 eggs, lightly beaten
1 9-inch pie crust
whipped cream

Preheat oven to 425°F (220°C).

In food processor, purée sweet potaotes until smooth. Add butter; purée until smooth. Add amaretto, sugar, flour, cinnamon, nutmeg, salt and vanilla extract and purée until combined. Add the lightly beaten eggs and pulse until just incorporated.

Pour mixture into pie crust. Bake for 10 minutes. Lower the oven temperature to 325°F (165°C) and bake for 25-35 minutes more or until center is set. Turn oven off and open the door. Let cool in the oven for ½ hour. Decorate with whipped cream. Serves 8-10.

Pineapple Sweet Potato Pie

9-inch unbaked pastry shell
2 cups (480 ml) cooked mashed sweet potatoes
⅔ cup (160 ml) brown sugar
¼ cup (60 ml) half and half
2 tbs (30 ml) butter or margarine, melted
1 tsp (5 ml) vanilla extract
½ tsp (3 ml) cinnamon
¼ tsp (1 ml) nutmeg
¼ tsp (1 ml) salt
1 egg, beaten

Topping:
15¼-oz can (458 g) DEL MONTE Pineapple in its Own Juice
1 tsp (5 ml) cornstarch
1 tsp (5 ml) minced candied ginger

Preheat oven to 425°F (220°C).

Prepare pastry shell; set aside.

Combine sweet potatoes, brown sugar, half and half, butter or margarine, ½ tsp vanilla, cinnamon, nutmeg, salt and beaten egg; mix well.

Pour into pastry shell. Bake 25-30 minutes; cool.

Topping: Drain pineapple, reserving ½ cup juice. Dissolve cornstarch in reserved juice. Cook, stirring constantly, until thickened and translucent. Add ginger and remaining ½ tsp vanilla.

Arrange pineapple over pie. Spoon Topping over fruit. Garnish with whipped cream and chopped nuts, if desired. Serves 8.

Di Saronno
Sweet Potato Pie

Caribbean Fudge Pie

¼ cup (60 ml) butter or margarine, softened
¾ cup (180 ml) brown sugar, firmly packed
3 eggs
12-oz pkg (360 g) semisweet chocolate pieces, melted
2 tsp (10 ml) instant coffee powder
1 tsp (5 ml) rum extract or 1 tbs (15 ml) dark rum
¼ cup (60 ml) all-purpose flour
1 cup (240 ml) chopped DIAMOND Walnuts
½ cup (120 ml) DIAMOND Walnuts, halves or large pieces
9-inch unbaked pastry pie shell

Preheat oven to 375°F (190°C).

In large bowl, combine butter or margarine and brown sugar; beat until light and fluffy. Add eggs, 1 at a time, beating well after each addition. Add melted chocolate, instant coffee and rum extract to butter mixture; mix well. Stir in flour and 1 cup chopped walnuts; pour into pie shell. Decorate top with ½ cup walnut pieces.

Bake in lower third of oven at 375°F (190°C) for 25 minutes. Cool on wire rack. Chill before serving. Serve topped with whipped cream or ice cream, if desired. Store in refrigerator. Serves 8.

Chocolate-Mint Pie

¼ cup (60 ml) crushed peppermint candy
1 pkg BETTY CROCKER Chocolate French Silk
    Creamy Dessert Mix
¼ cup (60 ml) margarine (stick, not soft-style) or butter, melted
2¼ cups (540 ml) cold milk, divided
½ tsp (3 ml) mint or peppermint extract

Stir 2 tbs of the candy, contents of the crust mix envelope and melted margarine or butter in 8 or 9x1¼-inch pie plate with spoon until moistened. Press firmly against bottom and side.

Beat contents of the filling mix envelope, 1¾ cups cold milk and the mint extract in medium bowl with electric mixer on low speed until slightly thickened. Beat on highest speed at least 4 minutes. Do not underbeat. Spread on bottom of crust.

Beat contents of the topping mix envelope and ½ cup cold milk in small deep bowl with electric mixer on low speed 30 seconds. Beat on highest speed at least 2 minutes. Do not underbeat. Spoon over filling by large tablespoonfuls around edge.

Refrigerate at least 1½ hours, until set. Sprinkle remaining candy over topping just before serving. Store covered in refrigerator. Serves 8-10.

Note: If using skim milk, topping and filling will be slightly softer.

Chocolate-Mint Pie

Creamy Mocha Pie

*1 pkg BETTY CROCKER Chocolate French Silk
    Creamy Dessert Mix*
¼ cup (60 ml) margarine (stick not soft-style) or butter, melted
2 cups (480 ml) cold milk, divided
3 tbs (45 ml) coffee liqueur*
1-2 tbs (15-30 ml) caramel ice cream topping
1.4-oz bar (42 g) chocolate-coated toffee candy, coarsely crushed

Stir contents of crust mix envelope and melted margarine or butter in 8 or 9-inch pie plate with spoon until moistened. Press firmly against bottom and side.

Beat contnets of filling mix envelope, 1½ cups cold milk and the coffee liqueur in medium bowl with electric mixer on low speed until slightly thickened. Beat on highest speed at least 4 minutes. Do not underbeat. Spread over bottom of crust.

Beat contents of topping mix envelope and ½ cup cold milk in small deep bowl with electric mixer on low speed 30 seconds. Beat on highest speed at least 2 minutes. Do not underbeat.

Spoon over filling and spread gently. Drizzle caramel ice cream topping over pie; sprinkle with candy. Refrigerate at least 1½ hours, until set. Store covered in refrigerator. Serves 8-10.

Note: If using skim milk, topping ad filing will be slightly softer.

* Liqueur substitution: Stir 4 rounded tsp (20 ml) powdered instant coffee (dry) into filling mix (dry). Use 1¾ cups (415 ml) milk when preparing filling.

Mississippi Mud Pie

Opposite: Creamy Mocha Pie

Mississippi Mud Pie

4-oz bar (120 g) GHIRARDELLI Sweet Chocolate
½ cup (120 ml) butter
3 eggs
3 tbs (45 ml) light corn syrup
1 cup (240 ml) sugar
1 tsp (5 ml) vanilla
pinch salt
9-inch unbaked deep pastry pie shell
1 pint (480 ml) vanilla ice cream

Preheat oven to 350°F (180°C).

In heavy saucepan or microwave oven, melt chocolate with butter. Beat eggs; mix in corn syrup, sugar, vanilla and salt. Combine with chocolate mixture.

Pour into unbaked pie shell. Bake for 35-40 minutes or until top is cracked and filling is still soft. Cool to room temperature.

Top each wedge with a scoop of ice cream.
Serves 8-10.

Lemon Meringue Pie

1 prepared and baked 9-inch pie shell
⅔ cup (160 ml) WASHINGTON All-Purpose Flour
1½ cups (355 ml) sugar
¼ tsp (1 ml) salt
2 cups (480 ml) water
3 egg yolks, beaten
2 tbs (30 ml) butter or margarine
grated peel of lemon
⅓-½ cup (80-120 ml) lemon juice

Meringue:
3 egg whites
¼ tsp (1 ml) cream of tartar
6 tbs (90 ml) sugar

Preheat oven to 350°F (180°C).

Combine dry ingredients in saucepan. Gradually add water. Cook, stirring constantly, until mixture boils and is thick. Stir part of hot mixture into yolks. Blend well; return to hot mixture. Cook and stir 3-4 minutes longer, until mixture reaches 160°F (71°C). Stir in butter or margarine, lemon peel and lemon juice. Cool about 10 minutes.

Pour into baked crust.

Meringue: Beat egg whites and cream of tartar together to form soft peaks. Add sugar gradually; beat to stiff peaks. Spread on cooled filling. Bake about 15 minutes, until golden. Cool before serving. Serves 6.

Lemon Delight Pie

1 cup (240 ml) SUN•MAID Raisins
3 tbs (45 ml) plus ½ cup (120 ml) sugar, divided
3 cups (720 ml) plus 2 tbs (30 ml) water, divided
1 tbs (15 ml) cornstarch
1 pkg (4 serving size) lemon pudding/pie filling mix
2 egg yolks
1 cup (240 ml) dairy sour cream
9-inch baked pastry pie shell

In saucepan, combine raisins, 3 tbs sugar and 1 cup water. Simmer 15 minutes, stirring occasionally. Combine cornstarch and 2 tbs water; stir into raisin mixture. Cook until thickened; set aside.

In large saucepan, combine pie filling mix and remaining ½ cup sugar. Stir in remaining 2 cups water and egg yolks; blend well. Cook over medium heat, stirring constantly, about 5 minutes until mixture comes to a full boil and reaches 160°F (71°C). Stir in raisin mixture; cool.

Fold in sour cream; pour into pie shell. Refrigerate several hours, until chilled. Top with additional sour cream or meringue, if desired. Serves 8.

Cream Pie

¾ cup (180 ml) granulated sugar
⅓ cup (80 ml) sifted WASHINGTON All-Purpose Flour
¼ tsp (1 ml) salt
2 cups (480 ml) milk
3 egg yolks, beaten (reserve whites for meringue)
2 tbs (30 ml) butter or margarine
1 tsp (5 ml) vanilla
9-inch pie shell, baked

Combine dry ingredients in saucepan. Gradually stir in milk. Cook and stir until mixture boils. Cook 2 minutes longer over low heat.

Stir small amount of hot mixture into yolks. Blend well, return to hot mixture. Boil 2 minutes, stirring; cook until mixture reaches 160°F (71°C). Stir in butter or margarine and vanilla. Cool slightly.

Pour into baked crust. Top with meringue (whipped egg whites), whipped cream or fruit of your choice. Serves 6.

Banana Cream Pie: Slice 2-3 bananas into baked crust; pour filling over bananas.

Butterscotch Pie: Substitute brown sugar for granulated sugar. Double the amount of butter or margarine.

Chocolate Cream Pie: Increase sugar to 1 cup (240 ml) ; add 2 squares unsweetened chocolate to the milk mixture.

Coconut Cream Pie: Stir 1 cup (240 ml) flaked coconut into the filling before pouring it into the crust. Sprinkle ⅓ cup (80 ml) coconut over top of filling.

Date Cream Pie: Stir 1 cup (240 ml) chopped dates into the filling before pouring it into the crust.

Rum Pie: Substitute 1 tsp (5 ml) rum extract for vanilla.

Pineapple Cream Pie: Reduce sugar to ½ cup (120 ml) and milk to 1¼ cups (295 ml). Fold 1 cup (240 ml) well-drained pineapple into creamy mixture just before cooling.

Lemon Cream Pie: Omit vanilla. Stir in ¼ cup (60 ml) lemon juice and grated peel of 1 lemon to creamy mixture just before cooling.

Cream Pie

Chocolate Cream Pie

2 cups (480 ml) milk
2 eggs
2 egg yolks
1 cup (240 ml) sugar
¼ tsp (1 ml) salt
2 tbs (30 ml) all-purpose flour
2 tbs (30 ml) cornstarch
¼ cup (60 ml) SACO Baking Cocoa
4 tbs (60 ml) unsalted butter
1½ tsp (8 ml) vanilla extract
9-inch pie shell, baked
2 cups (480 ml) heavy or whipping cream
¼ cup (60 ml) sugar

Heat milk to a scald in medium saucepan (small bubbles should form around edges, but do not boil).

Lightly beat eggs and egg yolks in a medium mixing bowl.

In small bowl, combine sugar, salt, flour, cornstarch and cocoa. Slowly add dry ingredients to eggs, mixing well. Gradually pour hot milk into egg mixture, whisking constantly to prevent lumps.

Return mixture to saucepan; bring to a boil over medium heat, whisking constantly to prevent burning. Boil for 2-3 minutes or until mixture reaches 160°F (71°C). Remove from heat; stir in butter and vanilla.

Pour through a hand strainer into cooled pie shell. Cover with plastic wrap, pressing wrap directly onto pudding surface (prevents a skin from forming on top). Chill until set.

In large mixing bowl, place the cream and sugar together; refrigerate for 15 minutes. Beat until stiff peaks are formed. Remove plastic wrap and mound cream on top of filled pie. Serves 8-10.

Pie is best eaten soon after topped with cream. Refrigerate any leftover pie.

Boston Cream Pie

2½ cups (590 ml) sifted WASHINGTON Self-Rising Flour
1½ cups (355 ml) sugar
½ cup (120 ml) shortening
½ cup (120 ml) milk
3 eggs
1 tsp (5 ml) vanilla
¼ cup (60 ml) milk

Preheat oven to 350°F (180°C). Grease bottom only of two 8-inch layer pans.

Place first 4 ingredients in large mixing bowl. Blend on low speed then beat 2 minutes on medium speed. Add eggs, vanilla and milk. Blend on low speed, then beat 2 minutes on medium speed.

Pour into pans. Bake 25-30 minutes. Cool 10 minutes in pan. Remove, split each horizontally and fill with Cream Filling. Top with Chocolate Glaze or sprinkle with confectioners' sugar. Serve in wedge-shaped pieces. Yields 2 cakes, serves 12 each.

Cream Filling

5 tbs (75 ml) WASHINGTON Self-Rising Flour
½ cup (120 ml) sugar
½ tsp (3 ml) salt
2 cups (480 ml) scalded milk
2 eggs, slightly beaten
1 tsp (5 ml) vanilla

Combine flour, sugar and salt in top of double boiler. Stir in scalded milk and cook until thick. Continue cooking 15 minutes. Combine eggs with a little of hot mixture then pour it all back into hot mixture. Cook 3 minutes longer or until mixture reaches 160°F (71°C). Remove from heat; stir in vanilla. Cool. Fill split cake.

Opposite: Chocolate Cream Pie

Buttermilk Pie

9-inch unbaked pastry shell
¾ cup (180 ml) IMPERIAL Granulated Sugar
¼ cup (60 ml) all-purpose flour
½ tsp (3 ml) salt
½ cup (120 ml) butter, melted
3 eggs, beaten
½ cup (120 ml) buttermilk
1½ tsp (8 ml) vanilla or
1 tsp (5 ml) vanilla plus
1 tsp (5 ml) lemon extract

Preheat oven to 350°F (180°C).

In bowl, combine granulated sugar, flour and salt; add melted butter and beaten eggs; beat slightly with rotary beater. Stir in buttermilk, beating with spoon, then blending in vanilla or flavoring.

Pour into unbaked pastry shell. Bake for 45-50 minutes. Let cool before cutting. Serves 8.

Yuletide Raisinberry Pie

1 cup (240 ml) sugar
4 tsp (20 ml) cornstarch
½ tsp (3 ml) allspice or cinnamon
¾ cup (180 ml) orange juice
12-oz pkg (360 g) fresh or frozen whole cranberries
1½ cups (355 ml) SUN•MAID Raisins or Muscat Raisins
½ tsp (3 ml) grated lemon peel
½ tsp (3 ml) grated orange peel
pastry for 2-crust, 9-inch pie
beaten egg, for glaze

Preheat oven to 450°F (230°C).

In 3-quart saucepan, combine sugar, cornstarch and allspice or cinnamon. Gradually stir in orange juice, then cranberries, raisins and peels. Bring to boil; reduce heat and simmer until cranberries pop and mixture begins to thicken, 3-5 minutes. Cool to lukewarm.

Roll out ½ of the pastry on floured surface. Line 9-inch pie plate with pastry; flute edges. Spoon in filling.

Roll out remaining pastry; cut into strips ½-inch wide. Arrange in lattice pattern over filling; trim edges. Brush pastry with beaten egg; sprinkle lightly with additional sugar.

Bake for 10 minutes. Reduce heat to 375°F (190°C); continue baking 25-30 minutes or until filling is bubbly and crust is golden. Cover with foil as needed during baking to prevent over browning. Cool completely. Serve with ice cream or sweetened whipped cream, if desired. Serves 6.

Buttermilk Pie

Opposite: Yuletide Raisinberry Pie

Cream Cheese Pie

Filling:
2 8-oz pkgs (240 g each) cream cheese, softened
2 eggs, beaten
¾ cup (180 ml) sugar
1 tbs (15 ml) lemon juice
1 tsp (5 ml) McCORMICK/SCHILLING Pure Vanilla Extract

9-inch graham cracker crust, baked

Topping:
1 cup (240 ml) dairy sour cream
¼ cup (60 ml) sugar
1 tsp (5 ml) McCORMICK/SCHILLING Pure Vanilla Extract

Preheat oven to 350°F (180°C).

Filling: Place cream cheese, eggs, ¾ cup sugar, lemon juice and 1 tsp vanilla in large bowl and beat until light and smooth.

Pour into graham cracker crust. Bake 35 minutes. Remove from oven and set aside to cool 5 minutes. Do not turn oven off.

Topping: Place sour cream, ¼ cup sugar and 1 tsp vanilla in bowl and mix well. Spread carefully over top of pie.

Return pie to oven and bake 10 minutes. Cool to room temperature and place in refrigerator to chill 4 hours or overnight. Serves 6.

Opposite: Cream Cheese Pie

Almond Cream Cheese Pie with Strawberries

½ cup (120 ml) plus 2 tbs (30 ml) BLUE DIAMOND Blanched Whole Almonds, toasted, divided
1 cup (240 ml) flour, divided
½ cup (120 ml) plus 2 tbs (30 ml) sugar, divided
dash salt
6 tbs (90 ml) firm butter
3-5 tbs (45-75 ml) cold water
8 oz (240 g) cream cheese, softened
1 tsp (5 ml) vanilla extract
½ tsp (3 ml) almond extract
¼ cup (60 ml) hot water
1 envelope unflavored gelatin
1 cup (240 ml) heavy cream, whipped to soft peaks
2 pints (960 ml) fresh strawberries, cleaned and stems removed
¼ cup (60 ml) currant jelly
1 tbs (15 ml) water

Preheat oven to 400°F (205°C).

Finely grind ½ cup almonds with ½ cup flour in food processor. Add remaining ½ cup flour, 2 tbs sugar and salt. Add butter and mix with on-off bursts until mixture resembles coarse corn meal.* Do not overmix. Add enough water to just form dough. Shape dough into a ball and chill 30 minutes.

Roll dough out on lightly floured board. Fit into a 9-inch pie pan; chill 30 minutes. Prick bottom of pastry shell with fork. Line with wax paper, then fill with dried beans. Bake for 10 minutes. Remove paper and beans. Continue baking 10 minutes or until golden brown; reserve shell.

To prepare filling, beat cream cheese until smooth. Beat in remaining ½ cup sugar, vanilla and almond extract; reserve.

Over medium heat, combine hot water and gelatin until dissolved. Cool slightly; whisk thoroughly into whipped cream. Immediately fold whipped-cream-gelatin mixture into cream cheese mixture. Pour into prepared pie shell; smooth top with spatula. Chill 3 hours.

Garnish top of pie with whole strawberries. Whisk currant jelly and water over medium heat until melted; boil 30 seconds. Cool slightly. Glaze strawberries. If glaze becomes too thick, additional drops of water may be added. Finely chop remaining 2 tbs almonds and sprinkle over strawberries. Serves 6-8.

* To prepare by hand, finely grind ½ cup almonds with ½ cup flour in blender. Transfer to large bowl. Add remaining ½ cup flour, 2 tbs sugar and salt. With fingertips, work butter into flour mixture until mixture resembles coarse corn meal.

Chocolate Chunk Cookie Dough Cheese Pie

2 3-oz pkgs (90 g each) cream cheese, softened
⅓ cup (80 ml) granulated sugar
⅓ cup (80 ml) dairy sour cream
1 egg
½ tsp (3 ml) vanilla extract
6-oz pkg (180 g) chocolate crumb crust
Cookie Dough (recipe follows)

Preheat oven to 350°F (180°C).

In medium bowl, beat cream cheese and granulated sugar until blended; blend in sour cream, egg and vanilla. Pour into crust.

Prepare Cookie Dough; drop by teaspoonfuls evenly onto cream cheese batter. Bake 35-40 minutes or just until almost set in center. Cool completely. Refrigerate leftovers. Serves 8.

Cookie Dough

2 tbs (30 ml) butter or margarine, softened
¼ cup (60 ml) light brown sugar, packed
¼ cup (60 ml) all-purpose flour
1 tbs (15 ml) water
¼ tsp (1 ml) vanilla extract
1 cup (240 ml) HERSHEY'S Semi-Sweet Chocolate Chunks

In small bowl, beat butter or margarine and brown sugar; add flour, water and vanilla, beating until blended. Stir in chocolate chunks.

Chocolate Macaroon Heath Pie

½ cup (120 ml) butter or margarine, melted
3 cups (720 ml) shredded coconut
2 tbs (30 ml) all-purpose flour
½ gal (1.9 l) chocolate ice cream, softened
6-oz pkg (180 g) HEATH BITS, divided

Chocolate Chunk Cookie Dough Cheese Pie

Combine butter or margarine, coconut and flour. Press into a 9-inch pie pan. Bake at 375°F (190°C) for 10 minutes or until edges are light golden brown. Cool to room temperature.

Reserve ¼ cup Heath Bits and set aside. Combine ice cream and remaining Heath Bits. Spread over cooled crust. Sprinkle with reserved bits. Freeze at least 3 hours. Remove from freezer and let stand 10 minutes to soften before serving. Serves 6-8.

Baked Desserts

Clafoutis
Cobblers
Crisps
Betties
Buckles
BAKED
DESSERTS

Cherry Clafouti

2 16-oz cans (480 g each) sour pitted cherries
1 cup (240 ml) sugar, divided
4 tsp (20 ml) quick-cooking tapioca
1 tbs (15 ml) plus ½ tsp (3 ml) McCORMICK/SCHILLING
    Pure Vanilla Extract, divided
1 tsp (5 ml) lemon juice
¼ tsp (1 ml) McCORMICK/SCHILLING Pure Almond Extract
dash McCORMICK/SCHILLING Ground Cinnamon
1¼ cups (295 ml) milk
⅔ cup (160 ml) all-purpose flour
3 eggs
dash salt
2 tbs (30 ml) butter or margarine
cream, whipped cream or vanilla ice cream to serve, if desired

Preheat oven to 350°F (180°C). Grease bottom and sides of 2-quart oval, round or rectangular 2-inch deep baking pan.

Drain cherries, reserving ⅓ cup juice. Place cherries in large bowl. Add reserved ⅓ cup cherry juice, ⅔ cup sugar, tapioca, ½ tsp vanilla, lemon juice, almond extract and cinnamon. Mix well and set aside at room temperature.

Place milk, flour, remaining ⅓ cup sugar, eggs, remaining 1 tbs vanilla and salt in blender and blend 1 minute at highest speed. Pour 1½ cups batter into prepared pan. Set aside remaining batter.

Bake 10 minutes. Remove from oven and pour reserved cherry mixture over baked crust. Dot with butter or margarine and pour remaining batter evenly over cherries. Return to oven and bake 35 minutes. Serve immediately with cream, whipped cream or vanilla ice cream. Yields 12 ½-cup servings.

Opposite: Cherry Clafouti

Warm Cherry Puff

1 cup (240 ml) milk
2 eggs
½ cup (120 ml) biscuit baking mix
¼ cup (60 ml) sugar
¼ tsp (1 ml) almond extract
2 tbs (30 ml) margarine or butter, softened
21-oz can (630 g) COMSTOCK, THANK YOU or
    WILDERNESS Cherry or Light Cherry Pie Filling
    (or Peach or Apple Pie Filling)

Preheat oven to 400°F (205°C). Grease 10-inch pie pan or 11x7-inch baking pan.

Blend milk, eggs, biscuit mix, sugar, extract and margarine or butter in blender 15 seconds, or beat on high speed of mixer 1 minute.

Pour into pan. Spoon cherry filling over the top. Bake 25-30 minutes, until golden brown. Yields 8 servings.

Warm Cherry Puff

Pineapple Clafouti

15¼-oz can (458 g) DEL MONTE Pineapple Tidbits
    in its Own Juice
¼ cup (60 ml) sugar
¼ cup (60 ml) kirsch (cherry brandy)
1 tbs (15 ml) lemon juice
1 tsp (5 ml) cornstarch
⅓ cup (80 ml) DEL MONTE Natural Raisins
6-8 DEL MONTE Dried Apricots, chopped
3 eggs, separated
⅓ cup (80 ml) sugar
1 cup (240 ml) milk
⅔ cup (160 ml) flour
dash salt

Preheat oven to 325°F (165°C). Grease shallow, 2-quart baking dish.

Drain pineapple reserving juice in small saucepan. Add ¼ cup sugar, kirsch, lemon juice and cornstarch. Stir in raisins and apricots. Bring to boil. Reduce heat and cook, stirring constantly, 3 minutes. Remove from heat; add pineapple. Set aside 30 minutes.

Drain syrup into small serving dish. Spoon fruit evenly over bottom of baking dish.

Beat egg whites until soft peaks form; set aside. Beat together egg yolks and ⅓ cup sugar. Gradually add milk, flour and salt; mix until smooth and well blended. Fold egg whites into batter. Spread over fruit.

Place in center of oven. Bake 35-40 minutes. Dust with powdered sugar and cinnamon, if desired. Serve warm with reserved syrup. Yields 6-8 servings.

Apple Clafouti

2 23-oz jars (690 g each) MOTT'S Chunky Apple Sauce
⅔ cup (160 ml) seedless raisins
1 tsp (5 ml) cinnamon
1 cup (240 ml) all-purpose flour
1 tsp (5 ml) baking powder
½ tsp (3 ml) salt
¼ cup (60 ml) honey
¼ cup (60 ml) buttermilk
3 egg whites
confectioners sugar

Preheat oven to 400°F (205°C). Spray two 9-inch glass pie plates with cooking spray.

In a large bowl, combine applesauce, raisins and cinnamon. Set aside. In a separate bowl, stir together flour, baking powder and salt. In a medium bowl, mix honey, buttermilk and egg whites until slightly frothy. Add flour mixture to liquid mixture and whisk until blended.

Pour ½ cup batter into pie plates and bake for 4-5 minutes or until golden. Pour ½ of applesauce mixture over each plate and then pour remaining batter over each. Reduce heat to 350°F (180°C) and bake for 15-20 minutes until top is puffy and golden brown. Dust with confectioners sugar and let cool. Slice into wedges.
Yields 12 servings.

Pineapple Clafouti

Opposite: Apple Clafouti

Dutch Baby with Blueberry Sauce

Blueberry Sauce:
1 pint (480 ml) fresh or frozen North American blueberries
2 cups (480 ml) water
¼ cup (60 ml) sugar
2 tbs (30 ml) cornstarch
¼ tsp (1 ml) salt
2 tbs (30 ml) lemon juice
6 tbs (90 ml) butter or margarine

Dutch Baby Batter:
6 eggs
1½ cups (355 ml) low-fat milk
1½ cups (355 ml) flour

Preheat oven to 425°F (220°C). Use 10-inch ovenproof skillet or shallow baking dish.

Rinse and drain blueberries; add water and heat until warm. Combine sugar, cornstarch and salt; add to blueberries. Cook and stir until thickened and clear. Add lemon juice. Cool if desired.

Melt 3 tbs butter in skillet. Pour half of Batter into hot butter. Bake at 20 minutes or until puffy and golden. Spoon Blueberry Sauce into center of baked Dutch Baby. Sprinkle with confectioners sugar, if desired. Repeat with remaining batter. Yields 6 servings.

Dutch Baby Batter: Process eggs in blender or food processor at high 1 minute. With motor running, gradually add low-fat milk, then flour; blend 30 seconds longer.

Courtesy of the North American Blueberry Council.

Blueberry Cobbler with Maple Cream

2 pints (960 ml) fresh or frozen North American blueberries
⅔ cup (160 ml) sugar, divided
½ cup (120 ml) apple cider vinegar
2 tbs (30 ml) cornstarch
2 cups (480 ml) flour
2 tsp (10 ml) baking powder
½ tsp (3 ml) salt
⅓ cup (80 ml) butter or margarine
1 cup (240 ml) milk, divided
powdered sugar, optional

Maple Cream:
1 cup (240 ml) whipping cream
2 tbs (30 ml) maple syrup

Preheat oven to 400°F (205°C). Use six 12-oz baking dishes.

Rinse fresh blueberries; drain well. Combine blueberries, ½ cup sugar, cider vinegar and cornstarch. In a separate bowl, combine flour, remaining sugar, baking powder and salt; mix well. Cut in butter or margarine until mixture resembles cornmeal. Add ¾ cup milk; mix until dough leaves sides of bowl.

Turn dough onto lightly floured surface; roll to ¾-inch thickness. Cut into six 4-inch rounds.

Portion blueberry mixture into baking dishes. Top each with round of dough; brush with remaining milk. Bake 30 minutes or until topping browns and blueberries bubble. Cool 20 minutes before serving. Sprinkle with powdered sugar and serve with Maple Cream. Yields 6 servings.

Maple Cream: Beat whipping cream until thickened. Gradually add maple syrup; beat until stiff peaks form. Yields 2 cups.

Courtesy of the North American Blueberry Council.

Opposite: Dutch Baby with Blueberry Sauce

Peach Cobbler

1-lb 13-oz can (845 g) cling peach slices
½ cup (120 ml) plus 2 tbs (30 ml) sugar
1 cup (240 ml) plus 1 tbs (15 ml) sifted HECKER'S/
*   CERESOTA Unbleached Flour*
¼ tsp (1 ml) cinnamon
1 tsp (5 ml) baking powder
½ tsp (3 ml) salt
¼ cup (60 ml) butter
1 egg yolk
¼ cup (60 ml) milk, cream or half-and-half

Preheat oven to 425°F (220°C). Grease 9-inch round layer cake pan.

Drain peaches. Mix with ½ cup sugar, 1 tbs flour and cinnamon; set aside. Sift remaining flour and sugar, baking powder and salt together into mixing bowl. Cut in 2 tbs butter until mixture resembles coarse meal. Combine egg yolk and milk; add to flour mixture, mixing well.

Roll out to 9-inch circle; fit into cake pan. Reserve a little sugar-cinnamon mixture; lightly mix remainder with peaches. Turn peaches into pan over dough; sprinkle with cinnamon-sugar mixture. Dot with remaining butter.

Bake 22-25 minutes or until crust tests done. Cut into wedges; serve warm with cream. Yields 6-7 servings.

Fruit Cobbler Four Ways

1 cup (240 ml) all-purpose flour
1 cup (240 ml) sugar
1 tbs (15 ml) baking powder
dash salt
⅔ cup (160 ml) milk
¼ cup (60 ml) butter or margarine, diced
1 29-oz can (870 g) sliced peaches, drained, with juice reserved
½ tsp (3 ml) McCORMICK/SCHILLING Lemon Peel
¼ tsp (1 ml) McCORMICK/SCHILLING Ground Nutmeg
¼ tsp (1 ml) McCORMICK/SCHILLING Ground Cinnamon
cream, whipped cream or ice cream, to serve

Preheat oven to 350°F (180°C). Use 8x8x2-inch glass baking dish.

Combine flour, sugar, baking powder and salt in baking dish. Stir until well combined. Add milk and stir well. Dot surface of batter with butter. Arrange peaches over batter and pour reserved peach juice over. Sprinkle with lemon peel, nutmeg and cinnamon. Do not stir.

Bake 55-60 minutes or until golden crust has formed on top of cobbler. Serve warm with cream, whipped cream or ice cream. Yields 9 servings.

Apple Cobbler: Substitute peaches and peach juice with one 21-oz can (630 g) apple pie filling and 1 cup (240 ml) water. Do not stir. Proceed as directed above.

Cherry Cobbler: Replace peaches and peach juice with one 21-oz can (630 g) cherry pie filling and 1 cup (240 ml) water. Do not stir. Proceed as directed above.

Pineapple Cobbler: Replace peaches and peach juice with one 20-oz can (600 g) crushed pineapple in juice and 1 cup (240 ml) water. Do not stir. Proceed as directed above.

Opposite: Peach Cobbler

Apricot-Orange Cobbler

1-lb 14-oz can (875 g) apricot halves
¾ cup (180 ml) orange sections
½ tsp (3 ml) grated orange rind
¼ cup (60 ml) sugar
2 tbs (30 ml) cornstarch

Topping:
1 cup (240 ml) sifted PRESTO
⅓ cup (80 ml) light cream or milk
2 tbs (30 ml) margarine, melted
2 tsp (10 ml) sugar

Preheat oven to 400°F (205°C). Use 8x8x2-inch baking dish.

Drain apricot halves, reserving syrup. Arrange apricot halves and orange sections on bottom of baking dish. Sprinkle with orange rind. Combine sugar and cornstarch in medium saucepan. Stir in reserved syrup. Cook over medium heat, stirring constantly, until mixture comes to a boil; boil 1 minute. Pour cornstarch mixture over fruit. Heat in oven while preparing biscuit Topping.

Topping: Combine flour, cream and margarine. Stir just until moistened. Drop by tablespoon onto hot fruit. Sprinkle with the sugar. Continue baking 20-25 minutes or until golden. Serve warm with ice cream, if desired. Yields 6-8 servings.

Apple-Raisin Cobbler

Filling:
6 cups (1.4 l) sliced, peeled apples
⅔ cup (160 ml) sugar
3 tbs (45 ml) MINUTE Tapioca
1 tsp (5 ml) ground cinnamon
¼ tsp (1 ml) ground nutmeg
1 cup (240 ml) water
⅓ cup (80 ml) raisins
2 tbs (30 ml) margarine or butter

Biscuit Topping:
¾ cup (180 ml) flour
2 tbs (30 ml) sugar
1 tsp (5 ml) CALUMET Baking Powder
dash salt
¼ cup (60 ml) margarine or butter
3 tbs (45 ml) milk

Preheat oven to 375°F (190°C). Use ungreased 2-quart baking dish.

Mix apples, sugar, tapioca, cinnamon, nutmeg and water in large saucepan. Let stand 5 minutes. Stirring constantly, cook over medium heat until mixture comes to full boil.

Pour into baking dish. Sprinkle with raisins. Dot with margarine.

Biscuit Topping: Mix flour, 2 tbs sugar, baking powder and salt in large bowl. Cut in margarine. Stir in milk until soft dough forms.

Drop by tablespoonfuls onto hot fruit mixture. Bake 30 minutes or until topping is golden brown. Serve warm with whipped topping or ice cream, if desired. Yields 8 servings.

Opposite: Apricot-Orange Cobbler

Cranberry-Apple Cobbler

5 cups (1.2 l) sliced, peeled apples or pears
1¼ cups (295 ml) sugar
1 cup (240 ml) cranberries
3 tbs (45 ml) MINUTE Tapioca
½ tsp (3 ml) ground cinnamon
1 cup (240 ml) water
2 tbs (30 ml) margarine or butter
¾ cup (180 ml) flour
2 tbs (30 ml) sugar
1 tsp (5 ml) CALUMET Baking Powder
dash salt
¼ cup (60 ml) margarine or butter
3 tbs (45 ml) milk

Preheat oven to 375°F (190°C). Use 2-quart baking dish.

Mix apples or pears, sugar, cranberries, tapioca, cinnamon and water in a large saucepan. Let stand 5 minutes. Stirring constantly, cook on medium heat until mixture comes to full boil.

Pour into baking dish. Dot with margarine or butter.

Mix flour, 2 tbs sugar, baking powder and salt in large bowl. Cut in margarine or butter until mixture resembles coarse crumbs. Stir in milk until soft dough forms. Drop by tablespoonfuls onto hot apple mixture.

Bake 30 minutes or until topping is golden brown. Serve warm with whipped topping or ice cream, if desired. Yields 8 servings.

Pear Brown Betty

4 cups (960 ml) peeled, sliced pears
1 cup (240 ml) SUN•MAID Raisins
¼ cup (60 ml) orange juice
1 cup (240 ml) sugar
¾ cup (180 ml) all-purpose flour
½ tsp (3 ml) cinnamon
¼ tsp (1 ml) nutmeg
½ cup (120 ml) butter or margarine

Preheat oven to 375°F (190°C). USe 8-inch square baking pan.

In baking pan, combine pears, raisins and orange juice. In large bowl, combine sugar, flour, cinnamon and nutmeg; mix well. Using pastry blender or fork, cut in butter or margarine until mixture resembles coarse crumbs. Sprinkle evenly over pear mixture.

Bake 45 minutes or until lightly browned. Serve warm or at room temperature with ice cream or whipping cream, if desired. Yields 6 servings.

Pear Brown Betty

Apple Harvest Crisp

Apple Harvest Crisp

¾ cup (180 ml) plus 2 tbs (30 ml) DOMINO Granulated Sugar
2 tbs (30 ml) cornstarch
½ tsp (3 ml) ground cinnamon, plus a dash
dash ground nutmeg
5 cups (1.2 l) sliced, peeled apples
½ cup (120 ml) chopped dried fruit bits or raisins
¾ cup (180 ml) quick-cooking oats
¼ cup (60 ml) all-purpose flour
2 tbs (30 ml) butter or margarine
½ cup (120 ml) chopped nuts

Preheat oven to 375°F (190°C). Use deep-dish pie plate or 8x8x2-inch baking dish.

In bowl, combine ¾ cup sugar, cornstarch, ½ tsp cinnamon and nutmeg. Add apples and dried fruit or raisins, tossing gently to combine.

Turn into pie plate or baking dish.

In bowl, combine 2 tbs sugar, oats, flour and dash cinnamon. With 2 knives, pastry blender or fork, cut in butter or margarine until mixture is crumbly. Stir in nuts. Sprinkle evenly over fruit mixture.

Bake 35-40 minutes or until fruit is tender and crumbs are golden brown. Serve warm and, if desired, with vanilla ice cream or softly whipped cream. Yields 6 servings.

Microwave directions: Prepare recipe according to above directions using a microwave-safe dish. Place on an inverted plate to slightly elevate dish in the oven. Cook at high 8-9 minutes or until fruit is tender, rotating dish once if necessary.

Cran-Apple Crisp

2 21-oz cans (630 g each) COMSTOCK, THANK YOU
*   or WILDERNESS Cranberry Classics Apple Cranberry*
*   or Apple Pie Filling*
¼ cup (60 ml) flour
¼ cup (60 ml) quick oats
¼ cup (60 ml) brown sugar
¾ tsp (4 ml) ground cinnamon
¼ cup (60 ml) chopped nuts, optional
2 tbs (30 ml) butter or margarine

Preheat oven to 400°F (205°C). Use shallow 1½-quart casserole dish.

Pour apple cranberry or apple filling into casserole dish.

In a small bowl, mix flour, oats, brown sugar, cinnamon and nuts. Cut in butter or margarine until mixture is crumbly. Sprinkle over filling.

Bake 25 minutes or until topping is golden brown. Cool on rack. Top with scoop of nondairy whipped topping or ice cream, if desired. Yields 6-8 servings.

Indian Fruit Crisp

4 cups (960 ml) fresh sliced pears, peaches or apples
¼ cup (60 ml) sugar
½ tsp (3 ml) ginger, nutmeg or cinnamon
grated peel of 1 lemon
1 tbs (15 ml) lemon juice
½ cup (120 ml) INDIAN HEAD Corn Meal
¾ cup (180 ml) WASHINGTON All-Purpose Flour
½-¾ cup (120-180 ml) sugar
⅓ cup (80 ml) butter or margarine

Preheat oven to 400°F (205°C). Grease 1½-quart baking dish.

Combine first 5 ingredients in bowl. Place in baking dish. Set aside.

Combine remaining ingredients by cutting in butter or margarine until crumbly. Sprinkle over fruit mixture.

Bake 35-40 minutes. Serve warm with cream. Yields 6 servings.

Indian Fruit Crisp

Opposite:
Cran-Apple Crisp

Pears Anna

3 tbs (45 ml) melted butter, divided
3 tbs (45 ml) brown sugar, packed
3 tbs (45 ml) flour
dash ground ginger
8 cups (1.9 l) cored and thinly sliced USA Bosc pears
1 tsp (5 ml) grated orange peel

Preheat oven to 400°F (205°C). Coat a 9-inch ovenproof skillet with 1 tbs butter.

Combine brown sugar, flour and ginger; set aside.

Layer half pear slices in pan, spoke-fashion, with stem ends toward center; sprinkle layer with half sugar mixture. Repeat layers. Top with remaining melted butter and orange peel.

Cook, uncovered, over medium heat 10 minutes. Bake, uncovered, 30 minutes; baste once. Yields 6 servings.

Courtesy of the Oregon Washington California Pear Bureau.

Pears Anna

Blueberry Buckle

¾ cup (180 ml) sugar
¼ cup (60 ml) butter or margarine
2 eggs
1 tsp (5 ml) vanilla extract
2 cups (480 ml) flour
2 tsp (10 ml) baking powder
½ tsp (3 ml) salt
½ cup (120 ml) buttermilk
2½ cups (590 ml) fresh or frozen North American blueberries

Streusel Topping:
¼ cup (60 ml) granulated sugar
¼ cup (60 ml) brown sugar, packed
¼ cup (60 ml) flour
¼ cup (60 ml) butter or margarine
½ tsp (3 ml) ground cinnamon

Preheat oven to 375°F (190°C). Lightly grease 9-inch square baking pan.

Cream sugar and butter or margarine; beat in eggs and vanilla. Combine flour, baking powder and salt. Add flour mixture and buttermilk alternately to batter. Stir in berries.

Streusel Topping: Blend sugar, packed brown sugar, flour, butter or margarine and ground cinnamon until crumbly.

Spread batter in baking pan. Sprinkle with Streusel Topping. Bake 25-30 minutes or until wooden pick inserted near center comes out clean. Yields 9 servings.

Courtesy of the North American Blueberry Council.

Buttermilk Blueberry Buckle

2 cups (480 ml) all-purpose flour
2 tbs (30 ml) SACO Buttermilk Blend
1 tsp (5 ml) baking powder
¼ tsp (1 ml) baking soda
½ tsp (3 ml) salt
1 cup (240 ml) sugar
¼ cup (60 ml) soft shortening
1 egg
½ cup (120 ml) water
2 cups (480 ml) frozen or fresh blueberries

Topping:
½ cup (120 ml) sugar
⅓ cup (80 ml) flour
½ tsp (3 ml) cinnamon
¼ cup (60 ml) butter or margarine, softened

Preheat oven to 375°F (190°C). Grease and flour 9x9-inch pan.

Sift the flour, buttermilk blend, baking powder, baking soda and salt together and set aside. In a separate mixing bowl cream together the sugar and shortening until fluffy. Add egg and beat thoroughly. Blend in water. Add the dry ingredients to the wet and mix just until smooth. Do not overbeat. Fold blueberries into batter. Spread batter in pan.

Topping: Mix the sugar, flour, cinnamon and soft butter together in a small mixing bowl. Sprinkle over top of the batter.

Bake 45-50 minutes or until tested done. Best served warm. When using frozen berries add 10-12 minutes to baking time. Yields 9 servings.

Buttermilk Blueberry Buckle

Cookies

Drop
Sugar
Chocolate
Lace
Shortbread
Slicing
Biscotti
Bar
Brownies
COOKIES

Original Nestlé Toll House Chocolate Chip Cookies

2¼ cups (540 ml) all-purpose flour
1 tsp (5 ml) baking soda
1 tsp (5 ml) salt
1 cup (240 ml) butter, softened
¾ cup (180 ml) granulated sugar
¾ cup (180 ml) brown sugar, packed
1 tsp (5 ml) vanilla extract
2 eggs
12-oz pkg (360 g) NESTLÉ TOLL HOUSE
  Semi-Sweet Chocolate Morsels
1 cup (240 ml) chopped nuts

Preheat oven to 375°F (190°C). Grease baking sheet.

Combine flour, baking soda and salt in bowl. Beat butter, granulated sugar, brown sugar and vanilla in large mixing bowl. Add eggs, one at a time, beating well after each addition. Gradually beat in flour mixture. Stir in morsels and nuts.

Drop by rounded tablespoons onto greased baking sheets. Bake 9-11 minutes or until golden brown. Let stand for 2 minutes; remove to wire racks to cool completely. Yields about 5 dozen cookies.

Pan Cookie Variation: Prepare dough as above. Spread into greased 15x10-inch jelly-roll pan. Bake in preheated 375°F (190°C) oven 20-25 minutes or until golden brown. Cool in pan on wire rack. Yields about 4 dozen bars.

Slice and Bake Variation: Prepare dough as above. Divide in half; wrap in wax paper. Chill for 1 hour or until firm. Shape each half into 15-inch log; wrap in wax paper. Chill for 30 minutes. Cut into ½-inch thick slices; place on ungreased baking sheets. Bake in preheated 375°F (190°C) oven 8-10 minutes or until golden brown. Let stand for 2 minutes; remove to wire racks to cool completely. Yields 5 dozen cookies.

May be stored in refrigerator for up to 1 week or in freezer for up to 8 weeks.

Baker's Peanut Butter Chocolate Chip Cookies

½ cup (120 ml) margarine or butter, softened
1 cup (240 ml) peanut butter
¾ cup (180 ml) brown sugar, firmly packed
¾ cup (180 ml) granulated sugar
1 tsp (5 ml) vanilla
2 eggs
1½ cups (355 ml) all-purpose flour
1 tsp (5 ml) baking soda
¼ tsp (1 ml) salt
12-oz pkg (360 g) BAKER'S Semi-Sweet Real Chocolate Chips
1 cup (240 ml) chopped nuts, optional

Preheat oven to 375°F (190°C). Use ungreased cookie sheets.

Beat margarine or butter, peanut butter, sugars, vanilla and eggs until light and fluffy. Mix in flour, baking soda and salt. Stir in chips and nuts, if desired.

Drop by rounded teaspoonfuls, 2 inches apart, onto cookie sheets. Bake for 8-10 minutes or until golden brown. Remove from cookie sheet to cool on wire racks. Yields about 6 dozen cookies.

Opposite:
Original Nestlé Toll House
Chocolate Chip Cookies

Yuletide Chocolate Chip Cookies

½ cup (120 ml) butter or margarine
⅔ cup (160 ml) brown sugar, packed
1 tsp (5 ml) brandy flavoring
3 tbs (45 ml) dark corn syrup
1 egg
1 cup (240 ml) diced candied mixed fruit
1⅓ cups (320 ml) flour, divided
1 tsp (5 ml) pumpkin pie spice
¾ tsp (4 ml) baking powder
¼ tsp (1 ml) salt
6 oz (180 g) GHIRARDELLI Semi-Sweet Chocolate Chips
⅓ cup (80 ml) chopped pecans
⅓ cup (80 ml) slivered almonds
⅓ cup (80 ml) currants
14 red candied cherries, quartered

Preheat oven to 350°F (180°C) 10 minutes before baking. Grease baking sheet.

Cream butter or margarine with brown sugar, brandy flavoring and corn syrup; add egg and beat until very light. Coat candied fruit with 1 tablespoon of the flour; set aside. Sift remaining flour with pumpkin pie spice, baking powder and salt. Stir dry ingredients into creamed mixture. Add fruit, chocolate chips, pecans, almonds and currants.

Chill dough 1 hour. Drop by heaping teaspoons onto baking sheet. Top each cookie with piece of cherry. Bake 8-10 minutes. Cool on rack. Store in covered container several days to soften and age. Yields 4½ dozen cookies.

Almond Butter Chocolate Chip Cookies

1 cup (240 ml) flour
½ tsp (3 ml) salt
½ tsp (3 ml) baking soda
½ cup (120 ml) butter, softened
½ cup (120 ml) almond butter*
½ cup (120 ml) light brown sugar, firmly packed
½ cup (120 ml) granulated sugar
1 egg, lightly beaten
1 tsp (5 ml) almond extract
½ cup (120 ml) BLUE DIAMOND Chopped Natural Almonds, toasted
½ cup (120 ml) semisweet chocolate chips

Preheat oven to 350°F (180°C). Grease cookie sheet.

Mix flour, salt and baking soda; reserve. Cream butter and almond butter. Beat in, one at a time, brown sugar, granulated sugar, egg and almond extract. Add flour mixture and blend well. Stir in almonds and chocolate chips.

Drop by teaspoonfuls onto cookie sheet. Bake until lightly browned, about 10 minutes. Cool on wire rack. Yields 4 dozen cookies.

*Note: To prepare ½ cup (120 ml) of almond butter, grind 1 cup (240 ml) toasted blanched whole almonds in food processor or blender until coarse in texture. With machine running, add ½ tbs (8 ml) vegetable oil and continue to process until texture is smooth. This recipe can be easily doubled or tripled when a large quantity of almond butter is desired.

Almond Butter
Chocolate Chip Cookies

Island Cookies

1⅔ cups (400 ml) all-purpose flour
¾ tsp (4 ml) baking powder
½ tsp (3 ml) baking soda
½ tsp (3 ml) salt
¾ cup (180 ml) butter or margarine, softened
¾ cup (180 ml) brown sugar, packed
¾ cup (180 ml) granulated sugar
1 tsp (5 ml) vanilla extract
1 egg
11½ oz (345 g) pkg NESTLÉ TOLL HOUSE Milk Chocolate
    Morsels, Semi-Sweet Chocolate Morsels, Semi-Sweet Mini
    Morsels, Mint-Chocolate Morsels, Premier White Morsels or
    Butterscotch Morsels
1 cup (240 ml) flaked coconut, toasted if desired
¾ cup (180 ml) chopped macadamia nuts or walnuts

Preheat oven to 375°F (190°C). Use ungreased baking
sheets.

Combine flour, baking powder, baking soda and salt
in small bowl. Beat butter or margarine, brown sugar,
granulated sugar and vanilla in large mixing bowl until
creamy. Beat in egg. Gradually beat in flour mixture.
Stir in morsels, coconut and nuts.

Drop by slightly rounded tablespoon onto baking
sheets. Bake 8-11 minutes or until edges are lightly
browned. Let stand for 2 minutes; remove to wire racks to
cool completely. Yields about 3 dozen cookies.

Triple Chocolate Cookies

1 cup (240 ml) all-purpose flour
1¾ cups (415 ml) NESTLÉ TOLL HOUSE Baking Cocoa
1 tsp (5 ml) baking soda
12-oz pkg (360 g) NESTLÉ TOLL HOUSE
    Semi-Sweet Chocolate Morsels, divided
⅓ cup (80 ml) butter or margarine, cut into pieces
14-oz can (420 ml) CARNATION Sweetened Condensed Milk
1 egg
1 tsp (5 ml) vanilla
½ cup (120 ml) chopped nuts

Preheat oven to 350°F (180°C). Lightly grease baking
sheets.

Combine flour, cocoa and baking soda in medium
bowl. Mix 1 cup morsels and butter or margarine in large,
heavy saucepan over low heat, stirring until smooth.
Remove from heat. Stir in sweetened condensed milk, egg
and vanilla; mix well. Stir in flour mixture. Stir in nuts and
remaining morsels (dough will be soft).

Drop dough by rounded tablespoons onto baking
sheets. Bake 8-10 minutes or until edges are set but centers
are still slightly soft. Let stand for 2 minutes; remove to
wire racks to cool completely. Yields 3½ dozen cookies.

Opposite:
Island Cookies *and*
Triple Chocolate Cookies

Mini Morsel Meringue Cookies

4 egg whites
½ tsp (3 ml) salt
½ tsp (3 ml) cream of tartar
1 cup (240 ml) granulated sugar
12-oz pkg (360 g) NESTLÉ TOLL HOUSE
*   Semi-Sweet Chocolate Mini Morsels*

Preheat oven to 300°F (150°C). Grease baking sheets.
   Beat egg whites, salt and cream of tartar in small mixing bowl until soft peaks form. Gradually add sugar; beat until stiff peaks form. Gently fold in morsels ⅓ at a time.   Drop by level tablespoons onto baking sheets. Bake 20-25 minutes or until meringues are dry and crisp. Let stand for 2 minutes; remove to wire racks to cool completely. Store in airtight containers. Yields 5 dozen cookies.

Chocolate Chunk
Whole Wheat Cookies

Chocolate Chunk Whole Wheat Cookies

2½ cups (590 ml) lightly-spooned whole wheat flour
¼ cup (60 ml) all-purpose flour
⅓ cup (80 ml) SACO Buttermilk Blend
½ tsp (3 ml) baking soda
1 cup (240 ml) butter, softened
1 tsp (6ml) vanilla extract
1½ cups (355 ml) dark brown sugar, firmly-packed
3 eggs
1 cup (240 ml) coarsely broken walnuts or pecans, optional
12-oz pkg (360 g) SACO Chocolate Chunks

Preheat oven to 375°F (190°C). Grease cookie sheets.
   Stir together whole wheat flour, all-purpose flour, buttermilk blend and baking soda in medium bowl until blended. Set aside. Beat butter, vanilla, brown sugar and eggs in large bowl with electric mixer until well blended and lighter in color. Gradually beat in the flour mixture on low speed, just until blended. Stir in nuts, if desired, and chocolate chunks.
   Drop rounded teaspoonfuls onto cookie sheets, spacing about 1½ inches apart. Bake 8-10 minutes. Yields 5 dozen cookies.

Opposite: Mini Morsel Meringue Cookies
and Frosted Maple Pecan White Chip Cookies (see page 370)

Chocolate Chocolate Chunk Cookies

1¾ cups (415 ml) flour
¼ tsp (1 ml) baking soda
1 cup (240 ml) butter, softened
1 cup (240 ml) granulated sugar
½ cup (120 ml) light brown sugar
1 tsp (5 ml) vanilla extract
⅓ cup (80 ml) SACO Premium Baking Cocoa
2 tbs (30 ml) light cream
12-oz pkg (360 g) SACO Chocolate Chunks
4 oz (120 g) SACO Chocolate Chunks, grated
1 cup (240 ml) chopped pecans, optional

Preheat oven to 350°F (180°C). Grease cookie sheets.

Sift together flour and baking soda; set aside. Cream butter and sugars together with mixer and add the vanilla; mix well. Add cocoa and beat until well blended. Add cream and, on low speed, gradually add flour mixture. Beat just until mixed. Stir in chocolate chunks and nuts, if desired.

Drop by heaping tablespoons onto cookie sheets; flatten cookie slightly. Bake for 12-13 minutes. The cookies should feel soft; do not overbake. Let cookies stand on cookie sheet for 2 minutes. Transfer to wire racks to cool. Yields 2 dozen cookies.

Chocolate Chocolate Chunk Cookies

Incredible Chocolate Chunk Cookies

1½ cups (355 ml) rolled oats
2 cups (480 ml) flour
½ tsp (3 ml) baking powder
1 tsp (5 ml) baking soda
½ tsp (3 ml) salt
1 cup (240 ml) butter, softened
1 cup (240 ml) sugar
1 cup (240 ml) light brown sugar
1 tbs (15 ml) vanilla extract
2 eggs
12-oz pkg (360 g) SACO Chocolate Chunks
1½ cups (355 ml) chopped walnuts

Preheat oven to 375°F (190°C). Grease cookie sheets.

Pulverize oats in blender or food processor to a fine powder. In small bowl mix ground oats, flour, baking powder, baking soda, and salt. In large bowl, combine butter, sugar, brown sugar and vanilla; beat until creamy. Beat in eggs. Gradually add oat and flour mixture. Stir in grated and whole chocolate chunks and nuts.

Drop by heaping tablespoons onto cookie sheets. Bake 10-12 minutes. Transfer to wire racks to cool. Yields 4 dozen cookies.

Opposite:
Incredible Chocolate
Chunk Cookies

Oatmeal-Prune Chocolate Chunk Cookies

2¼ cups (540 ml) flour
2 tsp (10 ml) baking powder
¾ tsp (4 ml) baking soda
1 tsp (5 ml) salt
1½ tsp (8 ml) ground cinnamon
1½ tsp (8 ml) ginger
1 cup (240 ml) butter, softened
½ cup (120 ml) granulated sugar
1 cup (240 ml) light brown sugar
1 egg
1 cup (240 ml) rolled oats
1 cup (240 ml) pitted prunes, chopped
1 cup (240 ml) coarsely chopped walnuts
12-oz pkg (360 g) SACO Chocolate Chunks

Preheat oven to 375°F (190°C). Grease cookie sheets.

In small bowl, sift together the flour, baking powder, baking soda, salt, cinnamon and ginger. In large bowl, cream the butter. Add both sugars and beat well. Beat in egg. Add the sifted dry ingredients. With a large wooden spoon stir in the rolled oats, prunes, nuts and chocolate chunks.

Roll large tablespoons of dough into balls, place 2 inches apart on cookie sheets. Flatten with a water-moistened fork, criss-cross fashion. Bake 12-15 minutes. Transfer to wire racks to cool. Yields 2-2½ dozen cookies.

Double Chocolate Chunk Mocha Cookies

4 squares BAKER'S Semi-Sweet Chocolate
½ cup (120 ml) margarine or butter, slightly softened
½ cup (120 ml) granulated sugar
¼ cup (60 ml) brown sugar, firmly packed
1 egg
1 tsp (5 ml) vanilla
2 tbs (30 ml) instant coffee
1 cup (240 ml) all-purpose flour
½ tsp (3 ml) CALUMET Baking Powder
¼ tsp (1 ml) salt
¾ cup (180 ml) chopped walnuts, optional
4 squares BAKER'S Semi-Sweet Chocolate

Preheat oven to 375°F (190°C). Grease cookie sheets.

Melt 1 square chocolate; set aside. Cut 3 squares chocolate into large (½-inch) chunks; set aside. Beat margarine or butter, sugars, eggs, vanilla and instant coffee until light and fluffy. Stir in 1 square melted chocolate. Mix in flour, baking powder and salt. Stir in chocolate chunks and walnuts, if desired. Refrigerate 30 minutes.

Drop dough by heaping tablespoonfuls, about 2 inches apart, onto cookie sheets. Bake 8 minutes or until lightly browned. Cool 5 minutes on cookie sheets. Remove and finish cooling on wire racks.

Melt 4 squares chocolate. Dip ½ of each cookie into melted chocolate. Let stand on waxed paper until chocolate is firm. Yields 2 dozen cookies.

Oatmeal-Prune Chocolate
Chunk Cookies

Opposite:
Double Chocolate Chunk
Mocha Cookies

Frosted Maple Pecan White Chip Cookies

3 cups (720 ml) all-purpose flour
2 tsp (10 ml) baking soda
2 cups (480 ml) brown sugar, packed
1 cup (240 ml) shortening
½ cup (120 ml) butter or margarine, softened
2 eggs
1 tsp (5 ml) maple flavoring
1 tsp (5 ml) vanilla extract
12-oz pkg (360 g) NESTLÉ TOLL HOUSE
    Premier White Morsels
½ cup (120 ml) chopped pecans
60 pecan halves

Maple Frosting:
4 cups (960 ml) powdered sugar
4-6 tbs (60-90 ml) milk
¼ cup (60 ml) butter or margarine, softened
1 tsp (5 ml) maple flavoring

Preheat oven to 350°F (180°C). Use ungreased baking sheets.

Combine flour and baking soda in medium bowl. Beat brown sugar, shortening, butter or margarine, eggs, maple flavoring and vanilla in large mixing bowl until creamy. Gradually beat in flour mixture. Stir in morsels and chopped pecans.

Drop by rounded tablespoons onto baking sheet. Bake 9-12 minutes or until light golden brown. Let stand for 2 minutes; remove to wire racks to cool completely. Spread with Maple Frosting; top each cookie with pecan half. Yields 5 dozen cookies.

Maple Frosting: Combine all ingredients in medium bowl; stir until smooth.

Hermits I

½ cup (120 ml) shortening
½ cup (120 ml) sugar
½ cup (120 ml) brown sugar, firmly packed
2 eggs
2 cups (480 ml) all-purpose flour
2 tsp (10 ml) baking powder
1 tsp (5 ml) cinnamon
½ tsp (3 ml) nutmeg
¼ tsp (1 ml) salt
¼ tsp (1 ml) cloves
1 cup (240 ml) SUN•MAID Raisins
¾ cup (180 ml) chopped DIAMOND Walnuts

Preheat oven to 350°F (180°C). Grease cookie sheets.

Combine shortening, sugar, brown sugar and eggs; beat until light and fluffy. Combine flour, baking powder, cinnamon, nutmeg, salt and cloves. Add to shortening mixture; mix well. Stir in raisins and walnuts.

Drop by teaspoonfuls onto cookie sheets. Bake in upper third of oven 12-15 minutes or until lightly browned. Yields 3 dozen cookies.

Opposite: Hermits I

Hermits II

2 eggs, beaten
1 cup (240 ml) sugar
½ cup (120 ml) milk
2 tsp (10 ml) vanilla
4 cups (960 ml) sifted PRESTO
1 tsp (5 ml) cinnamon
½ tsp (3 ml) cloves
½ tsp (3 ml) nutmeg
1 cup (240 ml) raisins
½ cup (120 ml) chopped nuts
¾ cup (180 ml) melted shortening

Preheat oven to 350°F (180°C). Grease cookie sheets.

Beat eggs well, add sugar and milk (to which the vanilla has been added). Add Presto which has been sifted with spices, raisins and nuts sprinkled with Presto. Add melted shortening and stir until blended.

Drop by teaspoonfuls onto cookie sheets and bake 10-12 minutes. Yields 6 dozen cookies.

Chewy Oat Bran Raisin Cookies

½ cup (120 ml) margarine or butter, softened
½ cup (120 ml) brown sugar, firmly packed
2 eggs
½ cup (120 ml) GRANDMA'S Unsulphured Molasses
1¼ cups (295 ml) all-purpose flour
2 tsp (10 ml) baking soda
½ tsp (3 ml) salt
1 tsp (5 ml) cinnamon
½ tsp (3 ml) ginger
1½ cups (355 ml) oat bran or rolled oats
1 cup (240 ml) raisins
1 cup (240 ml) chopped nuts

Preheat oven to 350°F (180°C) 10 minutes before baking. Grease cookie sheets.

In large bowl, beat margarine or butter and brown sugar until light and fluffy. Add eggs and molasses; beat well. Stir in remaining ingredients; mix well. Refrigerate 1-2 hours for ease in handling.

Drop by teaspoonfuls 2 inches apart onto prepared cookie sheets. Bake 10-15 minutes or until golden brown. Immediately remove from cookie sheets.
Yields 3-4 dozen cookies.

Hermits II

Opposite: Chewy Oat Bran Raisin Cookies

Sun Maid New Oatmeal Raisin Frost-Bites

3 tbs (45 ml) orange juice or orange-flavored liqueur
¾ cup (180 ml) SUN•MAID Raisins
½ cup (120 ml) butter or margarine, at room temperature
¾ cup (180 ml) sugar
1 large egg
2 tsp (10 ml) grated orange peel
1 cup (240 ml) all-purpose flour
1 tsp (5 ml) baking soda
1½ cups (355 ml) rolled oats
8 oz (240 g) white chocolate baking chips
1 tsp (5 ml) vegetable oil or shortening

Preheat oven to 350°F (180°C). Grease cookie sheets.

In small bowl, combine orange juice or liqueur and raisins; let stand overnight. In large bowl, beat butter or margarine and sugar until fluffy. Beat in egg and orange peel. In another bowl, combine flour and baking soda; stir into butter mixture. Add raisins, any soaking liquid, and oats; mix well.

Drop dough by rounded teaspoonfuls onto cookie sheets, spacing 2 inches apart; flatten slightly. Bake 10-12 minutes. Transfer to racks, and cool completely.

In small, deep, microwave-safe bowl, heat white chocolate chips and oil 3-4 minutes on low power, stirring once. Let stand 2 minutes, stir until smooth. Dip one-third of cookie in chocolate; set on waxed paper-lined baking sheets. Chill until chocolate is firm. Yields 3 dozen cookies.

Strip Variation: Divide dough into 4 equal portions. Place 2 portions, at least 6 inches apart, on baking sheet. With well-floured hands, pat each portion into a 12-inch long log (dough will be sticky); flatten each log to 1½ inches wide.

Bake until golden brown, 12-14 minutes. Let cool on baking sheets 2 minutes; cut logs diagonally into 1-inch-wide strips. Follow for dipping cookies. Yields 4 dozen cookies.

Buttermilk-Oatmeal-Nut Cookies

1¾ cups (180 ml) sifted HECKERS/CERESOTA
    Unbleached Flour
¾ tsp (4 ml) baking soda
1 cup (240 ml) shortening
1½ cups (355 ml) brown sugar, firmly packed
1 tsp (5 ml) salt
½ tsp (3 ml) cinnamon
½ tsp (3 ml) cloves
¼ cup (60 ml) buttermilk or sour milk
2 eggs
1½ cups (355 ml) uncooked rolled oats
1 cup (240 ml) chopped nuts

Preheat oven to 375°F (190°C). Grease cookie sheet.

Sift together flour and soda. Combine shortening, brown sugar, salt, cinnamon, cloves, buttermilk or sour milk and eggs; beat vigorously. Mix in flour, oats and nuts.

Drop mixture by teaspoonfuls, 2 inches apart, onto prepared cookie sheet. Bake 10-15 minutes. Yields 3 dozen cookies.

Chocolate Raisin Oat Cookies

1 cup (240 ml) butter or margarine, softened
1½ cups (355 ml) brown sugar, firmly packed
2 eggs
2 tsp (10 ml) vanilla
6 oz (180 g) semisweet chocolate pieces, melted
2 cups (480 ml) all-purpose flour
2 tsp (10 ml) baking soda
2½ cups (590 ml) rolled oats
1½ cups (355 ml) SUN•MAID Raisins

Preheat oven to 350°F (180°C). Grease cookie sheets.

Combine butter or margarine, brown sugar, eggs and vanilla in large bowl; beat until light and fluffy. Blend in melted chocolate. Combine flour and baking soda. Stir into butter mixture; mix well. Stir in oats and raisins.

Drop by tablespoonfuls onto cookie sheets. Bake in upper third of oven, 10-12 minutes. Remove from cookie sheets; cool on wire racks. Yields 4 dozen cookies.

Oatmeal Chocolate Walnut Cookies

½ cup (120 ml) butter, softened
½ cup (120 ml) margarine, softened
1 cup (240 ml) JACK FROST Dark Brown Sugar, packed
1 cup (240 ml) JACK FROST Granulated Sugar
2 large eggs
2 tbs (30 ml) milk
2 tsp (10 ml) vanilla
2 cups (480 ml) all-purpose flour
1 tsp (5 ml) baking powder
1 tsp (5 ml) baking soda
1 tsp (5 ml) salt
2¼ cups (540 ml) quick-cooking oats
12 oz (360 g) semisweet chocolate chips
1 cup (240 ml) coarsely chopped walnuts

Preheat oven to 350°F (180°C) 10 minutes before baking. Grease cookie sheets.

In large mixing bowl, cream butter, margarine and sugars; add eggs, milk and vanilla and beat until light and fluffy. In medium bowl, stir together flour, baking powder, baking soda, salt and oats. Add to creamed mixture until blended. Stir in chocolate chips and nuts. Cover and refrigerate for at least 1 hour.

Drop by teaspoonfuls onto cookie sheets. Bake 10-12 minutes or until edges are slightly browned. (The tops of the cookies will still be moist and light colored.) Do not overbake. Remove from oven and let cool on cookie sheets for 5 minutes. Remove to wire racks to cool completely. Yields 4 dozen.

Gourmet Flavor Variations: Substitute the following for semisweet chocolate chips and walnuts:

2 cups (480 ml) coconut and 1 cup (240 ml) chopped hazelnuts

2 cups (480 ml) white chocolate chips and 1 cup (240 ml) chopped macadamia nuts

2 cups (480 ml) raisins or butterscotch chips and 1 cup (240 ml) chopped pecans

2 cups (480 ml) milk chocolate chips and 1 cup (240 ml) chopped or slivered almonds

2 cups (480 ml) candy coated chocolate pieces and 1 cup (240 ml) chopped peanuts

Oatmeal Chocolate Walnut Cookies

Oat Pineapple Drops

½ cup (120 ml) shortening
1 cup (240 ml) brown sugar
1 egg
2 cups (480 ml) sifted PRESTO
1 cup (240 ml) crushed pineapple
1 tsp (5 ml) vanilla
1 cup (240 ml) oats
½ cup (120 ml) chopped pecans or walnuts

Preheat oven to 350°F (180°C). Grease baking sheets.

Cream shortening, add sugar gradually. Add egg and beat well. Add sifted flour alternately with pineapple, to which vanilla has been added. Fold in oats and nuts.

Drop by teaspoonfuls onto baking sheet and bake 12-15 minutes. Yields 3 dozen cookies.

Oatmeal Snacks

2 eggs
¼ cup (60 ml) vegetable oil
½ cup (120 ml) GRANDMA Molasses
1 cup (240 ml) sifted, all-purpose flour
1⅓ cups (320 ml) oats
¾ cup (180 ml) shredded coconut
1 tsp (5 ml) cinnamon
½ cup (120 ml) chopped walnuts

Preheat oven to 350°F (180°C). Use ungreased cookie sheets

Beat eggs and mix in oil and molasses. Mix dry ingredients and nuts together, then incorporate into wet ingredients. Mix well.

Drop batter by teaspoonfuls onto cookie sheets. Flatten with fork. Bake 10 minutes. Yields 3 dozen cookies.

Sunshine Walnut Cookies

¾ cup (180 ml) shortening (part butter or margarine)
1 cup (240 ml) brown sugar, firmly packed
1 egg
¼ cup (60 ml) frozen orange juice concentrate, thawed
1 cup (240 ml) whole wheat flour
¼ cup (60 ml) nonfat dry milk
¼ cup (60 ml) wheat germ
1 tsp (5 ml) baking powder
¼ tsp (1 ml) cinnamon
1½ cups (355 ml) rolled oats
1 cup (240 ml) chopped DIAMOND Walnuts
½ cup (120 ml) SUN•MAID Raisins

Oat Pineapple Drops

Preheat oven to 350°F (180°C). Lightly grease cookie sheets.

Combine shortening, brown sugar and egg; beat until light and fluffy. Blend in orange juice concentrate. Combine flour, nonfat dry milk, wheat germ, baking powder and cinnamon; stir into shortening mixture. Stir in oats, walnuts and raisins.

Drop by heaping tablespoonfuls onto cookie sheets; flatten slightly to about 2½-inch diameter. Bake in upper third of oven for 12-15 minutes or until lightly browned. Cool 2-3 minutes. Using broad spatula, remove from cookie sheets; cool on wire racks. Yields 2½ dozen cookies.

Haight-Ashbury Granola Cookies

1 cup (240 ml) regular rolled oats
2 tbs (30 ml) oil
½ cup (120 ml) butter or margarine, softened
½ cup (120 ml) honey
½ cup (120 ml) brown sugar, packed
1 egg
1 tsp (5 ml) vanilla
1½ tsp (8 ml) cinnamon
¼ tsp (1 ml) allspice
¼ cup (60 ml) wheat germ
1½ cups (355 ml) unbleached flour
¾ tsp (4 ml) salt
½ tsp (3 ml) baking powder
½ tsp (3 ml) baking soda
¼ cup (60 ml) milk
¾ cup (180 ml) chopped dates
¾ cup (180 ml) chopped walnuts
¾ cup (180 ml) flaked coconut
6 oz (180 g) *GHIRARDELLI Semi-Sweet Chocolate Chips*

Preheat oven to 350°F (180°C). Grease cookie sheets.

Toss oats with oil and toast 15 minutes, stirring once. Cream butter or margarine with honey, brown sugar, egg, vanilla and spices. Mix in wheat germ. Stir flour with salt, baking powder and baking soda. Mix dry ingredients into creamed mixture alternately with milk. Stir in toasted oats, dates, nuts, coconut and chocolate chips.

Drop by teaspoonfuls onto greased baking sheet. Bake 9-10 minutes. Cool on rack. Yields 7 dozen cookies.

Redwood Camp Cookie Squares

½ cup (120 ml) butter or margarine
¼ cup (60 ml) sugar
½ cup (120 ml) brown sugar, packed
2 eggs, beaten
1½ tsp (8 ml) vanilla
½ cup (120 ml) quick rolled oats
1 cup (240 ml) unsifted flour
½ tsp (3 ml) baking soda
¼ tsp (1 ml) salt
dash cinnamon
½ cup (120 ml) chopped peanuts
6 oz (180 g) *GHIRARDELLI Semi-Sweet Chocolate Chips*

Preheat oven to 350°F (180°C). Grease 9x13-inch baking pan.

Lightly cream butter with sugar and brown sugar in large bowl. Add eggs and vanilla. (Mixture will be lumpy.) Stir flour with rolled oats, baking soda, salt and cinnamon. Mix dry ingredients into creamed mixture. Fold in peanuts and chocolate chips.

Spread dough into baking pan. Bake about 20 minutes. Cool before cutting into squares. To keep moist, wrap in foil. Yields 2 dozen squares.

Opposite:
Haight-Ashbury Granola Cookies

Sutter's Gold
Chocolate Chip Cookies

1 cup (240 ml) butter or margarine, softened
½ cup (120 ml) sugar
½ cup (120 ml) brown sugar, packed
2 eggs
2 tbs (30 ml) milk
1 tsp (5 ml) vanilla
2 cups (480 ml) unsifted flour
1 tsp (5 ml) baking powder
½ tsp (3 ml) baking soda
½ tsp (3 ml) salt
12-oz pkg (360 g) GHIRARDELLI Semi-Sweet Chocolate Chips
3 cups (720 ml) breakfast wheat cereal flakes
cinnamon sugar

Preheat oven to 350°F (180°C). Grease cookie sheets.

Cream butter or margarine with sugar, brown sugar, eggs, milk and vanilla in large bowl. Stir flour with baking powder, baking soda and salt; blend into creamed mixture. Stir in chocolate chips and cereal.

Drop by teaspoonfuls onto baking sheet. Sprinkle with cinnamon sugar. Bake 10 minutes. Cool on rack. Yields 6 dozen cookies.

Golden Nugget Cookies

¾ cup (180 ml) butter or margarine
1 cup (240 ml) sugar
1 egg
½ tsp (3 ml) vanilla
½ tsp (3 ml) cinnamon
½ tsp (3 ml) nutmeg
1 cup (240 ml) mashed ripe bananas
1½ cups (355 ml) flour
½ tsp (3 ml) salt
½ tsp (3 ml) baking soda
1 cup (240 ml) quick rolled oats
6 oz (180 g) GHIRARDELLI Semi-Sweet Chocolate Chips

Preheat oven to 375°F (190°C). Grease baking sheets.

Cream butter or margarine with sugar, egg, vanilla, cinnamon and nutmeg in large bowl. Mix in bananas. Combine flour, salt and baking soda; stir into creamed mixture. Fold in oats and chocolate chips.

Drop by teaspoonfuls onto baking sheet. Bake 8-10 minutes. Cool on rack. Yields 3 dozen cookies.

Sutter's Gold Chocolate Chip Cookies

Opposite: Golden Nugget Cookies

381

Chocolate Kiss Kisses

½ cup (120 ml) sugar
½ cup (120 ml) FLEISCHMANN'S Margarine, softened
1 egg
⅓ cup (80 ml) unsweetened cocoa
1 tsp (5 ml) vanilla extract
1 cup (240 ml) all-purpose flour
1 tsp (5 ml) baking soda
24 chocolate candy hugs or kisses

Preheat oven to 350°F (180°C). Use ungreased baking sheet.

In large bowl, with electric mixer at medium speed, beat sugar and margarine until creamy. Blend in egg, cocoa and vanilla. Combine flour and baking soda; stir in egg mixture.

Drop by level tablespoons, 2 inches apart, on baking sheets. Bake 7-9 minutes or until puffed and slightly set; remove from oven. Immediately, top each with a candy hug or kiss, pressing lightly into center of each cookie. Cool completely on wire racks. Store in airtight container. Yields 2 dozen cookies.

Cocoa Peanut Butter Kisses

½ cup (120 ml) unsalted butter, softened
¾ cup (180 ml) brown sugar, packed
¼ cup (60 ml) sugar
½ cup (120 ml) peanut butter, room temperature
1 tsp (5 ml) vanilla extract
1 egg
1½ cups (355 ml) all-purpose flour
¼ cup (60 ml) SACO Baking Cocoa
1 tsp (5 ml) baking soda
¼ tsp (1 ml) salt
42-48 chocolate kisses, unwrapped

Preheat oven to 350°F (180°C). Grease baking sheets.

Beat butter with brown sugar, sugar and peanut butter with electric mixer for 1 minute on medium speed. Add vanilla and egg, mixing until combined. Sift flour, cocoa, baking soda and salt. Add dry ingredients to butter mixture, beating until combined.

Shape dough into 1-inch balls. Place 2 inches apart on prepared baking sheets. Bake 8-10 minutes. Remove from oven and immediately top each cookie with a chocolate kiss, pressing into the cookie. Let cool until chocolate firms up. Yields 3½-4 dozen cookies.

Opposite: Chocolate Kiss Kisses

Cocoa Peanut Butter Kisses

Peanut Butter Cookies

½ cup (120 ml) shortening
½ cup (120 ml) peanut butter
½ cup (120 ml) granulated sugar
½ cup (120 ml) brown sugar
1 egg
1¼ cups (295 ml) sifted PRESTO

Preheat oven to 350°F (180°C). Grease baking sheets.

Cream shortening, add peanut butter and blend well. Gradually add both sugars and mix well. Add unbeaten egg and mix thoroughly. Add sifted flour and shape into small balls with hands.

Put on baking sheet about 2 inches apart and bake 15-20 minutes. Yields 2-2½ dozen cookies.

Old-Fashioned Molasses Cookies

Old-Fashioned Molasses Cookies

4 cups (960 ml) sifted all-purpose flour
2 tsp (10 ml) ARM & HAMMER Baking Soda
2 tsp (10 ml) ground ginger
1 tsp (5 ml) cinnamon
dash salt
1½ cups (355 ml) molasses
⅔ cup (160 ml) butter-flavored shortening
⅓ cup (80 ml) boiling water
granulated sugar for garnishing

Preheat oven to 375°F (190°C). Use ungreased baking sheets.

Sift together flour, baking soda, spices and salt. Combine molasses, shortening and water in large bowl. Add dry ingredients to liquid and blend well. Cover and chill several hours or overnight.

Turn onto well-floured board. Using floured rolling pin, roll to ¼-inch thickness. Cut with 3½-inch floured cookie cutter.

Sprinkle with sugar and place on baking sheets. Bake 12 minutes. Cool on racks. Yields 3 dozen cookies.

Opposite: Peanut Butter Cookies

Soft Carrot Nut Molasses Cookies

1 cup (240 ml) sugar
¾ cup (180 ml) FLEISCHMANN'S Margarine, softened
½ cup (120 ml) BRER RABBIT Light or Dark Molasses
1 egg
½ cup (120 ml) vanilla-flavored yogurt
2¾ cups (660 ml) all-purpose flour
2 tsp (10 ml) baking soda
1 tsp (5 ml) ground cinnamon
1 cup (240 ml) shredded carrots
¾ cup (180 ml) chopped PLANTERS Walnuts
¾ cup (180 ml) seedless raisins
1¼ cups (295 ml) confectioners sugar
2-3 tbs (30-45 ml) water
additional chopped PLANTERS Walnuts

Preheat oven to 375°F (190°C). Grease and flour baking sheets.

In bowl, with electric mixer at high speed, beat sugar and margarine until creamy. At medium speed, blend in molasses, egg and yogurt until smooth. Combine flour, baking soda and cinnamon; stir into molasses mixture with carrot, walnuts and raisins.

Drop dough by tablespoonfuls about 2 inches apart onto prepared baking sheets. Bake 8-10 minutes or until lightly browned. Remove from baking sheet; cool on wire rack.

Blend confectioners sugar and water until smooth. Spread icing over prepared cookies and sprinkle with additional chopped nuts. Yields 4-5 dozen cookies.

Soft Carrot Nut Molasses Cookies

Cocoa Date Drop Cookies

½ cup (120 ml) shortening
¾ cup (180 ml) sugar
1 egg
2 cups (480 ml) sifted PRESTO
2 tbs (30 ml) cocoa
½ cup (120 ml) milk
1 tsp (5 ml) vanilla
¾ cup (180 ml) chopped dates

Preheat oven to 350°F (180°C). Grease baking sheets.

Cream shortening, add sugar gradually. Add egg and beat well. Add Presto sifted with cocoa alternately with milk to which the vanilla has been added. Stir in dates sprinkled with flour.

Drop by teaspoonfuls onto baking sheets and bake 12-15 minutes. Yields 3 dozen cookies.

Opposite: Cocoa Date Drop Cookies

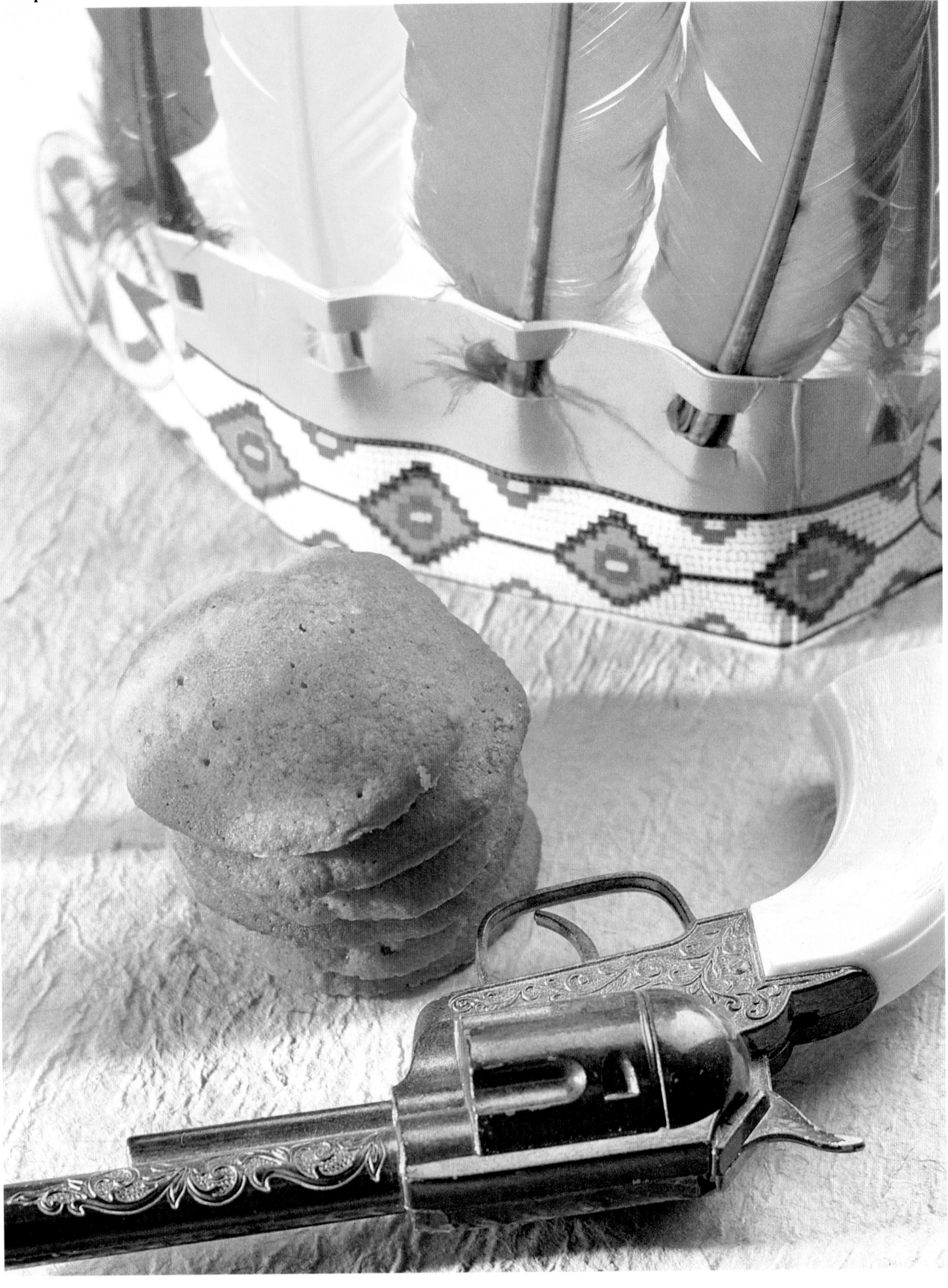

Pumpkin Walnut Cookies

½ cup (120 ml) butter or margarine, softened
1½ cups (355 ml) brown sugar, firmly packed
2 eggs
1 cup (240 ml) cooked or canned pumpkin
1 tsp (5 ml) vanilla
2½ cups (590 ml) all-purpose flour
1 tbs (15 ml) baking powder
2 tsp (10 ml) pumpkin pie spice
1½ cups (355 ml) coarsely chopped DIAMOND Walnuts

Preheat oven to 375°F (180°C). Grease cookie sheets.

Combine butter and brown sugar; beat until light and fluffy. Beat in eggs, one at a time; stir in pumpkin and vanilla. Combine flour, baking powder and pumpkin pie spice. Add to butter mixture; mix well. Stir in walnuts.

Drop by rounded teaspoonfuls 1 inch apart onto cookie sheets. Bake in upper third of oven for 12-14 minutes. Remove from cookie sheets; cool on wire racks. Yields 4 dozen cookies.

Frosted Pumpkin Cookies

2 cups (480 ml) all-purpose flour
1 tsp (5 ml) baking powder
1 tsp (10 ml) ground cinnamon
½ tsp (3 ml) baking soda
½ tsp (3 ml) ground nutmeg
1 cup (240 ml) butter, softened
¾ cup (180 ml) JACK FROST Granulated Sugar
¾ cup (180 ml) JACK FROST Brown Sugar, packed
1 egg
1 cup (240 ml) canned pumpkin
2 tsp (10 ml) vanilla
½ cup (120 ml) raisins
½ cup (120 ml) chopped walnuts

Cream Cheese Frosting:
3-oz pkg (90 g) cream cheese
¼ cup (60 ml) butter
1 tsp (5 ml) vanilla
2 cups (480 ml) JACK FROST Confectioners Sugar
chopped nuts, garnish

Preheat oven to 350°F (180°C). Grease cookie sheets.

In small mixing bowl, combine flour, baking powder, cinnamon, soda and nutmeg. Set aside. In large mixing bowl, beat butter 1 minute. Add granulated sugar and brown sugar. Beat until fluffy. Add egg, pumpkin and vanilla; beat well. Add dry ingredients to beaten pumpkin mixture; mix until well blended. Stir in raisins and walnuts.

Drop by teaspoonfuls 2 inches apart onto cookie sheets. Bake 10-12 minutes. Cool on cookie sheet for 2 minutes then place on wire rack to finish cooling. Yields 4 dozen cookies.

Cream Cheese Frosting: In a mixing bowl, beat cream cheese, butter and vanilla until light and fluffy. Gradually add confectioners sugar, beating until smooth. Frost tops of cookies. Garnish with chopped nuts.

Frosted Pumpkin Cookies

Butterscotch Buttermilk Drop Cookies

½ cup (120 ml) butter or margarine, softened
1½ cups (355 ml) brown sugar, packed
2 eggs
1 tsp (5 ml) vanilla
2½ cups (590 ml) all-purpose flour
1 tsp (5 ml) baking soda
½ tsp (3 ml) baking powder
½ tsp (3 ml) salt
¼ cup (60 ml) SACO Buttermilk Blend
1 cup (240 ml) water
⅔ cup (160 ml) walnuts or pecans, chopped

Brown Butter Frosting:
½ cup (120 ml) butter or margarine
2 cups (480 ml) sifted powdered sugar
2-4 tbs (30-60 ml) boiling water

Preheat oven to 350°F (180°C). Lightly grease baking sheets.

Beat butter or margarine until light; add brown sugar and cream together until mixture is light and fluffy. Beat in eggs and vanilla and blend thoroughly. In a separate bowl, sift together flour, baking soda, baking powder, salt and buttermilk blend. Add water alternately with dry ingredients to creamed mixture and stir just until ingredients are well mixed. Do not overbeat. Stir in chopped nuts.

Drop round tablespoonfuls of dough about 2½ inches apart onto baking sheets. Bake 10-12 minutes or until browned and barely firm to touch. Remove cookies and cool on racks. Frost with Brown Butter Frosting. Yields 4-5 dozen cookies.

Brown Butter Frosting: Melt butter in small saucepan and cook over medium heat, stirring constantly, until butter stops bubbling and is nut-brown in color. Combine with sifted powdered sugar and boiling water. Beat until smooth and of spreading consistency. Yields enough to frost 5 dozen cookies.

Opposite:
Applesauce Buttermilk
Drop Cookies

Applesauce Buttermilk Drop Cookies

2¾ cups (650 ml) all-purpose flour
1½ cups (355 ml) brown sugar, packed
1 tsp (5 ml) salt
½ tsp (3 ml) baking soda
¼ cup (60 ml) SACO Buttermilk Blend
¾ cup (180 ml) applesauce
½ cup (120 ml) shortening
2 eggs
1 tsp (5 ml) cinnamon
1 tsp (5 ml) vanilla
¼ tsp (1 ml) cloves
1 cup (240 ml) raisins
1 cup (240 ml) chopped nuts

Preheat oven to 375°F (190°C). Use ungreased cookie sheets.

Mix all ingredients together. Do not overbeat. If dough is soft, cover and refrigerate.

Drop dough by rounded teaspoonfuls, about 2 inches apart, onto cookie sheets. Bake until almost no indentation remains when touched, about 10 minutes. Immediately remove from cookie sheet. Cool. Spread with Brown Butter Frosting (above recipe). Yields 4½-5 dozen cookies.

Cinnamon Buttermilk Drop Cookies

½ cup (120 ml) shortening (part butter)
1 cup (240 ml) sugar
1 egg
¾ cup (180 ml) water
1 tsp (5 ml) vanilla
2 cups (480 ml) all-purpose flour
½ tsp (3 ml) baking soda
½ tsp (3 ml) salt
3 tbs (45 ml) SACO Buttermilk Blend
¼ cup (60 ml) granulated sugar
1 tsp (5 ml) cinnamon

Preheat oven to 400°F (205°C) 10 minutes before baking. Lightly grease baking sheets.

Mix shortening, sugar and egg thoroughly. Stir in water and vanilla. Sift flour, baking soda, salt and buttermilk blend. Stir in. Do not overbeat. Chill dough.

Drop rounded teaspoonfuls of dough about 2 inches apart on baking sheets. Sprinkle with mixture of ¼ cup sugar and 1 tsp cinnamon. Bake 8-10 minutes or until set, but not brown. Yields 4 dozen cookies.

Apple Butter Cookies

2 cups (480 ml) all-purpose flour
1 tsp (5 ml) salt
1 tsp (5 ml) baking soda
¼ tsp (1 ml) cloves
¼ tsp (1 ml) ground nutmeg
1 tsp (5 ml) ground cinnamon
¼ cup (60 ml) margarine, softened
1 cup (240 ml) sugar
1 egg
1 cup (240 ml) quartered dates
1 cup (240 ml) seedless raisins
1 cup (240 ml) MUSSELMAN'S Apple Butter

Preheat oven to 375°F (190°C). Grease baking sheets.

Combine dry ingredients. In another bowl, cream margarine and sugar and spices; stir in egg, dates and raisins. Stir in dry ingredients alternately with apple butter.

Drop by rounded teaspoonfuls 2 inches apart onto baking sheets. Bake about 12 minutes. Yields 4 dozen cookies.

Apple Butter Cookies

Buttermilk Orange Cookies

1 cup (240 ml) butter or margarine, softened
1½ cups (355 ml) brown sugar
2 eggs
1 tsp (5 ml) vanilla
2 tbs (30 ml) grated orange peel
½ tsp (3 ml) salt
1 cup (240 ml) buttermilk or sour milk
½ tsp (3 ml) baking soda
3 cups (720 ml) WASHINGTON Self-Rising Flour

Frosting:
3 tbs (45 ml) melted butter
2 cups (480 ml) confectioners sugar
3 tbs (45 ml) orange juice
1 tsp (5 ml) grated orange peel

Preheat oven to 400°F (205°C) 10 minutes before baking. Grease baking sheets or pans.

Place first 6 ingredients in bowl. Beat together until light and fluffy. Dissolve baking soda in buttermilk or sour milk. Add to flour; beat until smooth. Chill.

Drop by teaspoonfuls, 3 inches apart, onto baking sheets. Bake 8-10 minutes, until golden. Frost while warm. Yields 4 dozen cookies.

Frosting: Combine all ingredients. Frost warm cookies..

Opposite: Buttermilk Orange Cookies

Sugar Cookies I

1 cup (240 ml) DOMINO Granulated Sugar
¼ cup (60 ml) butter or margarine, softened
½ tsp (3 ml) salt
1 egg
1 tsp (5 ml) grated lemon rind
1 tsp (5 ml) vanilla extract
2¼ cups (540 ml) all-purpose flour
1 tsp (5 ml) baking powder
additional DOMINO Granulated Sugar

Preheat oven to 350°F (180°C). Use ungreased baking sheets.

In large bowl, cream sugar, butter or margarine and salt. Beat in egg, lemon rind, and vanilla until light and fluffy. Sift together flour and baking powder. Gradually stir into creamed ingredients.

On floured board, using floured rolling pin, roll dough until ⅛-inch thick. Cut into fancy shapes.

Place on baking sheets. Sprinkle generously with additional sugar. Bake 9-12 minutes or until lightly browned around the edges. Cool on racks.
Yields 5 to 7 dozen cookies.

Sugar Cookies II

1 cup (240 ml) butter or margarine, softened
1 cup (240 ml) vegetable oil
2 large eggs
1 cup (240 ml) JACK FROST Granulated Sugar
1 cup (240 ml) JACK FROST Confectioners Sugar
2 tsp (10 ml) vanilla
4¼ cups (1 l) all-purpose flour
½ tsp (3 ml) salt
1 tsp (5 ml) baking soda
1 tsp (5 ml) cream of tartar
½ cup (120 ml) JACK FROST Granulated Sugar*

Preheat oven to 350°F (180°C). Use ungreased cookie sheets.

In a large mixing bowl, cream butter or margarine, oil, eggs, sugars and vanilla. In another bowl, stir together flour, salt, baking soda and cream of tartar. Add to creamed mixture. Beat until smooth. Form into 1-inch balls and roll in granulated sugar, coating on all sides. Dough will be very soft.

Place on cookie sheet and flatten with decorative cookie press or bottom of a glass. Bake 10 to 12 minutes or until light golden brown. Let cool on sheet for 2 minutes before placing on cooling rack. Yields 4 dozen cookies.

*Option: Add ½ tsp (3 ml) cinnamon to the sugar before rolling the formed balls in it.

Sugared Vanilla Wafers

1½ cups (355 ml) sugar
1 cup (240 ml) butter or margarine, softened
2 eggs
1 tbs (15 ml) McCORMICK/SCHILLING Pure Vanilla Extract
2 tsp (10 ml) baking powder
3 cups (720 ml) sifted all-purpose flour
2 tbs (30 ml) milk
sugar for rolling and sprinkling
McCORMICK/SCHILLING Cinnamon Sugar, if desired

Preheat oven to 400°F (205°C). Lightly grease cookie sheets.

Place sugar and butter or margarine in large mixing bowl and cream with electric mixer until light and fluffy. Beat in eggs and vanilla. Gradually add baking powder to sifted flour and sift again. Gradually add to butter mixture, mixing well. Stir in milk and mix until well combined. Cover and refrigerate at least 2 hours.

Lightly flour work surface and sprinkle with 1 tbs sugar. Roll out chilled dough to ⅛-inch thickness and cut with 2-inch cookie cutters.

Place cookies 1 inch apart on prepared cookie sheets and sprinkle with sugar or cinnamon sugar. Bake 6 to 8 minutes. Remove from cookie sheets and place on wire racks to cool. Yields 5 dozen cookies.

Coconut Cookies

¾ cup (180 ml) butter or margarine, softened
½ cup (120 ml) sugar
1 egg
½ tsp (3 ml) vanilla
½ tsp (3 ml) almond extract
2¼ cups (540 ml) sifted WASHINGTON All-Purpose Flour
1⅓ cups (320 ml) shredded coconut
small amount milk
¼ cup (60 ml) sugar, approximately

Preheat oven to 400°F (205°C) 10 minutes before baking. Grease baking sheets or pans.

Place butter or margarine, sugar, egg, vanilla and almond extract in bowl. Beat together until light and fluffy. Stir in flour and coconut. Blend well. Divide in half; wrap in wax paper. Chill 30 minutes.

Roll on lightly floured surface to ⅛-inch thickness. Cut with floured cookie cutter.

Place on baking sheet. Brush tops with milk. Sprinkle generously with sugar. Bake about 6 minutes, until edges turn golden. Yields 5 dozen cookies.

Butterscotch Ice Box Cookies

3½ cups (840 ml) sifted WASHINGTON All-Purpose Flour
1 tsp (5 ml) baking soda
1 tsp (5 ml) salt
1 cup (240 ml) chopped nuts
1 cup (240 ml) soft butter or margarine
2 cups (480 ml) dark brown sugar
2 eggs
1 tsp (5 ml) vanilla

Preheat oven to 375°F (190°C) 10 minutes before baking. Use 2 ungreased baking sheets or pans.

Place flour, baking soda, salt and chopped nuts in bowl. Stir to blend. Set aside. Blend butter or margarine, brown sugar, eggs and vanilla together in large mixing bowl; beat until light and fluffy. Stir in flour mixture.

Shape dough into 2 rolls, 2 inches in diameter. Wrap each in foil or waxed paper. Chill 24 hours or more.

Slice dough ⅛-inch thick. Bake 8-10 minutes until golden. Remove from pan at once. Cool on wire rack. Yields 6-7 dozen cookies.

Above: Butterscotch Ice Box Cookies

Strawberry Linzer Cookies

1 cup (240 ml) FLEISCHMANN'S Margarine, softened
1 cup (240 ml) sugar
2½ cups (590 ml) all-purpose flour
½ cup (120 ml) finely chopped pecans
2 tsp (10 ml) finely grated lemon peel
½ cup (120 ml) strawberry preserves
confectioners sugar

Preheat oven to 325°F (165°C) 10 minutes before baking. Use ungreased baking sheets.

In large bowl, with electric mixer at medium speed, beat margarine and sugar until creamy. Mix flour, pecans and lemon peel; stir into margarine mixture until blended. Cover; chill 2 hours.

Divide dough in half. On floured surface, roll half the dough to ⅛-inch thickness. With a floured 2½-inch cookie cutter, cut out circles; using a smaller 1½-inch circle cutter, cut out centers from half the circles. Repeat with remaining dough, rerolling scraps as necessary.

Place circles on baking sheets. Bake 10-12 minutes or until lightly browned. Remove from sheets; cool on wire rack.

Spread about 1 tsp preserves on top of whole cookie; top with cookie with hole in it. Sprinkle with confectioners sugar if desired. Yields 2 dozen cookies.

Strawberry Linzer Cookies

Nutty Chocolate Snowball Cookies

1 cup (240 ml) butter or margarine, softened
¾ cup (180 ml) light brown sugar, packed
1 egg
1 tsp (5 ml) vanilla extract
2 cups (480 ml) all-purpose flour
½ cup (120 ml) HERSHEY'S European Style Cocoa
    or HERSHEY'S Cocoa
1 tsp (5 ml) baking powder
¼ tsp (1 ml) baking soda
3 tbs (45 ml) milk
¾ cup (180 ml) finely chopped macadamia nuts or other nuts
powdered sugar

Preheat oven to 350°F (180°C) 10 minutes before baking. Use ungreased cookie sheets.

In large bowl, beat butter or margarine, brown sugar, egg and vanilla until blended. Stir together flour, cocoa, baking powder and baking soda; add milk to butter mixture until well blended. Stir in nuts. Refrigerate until firm enough to handle, at least 2 hours.

Shape dough into 1-inch balls; place 2 inches apart on cookie sheet.

Bake 8 to 10 minutes or until set. Remove from cookie sheet to wire rack. Cool completely; roll in powdered sugar. Store in airtight container. Yields 4 dozen cookies.

Kris Kringle Fudge Cookies

¼ cup (60 ml) butter or margarine, melted
⅓ cup (80 ml) HERSHEY'S Cocoa or HERSHEY'S
    European Style Cocoa
1 cup (240 ml) all-purpose flour, divided
1 cup (240 ml) sugar
2 eggs
1 tsp (5 ml) vanilla extract
1 tsp (5 ml) baking soda
¼ tsp (1 ml) salt
¼ cup (60 ml) chopped pecans
powdered sugar

Preheat oven to 300°F (150°C). Grease cookie sheet.

In large bowl, stir cocoa into melted butter or margarine; cool slightly. Stir in ½ cup flour, sugar, eggs, vanilla, baking soda and salt; beat until well blended. Stir in remaining ½ cup flour and pecans until blended. Cover; refrigerate until firm, about 3 hours.

Shape dough into 1-inch balls; roll in powdered sugar. Place 3 inches apart on prepared cookie sheet. Bake 10-12 minutes until tops have crackled appearance and are set. Yields 2½ dozen cookies.

Kris Kringle
Fudge Cookies

Cocoa Refrigerator Cookies

1½ cups (355 ml) all-purpose flour
¼ cup (60 ml) cocoa
1½ tsp (8 ml) DAVIS Baking Powder
dash salt
½ cup (120 ml) FLEISCHMANN'S Margarine, softened
1 cup (240 ml) sugar
1 large egg
prepared vanilla or chocolate frosting, optional
white and dark chocolate, melted, optional

Preheat oven to 375°F (190°C) 10 minutes befor baking. Grease baking sheets.

In medium bowl, sift together flour, cocoa, baking powder and salt; set aside.

In large bowl, with electric mixer at medium speed, beat margarine and sugar until creamy; beat in egg. Gradually blend in flour mixture.

Divide dough in half. Shape each half into a 10-inch long log, about 1½ inches in diameter. Wrap in waxed paper; chill until firm, at least 4 hours or up to a week.

Unwrap dough and cut into ¼-inch slices. Place slices 1 inch apart on baking sheets. Bake 10-12 minutes. Remove from sheets; cool on wire racks. Decorate as desired. Store in airtight container. Yields 6 dozen cookies.

Chocolate Sandwich Cookies: Sandwich 2 cookies with frosting; drizzle top with melted white and dark coating chocolate if desired. Place on waxed paper and let stand until coating sets.

Festive Chocolate Wafers: Drizzle cookies with melted white and dark chocolate; place on waxed paper until chocolate sets.

Chocolate Dipped Wafers: Dip cookies halfway into melted white and dark chocolate; place on waxed paper until coating sets.

Chocolate Sugar Cookies

3 squares BAKER'S Unsweetened Chocolate
1 cup (240 ml) margarine or butter
1 cup (240 ml) sugar
1 egg
1 tsp (5 ml) vanilla
2 cups (480 ml) all-purpose flour
1 tsp (5 ml) baking soda
¼ tsp (1 ml) salt
additional sugar

Preheat oven to 375°F (190°C) 10 minutes before baking. Use ungreased cookie sheets.

Microwave chocolate and margarine or butter in large microwave-safe bowl on high 2 minutes or until margarine is melted. Stir until chocolate is completely melted. Stir 1 cup sugar into melted chocolate mixture until well blended. Stir in egg and vanilla until completely mixed. Mix in flour, baking soda and salt. Refrigerate 30 minutes.

Shape dough into 1-inch balls; roll in additional sugar. Place on cookie sheets. (If a flatter, crispier cookie is desired, flatten ball with bottom of drinking glass.)

Bake for 8 to 10 minutes or until set. Remove from cookie sheets to cool on wire racks. Yields 3½ dozen cookies.

Jam-Filled Chocolate Sugar Cookies: Prepare Chocolate Sugar Cookie dough as directed; roll in finely chopped nuts in place of sugar. Make indentation in each ball; fill center with your favorite jam. Bake as directed.

Chocolate-Caramel Sugar Cookies: Prepare Chocolate Sugar Cookie dough as directed. Roll in finely chopped nuts in place of sugar. Make indentation in each ball; bake as directed. Microwave one 14-oz pkg (420 g) Kraft Caramels with 2 tbs (30 ml) milk in micro-safe bowl on high 3 minutes or until melted, stirring after 2 minutes. Fill centers of cookies with caramel mixture. Drizzle with 3 melted Baker's Semi-Sweet Chocolates.

Opposite: Cocoa Refrigerator Cookies

Chocolate Mint Windmill Cookies

4-oz bar (120 g) GHIRARDELLI Semi-Sweet Chocolate
½ cup (120 ml) butter or margarine, softened
½ cup (120 ml) sugar
¼ cup (60 ml) brown sugar, packed
1 egg
¼ cup (60 ml) sour cream
2 cups (480 ml) unsifted flour
½ tsp (3 ml) baking powder
½ tsp (3 ml) salt
dash baking soda
1 tsp (1 ml) vanilla
¼ tsp (1 ml) peppermint extract
3 drops green or red food coloring

Preheat oven to 375°F (190°C). Use ungreased baking sheet.

In double boiler, melt chocolate over 1-inch simmering water. Cream butter or margarine with sugar and brown sugar; mix in egg and sour cream. Stir flour with baking powder, salt and baking soda. Gradually add dry ingredients to creamed mixture.

Divide dough in half. Add melted chocolate and the vanilla to half; add peppermint extract and food coloring to other half. Chill dough about 1 hour or until firm. Between 2 pieces of waxed paper, roll each half into a rectangle ⅛-inch thick. Place peppermint half on top of chocolate half and roll as for jelly roll. Wrap in waxed paper; chill. Cut in ¼-inch slices.

Place on baking sheet. Bake 8-10 minutes. Yields 3½ dozen cookies.

Cocoa-Walnut Crescents

Cocoa-Walnut Crescents

1 cup (240 ml) FLEISCHMANN'S Margarine, softened
⅔ cup (160 ml) powdered sugar
⅓ cup (80 ml) unsweetened cocoa
1 tsp (5 ml) vanilla extract
dash salt
1⅔ cups (400 ml) all-purpose flour
1 cup (240 ml) finely chopped PLANTERS Walnuts
Powdered Sugar Glaze
chopped walnuts

Preheat oven to 325°F (165°C). Lightly grease baking sheets.

In small bowl, with electric mixer at medium speed, beat margarine and sugar until light and fluffy. Add cocoa, vanilla and salt; mix at low speed until blended. Mix in flour and walnuts. Cover; chill dough for 1 hour.

Divide dough into 6 portions. Working with one portion at a time, roll into 18-inch long strips. Cut each strip into twelve 1½-inch pieces. Form into crescent shapes, tapering the ends.

Place on baking sheets. Repeat with remaining dough. Bake 15-18 minutes. Remove from baking sheets; cool completely on wire rack. Drizzle with Powdered Sugar Glaze; sprinkle with chopped nuts. When set, store in airtight container. Yields 6 dozen crescents.

Powdered Sugar Glaze: Mix ½ cup powdered sugar with enough water to create a pourable consistency.

Opposite:
Chocolate Mint Windmill Cookies

Molasses Ginger Bites

½ cup (120 ml) butter, softened
½ cup (120 ml) sugar
½ cup (120 ml) molasses
2 eggs
1 tsp (5 ml) baking soda
1 tsp (5 ml) McCORMICK/SCHILLING Ginger
½ tsp (3 ml) McCORMICK/SCHILLING Cinnamon
3¼ cups (780 ml) flour
1 tsp (5 ml) McCORMICK/SCHILLING Pure Vanilla Extract
powdered sugar

Preheat oven to 350°F (180°C). Use ungreased cookie sheets.

Cream butter with sugar. Beat in molasses and eggs. Combine next four ingredients and add gradually, mixing well. Stir in vanilla extract.

On board dusted with powdered sugar, roll out small amount of dough at a time, to ⅛-inch thickness. Cut out cookies using very small, 1-1¼-inch cutters, or use a knife to cut 1-inch squares.

Bake on cookie sheets 5 minutes. Cool on wire racks. Yields 12½ dozen tiny cookies.

Crisp Old-Fashioned Ginger Snaps

2 cups (480 ml) HECKERS/CERESOTA Unbleached Flour
2 tsp (10 ml) baking soda
1 tsp (5 ml) ground cinnamon
¾ tsp (4 ml) ground ginger
½ tsp (3 ml) ground cloves
¾ cup (180 ml) shortening
1 cup (240 ml) sugar
¼ cup (60 ml) molasses
1 egg

Preheat oven to 350°F (180°C). Grease cookie sheets.

Sift together flour, baking soda, cinnamon, ginger and cloves. Cream shortening and sugar until light; add molasses and egg and cream well. Mix in sifted dry ingredients until well blended.

Shape into small balls, place on cookie sheets (allow room for cookies to spread). Flatten slightly. Bake 10-12 minutes. Remove from cookie sheet; cool on rack. Yields 3 dozen cookies.

Molasses Ginger Bites

Gingerbread Delights

½ cup (120 ml) shortening
½ cup (120 ml) sugar
½ cup (120 ml) GRANDMA'S Molasses
1 egg, separated
2 cups (480 ml) sifted all-purpose flour
½ tsp (3 ml) salt
½ tsp (3 ml) baking soda
1 tsp (5 ml) baking powder
1 tsp (5 ml) cloves
1½ tsp (8 ml) cinnamon
½ tsp (3 ml) nutmeg
1 tsp (5 ml) ginger
raisins and nuts for eyes and buttons
Vanilla Frosting

Preheat oven to 350°F (180°C). Use ungreased cookies sheets.

Beat shortening, sugar, and molasses. Add egg yolk and mix well (keep egg white for the frosting). Sift flour, salt, baking soda, baking powder and spices together. Blend in with other ingredients and mix well. Refrigerate on a lightly floured board.

Roll out the dough to ¼-inch thickness. With 5-inch long cookie cutter, cut out gingerbread-men. Place on cookie sheet. Decorate with raisins or nuts. Bake 8-10 minutes. Cool and then decorate with vanilla frosting. Yields 2 dozen cookies.

Vanilla Frosting: Sift 1¼ cups (295 ml) confectioners' sugar and a pinch of cream of tartar. Add egg white and ¼ tsp (1 ml) vanilla. With mixer, beat mixture until stiff. Cover with a moistened towel until needed.

Almond Pretzel Cookies

1 cup (240 ml) sliced natural almonds
1 cup (240 ml) butter, softened
1½ cups (355 ml) sugar
1 egg
¼ cup (60 ml) evaporated milk
1 tsp (5 ml) almond extract
1 tsp (5 ml) vanilla extract
3½ cups (840 ml) unsifted flour
1 tsp (5 ml) baking powder

Preheat oven to 300°F (150°C). Use ungreased cookie sheets.

Crush almonds with rolling pin. Cream butter and sugar. Beat in egg, evaporated milk, almond and vanilla extracts. Combine flour and baking powder; stir into creamed mixture, until dough forms.

Divide dough into 24 equal pieces. Roll each piece into a rope about 10 inches long, then roll in crushed almonds and curve into a pretzel shape on cookie sheets.

Bake 15 minutes or until light golden on bottoms. Cool a few minutes, then transfer to wire racks to cool. Yields 2 dozen cookies.

Courtesy of the Almond Board of California.

Opposite: Almond Pretzel Cookies

Cinnamon Sandies

1 cup (240 ml) butter or margarine, softened
1½ cups (355 ml) confectioners sugar, divided
2 tsp (10 ml) McCORMICK/SCHILLING Pure Vanilla Extract
1 tbs (15 ml) water
2 cups (480 ml) all-purpose flour
1 cup (240 ml) finely chopped nuts
2 tsp (10 ml) McCORMICK/SCHILLING Ground Cinnamon

Preheat oven to 300°F (150°C). Use ungreased cookie sheets.

Place butter or margarine and ½ cup confectioners sugar in large mixing bowl and cream until light and fluffy. Stir in vanilla and water. Gradually add flour and mix well. Stir in nuts.

Shape teaspoonfuls of dough into crescents and place 1 inch apart on cookie sheets. Bake for 20 minutes or until very lightly browned. Sift remaining 1 cup sugar with cinnamon and roll hot cookies in mixture. Place on wire racks to cool. When cool, roll again in sugar mixture. Yields 5 dozen cookies.

Cinnamon Sledges

1 cup (240 ml) butter or margarine, softened
1 cup (240 ml) sugar
1 egg, separated
2 cups (480 ml) sifted all-purpose flour
1 tbs (15 ml) McCORMICK/SCHILLING Ground Cinnamon
½ cup (120 ml) chopped pecans

Preheat oven to 300°F (150°C). Use ungreased 15x12-inch cookie sheet.

Place butter and sugar in large mixing bowl and cream with electric mixer at high speed until light and fluffy. Add egg yolk and beat well. Add flour and cinnamon and mix at low speed until well blended.

Spread dough on cookie sheet, leaving 1½-inch border to allow for spreading. Beat egg white in small bowl with fork until foamy. Brush over top of dough. Sprinkle with nuts and lightly press nuts into dough.

Bake 45-50 minutes. Cut into 2-inch squares while still hot. Remove form cookie sheet and place on wire racks to cool. Yields 3 dozen cookies.

Opposite: Cinnamon Sledges

Anise-Flavored Pfefernüsse

1 cup (240 ml) light brown sugar, firmly packed
½ cup (120 ml) butter or margarine, softened
2 eggs
1 tsp (5 ml) McCORMICK/SCHILLING Pure Vanilla Extract
½ tsp (3 ml) McCORMICK/SCHILLING Pure Lemon Extract
½ tsp (3 ml) McCORMICK/SCHILLING Pure Anise Extract
1 tsp (5 ml) baking powder
1 tsp (5 ml) McCORMICK/SCHILLING Ground Cinnamon
½ tsp (3 ml) salt
½ tsp (1 ml) McCORMICK/SCHILLING Ground Black Pepper
dash McCORMICK/SCHILLING Ground Nutmeg
dash McCORMICK/SCHILLING Ground Cloves
2¾ cups (650 ml) sifted all-purpose flour
confectioners sugar

Preheat oven to 375°F (190°C) 10 minutes before baking. Use ungreased baking sheets.

Place brown sugar and butter or margarine in large mixing bowl. Cream with electric mixer until smooth and fluffy. Beat in eggs and extracts. Add remaining ingredients except confectioners sugar to sifted flour and sift again. Gradually add to butter mixture, mixing well. Cover and refrigerate 2 hours.

Shape teaspoonfuls of dough into ovals and place 1 inch apart on cookie sheets. Bake 10 minutes. Remove from cookie sheets and place on wire racks. Sprinkle with confectioners sugar while cookies are still warm. When cookies are cool, store in airtight containers. Yields 4½-5 dozen cookies.

Anise-Flavored Pfefernüsse

Pecan Cookie Balls

1 cup (240 ml) butter or margarine, softened
2½ cups (590 ml) sifted confectioners sugar, divided
2 tsp (10 ml) McCORMICK/SCHILLING Pure Vanilla Extract
½ tsp (3 ml) McCORMICK/SCHILLING Ground Nutmeg
dash salt
2 cups (480 ml) sifted all-purpose flour
2 cups (480 ml) finely chopped pecans

Preheat oven to 350°F (180°C). Use ungreased cookie sheets.

Place butter or margarine in large mixing bowl and cream until fluffy. Add ½ cup confectioners sugar, vanilla, nutmeg, and salt. Cream until thoroughly mixed. Stir in flour and pecans.

Shape dough into 1-inch balls and place 1 inch apart on cookie sheets. Bake 15 minutes. Remove from cookie sheets and immediately roll hot cookies in remaining 2 cups confectioners sugar. Place sugared cookies on wire racks and set aside to cool. When cool, roll again in sugar. Yields 4-5 dozen cookies.

Date Sticks

½ cup (120 ml) butter or margarine, softened
1 cup (240 ml) sugar
1 egg
1 tsp (5 ml) McCORMICK/SCHILLING Pure Vanilla Extract
1 tsp (5 ml) McCORMICK/SCHILLING Lemon Peel
2 cups (480 ml) all-purpose flour
1 tsp (5 ml) McCORMICK/SCHILLING Ground Cinnamon
½ tsp (3 ml) baking powder
¼ tsp (1 ml) baking soda
¼ tsp (1 ml) salt
dash McCORMICK/SCHILLING Ground Nutmeg
1 cup (240 ml) chopped dates

Preheat oven to 350°F (180°C). Lightly grease cookie sheets.

Place butter or margarine in large mixing bowl and cream with electric mixer until fluffy. Gradually add sugar and beat until light and fluffy. Beat in egg, vanilla and lemon peel. Sift flour with cinnamon, baking powder, baking soda, salt and nutmeg. Gradually add to creamed mixture, mixing at low speed until well blended. Stir in dates.

Shape dough into thin sticks about 1½ inches long. Place 1 inch apart on prepared cookies sheets. Bake 15-20 minutes. Remove from cookie sheets and place on wire racks to cool. Yields 6 dozen sticks.

Pecan Cookie Balls

Opposite: Date Sticks

Thumbprint Cookies

½ cup (120 ml) butter or margarine
½ cup (120 ml) sugar
1 egg, separated
½ tsp (3 ml) vanilla
1 cup (240 ml) all-purpose flour
¼ tsp (1 ml) salt
1 cup (240 ml) finely chopped DIAMOND Walnuts
jam or candied cherries

Preheat oven to 350°F (180°C). Use ungreased cookie sheets.

Combine butter or margarine, sugar, egg yolk and vanilla; beat until light and fluffy. Combine flour and salt; stir into butter mixture. Shape into 1-inch balls. Slightly beat egg white with fork. Dip balls in egg white; roll each in walnuts.

Place 1 inch apart on cookie sheets; press thumb gently in center of each cookie. Bake in upper third of oven for 10-12 minutes or until set. Remove from cookie sheets; cool on wire racks. Fill thumbprints with jam or candied cherries. Yields 2 dozen cookies.

Chocolate Variation: Melt 1 square unsweetened chocolate, blend into butter mixture.

Russian Raisin Teacakes

1 cup (240 ml) butter or margarine, softened
¼ cup (60 ml) confectioners sugar
1 tsp (5 ml) vanilla
2 cups (480 ml) all-purpose flour
1 cup (240 ml) chopped DIAMOND Walnuts
1 cup (240 ml) SUN•MAID Raisins, chopped or
    SUN•MAID Zante Currants
powdered sugar, for rolling

Preheat oven to 350°F (180°C) 10 minutes before baking. Use ungreased cookie sheets.

Combine butter, confectioners sugar and vanilla; beat until light and fluffy. Stir in flour, walnuts and raisins. Cover; refrigerate until firm.

Shape dough into 1-inch balls. Place on cookie sheets. Bake in upper third of oven for 10 minutes. Roll warm cookies in confectioners sugar. Cool; roll again in confectioners sugar. Yields 4 dozen cookies.

Black-Eyed Susans

½ cup (120 ml) butter or margarine, softened
½ cup (120 ml) peanut butter
1 cup (240 ml) sugar
1 egg
1 tsp (5 ml) vanilla
1¼ cups (295 ml) all-purpose flour
½ tsp (3 ml) baking powder
¼ tsp (1 ml) salt

Filling:
1½ cups (355 ml) SUN•MAID Raisins
¾ cup (180 ml) orange juice
⅓ cup (80 ml) sugar
¾ tsp (4 ml) grated orange peel

Preheat oven to 350°F (180°C). Use ungreased cookie sheets.

Combine butter or margarine, peanut butter, sugar, egg and vanilla; beat until light and fluffy. Combine flour, baking powder and salt. Stir into butter mixture; mix well. Cover; refrigerate until firm.

Combine all Filling ingredients. Cook over medium heat, stirring frequently, until sugar dissolves and mixture thickens slightly; cool.

On lightly floured surface, roll out dough to ⅛-inch thickness. Cut into 2-inch rounds with cookie cutter. Place a teaspoon of Filling on center of half the dough rounds. Cut small circles from centers of remaining dough rounds; place on top of filled rounds. Press edges lightly together to seal.

Place on cookie sheets. Bake in upper third of oven 10-12 minutes. Remove from cookie sheets; cool on wire rack. Yields 2½ dozen cookies.

Opposite: Thumbprint Cookies

Filled Benne Lace Cookies

⅓ cup (80 ml) McCORMICK/SCHILLING Sesame Seeds
¼ cup (80 ml) butter
¼ cup (60 ml) light corn syrup
¼ cup (60 ml) light brown sugar, firmly packed
½ cup (120 ml) plus 2 tbs (30 ml) sifted all-purpose flour
¼ tsp (1 ml) baking powder
¼ tsp (1 ml) McCORMICK/SCHILLING Ground Cinnamon
3 oz (90 g) sweet baking chocolate

Preheat oven to 350°F (180°C). Lightly grease cookie sheets.

Place sesame seeds in shallow baking pan and toast in preheated oven 15 minutes or until golden brown. Set aside to cool.

Reduce oven temperature to 325°F (165°C).

Place butter, corn syrup and brown sugar in top of double boiler over (not in) boiling water. Cook just until butter has melted. Stir to combine and remove from heat. Sift flour, baking powder and cinnamon in a large bowl and add butter mixture. Stir into reserved sesame seeds and mix well.

Drop by ½ teaspoonfuls 3 inches apart onto prepared cookie sheets. Bake 8 minutes. Remove from oven and cool on cookie sheets 2 minutes. Remove from cookie sheets with thin flexible spatula and place on flat work surface. Let cool on flat surface.

Melt chocolate over low heat. Spread 1 cookie with thin coating of chocolate. Place second cookie on top of chocolate to make "sandwich." Repeat with remaining cookies and chocolate, making only 1 cookie "sandwich" at a time. Work quickly before chocolate cools. Yields 3 dozen filled cookies.

Tip: For best results, and nice crisp cookies, choose a dry, sunny day to make them.

Filled Benne Lace Cookies

Walnut Lace Cookies

½ cup (120 ml) butter or margarine
⅔ cup (160 ml) sugar
½ cup (120 ml) light corn syrup
1 tbs (15 ml) brandy or milk
1 cup (240 ml) all-purpose flour
¾ cup (180 ml) finely chopped DIAMOND Walnuts

Preheat oven to 350°F (180°C). Cut a sheet of aluminum foil into 6-inch squares; arrange 2-4 squares on each cookie sheet. Lightly grease each square.

In small saucepan, combine butter or margarine, sugar, corn syrup and brandy or milk; stir over low heat until butter is just melted. Remove from heat; stir in flour and walnuts.

Drop by slightly rounded teaspoonfuls onto center of each greased foil square. Bake in upper third of oven for 6-7 minutes or until cookies are evenly golden. Cool about 30 seconds.

Using metal spatula, loosen edge of cookie from foil and peel off foil. Quickly roll cookie around handle of wooden spoon to shape. Working quickly, repeat with remaining cookies.* Foil squares may be reused to bake remaining cookies. Yields 4 dozen cookies.

*It is best to work with only a few cookies at a time because they quickly become too crisp to roll. If cookies become too crisp, return to oven for few seconds to soften.

Lace Cookie Cup Variation: For each, use 1 tbs batter. Bake for 8-10 minutes. Loosen from foil; drape over bottom of small custard cup. Yields 2 dozen cups.

Spritz

1 cup (240 ml) soft butter or margarine
1 cup (240 ml) confectioners sugar
3 egg yolks
1 tsp (5 ml) vanilla or almond flavoring
2 cups (480 ml) sifted WASHINGTON All-Purpose Flour

Preheat oven to 375°F (190°C). Use 2 ungreased baking sheets or pans.

Place first 4 ingredients in bowl. Beat together until light and fluffy. Stir in part of flour; work remainder in with the hands.

Fill cookie press; form cookies on baking sheet. Bake 4-6 minutes, until delicately brown on edges. Remove from sheet while warm. Yields 4-4½ dozen cookies.

Walnut Lace Cookies

Classic Shortbreads

1½ cups (355 ml) flour
¾ cup (180 ml) JACK FROST Confectioners Sugar
¼ tsp (1 ml) salt
1 cup (240 ml) butter, softened
1 tsp (5 ml) almond extract

Preheat oven to 350°F (180°C). Butter shortbread mold.

In large mixing bowl, combine all ingredients.

Pour dough into shortbread mold, press firmly. Bake 45 minutes or until light golden brown. Allow to cool in mold, about 1 hour. Run knife around perimeter of shortbread to loosen edges. Turn upside down on serving plate. Cut or break into wedges. Yields 6 servings.

California Shortbread Bars

1 cup (240 ml) butter, softened
1 cup (240 ml) light brown sugar
1 egg yolk
1 tsp (5 ml) vanilla extract
½ tsp (3 ml) grated orange peel
¼ tsp (1 ml) almond extract
2 cups (480 ml) flour
1 cup (240 ml) natural California almonds, toasted
12-oz pkg (360 g) semisweet chocolate chips

Preheat oven to 350°F (180°C). Grease 9x12-inch baking pan.

Cream butter with brown sugar until light and fluffy. Beat in egg yolk. Beat in vanilla, orange peel and almond extract. Stir in flour and ½ cup almonds.

Spread dough into baking pan. Bake 25 minutes, until golden brown. Remove from oven; sprinkle top evenly with chocolate chips. Return pan to oven for 30 seconds. Remove from oven and spread melted chocolate chips evenly over surface. Sprinkle with remaining ½ cup almonds. Cool. Cut into bars to serve. Yields 2 dozen bars.

Courtesy of the Almond Board of California.

Chocolate Shortbread Cookies

1 cup (240 ml) cold unsalted butter, cut into ½-inch cubes
¾ cup (180 ml) sugar
1¾ cups (415 ml) all-purpose flour
¼ tsp (1 ml) salt
½ cup (120 ml) SACO Baking Cocoa

Preheat oven to 300°F (150°C). Lightly grease baking sheets.

Beat butter and sugar together on low speed for 30 seconds, then on medium speed for 30-45 seconds. Stir flour, salt and cocoa together and add to butter, mixing on low speed for 1 minute. Continue beating on medium speed for 1 minute until dough comes together.

Form 1-inch balls of dough and place on baking sheets, 2 inches apart. Press flat to ⅜-inch thickness. Bake for 25-35 minutes; until cookies are firm at the edges. Cool before storing.

Dough can also be shaped into a log 1½ inches in diameter, rolled in Demerara raw sugar or coarse sugar, chilled, sliced ⅜-inch thick and baked as directed. Store in an airtight container. Yields 2½-3 dozen cookies.

Chocolate Almond Shortbread

¾ cup (18 ml) butter or margarine, softened
1¼ cups (295 ml) powdered sugar
6 squares BAKER'S Semi-Sweet Chocolate, melted and cooled
1 tsp (5 ml) vanilla
1 cup (240 ml) all-purpose flour
¼ tsp (1 ml) salt
1 cup (240 ml) toasted ground blanched almonds
½ cup (120 ml) toasted chopped almonds

Preheat oven to 250°F (120°C). Use ungreased cookie sheet.

Beat butter or margarine and sugar until light and fluffy. Stir in chocolate and vanilla. Mix in flour, salt and ground almonds.

Shape dough into 12x9-inch rectangle on cookie sheet. Sprinkle with chopped almonds; press lightly into dough. Bake 45-50 minutes or until set. Cool on cookie sheet; cut into bars. Yields 3 dozen bars.

Opposite: Classic Shortbreads

Butterscotch Shortbread

½ cup (120 ml) brown sugar, packed
¼ cup (60 ml) granulated sugar
½ cup (120 ml) margarine or butter, softened
½ cup (120 ml) shortening
2¼ cups (540 ml) GOLD MEDAL All-Purpose Flour*
½ tsp (3 ml) salt

Preheat oven to 300°F (150°C). Use ungreased cookie sheets.

Mix sugars, margarine or butter and shortening in medium bowl thoroughly. Stir in flour and salt. Roll dough about ¼-inch thick on floured, cloth-covered surface. Cut into 1½x1-inch shapes.

Place on cookie sheets. Bake 20-25 minutes or until set (cookies will not brown). Immediately remove from cookie sheet. About 3 dozen cookies.

* Do not use self-rising flour in this recipe.

Traditional Lemon Shortbread

2¾ cups (650 ml) all-purpose flour
1 cup (240 ml) DOMINO Lemon Flavored Confectioners Sugar
¼ tsp (1 ml) salt
1½ cups (355 ml) butter or margarine, softened
1 tsp (5 ml) vanilla extract
DOMINO Lemon Flavored Confectioners Sugar

Preheat oven to 325°F (165°C). Use two 8-inch round cake pans.

In large bowl, combine flour, confectioners sugar and salt. Cut butter or margarine into small pieces. Add butter or margarine and vanilla to flour mixture. Stir mixture with fork to moisten, then with lightly-floured hand, combine until blended and mixture holds together.

Pat dough evenly into cake pans. With fork, prick dough in many places to make an attractive pattern. Bake 40 minutes or until golden. Remove from oven, immediately cut each round into 16 wedges. Cool. To serve, sprinkle with lemon-flavored confectioners sugar. Carefully remove cookies from pans. Yields 2½ dozen cookies.

Royal Walnut Shortbread

1 cup (240 ml) butter, softened
¾ cup (180 ml) powdered sugar
1 tsp (5 ml) vanilla
1½ cups (355 ml) all-purpose flour
1 cup (240 ml) chopped DIAMOND Walnuts
12 large pieces DIAMOND Walnuts

Preheat oven to 325°F (165°C). Use ungreased 9-inch tart pan.

Combine butter, powdered sugar and vanilla; beat until light and fluffy. Add flour; mix well. Stir in chopped walnuts.

Press dough into tart pan with removable bottom. Score dough with fork into 12 pie-shaped wedges; place 1 large walnut piece on each wedge. Place pan on cookie sheet. Bake about 40 minutes or until very lightly golden. Cool in pan, cut into wedges. Yields 1 dozen cookies.

To use food processor: Place butter, powdered sugar, vanilla and flour in food processor. Process until mixture resembles coarse crumbs. Add chopped walnuts. Process just until evenly mixed. Bake as above.

Spiced Shortbread

1¼ cups (295 ml) butter or margarine, softened
¼ tsp (1 ml) McCORMICK/SCHILLING Pure Almond Extract
dash McCORMICK/SCHILLING Ground Mace
dash McCORMICK/SCHILLING Ground Nutmeg
2½ cups (590 ml) sifted all-purpose flour
1 cup (240 ml) confectioners sugar
dash salt

Preheat oven to 250°F (120°C).

Place butter or margarine in large mixing bowl and beat with electric mixer at low speed until fluffy. Add almond extract, mace, and nutmeg. Add flour, confectioners sugar and salt gradually. Mix thoroughly by hand. Do not use electric mixer.

Press firmly into 8x1-inch round shortbread mold, or place on ungreased cookie sheet and form into 8-inch circle. Bake in preheated oven 2½ hours. Cool in pan on wire rack 30 minutes. Turn out onto serving plate. Yields 1 dozen cookies.

Almond Cream Cheese Cookies

3 oz (90 g) cream cheese, softened
1 cup (240 ml) butter, softened
1 cup (240 ml) sugar
1 egg yolk
1 tbs (15 ml) milk
dash almond extract
2½ cups (590 ml) sifted cake flour
*1 cup (240 ml) BLUE DIAMOND Sliced Natural Almonds,
    toasted*

Preheat oven to 325°F (165°C) 10 minutes before baking. Use ungreased cookie sheets.

Beat cream cheese with butter and sugar until fluffy. Blend in egg yolk, milk and almond extract. Gradually mix in cake flour. Gently stir in almonds. Dough will be sticky.

Shape dough between wax paper into 2 logs, 12 inches long and 1½ inches in diameter. Chill until very firm.

Cut logs into 1¼-inch slices. Bake on cookie sheets for 10-15 minutes or until edges are golden. Cookies should not be brown. Yields 4 dozen cookies.

Anise Cookies

½ cup (120 ml) butter or margarine, softened
1 cup (240 ml) sugar
1 egg
½ tsp (3 ml) McCORMICK/SCHILLING Pure Vanilla Extract
1½ tsp (8 ml) baking soda
½ tsp (3 ml) salt
1¾ cups (415 ml) sifted all-purpose flour
1½ tsp (8 ml) McCORMICK/SCHILLING Anise Seed

Preheat oven to 400°F (205°C) 10 minutes before baking. Lightly grease cookie sheets.

Place butter or margarine and sugar in large mixing bowl and cream until light and fluffy. Add egg and vanilla and mix well. Add baking powder and salt to sifted flour and sift again. Gradually add dry ingredients and anise seed to butter mixture, mixing thoroughly after each addition.

Shape dough into roll and wrap in wax paper. Refrigerate at least 2 hours.

Cut chilled dough into thin slices and place 1 inch apart on prepared cookie sheets. Bake 8 minutes or until golden brown. Remove from cookie sheets and place on wire racks to cool. Yields 5 dozen cookies.

Orange Pecan Crisps

*1½ cups (355 ml) sifted HECKERS/CERESOTA
    Unbleached Flour*
½ tsp (3 ml) baking soda
¾ tsp (4 ml) salt
½ cup (120 ml) shortening, softened
½ cup (120 ml) granulated sugar
½ cup (120 ml) brown sugar, firmly packed
1 egg
1 tbs (15 ml) grated orange rind
1 tbs (15 ml) orange juice
½ cup (120 ml) chopped pecans

Preheat oven to 375°F (190°C) 10 minutes before baking. Use ungreased cookie sheets.

Sift together flour, soda and salt. Cream shortening, sugars, egg, grated orange rind and orange juice. Add flour mixture and pecans gradually; mix well.

Shape into roll, wrap and chill.

Slice dough ⅛-¼-inch thick; place on cookie sheest. Bake until golden brown, about 10 minutes. Yields 5 dozen cookies.

Orange Pecan Crisps

Refrigerator Cookies with Five Variations

¾ cup (180 ml) butter
1 cup (240 ml) sugar
1 egg
1 tsp (5 ml) McCORMICK/SCHILLING Pure Vanilla Extract
dash salt
2 cups (480 ml) all-purpose flour

Preheat oven to 350°F (180°C) 10 minutes before baking. Use ungreased cookie sheets.

Place butter and sugar in mixing bowl. Beat with electric mixer to cream. Add egg, vanilla and salt. Beat until well combined. Stir in flour to make smooth dough.

Divide dough in half and form each half into cylinder about 1½ inches wide and 9 inches long. Wrap each half tightly in wax paper and refrigerate at least 5 hours or overnight. (Wrapped dough may be frozen up to 3 weeks.)

Cut dough into ¼-inch thick slices. Arrange slices 1½ inches apart on cookie sheets. Bake 12-15 minutes or until golden brown. Remove from cookie sheets and cool completely on wire racks. Yields 3 dozen cookies.

Poppy Seed Cookies: Add ½ cup (120 ml) McCormick/ Schilling Poppy Seeds and ½ tsp (3 ml) McCormick/ Schilling Ground Cinnamon to dough before adding flour.

Gingersnaps: Reduce butter to ½ cup (120 ml) and add ¼ cup (60 ml) molasses to butter-sugar mixture. Add 2 tsp (10 ml) McCormick/Schilling Ground Ginger, ½ tsp (3 ml) McCormick/Schilling Ground Cinnamon, and ¼ tsp (1 ml) McCormick/Schilling Ground Cloves before adding flour.

Lemon-Clove Cookies: Eliminate vanilla and substitute ½ tsp (3 ml) McCormick/Schilling Pure Lemon Extract. Add ¼ tsp (1 ml) McCormick/Schilling Ground Cloves before adding flour. Stir 2 tbs (30 ml) lemon juice into 1¼ cups (295 ml) confectioners sugar. Spread or drizzle over cooled cookies.

Almond Crescents: Reduce butter to ½ cup (120 ml). Eliminate vanilla and substitute ½ tsp (3 ml) McCormick/ Schilling Pure Almond Extract. Add ½ cup (120 ml) finely ground unblanched almonds before adding flour. Roll each ¼-inch slice into 2-inch cylinder. Bend cylinders to form crescents. Roll baked and cooled cookies in confectioners sugar.

Thumbprint Cookies: Reduce butter to ½ cup (120 ml). Add ¼ tsp (1 ml) McCormick/Schilling Ground Cardamom and 1 tsp (5 ml) McCormick/Schilling Orange Peel before adding flour. Roll each ¼-inch slice into small ball. Press thumb into center of ball and fill indentation with a dash of raspberry preserves.

Currant Slice 'n Bake Cookies

1 cup (240 ml) butter, softened
1 cup (240 ml) confectioners sugar
½ cup (120 ml) sugar
1 egg
2 tsp (10 ml) vanilla
2¼ cups (540 ml) all-purpose flour
½ tsp (3 ml) baking soda
1 cup (240 ml) SUN•MAID Zante Currants or Raisins

Preheat oven to 350°F (180°C) 10 minutes before baking. Use ungreased cookie sheets.

Combine butter, confectioners sugar, sugar, egg and vanilla; beat until light and fluffy. Combine flour and baking soda. Stir into butter mixture; mix well. Stir in currants or raisins.

Shape into 12-inch roll. Wrap; refrigerate until firm.

Cut dough into ¼-inch slices. Place on cookie sheets. Bake in upper third of oven 10-12 minutes. Cool on wire racks. Yields 4 dozen cookies.

Chocolate Variation: Blend 2 oz (60 g) melted semi-sweet chocolate into butter mixture.

Refrigerator Cookies

Chocolate Almond Biscotti I

2½ cups (590 ml) all-purpose flour
¾ cup (180 ml) SACO Baking Cocoa
2 cups (480 ml) sugar
½ tsp (3 ml) salt
1 tsp (5 ml) baking powder
4 eggs
1 egg yolk
1 tsp (5 ml) vanilla extract
7 oz (210 g) whole almonds or hazelnuts or a combination

Preheat oven to 350°F (180°C). Grease 2 baking sheets.

In large mixing bowl, combine flour, cocoa, sugar, salt and baking powder. In separate bowl combine eggs, egg yolk and vanilla, beating lightly. Add eggs to dry ingredients, mixing on low speed until combined. Add nuts and continue mixing until well combined.

Shape dough into 3 logs (dough will be sticky; wetting your hands will help). Place on 2 baking sheets. Logs should be ¾-inch thick and 3½-4 inches wide. Bake for 25-30 minutes. Remove from oven and allow to cool for 15-20 minutes.

Slice logs on the diagonal ½-inch thick, using a knife with a serrated blade. Place slices on baking sheets, cut side down, and return to a 325°F (165°C) oven. Bake for 15 minutes. Turn cookies over and return to oven for 15 minutes.

Allow cookies to cool before packing in airtight container. Cookies will be very hard and will keep several weeks at room temperature. Yields 3 dozen biscotti.

If desired, cookies can be dipped halfway in melted chocolate, chilling briefly to harden chocolate if necessary. Biscotti are delicious dunked in coffee and eaten.

Chocolate Almond Biscotti II

½ cup (120 ml) whole natural almonds
⅓ cup (80 ml) butter
¾ cup (180 ml) sugar
2 eggs
¾ tsp (4 ml) almond extract
1¾ cups (415 ml) flour
½ cup (120 ml) unsweetened cocoa powder
1½ tsp (8 ml) baking powder
¼ tsp (1 ml) salt

Spread almonds in a single layer in shallow pan. Place in cold oven; toast at 350°F (180°C), 8-10 minutes, stirring occasionally, until lightly toasted. Remove from pan to cool then chop into ¼-inch pieces.

Meanwhile, cream butter and sugar until fluffy; beat in eggs. Stir in almond extract. In a separate bowl, mix together remaining ingredients, except almonds; stir into butter mixture. Stir in almonds.

On a lightly floured board, roll dough into 2 ropes the length of a baking sheet. Place on an ungreased baking sheet and bake at 325°F (165°C), 25-30 minutes until set. Remove form baking sheet and let cool 5 minutes.

Slice diagonally into ½-inch slices; lay slices flat on baking sheet and return to oven for 10 minutes to dry out, turning slices over halfway through baking. Cool. Store in a tightly covered container. Yields about 3 dozen biscotti.

Courtesy of the Almond Board of California.

Opposite: Chocolate Almond Biscotti I

Chocolate Walnut Biscotti

½ cup (120 ml) margarine or butter
¾ cup (180 ml) sugar
2 eggs
1 tsp (5 ml) vanilla
2 cups (480 ml) flour
1½ tsp (8 ml) CALUMET Baking Powder
¼ tsp (1 ml) salt
4 squares BAKER'S Semi-Sweet Chocolate, chopped
1 cup (240 ml) chopped DIAMOND Walnuts

Preheat oven to 325°F (165°C). Grease and flour cookie sheets.

Beat margarine or butter and sugar until light and fluffy. Beat in eggs and vanilla. Mix in flour, baking powder and salt. Stir in chocolate and walnuts.

Shape dough into two 14x1½-inch slightly flattened logs. Place 2 inches apart on prepared cookie sheets. Bake 25 minutes or until lightly browned.

Place on cutting board; cool 5 minutes. Using serrated knife, cut each log into diagonal slices about ¾-inch thick. Place slices upright on cookie sheet ½ inch apart. Bake 10 minutes or until slightly dry. Cool on wire racks. Yields 3 dozen biscotti.

Chocolate-Dipped Biscotti: Melt 8 squares Baker's Semi-Sweet Chocolate. Dip ½ of each biscotti into melted chocolate. Place on wax paper-lined tray. Refrigerate until chocolate is firm.

Coconut-Almond Cookie Cups with Strawberry Whipped Cream

1 tbs (15 ml) butter, softened
1 tbs (15 ml) flour
1 egg white
¼ cup (60 ml) sugar
1 tbs (15 ml) flour
pinch salt
3 tbs (45 ml) butter, melted and cooled
⅓ cup (80 ml) sliced almonds
¼ cup (60 ml) shredded sweetened coconut

Strawberry Whipped Cream:
4-6 large DRISCOLL Strawberries, washed and hulled
½ cup (120 ml) whipping cream
1 tbs (15 ml) confectioners sugar

Variation: Raspberries and Ricotta
½ cup (120 ml) part-skim ricotta cheese
3 tbs (45 ml) plain or vanilla nonfat yogurt
3 tbs (45 ml) raspberry jelly
dash vanilla extract
6-oz pkg (180 g) DRISCOLL Raspberries, rinsed

Preheat oven to 325°F (165°C). Butter 2 large baking sheets with 1 tbs butter and dust with the 1 tbs flour or use a nonstick baking sheet.

Beat egg white with whisk until frothy. Add sugar and beat until sugar is almost dissolved (peaks will not form). Blend in flour and salt, then butter, almonds and coconut; mix well.

Using a measuring tablespoon, drop batter onto baking sheets to form 6 round cookies, leaving at least 4 inches between each cookie. With back of tablespoon or spatula, spread cookie batter evenly until cookies are about 4-5 inches in diameter. (The batter will spread considerably as it bakes). Bake until cookies are completely browned, about 15-18 minutes.

Immediately remove baking sheet from oven. Using spatula, carefully lift each cookie from sheet and quickly invert over an upside down coffee or tea cup or a small can. Cookie will droop slightly over sides of cup or can to form a cup shape. Let cool completely. If not using cookies immediately, carefully store in airtight container up to 3 days.

Strawberry Whipped Cream: In small bowl, mash berries with a fork. In a separate prechilled bowl, whip cream and confectioners' sugar until stiff. Add berries and beat to blend. Cover and refrigerate up to 1 hour, if not using immediately.

Raspberries and Ricotta: Measure all ingredients except raspberries into food processor or blender container. Process or blend until smooth. Stir in raspberries just until lightly crushed. Cover and refrigerate.

To serve, arrange cookie cup on dessert plate. Fill with Strawberry Whipped Cream or Raspberries and Ricotta. Serve with additional whole berries Driscoll Raspberries and/or Driscoll Strawberries, rinsed and hulled.

Opposite: Chocolate Walnut Biscotti

Raisin Biscotti

½ cup (120 ml) butter, softened
1 cup (240 ml) sugar
3 eggs, divided
1 tbs (15 ml) anise seeds
2 tsp (10 ml) grated lemon peel
2 tsp (10 ml) grated orange peel
3 cups (720 ml) all-purpose flour
½ tsp (3 ml) baking powder
¼ tsp (1 ml) baking soda
1 cup (240 ml) DIAMOND Chopped Walnuts
1 cup (240 ml) SUN•MAID Raisins

Preheat oven to 350°F (180°C). Grease cookie sheets.

Combine butter, sugar and 2 eggs plus 1 egg yolk (reserve remaining egg white); beat until light and fluffy. Stir in anise seeds, lemon peel and orange peel. Combine flour, baking powder and baking soda. Stir into butter mixture; mix well. Stir in walnuts and raisins.

Divide dough in half. Shape each half into a 12-inch roll. Place rolls on cookie sheets, allowing space in between for spreading. Press tops of rolls to flatten slightly. Slightly beat egg white; brush over rolls.

Bake in upper third of oven for 30 minutes or until lightly browned.

Remove from oven; reduce temperature to 325°F (165°C). Using sharp knife, cut rolls diagonally into ½-inch slices. Place slices, cut side down, on cookie sheet. Return to oven and bake at 325°F (165°C) for an additional 10-12 minutes or until almost dry. Cool on wire racks. Yields 4 dozen biscotti.

Tip: Biscotti can be made ahead and stored for weeks in airtight container. For an elegant touch, dip biscotti in 6 oz (180 g) semisweet chocolate, melted.

Raisin Biscotti

Chocolate Molasses Cups

3 refrigerated pie crusts
½ cup (120 ml) GRANDMA'S Unsulphured Molasses
2 eggs
¼ cup (60 ml) sugar
6-oz pkg (180 g) semi-sweet chocolate chips
½ cup (120 ml) chopped walnuts
powdered sugar

Above: Chocolate Molasses Cups

Allow crust packages to sit at room temperature for 15-20 minutes.

Preheat oven to 350°F (180°C). Use three 12-cup muffin pans.

Unfold each pie crust; peel off top plastic sheets. Press out fold lines. Invert and remove remaining plastic sheets. Cut 12 2½-inch circles from each pie crust. Press into bottom and up sides of mini-muffin/gem pan.

In medium bowl, combine molasses, eggs and sugar; beat until smooth. Stir in chocolate chips and walnuts.

Spoon into pastry lined cups, filling each ⅔ full. Bake for 20-25 minutes or until filling is set. Cool completely. Remove from pans. Sprinkle with powdered sugar. Yields 3 dozen cups.

Chocolate Chip Rugelach

1 cup (240 ml) butter or margarine, slightly softened
2 cups (480 ml) all-purpose flour
1 cup (240 ml) vanilla ice cream, softened
½ cup (120 ml) strawberry jam
1 cup (240 ml) BAKER'S Semi-Sweet Real Chocolate Chips
1 cup (240 ml) finely chopped nuts
powdered sugar

Preheat oven to 350°F (180°C) 10 minutes before baking. Use ungreased cookie sheet.

Beat butter or margarine and flour. Beat in ice cream until well blended. Divide dough into 4 balls; wrap each in waxed paper. Refrigerate until firm, about 1 hour.

Roll dough, one ball at a time, on floured surface into 11x6-inch rectangle, about ⅛-inch thick. Spread with 2 tbs of the jam; sprinkle with ¼ cup of the chips and ¼ cup of the nuts. Roll up lengthwise like a jelly roll.

Place on cookie sheet. Cut 12 diagonal slits in roll, being careful not to cut all the way through. Repeat with the remaining dough. Bake for 35 minutes or until golden brown. Cool 5 minutes on cookie sheet. Cut through each roll; separate pieces. Finish cooling on wire racks. Sprinkle with powdered sugar, if desired. Yields 4 dozen rugelach.

Raisin Rugelach

1 cup (240 ml) butter or margarine, softened
8 oz (240 g) cream cheese, softened
2 cups (480 ml) all-purpose flour
¾ cup (180 ml) SUN•MAID Raisins
¾ cup (180 ml) DIAMOND Walnuts, finely chopped
½ cup (120 ml) mini semisweet chocolate chips
⅔ cup (160 ml) sugar
2 tsp (10 ml) cinnamon
3 tbs (45 ml) butter or margarine, melted

Preheat oven to 350°F (180°C) 10 minutes before baking. Grease baking sheets.

In mixing bowl, cream butter or margarine and cream cheese. Gradually stir in flour; mix until smooth. Form dough into 3 equal balls; flatten slightly. Wrap and chill at least 3 hours or overnight.

Combine raisins, walnuts, chocolate chips, sugar and cinnamon; set aside.

To bake, roll one ball of dough on floured surface to 12-inch circle. Brush with 1 tbs of the butter or margarine; sprinkle with ⅓ of the raisin mixture. Roll over filling with rolling pin to press slightly into dough. Cut into pie-shaped wedges. Roll each wedge jelly-roll fashion, beginning from wide end.

Place on baking sheets, points down. Repeat with remaining balls of dough. If desired, brush tops with additional melted butter; sprinkle with additional cinnamon and sugar. Bake about 25 minutes or until golden. Cool on wire racks. Yields 3 dozen rugelach.

Opposite: **Raisin Rugelach**

Raisin Molasses Gems

¾ cup (180 ml) shortening
1 cup (240 ml) sugar
¼ cup (60 ml) molasses
1 egg
2 cups (480 ml) all-purpose flour
2 tsp (10 ml) baking soda
1 tsp (5 ml) cinnamon
½ tsp (3 ml) cloves
½ tsp (3 ml) ginger
¼ tsp (1 ml) salt
1 cup (240 ml) SUN•MAID Raisins

Preheat oven to 350°F (180°C) 10 minutes before baking. Grease cookie sheets.

Combine shortening and sugar; beat until light and fluffy. Add molasses and egg; blend well. Combine flour, baking soda, cinnamon, cloves, ginger and salt. Add to molasses mixture; mix well. Stir in raisins.

Cover; refrigerate until firm.

Shape dough into 1-inch balls; roll in sugar. Place 2 inches apart on cookie sheets. Bake in upper third of oven for 10-12 minutes or until set. Cool 1 minute; remove from cookie sheets. Cool on wire racks. Yields 3 dozen cookies.

Hamentashen

4 eggs, slightly beaten
¾ cup (180 ml) corn oil
¾ cup (180 ml) sugar
grated rind of 1 orange
5 cups (1.2 l) sifted PRESTO
Lekvar* or apple butter

Preheat oven to 350°F (180°C) 10 minutes before baking. Grease cookie sheets.

Combine slightly beaten eggs, corn oil, sugar and orange rind. Beat until mixture is fluffy and thick. Gently stir in flour. Chill about 1½ hours or until firm.

Divide dough into quarters. Roll out each on floured board or cloth to ⅛-inch thickness. Cut into 2½ or 3-inch circles and place on cookie sheets. Spoon 1 tbs Lekvar into center of each. Form tricorns, bringing up edges of dough almost to center and making three seams. (Some filling should show in center.) Pinch seams together tightly.

Bake 15-20 minutes or until golden brown.
Yields 6 dozen 2½-inch or 4 dozen 3-inch cookies.

*A traditional Hungarian fruit filling, a thick soft spread, usually made of apricots or prunes and sugar.

Raisin Molasses Gems

Opposite: Hamentashen

Chocolate Walnut Puffs

2 egg whites
¼ tsp (1 ml) cream of tartar
dash salt
½ cup (120 ml) sugar
6 oz (180 g) semisweet chocolate chips, melted
½ tsp (3 ml) vanilla
¾ cup (180 ml) chopped DIAMOND Walnuts

Preheat oven to 350°F (180°C). Grease cookie sheets.

Combine egg whites, cream of tartar and salt; beat to a fine foam. Gradually add sugar; beat until stiff peaks form. Fold in chocolate, vanilla and walnuts.

Drop by teaspoonfuls onto cookie sheets. Bake in upper third of oven for 10 minutes. Using broad spatula immediately remove from cookie sheets; cool on wire racks. Yields 3 dozen cookies.

Snowflake Macaroons

2⅔ cups (640 ml) BAKER'S ANGEL FLAKE Coconut
⅔ cup (160 ml) sugar
6 tbs (90 ml) flour
¼ tsp (1 ml) salt
4 egg whites
1 tsp (5 ml) almond extract

Preheat oven to 325°F (165°C). Lightly grease and flour cookie sheets.

Mix coconut, sugar, flour and salt in bowl. Stir in egg whites and almond extract until well blended.

Drop by teaspoonfuls onto cookie sheets. Bake 20 minutes or until edges of cookies are golden brown. Immediately remove from cookie sheets. Cool on wire racks. Drizzle with melted Baker's Semi-Sweet Chocolate, if desired. Yields 3 dozen cookies.

Chocolate Macaroons: Stir in 2 squares melted Baker's Semi-Sweet Chocolate before baking.

Snowflake Macaroons

Opposite: Chocolate Walnut Puffs

Madeleines

4 eggs
1¼ cups (295 ml) superfine sugar
2 cups (480 ml) sifted cake flour
1 tsp (5 ml) McCORMICK/SCHILLING Pure Vanilla Extract
dash McCORMICK/SCHILLING Ground Mace
1 cup (240 ml) butter or margarine, melted and cooled to room
*   temperature*
confectioners sugar for sprinkling, if desired

Preheat oven to 350°F (180°C). Lightly grease 24 2½-inch madeleine molds.

Separate eggs and set egg whites aside. Place egg yolks and superfine sugar in 2-quart bowl and beat until light colored and creamy. Stir in flour, vanilla and mace, mixing well. Gradually beat melted butter into flour mixture.

Place egg whites in mixing bowl and beat with electric mixer until soft peaks form when beaters are lifted. Fold egg whites into batter, folding gently until no streaks are visible. Spoon batter into prepared madeleine molds, filling molds ⅔ full. Bake for 15 minutes. Remove from molds and cool on wire rack. Sprinkle with confectioners sugar before serving. Yields 2 dozen madeleines.

Nutty Chocolate Chunk Bars

3 eggs
1 cup (240 ml) JACK FROST Granulated Sugar
1 cup (240 ml) JACK FROST Brown Sugar, packed
1 cup (240 ml) chunky peanut butter
¾ cup (180 ml) butter
2 tsp (10 ml) baking soda
2 tsp (10 ml) vanilla
1 cup (240 ml) oat bran
3½ cups (840 ml) quick -ooking oats
1 cup (240 ml) Spanish peanuts
12-oz pkg (360 g) semi-sweet chocolate chunks

Preheat oven to 350°F (180°C). Grease 15x10x2-inch pan.

In large mixing bowl, beat eggs, granulated sugar and brown sugar. Add peanut butter, butter, baking soda, vanilla and oat bran. Mix well. Stir in quick cooking oats, peanuts and chocolate.

Spread mixture into prepared pan. Bake 20-25 minutes. Yields 3 dozen bars.

Nutty Chocolate Chunk Bars

Hoosier Bars

1½ cups (355 ml) all-purpose flour
1 tsp (5 ml) baking soda
1 cup (240 ml) brown sugar, packed and divided
½ cup (120 ml) granulated sugar
½ cup (120 ml) butter or margarine, softened
2 eggs, separated
1 tsp (5 ml) vanilla extract
12-oz pkg NESTLÉ TOLL HOUSE Semi-Sweet
     Chocolate Morsels, divided
¾ cup (180 ml) honey roasted peanuts, divided

Preheat oven to 325°F (165°C). Grease 13x9-inch baking pan.

Combine flour and baking soda in small bowl. Beat ½ cup brown sugar, granulated sugar and butter in large bowl until creamy. Beat in egg yolks and vanilla. Gradually beat in flour mixture until crumbly. Stir in 1½ cup morsels and ½ cup nuts.

Press dough onto bottom of prepared baking pan.

Beat egg whites in small mixer bowl until soft peaks form. Gradually beat in remaining brown sugar until stiff peaks form; spread over dough. Sprinkle with remaining morsels and remaining nuts.

Bake 35-40 minutes or until top is set and lightly browned. Cool in pan on wire rack for 20 minutes. Cut into bars while still warm. Yields 3 dozen bars.

Opposite: Hoosier Bars

Holiday Red Raspberry Chocolate Bars

2½ cups (590 ml) all-purpose flour
1 cup (240 ml) sugar
¾ cup (180 ml) finely chopped pecans
1 cup (240 ml) butter or margarine, softened
1 egg
12-oz jar (360 g) seedless red raspberry jam
1⅔ cups (400 ml) HERSHEY'S Milk Chocolate Chips,
  Semi-Sweet Chocolate Chips or Raspberry Chips

Heat oven to 350°F (180°C). Grease 13x9x2-inch baking pan.

In large bowl, stir together flour, sugar, pecans, butter or margarine and egg until crumbly; set aside 1½ cups crumb mixture.

Press remaining crumb mixture onto bottom of prepared pan; spread jam over top. Sprinkle with chocolate chips. Crumble remaining crumb mixture over top.

Bake 40-45 minutes or until lightly browned. Cool completely in pan on wire rack; cut into bars. Yields 3 dozen bars.

Chewy Hazelnut Bars

1 lb (455 g) JACK FROST Dark Brown Sugar
¾ cup (180 ml) butter
2 eggs
2 tsp (10 ml) vanilla
2 cups (480 ml) all-purpose flour
2 tsp (10 ml) baking powder
½ tsp (3 ml) salt
1 cup (240 ml) chopped hazelnuts, pecans or walnuts
1 cup (240 ml) semisweet chocolate chips

Preheat oven to 350°F (180°C). Butter an 11x8-inch baking pan.

In a microwave-safe bowl, heat brown sugar and butter until butter melts, about 2 minutes on high. Let cool to room temperature. In a mixing bowl, beat brown sugar mixture, eggs and vanilla until well blended. In large bowl, combine flour, baking powder, and salt; add to butter mixture. Stir in nuts and chocolate chips.

Spread mixture evenly in prepared pan. Bake 35-40 minutes. Cool completely and cut into 2-inch squares. Yields 20 bars.

Chewy Hazelnut Bars

Opposite:
Holiday Red Raspberry
Chocolate Bars

Chewy Walnut Squares

1 cup (240 ml) brown sugar, firmly packed
1 tsp (5 ml) vanilla
1 egg
½ cup (120 ml) all-purpose flour
¼ tsp (1 ml) baking soda
¼ tsp (1 ml) salt
1 cup (240 ml) chopped DIAMOND Walnuts

Preheat oven to 350°F (180°C). Grease an 8-inch square pan.

In medium bowl, combine brown sugar, vanilla and egg; beat well. Combine flour, baking soda and salt. Add to sugar mixture; stir just until dry ingredients are moistened. Fold in walnuts; spread in pan.

Bake 20 minutes or until lightly browned. Cool completely; cut into squares. (Cookies will appear underdone when baked. Once cooled, they become firmer with crisp, crusty layers and soft, chewy centers.)
Yields 16 squares.

Date-Nut Bars

3 eggs, separated
1 cup (240 ml) sugar, divided
½ tsp (3 ml) vanilla
1 cup (240 ml) WASHINGTON Self-Rising Flour
1 cup (240 ml) nuts, chopped
1 cup (240 ml) dates, chopped

Preheat oven to 325°F (180°C). Grease 13x9-inch pan.

Place egg whites in bowl; beat until foamy. Add ½ cup sugar gradually; beat until stiff. Set aside. Beat together yolks, ½ cup sugar and vanilla until thick and lemon colored. Combine flour, nuts and dates; fold into egg yolk mixture. Fold in egg whites mixture.

Spoon into pan. Bake 25-30 minutes. Cool; cut into bars; roll in confectioners sugar, if desired.
Yields 2 dozen bars.

Pecan Bars

⅓ cup (80 ml) butter or margarine
⅓ cup (80 ml) brown sugar
1⅓ cups (400 ml) sifted WASHINGTON Self-Rising Flour
¼ cup (60 ml) chopped pecans

Topping:
2 eggs, beaten
¾ cup (180 ml) dark corn syrup
¼ cup (60 ml) brown sugar
3 tbs (45 ml) WASHINGTON All-Purpose Flour
½ tsp (3 ml) salt
1 tsp (5 ml) vanilla
¾ cup (180 ml) chopped pecans

Preheat oven to 350°F (180°C). Grease 13x9-inch pan.

Place butter and brown sugar in bowl. Cream together thoroughly. Stir in flour and pecans. Press into bottom of pan. Bake 10 minutes.

Topping: Combine first 6 ingredients in order given. Stir in pecans. Spread topping over hot crust. Bake 25-30 minutes more. Cool in pan. Cut in squares.
Yields 2 dozen bars.

Brickle Chips Pecan Dream Bars

1 cup (240 ml) butter
1 cup (240 ml) brown sugar
1 egg yolk
1 tsp (5 ml) vanilla
2 cups (480 ml) flour
6-oz pkg (180 g) BITS 'O BRICKLE
½ cup (120 ml) finely chopped pecans

Preheat oven to 350°F (180°C). Use an ungreased 15½x10½-inch jelly roll pan.

With mixer, cream butter well; blend in brown sugar, egg yolk and vanilla. By hand, mix in flour, ⅔ cups Bits 'O Brickle and nuts.

Press into jelly roll pan. Bake 18-20 minutes or until lightly browned. Remove from oven and immediately sprinkle remaining Bits 'O Brickle over top. Cool slightly but cut while warm. Yields 2 dozen bars.

Opposite: Date-Nut Bars

Breakfast Bars

¾ cup (180 ml) all-purpose flour
¾ cup (180 ml) toasted wheat germ
¼ cup (60 ml) sugar
½ tsp (3 ml) baking powder
½ tsp (3 ml) cinnamon
¼ cup (60 ml) butter or margarine, melted
¼ cup (60 ml) honey
1 egg
½ tsp (3 ml) vanilla
1 cup (240 ml) SUN•MAID Raisins
½ cup (120 ml) DIAMOND Chopped Walnuts

Heat oven to 350°F (180°C). Grease 8-inch square pan.

Combine flour, wheat germ, sugar, baking powder and cinnamon. Stir in butter or margarine, honey, egg and vanilla; mix well. Stir in raisins and walnuts.

Press mixture firmly into pan. Bake 20-25 minutes or until lightly browned. Yields 10 bars.

Date-Filled Spiced Oat Squares

1 cup (240 ml) chopped dates
⅓ cup (80 ml) water
¼ cup (60 ml) sugar
¼ cup (60 ml) chopped walnuts
4 tsp (20 ml) lemon juice
1 tsp (5 ml) McCORMICK/SCHILLING Pure Vanilla Extract
1 cup (240 ml) light brown sugar, firmly packed
½ cup (120 ml) butter or margarine, softened
3 cups (720 ml) rolled oats
½ tsp (3 ml) McCORMICK/SCHILLING Ground Cinnamon
¼ tsp (1 ml) McCORMICK/SCHILLING Ground Allspice

Preheat oven to 350°F (180°C). Grease 13x9x2-inch baking pan.

Place dates, water, sugar, walnuts and lemon juice in saucepan and stir to combine. Cook over low heat, stirring frequently, until thickened, about 5 minutes. Remove from heat, stir in vanilla and set aside. Cream brown sugar and butter or margarine in large bowl. Stir in rolled oats, cinnamon, and allspice.

Press half of oat mixture firmly in bottom of baking pan. Spread reserved date mixture evenly over and sprinkle with remaining half of oat mixture. Press firmly. Bake 15 minutes. Cool in pan on wire rack. Cut 4 rows down length of pan and 5 rows across width of pan to make 20 squares, each about 2x2 inches. Yields 20 squares.

Chocolate Date Bars

4 squares BAKER'S Semi-Sweet Chocolate
2 cups (480 ml) chopped dates
¾ cup (180 ml) water
⅓ cup (80 ml) corn syrup
¾ cup (180 ml) margarine or butter, slightly softened
1 cup (240 ml) brown sugar, firmly packed
1¾ cups (415 ml) all-purpose flour
½ tsp (3 ml) baking soda
¼ tsp (1 ml) salt
1½ cups (355 ml) quick-cooking oats

Preheat oven to 400°F (205°C). Grease 13x9-inch pan.

Microwave chocolate, dates, water and corn syrup in large microwave-safe bowl on high 3 minutes; stir. Microwave 2 minutes longer or until thickened. Or mix chocolate, dates, water and corn syrup in 1-quart saucepan; stir over low heat until thickened. Cool.

Beat margarine or butter and sugar in separate bowl. Mix in flour, baking soda and salt. Stir in oats. Press half the mixture evenly into prepared pan. Spread with chocolate mixture; top with the remaining oat mixture. Bake for 25 minutes or until topping is golden brown. Cool in pan; cut into bars. Yields 3 dozen bars.

Chocolate Date Bars

Fabulous Fig Bars

2 8-oz pkgs (240 g each) BLUE RIBBON or
    SUN•MAID Calimyra or Mission Figs
½ cup (120 ml) chopped DIAMOND Walnuts
⅓ cup (80 ml) sugar
¼ cup (60 ml) rum or orange juice
2 tbs (30 ml) hot water
½ cup (120 ml) butter, softened
1 cup (240 ml) brown sugar, packed
1 egg
1½ cups (355 ml) flour
½ tsp (3 ml) baking soda
1¼ cups (295 ml) old-fashioned oats

Rum Glaze:
½ cup (120 ml) confectioners sugar
3-4 tsp (15-20 ml) rum or orange juice

Preheat oven to 350°F (180°C). Coat 13x9-inch baking pan with vegetable cooking spray.   Cut stems from figs and coarsely chop. In small bowl, combine figs, walnuts, sugar, rum or orange juice and hot water. Set aside.

In mixing bowl, beat butter and brown sugar until creamy. Add egg and mix until smooth. Stir in flour and baking soda; blend in oats to make a soft dough. Reserve 1 cup dough.

With floured fingertips, press thin layer of remaining dough into bottom of prepared pan. Firmly pat fig mixture over dough. Drop reserved dough by teaspoonfuls over top, allowing fig mixture to show between drops. Bake 30 minutes or until golden brown. Cool completely in pan. Drizzle with rum glaze. Cut into bars. Yields 3 dozen bars.

Rum Glaze: Stir together confectioners sugar and rum or orange juice until smooth.

Fabulous Fig Bars

Opposite:
Microwave Peanut Butter
and Jam Bars

Microwave Peanut Butter and Jam Bars

6 tbs (90 ml) butter or margarine, softened
⅓ cup (80 ml) peanut butter
⅓ cup (80 ml) DOMINO Light Brown Sugar, firmly packed
⅓ cup (80 ml) DOMINO Granulated Sugar
1 egg
1⅔ cups (400 ml) all-purpose flour
⅔ cup (160 ml) strawberry jam or preserves

Use 8-inch square glass baking dish.

Beat butter or margarine , peanut butter, sugars and egg well. Add flour and beat on low speed until mixture is crumbly. Reserve 1 cup crumbs.

Press remaining crumbs into baking dish. Place on an inverted plate to elevate dish in microwave oven.

Cook at medium 6½ minutes or until base looks dry, rotating dish, if necessary. Spread jam to within ½-inch of edge of base. Sprinkle with reserved crumbs. Cook at medium 6-7 minutes, or until jam bubbles near the center, rotating dish once. Cool. Yields 16 bars.

Walnut Linzer Bars

¾ cup (180 ml) butter or margarine, softened
¾ cup (180 ml) sugar
1 egg
1 tsp (5 ml) cinnamon
1 tsp (5 ml) grated lemon peel
¼ tsp (1 ml) cloves
¼ tsp (1 ml) salt
2 cups (480 ml) all-purpose flour
1 cup (240 ml) ground DIAMOND Walnuts
1 cup (240 ml) raspberry or apricot jam
confectioners sugar, optional

Preheat oven to 325°F (165°C). Grease 9-inch square pan.

Combine butter or margarine, sugar, egg, cinnamon, lemon peel, cloves and salt; beat until light and fluffy. Add flour and walnuts; mix well. Set aside ¾ cup dough for lattice top.

Press remaining dough into pan; spread with jam.

Out of the ¾ cup dough, make pencil-shaped strips by rolling on floured board with palms of hands. Arrange strips in lattice over jam.

Bake 45 minutes or until lightly browned. Cool completely. Sprinkle with confectioners sugar, if desired. Cut into bars. Yields 20 bars.

Applesauce Spice Bars

½ cup (120 ml) butter or margarine, softened
1 cup (240 ml) brown sugar, firmly packed
1 egg
2 cups (480 ml) all-purpose flour
1 tsp (5 ml) cinnamon
1 tsp (5 ml) allspice
½ tsp (3 ml) baking soda
¼ tsp (1 ml) salt
1 cup (240 ml) applesauce
1 cup (240 ml) DIAMOND Chopped Walnuts
1 cup (240 ml) SUN•MAID Raisins

Glaze:
1½ cups (355 ml) powdered sugar
2 tbs (30 ml) milk
½ tsp (3 ml) vanilla

Preheat oven to 350°F (180°C). Grease 13x9-inch pan.

Combine butter, brown sugar and egg; beat until light and fluffy. Combine flour, cinnamon, allspice, baking soda and salt; add to butter mixture alternately with applesauce. Stir in walnuts and raisins.

Spread batter in pan. Bake 20-25 minutes or until golden brown. Cool 5 minutes. Combine all Glaze ingredients; blend well. Spread over warm surface. Cool completely; cut into bars. Yields 2 dozen bars.

Walnut Fruit Squares

1½ cups (355 ml) sifted flour
½ cup (120 ml) sugar
¾ cup (180 ml) butter or margarine, softened
¾ cup (180 ml) chopped walnuts
8-oz can (240 g) DEL MONTE Crushed Pineapple
   in its Own Juice
8-oz pkg (240 g) cream cheese, softened
½ cup (120 ml) powdered sugar
17-oz can (510 g) DEL MONTE Fruit Cocktail, drained

Preheat oven to 350°F (180°C). Use 13x9-inch pan.

Combine flour and sugar; cut in butter or margarine. Stir in nuts. Press into bottom of pan. Bake 25 minutes. Cool.

Drain pineapple reserving 1 tbs juice. Combine reserved juice, cream cheese and powdered sugar; beat until fluffy. Fold in fruits. Spread over crust. Chill overnight before serving. Will hold wet for several days. Yields 1 dozen squares.

Walnut Fruit Squares

Apricot Delights

⅓ cup (80 ml) butter or margarine, softened
¼ cup (60 ml) sugar
1⅓ cups (320 ml) all-purpose flour, divided
1 cup (240 ml) brown sugar, firmly packed
½ tsp (3 ml) baking powder
2 eggs, beaten
1 tsp (5 ml) vanilla
1 cup (240 ml) cooked, dried apricots*
1 cup (240 ml) chopped DIAMOND Walnuts

Preheat oven to 350°F (180°C). Use ungreased 9-inch square pan.

Combine butter or margarine and sugar; beat until light and fluffy. Add 1 cup flour; mix well. Spread mixture in pan. Bake for 20 minutes or until lightly browned.

Meanwhile, combine remaining ⅓ cup flour, brown sugar and baking powder; mix well. Add eggs and vanilla; blend well. Stir in apricots and walnuts; spread over partially baked base.

Return to oven; bake for an additional 30 minutes. Cool completely; cut into squares. Yields 20 bars.

*To cook, combine apricots and 1 cup (240 ml) water in saucepan. Bring to a boil; reduce heat and simmer for 10 minutes. Drain; chop apricots.

Buttermilk Cranberry Bars

3 cups (720 ml) all-purpose flour
½ tsp (3 ml) baking powder
½ tsp (3 ml) baking soda
½ tsp (3 ml) salt
¼ cup (60 ml) SACO Buttermilk Blend
½ cup (120 ml) butter or margarine
1 cup (240 ml) sugar
¾ cup (180 ml) brown sugar, packed
¼ cup (60 ml) water
2 tbs (30 ml) orange juice
1 egg
1 cup (240 ml) chopped walnuts
2½ cups (590 ml) fresh or frozen cranberries, coarsely chopped
1 tsp (5 ml) grated orange peel, optional

Cream Cheese Frosting:
3-oz pkg (90 g) cream cheese
1 tbs (15 ml) milk
2½ cups (590 ml) sifted powdered sugar
1 tsp (5 ml) vanilla

Preheat oven to 350°F (180°C). Grease 15x10½x1½-inch pan.

Sift together flour, baking powder, baking soda, salt, and buttermilk blend; set aside.

Beat butter or margarine, sugar and brown sugar in a large bowl until smooth. Stir in water, orange juice and egg. Stir into dry ingredients until dough is smooth. Do not overbeat. Fold in nuts, cranberries and orange peel. Dough will be stiff.

Pour into prepared pan. Bake 25-30 minutes. Frost with Cream Cheese Frosting. Yields 2½ dozen bars.

Cream Cheese Frosting: Blend cream cheese with milk. Add powdered sugar and enough milk to make a frosting of spreading consistency. Add vanilla.

Buttermilk Treasure Bars

½ cup (120 ml) brown sugar, packed
½ cup (120 ml) granulated sugar
½ cup (120 ml) margarine
2 eggs, beaten
1 tsp (5 ml) vanilla
2 cups (480 ml) all-purpose flour
½ tsp (3 ml) baking powder
½ tsp (3 ml) salt
½ tsp (3 ml) baking soda
¼ cup (60 ml) SACO Buttermilk Blend
¾ cup (180 ml) water
1 cup (240 ml) maraschino cherries, sliced
1 cup (240 ml) chopped walnuts
1 cup (240 ml) SACO Chocolate Chunks

Vanilla Butter Frosting:
⅓ cup (80 ml) butter or margarine, softened
2 cups (480 ml) powdered sugar
1 tsp (5 ml) vanilla
2 tbs (30 ml) milk, approximately

Preheat oven to 325°F (165°C). Grease 15½x10½x1½-inch pan.

Cream sugars and margarine together. Add eggs and vanilla. Sift together flour, baking powder, salt, baking soda and buttermilk blend. Add sifted dry ingredients, alternating with water to creamed mixture, and stir just until ingredients are well mixed. Do not overbeat. Stir in cherries, nuts and chocolate chunks.

Spread in prepared pan. Bake 30 minutes. Frost with Vanilla Butter Frosting. Yields 2½ dozen bars.

Vanilla Butter Frosting: Blend butter or margarine and sugar. Stir in vanilla and milk. Beat until frosting is smooth and of spreading consistency.

Oatmeal Scotchie Bars

1 pkg PILLSBURY MOIST SUPREME Yellow Cake Mix
½ cup (120 ml) brown sugar, firmly packed
½ cup (120 ml) margarine or butter, melted
2 eggs
1 cup (240 ml) corn flakes cereal
1 cup (240 ml) butterscotch chips
6 oz (180 g) quick-cooking rolled oats

Preheat oven to 350°F (180°C). Grease 13x9-inch baking pan.

In large bowl, combine cake mix, brown sugar, margarine and eggs; stir by hand until well blended. Add cereal, butterscotch chips and oats; mix well.

Spread in pan. Bake for 30-40 minutes or until golden brown. Cool completely. Cut into bars.
Yields 4 dozen bars.

Low-Fat Blueberry Ricotta Bars

Low-Fat Blueberry Ricotta Bars

2 tbs (30 ml) vegetable oil
½ cup (120 ml) MOTT'S Natural Apple Sauce
¾ cup (180 ml) granulated sugar
1 egg
1 egg white
1 cup (240 ml) all-purpose flour
1 tsp (5 ml) baking powder
½ tsp (3 ml) baking soda
¼ tsp (1 ml) salt
¼ cup (60 ml) skim milk
½ tsp (3 ml) vanilla extract

Filling:
1 cup (240 ml) fresh or frozen blueberries
¼ cup (60 ml) granulated sugar
½ tsp (3 ml) ground cinnamon

Topping:
2 egg whites, slightly beaten
1 cup (240 ml) nonfat ricotta cheese
⅓ cup (80 ml) granulated sugar
¼ tsp (1 ml) vanilla extract

Preheat oven to 375°F (190°C). Spray 9x9-inch baking pan with nonstick cooking spray.

In a large bowl, mix together vegetable oil, applesauce, granulated sugar, whole egg and egg white.

Prepare crust. In a separate medium bowl, mix together flour, baking powder, baking soda and salt. Add flour mixture to applesauce mixture alternately with skim milk. Add vanilla extract and mix until blended.

Filling: In a small bowl, mix together blueberries with granulated sugar and cinnamon.

Topping: In a separate medium bowl, combine beaten egg whites, non-fat ricotta cheese, granulated sugar and vanilla extract. Mix well until ingredients are combined.

Place crust mixture on bottom of prepared pan and flatten to make an even layer. Layer blueberry mixture on top of crust, then top with ricotta mixture. Bake for 60 minutes until inserted toothpick comes out clean. Cool for 20 minutes and cut into bars. Yields 1 dozen bars.

Opposite: Oatmeal Scotchie Bars

Philly Cheesecake Bars

Crust:
½ cup (120 ml) butter
¼ cup (60 ml) sugar
½ tsp (3 ml) vanilla
1 cup (240 ml) flour

Filling:
3 8-oz pkgs (240 g each) *PHILADELPHIA BRAND*
    Cream Cheese, softened
¾ cup (180 ml) sugar
1 tsp (5 ml) vanilla
3 eggs

Preheat oven to 350°F (180°C). Use 13x9-inch baking pan.
    Crust: Beat butter, sugar and vanilla in small bowl with electric mixer on medium speed until light and fluffy. Gradually add flour, mixing on low speed until blended. Press onto bottom of pan; prick with fork. Bake 20 minutes or until edges are light golden brown.
    Filling: Beat cream cheese, sugar and vanilla with electric mixer on medium speed until well blended. Add eggs; mix just until blended.
    Pour over crust. Bake 45 minutes or until center is almost set. Refrigerate 4 hours or overnight.
Yields 1½ dozen bars.

Marbled Cheesecake Bars

Crust:
1 cup (240 ml) all-purpose flour
1 cup (240 ml) chopped pecans
½ cup (120 ml) margarine or butter, softened
½ cup (120 ml) brown sugar, firmly packed

Topping:
½ bar *GHIRARDELLI* Bittersweet Chocolate,
    broken into 1-inch pieces
3 8-oz pkgs (240 g each) cream cheese, softened
¾ cup (180 ml) granulated sugar
1 tsp (5 ml) vanilla
3 eggs

Preheat oven to 325°F (165°C). Use ungreased 8 or 9-inch square baking pan.
    Combine flour, pecans, margarine or butter and brown sugar; mix well. Press onto bottom of pan. Bake 15-17 minutes or until light golden brown. Cool.
    Topping: Melt chocolate slowly in double boiler, remove from heat. (You may also melt chocolate in glass or metal bowl placed over pan of boiling water, to form double boiler. Remove pan from stove. Cover and let stand 5 minutes.) Stir until smooth and set aside.
    In a large bowl of electric mixer, beat cream cheese, granulated sugar and vanilla until well blended. Add eggs, one at a time, mixing well after each addition. Reserve 1 cup batter; set aside. Combine chocolate and remaining batter; mix well.
    Pour chocolate batter over crust. Pour plain batter over chocolate batter. Swirl batters with a knife to marbleize. Bake 30-35 minutes or until center is set. Chill several hours; store in refrigerator. Yields 16 bars.

Opposite: **Philly Cheesecake Bars**

Fudge Cheesecake Bars

4 4-oz bars (120 g each) HERSHEY'S Unsweetened
  Baking Chocolate, broken into pieces
1 cup (240 ml) butter or margarine
2½ cups (590 ml) sugar, divided
4 eggs
1 tsp (5 ml) vanilla extract
2 cups (480 ml) all-purpose flour
8-oz pkg (240 g) cream cheese, softened
13-oz pkg (390 g) HERSHEY'S HUGS Chocolates
  or HUGS WITH ALMONDS Chocolates, divided

Preheat oven to 350°F (180°C). Grease 13x9x2-inch
baking pan.

In large microwave-safe bowl, place baking chocolate
and butter or margarine. Microwave at high 2-2½ minutes, stirring after each minute, until butter and chocolate
are completely melted. Beat in 2 cups sugar, 3 eggs and
vanilla until blended. Stir in flour; spread batter into
prepared pan.

In small bowl, beat cream cheese, remaining ½ cup
sugar and remaining egg. Remove wrappers from 12
chocolate pieces; coarsely chop and stir into cream cheese
mixture. Drop by dollops over chocolate mixture in pan.
With knife, swirl chocolate up onto top for marbled effect.

Bake 35-40 minutes or just until set. Cool completely
in pan on wire rack; cut into bars. Remove wrappers from
remaining chocolate pieces; press on top. Cover; refrigerate. Yields 3 dozen bars.

Lemon Cheese Bars

1 cup (240 ml) all-purpose flour
½ cup (120 ml) finely chopped walnuts
6 tbs (90 ml) butter or margarine, softened
1½ cup (120 ml) DOMINO Lemon-Flavored
  Confectioners Sugar, divided
8-oz pkg (240 g) cream cheese, softened
1 tbs (15 ml) milk
½ tsp (3 ml) vanilla extract
1 egg

Preheat oven to 350°F (180°C). Lightly grease 8x8-inch
baking pan.

In medium bowl, mix flour, walnuts, butter or margarine and ½ cup confectioners sugar until blended (mixture
will be crumbly). Reserve ½ cup crumb mixture; pat
remaining mixture into bottom of pan.

Bake 20 minutes or until lightly browned. Meanwhile,
in small bowl, with mixer at low speed, beat cream cheese
until fluffy. Add milk, vanilla, egg and remaining 1 cup
confectioners sugar; beat until smooth.

Remove baking pan from oven; pour cheese mixture
over baked layer in pan; sprinkle with reserved crumb
mixture. Bake 35 minutes longer or until golden. Remove
from pan to cool, then refrigerate until cold. To serve,
sprinkle with lemon-flavored confectioners sugar. Cut into
bars. Yields 15 bars.

Strawberry Cheese Bars: Substitute ½ cup (120 ml)
Domino Strawberry-Flavored Confectioners' Sugar for
Lemon-Flavored Confectioners Sugar.

Opposite: Lemon Cheese Bars

Pumpkin Streusel Squares

1¾ cups (415 ml) unsifted flour
⅓ cup (80 ml) packed brown sugar
⅓ cup (80 ml) granulated sugar
1 cup (240 ml) cold margarine or butter, cut into small pieces
1 cup (240 ml) chopped nuts
15-oz can (450 g) COMSTOCK, THANK YOU
    or WILDERNESS Pure Pumpkin
14-oz can (420 ml) sweetened condensed milk
2 eggs
1 tsp (5 ml) ground cinnamon
½ tsp (3 ml) ground allspice
½ tsp (3 ml) salt, optional

Preheat oven to 350°F (180°C). Use 12x7-inch baking dish

In medium bowl, combine flour and sugars. Cut in margarine until crumbly. Stir in nuts. Reserving 1 cup crumb mixture, press remainder firmly on bottom and halfway up sides of baking dish.

In large mixing bowl, combine remaining ingredients. Mix well. Pour into prepared dish. Top with reserved crumb mixture. Bake 55 minutes or until golden. Cool. Serve with ice cream, if desired. Refrigerate leftovers. Yields 8-10 squares.

Pumpkin Streusel Squares

Luscious Lemon Bars

¾ cup (180 ml) margarine or butter, softened
¾ cup (180 ml) sugar
1 egg
2 tsp (10 ml) vanilla extract
2¼ cups (540 ml) all-purpose flour
15-oz can (450 g each) COMSTOCK, THANK YOU
    or WILDERNESS Lemon Pie Filling
confectioners sugar

Preheat oven to 375°F (190°C). Grease baking sheet.

In large mixing bowl with electric mixer, beat margarine, sugar, egg and vanilla until well blended. Mix in flour until incorporated.

Divide dough in half. With your hands, shape each half into log about 14 inches long and 1½ inches wide. Place on baking sheet. Using the handle of a wooden spoon, or your finger, make a depression along the center of each log, about ½-inch wide. Spoon in lemon filling, mounding slightly.

Bake for 20-25 minutes or until tops are set and bottoms are golden. Let cool 2 minutes and loosen bottoms with spatula. Sprinkle with confectioners sugar. Cool completely before cutting into 1-inch diagonal slices. Yields 2 dozen bars.

Above: Luscious Lemon Bars

Almond Lemon Bars

¾ cup (180 ml) flour
¾ cup (180 ml) BLUE DIAMOND Sliced Natural Almonds,
    toasted, divided
¼ cup (60 ml) confectioners sugar
½ cup (120 ml) butter, melted
1 cup (240 ml) sugar
2 eggs, beaten
2 tbs (30 ml) lemon juice
2 tsp (10 ml) grated lemon peel
½ tsp (3 ml) baking powder
¼ tsp (1 ml) vanilla extract
¼ tsp (1 ml) almond extract
pinch salt

Icing:
1½ cups (355 ml) powdered sugar
2 tbs (30 ml) lemon juice
1 tsp (5 ml) vanilla extract
1 tsp (5 ml) water

Preheat oven to 350°F (180°C). Grease 8-inch square
baking pan.

Combine flour, ½ cup almonds, confectioners sugar
and melted butter.

Press mixture into the bottom of baking pan. Bake
15-20 minutes or until lightly browned and firm to touch.

Meanwhile, beat together sugar, eggs, lemon juice,
lemon peel, baking powder, extracts and salt. Pour over
baked crust and continue baking 25 minutes or until
golden brown and set.

Cool on wire rack to room temperature. While bars
cool, combine Icing ingredients and spread over top.
Sprinkle top with remaining ¼ cup almonds. Allow the
glaze to harden about 15 minutes and cut into bars.
Yields 16 bars.

Triple Good Bars

2 cups (480 ml) SUN•MAID Raisins
14-oz can (420 ml) sweetened condensed milk
1 tbs (15 ml) lemon juice
1 tbs (15 ml) grated lemon peel
1 cup (240 ml) butter or margarine, softened
1⅓ cups (320 ml) brown sugar, firmly packed
1½ tsp (8 ml) vanilla
1 cup (240 ml) all-purpose flour
½ tsp (3 ml) baking soda
¼ tsp (1 ml) salt
2½ cups (590 ml) rolled oats
1½ cups (355 ml) DIAMOND Chopped Walnuts

Preheat oven to 375°F (180°C). Grease 13x9-inch pan.

In medium saucepan, combine raisins, sweetened
condensed milk, lemon juice and lemon peel. Cook over
medium heat, stirring constantly, just until mixture begins
to bubble; cool slightly. Combine butter, brown sugar and
vanilla; beat until light and fluffy. Add flour, baking soda
and salt; mix well. Stir in oats and walnuts. Reserve 2 cups
oat mixture for topping.

Press remaining oat mixture into pan. Spread raisin
mixture to within ½ inch of edges. Sprinkle with reserved
oat mixture; press lightly. Bake 25-30 minutes or until
golden brown. Cool completely; cut into bars.
Yields 4 dozen bars.

Triple Good Bars

Pineapple Bars

8¼-oz can (248 g) crushed pineapple
¾ cup (180 ml) sugar, divided
1 tbs (15 ml) plus ¾ cup (180 ml) flour
2 eggs
½ tsp (3 ml) baking powder
½ tsp (3 ml) salt
1 cup (240 ml) rolled oats
½ cup (120 ml) brown sugar, packed
½ cup (120 ml) butter or margarine, melted, divided
½ cup (120 ml) sliced natural almonds

Preheat oven to 375°F (190°C). Butter 8-inch square pan.

Combine undrained pineapple, ¼ cup sugar and 1 tbs flour in saucepan; cook, stirring constantly, until mixture is thickened and clear. Lightly beat 1 egg; stir part of hot mixture into it, then mix with remaining hot mixture in saucepan. Cook, stirring, 2 minutes longer. Set aside.

Mix ¾ cup flour with baking powder, salt, oats, brown sugar and ¼ cup melted butter or margarine. Press into prepared pan; bake 10 minutes.

Mix remaining ¼ cup melted butter, remaining egg and remaining ½ cup sugar with the almonds. Spread pineapple filling evenly over baked crust; spoon almond mixture over the top. Bake 30 minutes longer. Cool and cut into bars. Yields 16 bars.

Courtesy of the Almond Board of California.

Above: Pineapple Bars

Great Day Cocoa Brownies

½ cup (20 ml) butter or margarine
1 cup (240 ml) sugar
2 eggs
1 tsp (5 ml) vanilla
⅔ cup (160 ml) unsifted flour
½ cup (120 ml) GHIRARDELLI Unsweetened Cocoa
½ tsp (3 ml) baking powder
¼ tsp (1 ml) salt
½ cup (120 ml) chopped walnuts

Preheat oven to 350°F (180°C). Butter an 8-inch square pan then line with wax paper.

In a food processor, place butter or margarine (cut into 4 pieces), sugar, eggs and vanilla into processor bowl; process about 15 seconds. (Or in mixer, cream softened butter with same ingredients.) Sift flour with cocoa, baking powder and salt; blend into creamed mixture. Fold in nuts.

Spread in prepared pan. Bake 20-25 minutes. Cool. Frost if desired (recipe below). Cut into squares. Yields 16 squares.

Quick Fudge Frosting For Brownies

3 tbs (45 ml) butter or margarine
⅓ cup (80 ml) GHIRARDELLI Unsweetened Cocoa
1½ cups (355 ml) confectioners sugar
2-3 tbs (30-45 ml) milk
½ tsp (3 ml) vanilla

Melt butter or margarine; remove from heat and add cocoa, stirring until smooth. Mix in confectioners sugar, 2 tbs milk and vanilla. Beat until thick, adding remaining milk, a little at a time, as needed. Beat until thick enough to spread. Frost brownies or single layer cake. Double recipe for a larger cake. Sprinkle with chopped nuts, if desired.

Buttermilk Cake-Style Brownies

2 cups (480 ml) all-purpose flour
6 tbs (90 ml) SACO Buttermilk Blend
¾ tsp (4 ml) baking soda
¼ tsp (1 ml) salt
2 cups (480 ml) sugar
1 cup (240 ml) butter or margarine
3 tbs (45 ml) SACO Baking Cocoa
1½ cups (355 ml) water
2 eggs
1 tsp (5 ml) vanilla

Preheat oven to 350°F (180°C). Grease 10½x15½x2½-inch pan.

Sift flour, buttermilk blend, baking soda and salt together into a mixing bowl. Mix in sugar and set aside. Melt butter or margarine in saucepan; add cocoa and water to butter and mix well. Add cocoa mixture to dry ingredients and mix until moistened. Do not overbeat. Add eggs, one at a time, and mix until smooth. Add vanilla. Batter will be very runny.

Pour batter into prepared pan. Bake 25-30 minutes. Frost with Chocolate Buttermilk Icing (see below) while still slightly warm.

Chocolate Buttermilk Icing

½ cup (120 ml) butter or margarine
3 tbs (45 ml) SACO Baking Cocoa
⅓ cup (80 ml) water
2 tbs (30 ml) SACO Buttermilk Blend
3½ cup (840 ml) confectioners sugar, sifted
1 tsp (5 ml) vanilla
1 cup (240 ml) chopped nuts, optional

Melt butter or margarine in saucepan; add cocoa and water and mix well. Stir in buttermilk blend and bring to a rapid boil. Remove from heat and add confectioners sugar, vanilla and nuts. Stir until consistency is smooth. Spread frosting on slightly warm cake or brownies.

Great Day Cocoa Brownies

One Bowl Brownies

4 squares BAKER'S Unsweetened Chocolate
¾ cup (180 ml) margarine or butter
2 cups (480 ml) sugar
3 eggs
1 tsp (5 ml) vanilla
1 cup (240 ml) all-purpose flour
1 cup (240 ml) chopped nuts, optional

Preheat oven to 350°F (180°C). Grease 13x9-inch pan.

Microwave chocolate and margarine or butter in large microwave-safe bowl on high 2 minutes or until margarine is melted. Stir until chocolate is completely melted. Stir sugar into melted chocolate mixture. Mix in eggs and vanilla until well blended. Stir in flour and nuts.

Spread in prepared pan. Bake 30-35 minutes or until toothpick inserted into center comes out with fudgy crumbs. Do not overbake. Cool in pan; cut into squares. Yields 2 dozen brownies.

Tip: For cakelike brownies, stir in ½ cup (120 ml) milk with the eggs and vanilla. Increase flour to 1½ cups (355 ml).

Tip: When using a glass baking dish, reduce oven temperature to 325°F (165°C).

Peanut Butter Swirl Brownies: Prepare One Bowl Brownie batter as directed, reserving 1 tbs (15 ml) of the margarine and 2 tbs (30 ml) of the sugar. Spread in greased 13x9-inch pan. Add reserved ingredients to ⅔ cup (160 ml) peanut butter; mix well.

Place spoonfuls of peanut butter mixture over brownie batter. Swirl with knife to marbelize. Bake at 350°F (180°C) for 30-35 minutes or until toothpick inserted in center comes out with fudgy crumbs. Cool in pan; cut into squares.

Tip: For more peanut butter flavor, use 1 cup (240 ml) peanut butter.

Rocky Road Brownies: Prepare One Bowl Brownies as directed. Bake at 350°F (180°C) for 30 minutes. Sprinkle 2 cups (480 ml) Kraft Miniature Marshmallows, 1 cup (240 ml) Baker's Semi-Sweet Real Chocolate Chips and 1 cup (240 ml) chopped nuts over brownies immediately after removing from oven. Continue baking 3-5 minutes or until topping begins to melt together. Cool in pan; cut into squares.

Chocolate Chip Brownies

½ cup (120 ml) butter or margarine, softened
¾ cup (180 ml) sugar
2 eggs
1 tsp (5 ml) vanilla
½ cup (120 ml) unsifted flour
⅓ cup (80 ml) GHIRARDELLI Unsweetened Cocoa
½ tsp (3 ml) baking powder
¼ tsp (1 ml) salt
8 oz (240 g) GHIRARDELLI Semi-Sweet Chocolate Chips
½ cup (120 ml) chopped nuts

Preheat oven to 350°F (180°C). Lightly butter 8-inch square pan and then line with wax paper.

Cream softened butter with sugar, eggs and vanilla. Stir flour with cocoa, baking powder and salt; blend into creamed mixture. Fold in chocolate chips and nuts.

Spread batter in pan. Bake 20-25 minutes. Cool. Cut into squares. Yields 16 squares.

Chocolate Chip Brownies

White Chips Brownies

1 cup (240 ml) all-purpose flour
½ cup (120 ml) NESTLÉ TOLL HOUSE Baking Cocoa
¾ tsp (4 ml) baking powder
¼ tsp (1 ml) salt
1¼ cups (295 ml) granulated sugar
¾ cup (180 ml) butter or margarine, melted
2 tsp (10 ml) vanilla extract
3 eggs
12-oz pkg (360 g) NESTLÉ TOLL HOUSE Premier
    White Morsels, divided

Preheat oven to 350°F (180°C). Grease 9-inch square baking pan.

Combine flour, cocoa, baking powder and salt in medium bowl. Beat sugar, butter or margarine and vanilla in large mixing bowl. Add eggs, one at a time, beating well after each addition. Gradually beat in flour mixture. Stir in 1½ cups morsels.

Pour into prepared pan. Bake 25-30 minutes or until wooden pick inserted near center comes out slightly sticky. Cool in pan on wire rack (brownies will sink in center when cooled).

Microwave remaining morsels in heavy-duty plastic bag on medium-high power for 45 seconds; knead. Microwave at additional 10-120 second intervals, kneading until smooth. Cut tiny corner from bag; squeeze to drizzle over brownies. Chill for few minutes before cutting.
Yields 16 brownies.

White Chips Brownies

Caramel-Layered Brownies

4 squares BAKER'S Unsweetened Chocolate
¾ cup (180 ml) margarine or butter
2 cups (480 ml) sugar
3 eggs
1 tsp (5 ml) vanilla
1 cup (240 ml) all-purpose flour
1 cup (240 ml) BAKER'S Semi-Sweet Real Chocolate Chips
1½ cups (355 ml) chopped nuts
14-oz pkg (420 g) KRAFT Caramels
⅓ cup (80 ml) evaporated milk

Preheat oven to 350°F (180°C). Grease 13x9-inch pan.

Microwave chocolate and margarine in large microwave-safe bowl on high 2 minutes or until margarine or butter is melted. Stir until chocolate is completely melted. Stir sugar into melted chocolate mixture. Mix in eggs and vanilla until well blended. Stir in flour. Remove 1 cup of batter; set aside.

Spread remaining batter in prepared pan. Sprinkle with chips and 1 cup of the nuts.

Microwave caramels and milk in same bowl on high 4 minutes, stirring after 2 minutes. Stir until caramels are completely melted and smooth. Spoon over chips and nuts, spreading to edges of pan. Gently spread reserved batter over caramel mixture. Sprinkle with the remaining ½ cup nuts.

Bake 40 minutes or until toothpick inserted into center comes out with fudgy crumbs. Do not overbake. Cool in pan; cut into squares. Yields 2 dozen brownies.

Walnut Crunch Brownies

Brownie Layer:
4 squares BAKER'S Unsweetened Chocolate
¾ cup (180 ml) margarine or butter
2 cups (480 ml) granulated sugar
4 eggs
1 tsp (5 ml) vanilla
1 cup (240 ml) all-purpose flour

Walnut Topping:
¼ cup (60 ml) margarine or butter
¾ cup (180 ml) brown sugar, firmly packed
2 eggs
2 tbs (30 ml) all-purpose flour
1 tsp (5 ml) vanilla
4 cups (960 ml) chopped walnuts

Preheat oven to 350°F (180°C). Grease 13x9-inch pan.

Brownie Layer: Microwave chocolate and ¾ cup margarine or butter in large microwave-safe bowl on high 2 minutes or until margarine is melted. Stir until chocolate is completely melted. Stir granulated sugar into melted chocolate mixture. Mix in eggs and vanilla until well blended. Stir in flour.

Spread in prepared pan.

Walnut Topping: Microwave ¼ cup margarine or butter and brown sugar in same bowl on high 1 minute or until margarine is melted. Stir in eggs, flour and vanilla until completely mixed. Stir in walnuts.

Spread mixture evenly over brownie batter. Bake 45 minutes or until toothpick inserted into center comes out with fudgy crumbs. Do not overbake. Cool in pan; cut into squares. Yields 2 dozen brownies.

Caramel-Layered Brownies

Following page: Walnut Crunch Brownies

Sweet and Spicy Brownies

4 squares unsweetened chocolate
¾ cup (180 ml) butter or margarine
2 cups (480 ml) granulated sugar
3 large eggs
1 cup (240 ml) all-purpose flour
1 tbs (15 ml) TABASCO Pepper Sauce
½ cup (120 ml) semi-sweet chocolate chips
½ cup (120 ml) chopped walnuts

Preheat oven to 350°F (180°C). Grease 9x9-inch baking pan.

In small saucepan, over medium-low heat, melt chocolate squares and butter or margarine, stirring frequently.

In large bowl, combine sugar, eggs, flour, pepper sauce and melted chocolate mixture until well blended. Stir in chocolate chips and chopped walnuts.

Spoon mixture into pan. Bake 35-40 minutes until toothpick inserted in center comes out clean. Cool in pan on wire rack. Yields 16 brownies.

German Sweet Chocolate Brownies

4-oz pkg (120 g) BAKER'S German Sweet Chocolate
¼ cup (60 ml) margarine or butter
¾ cup (180 ml) sugar
2 eggs
1 tsp (5 ml) vanilla
½ cup (120 ml) all-purpose flour
½ cup (120 ml) chopped nuts

Preheat oven to 350°F (180°C). Grease 8-inch square pan.

Microwave chocolate and margarine or butter in large microwave-safe bowl on high 2 minutes or until margarine is melted. Stir until chocolate is completely melted. Stir sugar into melted chocolate mixture. Mix in eggs and vanilla until well blended. Stir in flour and nuts.

Spread in prepared pan. Bake for 25 minutes or until toothpick inserted into center comes out with fudgy crumbs. Do not overbake. Cool in pan; cut into squares. Yields 16 brownies.

Chocolate Chunk Brownies

1 cup (240 ml) unsalted butter
3½ oz (105 g) unsweetened chocolate squares
3 tbs (45 ml) SACO Baking Cocoa
1½ cups (355 ml) all-purpose flour
½ tsp (3 ml) baking powder
¾ tsp (4 ml) salt
4 eggs
2 cups (480 ml) sugar
2 tsp (10 ml) vanilla extract
6 oz (180 g) SACO Chocolate Chunks

Preheat oven to 350°F (180°C). Grease 13x9x2-inch pan.

Melt butter and unsweetened chocolate together in double boiler or in microwave. Stir to combine and set aside to cool to room temperature. Sift cocoa, flour, baking powder and salt together; set aside. Beat eggs on medium speed 1 minute in large bowl. Gradually add the sugar to the eggs, beating to combine. Stir in vanilla and the room-temperature cocoa-butter mixture, just until combined. Stir in dry ingredients.

Pour into prepared pan. Sprinkle chocolate chunks evenly over batter. Bake 30-35 minutes or until center is set. Cool before cutting. Extra brownies freeze well. Yields 2 dozen brownies.

Double Espresso Brownies

Espresso Brownies:
1 cup (240 ml) all-purpose flour
½ tsp (3 ml) baking powder
¼ tsp (1 ml) salt
⅓ cup (80 ml) hot water
1 tbs (15 ml) instant espresso powder or crystals*
1 cup (240 ml) granulated sugar
½ cup (120 ml) butter or margarine
12-oz pkg (360 g) *NESTLÉ TOLL HOUSE*
    Semi-Sweet Chocolate Morsels, divided
3 eggs

Espresso Frosting:
½ cup (120 ml) whipping cream
1 tsp (5 ml) instant espresso powder or crystals*
½ cup (120 ml) sifted powdered sugar

Preheat oven to 350°F (180°C). Grease 9x9-inch baking pan.

Espresso Brownies: In small bowl, combine flour, baking powder and salt. In medium-size heavy saucepan, combine water and espresso; heat to dissolve. Stir in sugar and butter or margarine; cook over low heat, stirring constantly until mixture comes to a boil. Remove from heat; stir in 1 cup morsels until smooth. Stir in eggs one at a time, stirring well after each addition. Stir in dry ingredients.

Pour into prepared pan. Bake 25-30 minutes. Cool in pan.

Espresso Frosting: In small heavy saucepan, combine cream and espresso; heat to dissolve. Stir in remaining morsels from brownie recipe; stir until smooth. Remove from heat; stir in powdered sugar. Chill until spreading consistency. Spread over brownies; cut into 2½-inch squares. Yields 3 dozen brownies.

* For a milder coffee flavor, substitute Taster's Choice Freeze Dried Coffee Crystals for espresso.

Chocolate Mint Brownie Squares

½ cup (120 ml) butter or margarine
5 tbs (75 ml) SACO Baking Cocoa
1 cup (240 ml) sugar
2 eggs
½ cup (120 ml) all-purpose flour
2 tbs (30 ml) SACO Buttermilk Blend
½ tsp (3 ml) vanilla
¼ tsp (1 ml) salt
1 cup (240 ml) chopped nuts, optional

Mint Icing:
1 cup (240 ml) powdered sugar
2 tbs (30 ml) soft butter
1 tbs (15 ml) evaporated milk or half & half
½-1 tsp (3-5 ml) peppermint extract
1-2 drops green or red food coloring

Cocoa Glaze:
2 tbs (30 ml) butter
¼ cup (60 ml) SACO Baking Cocoa
3 tbs (45 ml) water
1¼ cups (295 ml) powdered sugar
½ tsp (3 ml) vanilla

Preheat oven to 350°F (180°C). Grease 9x9-inch square pan.

In medium saucepan, over low heat, melt butter or margarine. Stir in cocoa and sugar until well blended. Add eggs, one at a time, beating well after each addition. Add the flour, buttermilk blend, vanilla, and salt and stir well. Do not overbeat. Stir in chopped nuts.

Pour brownie mixture into prepared pan. Bake 30-35 minutes. Brownies are done when toothpick, inserted in center, comes out clean. Cool on wire rack. Frost with Mint Icing and Cocoa Glaze. Yields 12-16 brownies.

Mint Icing: Mix ingredients together and spread on brownies. Chill before adding Cocoa Glaze.

Cocoa Glaze: Melt butter over low heat. Add cocoa and water, stirring constantly, until mixture thickens. Do not boil. Remove from heat. Blend in powdered sugar and vanilla. Beat until smooth. Spread Glaze on top of Mint Icing and chill.

Opposite: Double Espresso Brownies

Chewy Pear Brownies, Microwave Method

2 eggs
1 cup (240 ml) sugar
⅔ cup (160 ml) butter or margarine, melted
1 tsp (5 ml) vanilla
¾ cup (180 ml) flour
⅓ cup (80 ml) unsweetened cocoa
1 tsp (5 ml) baking powder
½ tsp (3 ml) salt
1½ cups (355 ml) coarsely chopped USA Bartlett pears
½ cup (120 ml) chopped walnuts

Grease 9-inch square microwave-safe dish.

Beat eggs in mixing bowl. Blend in sugar, butter or margarine and vanilla; beat until sugar dissolves. Combine flour, cocoa, baking powder and salt. Stir into egg mixture until flour is evenly moistened and batter is smooth. Fold in pears and nuts.

Pour into prepared dish. Microwave at medium-high for 6 minutes. Turn one-quarter turn; microwave 2 minutes. Turn one-quarter again and microwave 2 minutes. Cool and cut into squares. Yields 16 brownies.

Conventional Method: Turn batter into greased 8-inch square baking pan. Bake at 350°F (180°C) 30-35 minutes.

Courtesy of Oregon Washington California Pear Bureau.

Above:
Chewy Pear Brownies, Microwave Method

Butterscotch Brownies

⅓ cup (80 ml) margarine
1 cup (240 ml) brown sugar, firmly packed
1 egg
½ cup (120 ml) chopped nuts
1 tsp (5 ml) vanilla
1 cup (240 ml) sifted PRESTO

Preheat oven to 350°F (180°C). Grease an 8x8x2-inch pan.

Blend margarine and sugar. Add egg; beat well. Mix in nuts and vanilla. Fold in sifted flour.

Spread in prepared pan. Bake 30-35 minutes or until golden brown. Cool; cut into squares. Yields 16 brownies.

Graham Brownies

1 cup (240 ml) sugar
½ cup (120 ml) FLEISCHMANN'S Margarine, melted
3 eggs, slightly beaten
1 tsp (4 ml) vanilla extract
22 squares HONEY MAID Chocolate Grahams,
    finely crushed, about 1½ cups (355 ml)
¾ cup (180 ml) PLANTER'S Walnuts, chopped

Preheat oven to 350°F (180°). Grease 8x8x2-inch baking pan.

In bowl, blend sugar, margarine, eggs and vanilla. Stir in graham crumbs until blended. Stir in walnuts.

Spread batter into prepared pan. Bake 30-35 minutes or until toothpick inserted comes out clean. Cool completely on wire rack. Cut into squares to serve. Yields 16 brownies.

Graham Brownies

469

Chocolate Chunk Blonde Brownies

½ cup (120 ml) margarine or butter, softened
1 cup (240 ml) brown sugar, firmly packed
4 eggs
2 tsp (10 ml) vanilla
2 cups (480 ml) all-purpose flour
1 tsp (5 ml) CALUMET Baking Powder
¼ tsp (1 ml) salt
8-oz pkg (240 g) BAKER'S Semi-Sweet Chocolate, coarsely chopped
1 cup (240 ml) chopped nuts

Preheat oven to 350°F (180°C). Grease 13x9-inch pan.

Beat margarine, sugars, eggs and vanilla until light and fluffy. Mix in flour, baking powder and salt until well blended. Stir in chocolate and nuts.

Spread in prepared pan. Bake 30 minutes or until toothpick inserted into center comes out with moist crumbs. Do not overbake. Cool in pan; cut into squares. Yields 2 dozen brownies.

Above: Chocolate Chunk Blonde Brownies

S'More Blonde Brownies

½ cup (120 ml) butter or margarine, softened

¾ cup (180 ml) sugar

1 egg

1¼ cups (295 ml) all-purpose flour

¾ cup (180 ml) graham cracker crumbs

1 tsp (5 ml) baking powder

1 cup (240 ml) marshmallow creme

5 1½-oz (45 g each) HERSHEY'S Milk Chocolate Bars
　　or Cookies 'N Mint Chocolate Bars, unwrapped and divided

½ tsp (3 ml) shortening (not butter, margarine or oil)

Preheat oven to 350°F (180°C). Grease 9-inch square baking pan.

In medium bowl, beat butter or margarine and sugar until blended. Add egg; beat until light and fluffy. Stir in flour, graham cracker crumbs and baking powder; beat until well blended.

Press half of dough in prepared pan; spread with marshmallow creme. Arrange 4½ chocolate bars over dough, breaking as needed to fit. Carefully press remaining flour mixture over chocolate bars, covering completely.

Bake 20-25 minutes or until lightly browned. Cool completely in pan on wire rack. In small microwave-safe bowl, place remaining ½ chocolate bar, broken into pieces, and shortening. Microwave at high 15-30 seconds or just until chocolate is melted when stirred. Drizzle over top. Cut into bars. Yields 16 brownies.

S'More Blond Brownies

Festive Fruited Vanilla Chip Brownies

½ cup (120 ml) butter or margarine, melted
1⅔ cups (400 ml) HERSHEY'S Vanilla Milk Chips, divided
2 eggs
¼ cup (60 ml) sugar
1¼ cups (295 ml) all-purpose flour
⅓ cup (80 ml) orange juice
¾ cup (180 ml) cranberries, chopped
¼ cup (60 ml) snipped dried apricots
½ cup (120 ml) coarsely chopped nuts
¼ cup (60 ml) light brown sugar, packed

Preheat oven to 325°F (165°C). Grease and flour 9-inch square baking pan.

Into melted butter, immediately stir in 1 cup vanilla chips; set aside.

In large bowl, beat eggs until foamy. Add sugar; beat until thick and pale yellow in color. Add flour, orange juice and reserved butter-chip mixture; beat just until combined. Spread half of batter, about 1¼ cups, into prepared pan. Bake 15 minutes until edges are lightly browned; remove form oven. Leave oven on.

Stir in cranberries, apricots and remaining ⅔ cup vanilla chips into reserved batter; spread over top of hot baked mixture. Stir together nuts and brown sugar; sprinkle over top.

Bake 25-30 minutes or until edges are lightly browned. Cool completely in pan on wire rack; cut into bars. Yields 16 brownies.

Cherry Cheese Brownies

16-oz can (480 g) Northwest dark sweet pitted cherries
15-oz pkg (450 g) brownie mix
2 eggs, divided
¼ cup (60 ml) vegetable oil
3-oz pkg (90 g) cream cheese, softened
2 tbs (30 ml) sugar
¾ cup (180 ml) flaked coconut
1 tsp (5 ml) almond extract
sweetened whipped cream, optional

Preheat oven to 350°F (180°C). Grease 9-inch square baking pan.

Drain cherries; reserve ¼ cup liquid. Combine brownie mix, 1 egg, oil and reserved cherry liquid; mix thoroughly. Reserve 12 cherries for garnish, if desired. Gently stir remaining cherries into brownie mixture; set aside. Combine cream cheese and sugar; mix well. Beat remaining egg and stir into cream cheese mixture with coconut and almond extract.

Spoon cream cheese mixture into prepared pan alternately with brownie mixture. Swirl mixtures together slightly. Bake 35-40 minutes or until toothpick inserted near center comes out clean. Cool. Cut into squares. If desired, serve with dollop of whipped cream and top with cherry. Yields about 1 dozen brownies.

Courtesy of the National Cherry Growers and Industries Foundation.

Cherry Cheese Brownies

Opposite:
Festive Fruited Vanilla Chip Brownies

Lunchbox Brownies

¼ cup (60 ml) margarine or butter
¾ cup (180 ml) shortening*
¾ cup (180 ml) cocoa*
2 cups (480 ml) IMPERIAL Granulated Sugar
4 eggs, beaten
1 tsp (5 ml) vanilla
1½ cups (355 ml) all-purpose flour
1 tsp (5 ml) baking powder
1 tsp (5 ml) salt
1 cup (240 ml) chopped nuts

Frosting
¼ cup (60 ml) margarine or butter**
5 tbs (75 ml) cocoa**
¼ cup (60 ml) milk
2 cups (480 ml) IMPERIAL 10X Powdered Sugar
1 tsp (5 ml) vanilla

* 4 squares unsweetened chocolate, melted can be substituted for the cocoa and margarine.
** 1½ squares unsweetened chocolate, melted, can be substituted for the cocoa and 1½ tbs margarine.

Melt margarine or butter and shortening in large saucepan over low heat; stir in cocoa. Remove from heat and add ImperialGranulated Sugar, eggs, vanilla, mixing thoroughly. Combine flour, baking powder, salt; stir into chocolate mixture. Add nuts and mix well. Spread in well-greased 13x9x2-inch pan. Bake in preheated oven at 350°F (180°C)
for 30-35 minutes. Spread with frosting while brownies are still warm. Cool; cut into 2-inch squares. Yields 24.

Frosting: Melt margarine in small saucepan over low heat. Stir in cocoa, milk, Imperial Powdered Sugar; mix well. Remove from heat and stir in vanilla. Spread over warm brownies.

Sensibly Delicious Double Chocolate Chip Brownies

12-oz pkg (360 g) NESTLÉ TOLL HOUSE
    Semi-Sweet Chocolate Morsels, divided
1 cup (240 ml) granulated sugar
½ cup (120 ml) unsweetened applesauce
2 tbs (30 ml) margarine
3 egg whites
1¼ cups (295 ml) all-purpose flour
¼ tsp (1 ml) baking soda
¼ tsp (1 ml) salt
1 tsp (5 ml) vanilla extract
⅓ cup (80 ml) chopped nuts

In large, heavy saucepan over low heat, melt 1 cup morsels, sugar, applesauce and margarine, stirring until smooth. Remove from heat. Add egg whites; stir well. Stir in flour, baking soda, salt and vanilla. Stir in remaining morels and nuts. Spread into greased 13x9-inch baking pan. Bake in preheated 350°F (180°C) oven for 16-20 minutes or just until set. Cool completely. Cut into 2-inch squares. Yields 24.

Opposite: Lunchbox Brownies

Sensibly Delicious Blonde Brownies

2¼ cups (540 ml) all-purpose flour
2½ tsp (13 ml) baking powder
½ tsp (3 ml) salt
1¾ cups (415 ml) packed brown sugar
6 tbs (90 ml) margarine, softened
2 egg whites
1½ tsp (8 ml) vanilla extract
⅓ cup (80 ml) water
12-oz pkg (360 g) NESTLÉ TOLL HOUSE
  Semi-Sweet Chocolate Morsels

In small bowl, combine flour, baking powder and salt. In large mixer bowl, beat sugar, margarine, egg whites and vanilla until smooth. Gradually beat dry ingredients alternately with water. Stir in morsels. Spread into greased 15x10-inch jelly-roll pan. Bake in preheated 350°F (180°C) oven for 20-25 minutes or until top is golden brown. Cool in pan. Cut into 2-inch squares. Yields 35.

Slenderific Brownie Snacking Cakes

½ cup (120 ml) HERSHEY'S European Style
  Cocoa or HERSHEY'S Cocoa
½ cup (120 ml) all-purpose flour
½ tsp (1 ml) baking powder
¼ cup (60 ml) canola vegetable oil
½ cup (120 ml) packed light brown sugar
½ cup (120 ml) granulated sugar
½ cup (120 ml) egg whites, beaten until foamy
2 tsp (10 ml) vanilla extract
powdered sugar, optional

Heat oven to 350°F (180°C). Grease 8-inch square pan. In small bowl, stir together cocoa, flour and baking powder. Set aside. In medium bowl, stir together vegetable oil, brown sugar and granulated sugar; stir in beaten egg whites and vanilla. Gradually stir in cocoa mixture until blended. Pour into prepared pan.

Bake 15-20 minutes or until brownie begins to pull away from side of pan. Cool completely in pan on wire rack. Just before serving, cut into bars or cut with cookie cutters; sprinkle with powdered sugar, if desired. Yields 12.

Sensibly Delicious
Blonde Brownies

Index